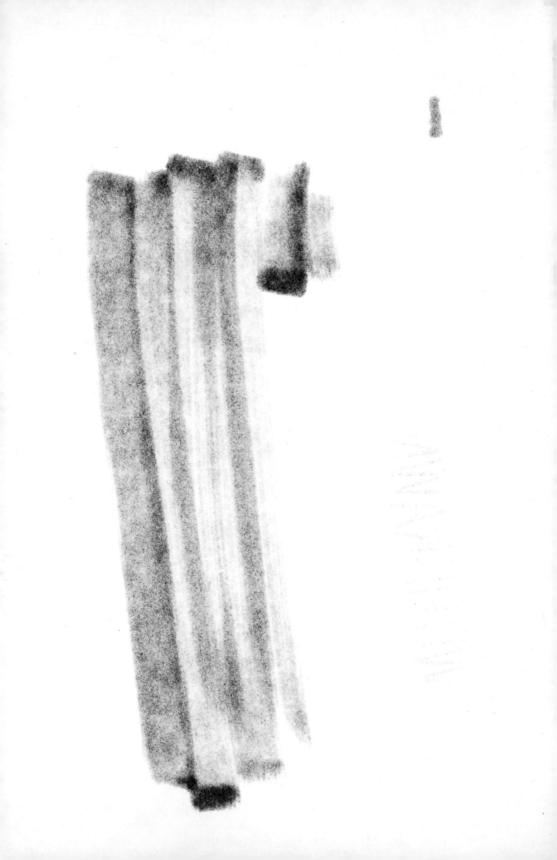

Existential Sociology

Homo sum; nihil humani a me alienum puto [I am a man; nothing human is alien to me], said the Latin playwright. And I would rather say, *Nullum hominen a me alienum puto* [I am a man; no other man do I deem a stranger]. For to me the adjective *humanus* is no less suspect than its abstract substantive *humanitus*, humanity. Neither "the human" nor "humanity," neither the simple adjective nor the substantivized adjective, but the concrete substantive — man. The man of flesh and bone; the man who is born, suffers, and dies — above all, who dies; the man who eats and drinks and plays and sleeps and thinks and wills; the man who is seen and heard; the brother, the real brother.

For there is another thing which is also called man, and he is the subject of not a few lucubrations, more or less scientific. He is the legendary featherless biped, the [political animal] of Aristotle, the social contractor of Rousseau, the *homo economicus* of the Manchester school, the *homo sapiens* of Linnaeus, or, if you like, the vertical mammal. A man neither of here nor there, neither of this age nor of another, who has neither sex nor country, who is in brief, merely an idea. That is to say, a no-man.

The man we have to do with is the man of flesh and bone — I, you, reader of mine, the other man yonder, all of us who walk solidly upon the earth. [Unamuno, 1954]

Existential Sociology

JACK D. DOUGLAS
Professor of Sociology
University of California, San Diego

JOHN M. JOHNSON
Associate Professor of Sociology
Arizona State University, Tempe

with

DAVID L. ALTHEIDE
JOHN P. ANDERSON
RICHARD H. BROWN
ANDREA FONTANA
JOSEPH A. KOTARBA
BARBARA PONSE
CAROL A. B. WARREN
RICHARD VAN DE WATER

CAMBRIDGE UNIVERSITY PRESS

CAMBRIDGE
LONDON   NEW YORK   MELBOURNE

Published by the Syndics of the Cambridge University Press
The Pitt Building, Trumpington Street, Cambridge CB2 1RP
Bentley House, 200 Euston Road, London NW1 2DB
32 East 57th Street, New York, NY 10022, USA
296 Beaconsfield Parade, Middle Park, Melbourne 3206, Australia

First published 1977

Printed in the United States of America
Typeset by Telecki Publishing Services, Yonkers, New York
Printed and bound by Vail-Ballou Press, Inc., Binghamton, New York

Library of Congress Cataloging in Publication Data

Douglas, Jack D

Existential sociology.

Bibliography: p.

Includes index.

1. Sociology. 2. Existentialism.
I. Johnson, John J., joint author. II. Title.
HM24.D7 301 76-47198

ISBN 0 521 21515 3 hard covers
ISBN 0 521 29225 5 paperback

Contents

Introduction

Existential sociology is defined descriptively as the study of human experience-in-the-world (or existence) in all its forms. The fundamental, but not exclusive, method of existential sociology is direct personal experience, including that of our own daily lives and that gained through more formal and explicitly defined research practice. The goal is to construct both practical and theoretical truths about that experience, to understand how we live, how we feel, think, act. Underlying this abstractly defined goal is a passion to understand the wellsprings of our actions and their consequences; where we came from and where we are going. And intertwined with this passion is a gut-level faith in the ultimate utility of such understanding to guide us toward realistic solutions to the social problems we confront in our daily lives.

This definition of existential sociology is purposely broad, partly vague, and definitely open. Any sociology that seeks to remain faithful to the entire gamut of human experience must not begin with narrow, preconceived goals, clearly defined boundaries, or absolutist concepts of methodological propriety. The definition is intended merely to point to human experience as the realm of our concern. The definition is not formulated to fit existing professional boundaries or conventions: Existential sociology intersects and overlaps with many other disciplines, such as humanistic and existential psychology. It is open-ended to inspire a creative search, not an assertion of preconceived answers. It intends an invitation to others to join this search for more truthful understanding of our daily lives, not a claim of theoretical membership or exclusiveness.

Any work entitled "existential sociology" immediately raises questions of the relations between existential philosophy and existential sociology. The relations between philosophy and sociology have always been important and controversial. Historically, philosophy has had major influences on the development of the important forms of sociological thought. Enlightenment philosophy had a profound impact on Durkheimian sociology, and the philosophy of Wilhelm Dilthey had a great effect on the sociology of Max Weber. (These and other relations are analyzed in Chapter 2.) The philosophical writings of Edmund Husserl, Henri Bergson, William James, and others had great influence on the thinking of the early American pragmatists and remain a source of inspiration for the more recently developed phenomenological sociologies, such as ethnomethodology. Analyses of these and other philosophical influences are found in several of this book's chapters. But the empiricist rhetoric of nineteenth-century science, which is still powerful in sociology, has rendered these influences controversial. Emile Durkheim, whose work has been taken as an exemplary model by most American sociologists, was anxious to show that his theories originated from the "things themselves," the objectlike social facts external to individual consciousness, and not from any form of philosophical speculation. He often hid the ways in which his thoughts had initially stemmed from philosophy and the ways in which philosophy continually influenced his epistemological and methodological thought.

Some questions concerning the relations between existential philosophy (or literature) and existential sociology are easily dealt with. Some readers, for example, may initially assume that an existential sociology follows in the steps of the philosophy, that we have assumed the philosophy to be essentially correct and are now busily imposing those ideas upon our own experience of the social world. Some readers of early efforts of phenomenological sociology have even gone so far as to criticize it because it dared to diverge from the sacrosanct writings of Husserl and others. Other readers may be tempted to fault most of this volume for deviance from the traditions of existential philosophy or literature. So we must emphasize from the beginning that, although there are some clear and distinct lines of development in intellectual history that underlie and support our sociological efforts, our work is grounded in the social experience of daily life, not in any body of abstract philosophical thought. We did not begin with existential philosophy or existential sociology, and we do not expect to end with any kind of existential philosophy. We began with social experience, conducted extensive social researches, and have arrived, we hope, at a creative theory of society that is thoroughly grounded in that social experience and research. In general, whatever connections exist between our sociological enterprise and philosphy have come *after* the experience and research that led us to see (retrospectively) the relations between what we were doing and what some philosophers were doing. We then found the philosophy to be a valuable intellectual *resource* in creating more general understanding of that experience. We use the philosophical insights where

they fit and help; we forget them where they do not.[1] The major point
to be emphasized here is that existential sociology begins with concrete,
socially situated experiences, and only after that attempts to build
more general, theoretical, abstract understandings of social life.[2] It
builds its methods as it goes in accord with the demands of the subject
matter and the desire to find progressively more general truths about
human existence. In these ways it is fundamentally distinct from most
traditional or classic forms of sociology. It draws upon that classic tradition in many ways, and we have all benefited greatly from the many
creative insights of that tradition. But when we do draw upon those insights, we try to refound or reconstruct their relevance upon the firmer
basis of our own social experience.

There are many specific similarities and differences between our
work and that of philosophers and others called existentialists. Both the
basic contributions and the basic problems of existential philosphy in
relation to our own work lie in the fundamental methods utilized to
know about the social world. In general terms, there are three different
but overlapping forms of knowing in sociology and all other sciences:
(1) *introspection* — the observation, description, and analysis of one's
own inner experiences or reflections; (2) *self-observation* — the description and analysis of one's own everyday, commonsense experience,
when alone or when in interaction with others; and (3) *systematic and
more controlled forms of observation* — those descriptions and analyses
carried out to discover the truth about some realm of social interaction.
Although it is true that these last two forms of knowing presuppose the
first, which is basic to all organized thought, all sociological theories
commonly rest on some combination of all three. But theories differ
greatly in the degree to which they rely on any particular form or any
particular combination of these.
The traditional mode of thought in philosophy is some form of introspection: some form of thinking about thinking, about the forms or
properties of reason, and about one's own conscious experience. The
ideal of philosophical thought has been clear since Socratic days: One
seeks knowledge of all things through knowledge of himself, his own

[1]We did not want to impose a neologism (e.g., experiential sociology) upon our enterprise because this would foster an image of a rationally defined and well-delimited
endeavor belonging to those who created the name and, moreover, would obscure
what similarities do exist between our ideas and those of existential philosophers
and writers. This would be contrary to our intentions and desires.
[2]Many phenomenologists and some others argue that this is impossible because our
experience is determined from the beginning by our shared linguistic symbols. But
this argument involves a basic misunderstanding about the fundamental importance
of feelings for symbolic experience and of man's perceptual openness to new experience in concrete situations. Much of Chapter 1 is devoted to a discussion of this.

forms of reason, consciousness, moral experience, and beliefs. Philosophers have occasionally appealed to the world of common experience and even at times to some degree of systematic observations. But their predominant appeals have been those concerning the subjective stuff of the mind: reason and knowledge. Vague dissatisfaction with existing forms of social science explanation has led to a contemporary revival of interest in this venerable but musty tradition; in *The Coming Crisis of Western Sociology*, for example, Alvin Gouldner promoted a conservation of this tradition by appealing to "radical" sentiments of the day.

One major stimulus of the early social movements of science in Western societies was a profound passion to achieve a more certain form of knowledge than seemed possible with this traditional, subjective form of philosophical thought. The scientific thinkers, who were reacting more against religious dogmatism than to philosophical traditionalism, found the "endless squabbling of the philosophers" repulsive. They sought to replace this with "the certainties of external, objective knowledge of the world." Their ideal was opposite to that of traditional philosophy: Instead of knowing the world through an examination of one's own thinking and experience, the scientist proposed knowledge of the external world first and, later, of thought itself by absolutely objectifying thought itself. By systematically controlling observations and thought in such ways that all ideas about the world, all knowledge, would be ultimately dependent upon or determined by the external world itself, they hoped to eliminate all concerns with the operations of knowing subjective mind. This ideal of absolute objectification of the world lingers in the rhetorical flourishes of positivist sociological thought, such as in the popular concern with verification procedures.

As might be expected, philosophers were not long in counterattacking. Hume and Kant especially tried to show that all forms of thought, including the most elementary scientific ideas about causality, were ultimately dependent upon or determined by the basic properties of thought itself, by the preexisting or a priori nature of the knowing mind. Although it is doubtful that these philosophical arguments convinced many scientists, by the middle of the twentieth century most serious natural and physical scientists had come, largely independently of philosphy, to recognize that absolute objectivity is a misconception (just as much as absolute subjectivity would be). More and more thoughtful scientists began to recognize that any concept of objectivity must depend ultimately, at least in part, upon the nature of the knowing mind and the situation of that knowing mind in the world. The centuries-old assumption by scientists that subject (knower) and object (known) can be effectively separated by experimental procedures — that experimental or other methodological protocol can produce the so-

called subject-object dualism — was completely undermined by developments within science itself. Many natural and physical scientists abandoned these inherited concepts of the categorical dichotomous separation of subject and object years before most social scientists were even
familiar with the problems.

Our previous empirical researches and experiences (Johnson, 1975;
Douglas, 1976) have pointed out several different features of the research process that show the impossibility of any absolute separation
between the knowing subject and the objects of knowledge. The conclusion that subject and object are interdependent has two fundamental
consequences for all social thought. First, it means that our traditional
ideas about objectivity in the social sciences must be either changed or
abandoned. This is a vital point to which we shall return. Second, the
denial of subject-object dualism means that any attempt to get at truth,
to rationalize our thoughts about the world, to make them more objective, or however one decides to phrase it, inevitably depends in significant part upon an analysis of the knowing mind itself and, most likely,
on other aspects of the human knower as well. Put differently, once the
rhetoric about treating thought and meaning as an object or "like a
thing" (as Durkheim put it) is seen for what it is, we recognize that the
truth of any study of the world ultimately depends upon the mind's
knowing itself: upon some form of systematic introspection and rational analysis.

The mere mention of introspection as the ultimate basis of knowledge raises the fear of solipsism in the minds of most traditional scientific thinkers. We present the most obvious arguments against this fear
that introspection leads to solipsism in the beginning of Chapter 3,
which examines the contributions of existential philosophy to theoretical sociology. But let us note here a further argument against solipsism.
Even if the reader is unconvinced by all the vast empirical evidence and
our arguments against the fears of solipsism, we can argue that our own
personal experiences deny its possibility. And no better support for our
denial can be found than our own experiences in putting together this
volume, a project that spanned several years. The ten contributors to
this volume represent a wide range of social backgrounds and past experiences, three different nationalities, a significant range of ages, a diversity of political sentiments and loyalties, and other important differences. Some of the contributors are close friends; others have never
met. Some of the contributors know each other quite well, but dislike
each other or have changed their feelings with the passage of time. And
the feelings involved in some of our disagreements, whether these are of
a situational or long-standing nature, are deep ones indeed. All these
kinds of experiences are not incidental to the theoretical arguments ad-

vanced in this book. Indeed, we have tried to learn from these experiences and to articulate their more general relevance for our sociological work. Nevertheless, despite our differences, we were able to join together for the practical purpose of completing our common enterprise. Thus, when we argue that all human understanding is necessarily problematic and that therefore we must fundamentally change the traditional ideas about scientific truth (as detailed in Chapter 1), our personal experiences in trying to bring about such a reconstruction tell us that abandonment of the traditional subject-object dualism does not entail a precipitous descent into solipsism. We criticize the traditional sociological enterprise in order to invite a more creative, more truthful, open-minded reconstruction, not to destroy or sweep away all earlier social thought.

Personal research experiences together with in-depth involvement in and understanding of our daily lives are the most distinctive features of existential sociology. These are the foundations from which any truthful theoretical understanding of American society must spring. Precisely what existential sociology consists of, why it is so essential, and how it differs from the earlier sociological perspectives are discussed in detail in Chapters 1 through 4. But the reader will also find many other important aspects and emphases in our work. The emphasis on brute being, on the relative independence and dominance of feelings over the cognitive and evaluative features of social action, is the most striking and perhaps the most controversial. Chapter 1 considers at some length the relevance of brute being to sociological understanding. Specific illustrations of the overriding importance of feelings for a truthful understanding of specific actions are found in the substantive researches concerning television newsworkers (Chapter 4), a community mental health clinic (Chapter 6), social welfare workers (Chapters 7 and 8), persons who experience chronic pain (Chapter 9), and members of gay communities (Chapter 10). In addition to these emphases on brute being, our researches and other personal experiences lead us to stress how situated (or contextualized) our everyday lives are, how problematic and uncertain most meanings and understandings are for societal members, and how much people are involved in hiding their private selves from public view. These features of daily life are most strikingly illustrated in Chapters 1 and 7 through 10. Added to these is an emphasis on the inevitability of politics in most complicated social settings of contemporary society. Substantive data for this emphasis are presented in Chapters 1, 4, 6, 7, and 8. Finally, throughout this book it is clear that we do not feel existential sociology is complete when an empirical description or analysis of some setting or series of actions has been accomplished. Within the constraints imposed on us by our varying natural abilities, we have tried, with what we hope is an appropriate sense of humility, to evaluate the implications of our descriptions and analyses, whether for sociology or social policy. An important point to be stressed here is that all these more specific aspects of our work have followed from our direct experiences, systematic observations, descriptions, and analyses, and not from any philosophical or theoretical predilections.

The specific emphases noted above provide a basis for distinguishing existential sociology from several other proposals advanced in recent years as alternatives to what has been the dominant intellectual motif in sociology: structural functionalism. Our emphasis on feelings, for example, distinguishes existential sociology from those programs that exclusively stress the cognitive aspects of social activities. These include the sociological followers of Husserlian and Schutzian phenomenology: Harold Garfinkel's "ethnomethodology" or "neopraxiology," Aaron Cicourel's "cognitive sociology," and John O'Neill's "wild sociology." All these represent an overreaction to the emphases structural functionalists placed on norms or values in their analyses. And some have matched the absolutism of sociological structural functionalism with their own brands, as exemplified by John O'Neill's assertion (1974:35) that "man is nothing else than the way he talks about himself." Our emphasis on the problematic and situated nature of meaningful experience contrasts both with the structuralism of Alvin Gouldner's "reflexive sociology" and Jurgen Habermas's "critical theory" and with the formalism of dramaturgical approaches in sociology. Our emphasis on the crucial importance of understanding the substantive rationality social actors use in their daily lives contrasts with the unexamined model of formal rationality found in exchange theory, the more recent versions of sociological behaviorism, and even some of the phenomenological sociologies. Our emphasis on the inevitability of politics in everyday life strikes a balance between those new alternatives that make no mention of politics and those that seem to consider all aspects of human existence as political in nature. Our emphasis on systematic research observations and the intimate relations between methodological problems and what is seen and known about the social world distinguishes existential sociology from Gouldner's and O'Neill's sociological introspection. And our evaluative interests contrast with the view of phenomenological description as the beginning and end of the sociological enterprise, as proposed or implied by Matza's "naturalism" and Hugh Mehan and Houston Wood's version of ethnomethodology. Both these last approaches, as well as some others, in our view, represent untenable denials that sociological work ever has direct or indirect moral or ethical implications.

Although this book is aimed at a fundamental reorientation of our understanding of our lives, and although certain emphases herein provide grounds for distinguishing existential sociology from other recently proposed alternatives in sociology, it is important to avoid the excesses that so easily arise when such so-called fundamentals are at issue. It is all too common for readers to seize the distinctive aspects of a theoretical understanding and treat them as the whole. This may be useful for debate or for other rhetorical purposes, but it is destructive of true understanding. By emphasizing the importance of feeling, for example, we never intend to deny the importance of symbolic thought and rationality. Without reason, the human animal would have been extinguished long ago by far more powerful animals; symbolic thought is clearly one of the most distinctive aspects of human existence. What we intend is simply to put first things first, to put these other aspects into the primordial context of human existence. By doing so, we do not deny their importance; rather, we make their nature and significance clearer. Nor do we intend by our emphasis on the concrete, individual, situated nature of our daily lives to deny that there exist shared meanings, patterns, or structures to our lives. On the contrary, we have tried to reintroduce considerations of the need for some shared meanings, for actual patterns and policy matters — considerations largely excluded by other new alternatives in sociology. But we have tried to show that any such ideas of sharedness (or patterns) must be seen in the context of the pluralistic, conflictual, and necessarily problematic nature of our lives. Chapters 4 and 8, for example, emphasize the need to consider both sharedness and problematicness, pluralistic variability and patterns. Nor does our emphasis on the individual's freedom and creativity in any way deny the importance of community, constraint, or power in our world. We have long stressed their importance (Douglas, 1971b), but they must be seen in the context of individual experience, which is the beginning and end of all such abstractions: There is no community, no constraint, no power when individuals do not build them and maintain them. Even Chapter 10, which emphasizes individual freedom and creativity in constructing a gay self, is based on the importance of community or membership meanings to those individuals. But we have tried to put first things first, to build the less basic upon the more basic. Nor does our emphasis upon the crucial distinction between private and public lives mean that we think public lives are unimportant or false. The realities are much more mixed; all parts of our lives are important, only to varying degrees. From our readers we ask for a balanced appraisal of all these considerations.

The reader should consult his or her own social experiences to assess whether we have successfully articulated important truths about our social world. Certainly there will be differences in substantive details between the limited numbers of settings we have studied and the vast range of experiences our readers have. But if we have articulated important truths about social existence, they should be clearly applicable to the experiences of our readers. Insofar as it still makes any sense to speak of a social science's objectivity, this is its foundation — our own everyday, commonsense experiences in society. When reading the arguments about the fundamental importance of love, hate, and all the other feelings in our lives, for example, the reader should consult his or her own life. The conclusion will almost certainly be that the point is obvious. Everyone knows immediately that he is a mass of complex, conflicting, momentarily changing feelings, and that this is where he lives, where his dreams, plans, and works begin and toward which they are directed. The reader may well find it ridiculous that we have had to make such a point of it. We hope, then, that he will see how ridiculous it has been for sociologists, all of whom purport to deal with matters of fundamental importance in social life, to have rarely mentioned feelings except to sweep them aside as residual epiphenomena unimportant to society or as unstudiable by the preconceived methods of "hard science." We hope he will see the obvious need to reconstruct such a science and accept our invitation to join us in this adventure to create more truthful understandings of our experiences.

Jack D. Douglas
John M. Johnson

April, 1977

About the contributors

David L. Altheide (Chapter 4) is Assistant Professor of Sociology at Arizona State University, where he teaches classes in the sociology of deviant behavior, mass communications, research methodology, and social theory. His pulications include *Creating Reality: How TV News Distorts Events* (Sage, 1976) and journal articles in *American Sociological Review, Journal of Work and Occupations, Pacific Sociological Review, Sociology and Social Research, Urban Life*, and others. He is currently involved in research concerning mass media accounts of energy and environmental problems.

John P. Anderson (Chapter 6) received his Ph.D. in sociology from Harvard University in 1971, served as a postdoctoral fellow at Duke University Medical Center between 1971 and 1973, and now works as a Research Associate in the Department of Community Mental Health at the University of California Medical School, San Diego.

Richard H. Brown (Chapter 2) is Associate Professor of Sociology at the University of Maryland at College Park, where he teaches classes in comparative sociology, the philosophy and sociology of knowledge, and social theory. His publications include *A Poetics for Sociology* (Cambridge University Press, 1977), *Structure, Consciousness and History* Cambridge University Press, 1977, coedited with Stanford Lyman), and many journal articles in several academic disciplines.

Jack D. Douglas (Chapter 1 and Appendix) is Professor of Sociology at the University of California, San Diego. He has written and edited twenty-five books in sociology, including *The Social Meanings of Suicide* (Princeton University Press, 1967), *American Social Order*

(Free Press, 1971), *Defining America's Social Problems* (Prentice-Hall, 1973), *Investigative Social Research* (Sage, 1976), and *The Nude Beach* (Sage, 1977, with Paul K. Rasmussen). He is currently completing a book entitled *Creative Deviance and Social Change.*

Andrea Fontana (Chapter 3) received his Ph.D. from the University of California, San Diego, in 1976 and is now Assistant Professor of Sociology at the University of Nevada, Las Vegas. Andy teaches classes in the sociology of deviance, formal organizations, gerontology, and social theory. He is the author of *The Last Frontier: The Social Meanings of Old Age in America* (Sage, 1977) and a forthcoming book of readings, *Culture and Old Age,* coedited with Frederick Preston.

John M. Johnson (Chapters 5, 7, and 8) is Associate Professor of Sociology at Arizona State University, where he teaches classes in the sociology of deviant behavior, social problems, and social theory. His major publications include *Doing Field Research* (Free Press, 1975), *Official Deviance* (Lippincott, 1977, coedited with Jack D. Douglas), and several book chapters and journal articles. He is currently involved in research on child battering, abuse, and neglect.

Joseph A. Kotarba (Chapter 9) is now a Ph.D. candidate in sociology at the University of California, San Diego. One of his earlier publications, "American Acupuncturists: The New Entrepreneurs of Hope," published in *Urban Life* (July 1975), won the 1975 Student Paper Competition Award of the Pacific Sociological Association. He is currently pursuing his research interests in alcoholism, drinking driving, tavern sociability, and the use of unorthodox medical practices.

Barbara Ponse (Chapter 10) received her Ph.D. in sociology from the University of Southern California and is now Assistant Professor of Sociology at Washington University, Saint Louis. Her dissertation research will be published in *Identities in the Lesbian World* (Greenwood Press, forthcoming).

Carol A. B. Warren (Chapter 10) is Assistant Professor of Sociology at the University of Southern California, where she teaches classes in the sociology of deviance, everyday life, human sexuality, and qualitative methods. She is author of *Identity and Community in the Gay World* (Wiley, 1974), *Social Problems in the Seventies* (General Learning Press, 1974, with Sharon K. Davis), *Sociology:*

Change and Continuity (Dorsey Press, 1977), and many journal articles in sociology.

Richard Van de Water (Chapter 3) is a Ph.D. candidate in sociology at the University of California, San Diego. He is interested in the philosophical assumptions of sociological theories.

PART I

Aspects of existential sociology

1

Existential sociology

JACK D. DOUGLAS

The revolt of brute being is an overriding fact of modern history. *Brute being* is that core of feeling and perception that is our innermost selves, our beings. Modern man is rediscovering his brute being, freeing his being, and thereby willing and creating a new self and a new world. Instead of striving vainly to transcend himself, to become some *thing* other than what he is, or submitting out of fear to externally forced repressions of his self and to continued hiding of his self behind elaborate fronts and self-deceptions, he is choosing to search for, to create, and then to fulfill his being. Everywhere modern men have asserted their human existence over other-worldly essences, their subjective beings over the absolutist domination of external objects, their creative feelings over oppressive moralism, the immediate reality of their perceptions over traditionally dictated forms, their self-willed desires over externally imposed repressions, their individual freedoms over collectivist tyrannies. This revolt is now shaking and transforming millions of individual lives, many mass societies, and all intellectual disciplines. We changed our lives first, then our thinking about our lives; now we will use this new form of thinking to change our lives further.

This bald assertion is too simplistic and apocalyptic. Our modern world is complex, highly varied, and full of confusing countertrends. No doubt this revolt, like all revolts, involves its own dangers of excess. Most importantly, it raises serious problems of social order, and these arouse deep anxieties that can produce tyrannical repressions. But, regardless of these modifications and cautions, I believe the crucial force of change, or revitalization, and of creativity in our modern world is this revolt of brute being.

The revolt of brute being, of the man-of-flesh-and-bone-in-the-world, is the dominant thrust of existential thought — in literature, philosophy, theology, psychology, and sociology. Although they are not the first to do so, the existential livers and thinkers, with their many allies working

3

under different banners, have challenged the traditional absolutist forms
of thought and society more successfully than any earlier thinkers.
They have dissected, challenged, attacked, and striven to replace the
traditional absolutist forms of science, which in the past century have
held a sacred place comparable to that occupied by religion in the medieval world; of morality, which has oppressed our everyday lives with its
concept of a homogeneous set of abstract, universal principles enforced
by terrible stigmas and pain; and of bureaucratic controls, which have
progressively herded us all into abstract categories of inhuman data to
be processed.

Like earlier challenges to absolutist forms of thought and society,
this existential challenge may be put down by the absolutists, who have
both good reason to fear its consequences and deep anxieties inspired
by growing social conflict and change. But there is no doubt that existential thought has already been a major challenge to absolutist thought
and that this challenge is increasing today. In recent years the study of
man and society has also increasingly been challenged by the same
changes in our lives that have inspired existential thought and by existential thought itself.

A systematic presentation of the basic ideas of existential sociology
must begin with the question, What do we want to know about human
beings? The obvious answer is that we are concerned with understanding
the social world, rather than the physics of perception, neurophysiology,
cell physiology, the chemistry of life, or any of the other aspects of life.
But that answer masks the many problems involved in deciding which
realm of phenomena we are trying to understand. Just as functional
sociology involved a radical shift in the definition of the relevant realm
of reality, so does existential sociology involve a radical shift from the
realm defined as relevant by the functional sociologists and even by
most of the phenomenological sociologists.

Existential sociology does not begin with a definition of its subject
matter, theoretical paradigm, or set of assumptions about proper scientific methods. Existential sociology begins only with the goal of truthfully understanding man in society. We seek to understand the total
man in his total natural social environment. Nothing about man in
society is irrelevant to our study; nothing about what is truly important
in his life is prejudged or predefined. We take the complete man- and
woman-of-flesh-and-bone in the concrete social situations in which we
find them. Our decisions about what is important, and in what ways,
are based on what we experience and observe about those complete individuals in concrete situations. Our decisions about how we know these
things are based on our experience and our analyses within that experi-

ence of how one does, in fact, know the world. We do not stand outside experience and impose prejudged criteria of scientific methods upon that experience. We do not put society on the rack and try to torture the truth out of it by absolutist scientific methods. We seek truth in the ways we find necessary in the natural social world. We *create* truth from within by finding what works, what enables us to understand, explain, piece together, and partially predict our social world. Our knowledge necessarily remains partially relative, situated, and reflexive, though we continually strive to push it beyond our own immediate situations. We strive to describe and analyze the methods we have used in our concrete studies and to extend these, as we find them useful or workable, to new studies (for a discussion of our methods, see Johnson, 1975; Douglas, 1976).

To demonstrate the significance of this approach to the social world, this chapter briefly examines the development of the major classic sociological perspectives, presents an overview of some of the major conclusions of existential sociology, and then describes some of its most important details.

Classical sociological perspectives

Classical sociology was dominated by a taken-for-granted paradigm of social explanation or theory that we might call the *objective paradigm* (see Chapter 2). The goal was to produce a science of society, and *science* meant the traditional, nineteenth-century natural science aimed at producing knowledge that was "absolutely objective." This goal meant that all social knowledge had to be tied to or made dependent on nonsubjective, absolutely objective phenomena. The history of the traditional philosophy of science made it apparent that the only phenomena that fit that requirement were externally (physically) observable objects or events.

The first major foray into the scientific study of man, social mechanism, took the implications of this requirement literally: Only externally observable phenomena were considered. Man was seen as simply another mechanism, literally a form of clockworks in the early Cartesian works. Man had thoughts, feelings, intentions, and other subjective phenomena; but these were excluded from consideration or, in the case of the Cartesians, considered independent complements of the mechanistic clockworks or possibly epiphenomena — the "mentalistic excrescences" of the brain. Over several centuries the mechanists produced thousands of scholarly works that attempted to explain (supposedly) externally perceivable events in terms of other externally observable events. That is, both the dependent and independent variables, the things explained and those explaining, were externally observable events or phenomena. For example, the mechanists argued that death rates or suicide rates were caused by climatic conditions, such as temperature, or by altitude, or by phases of the moon, or by menstrual cycles, or by thyroid disorders. Not surprisingly, this initial thrust of the science of man led primarily to the development of demography, which until recently retained its head-counting orientation and is still the social science most concerned with externally perceivable things — human bodies.

It was only with tremendous difficulty and soul searching, combined with ingenious ideas and possibly some casuistry, that the classical structural-functional paradigm of social theory grew out of and progressively diverged from this mechanistic model. If one follows the scientific literature on any social subject, such as suicide, through the nineteenth century, he finds a slow development toward considering social meanings as the causes of these externally perceivable events. The fundamental things to be explained, the dependent variables, were still considered externally observable events. These were the social actions (behavior, events), such as suicide, or the institutions, such as capitalism. But increasingly, the first factor in the equation (the independent, causal factor) was some kind of social meaning, especially values. At first these were included as one part of the explanation, along with phases of the moon and everything else (e.g., Morselli, 1903), but by the time of Durkheim and Weber, they were seen as the crucial independent variables, the sole explanation of social action. Because inclusion of this "subjective stuff" imperiled the scientific status of the work, these social meanings were considered to be objectlike in the sense that they could be analyzed as if they were objects. (This argument was more extreme and simplistic in Durkheim than in Weber, and this made Durkheim more acceptable as a model to the later American sociologists, who were committed to making sociology a "real" science.) The usual method was to show that one set of externally observable phenomena, such as divorce rates or rates of widowhood, were causes of another set of externally observable phenomena, such as suicide rates, and to infer, presumably in a completely objective, nonproblematic fashion, that the two were causally related through some necessary, meaningful connection. In this way social meanings were bootlegged into scientific social theory. They were introduced in the guise of objects.

This bootlegging operation became less desirable as the developments of logical positivism led sociologists and others increasingly to believe that objectivity was guaranteed by the methods or procedures of observation and verification, rather than by the nature of the phenomena being studied. Sociologists came increasingly to believe that as long as they observed the subjective phenomena as if they were objects, by following the canons of experimental science, the results were objective. Social meanings, specifically values, could be scientifically determined by "hard methods," such as the use of experimental questionnaires that supposedly prevented the experimenter from biasing the findings by excluding him as much as possible from the situation being observed. (Mail-order questionnaires analyzed by hired data coders became the purest form of science for many.) The paradigm in its most general form, as proposed by the functionalists, still assumed that the dependent variables to be explained were social actions and, as such, presumably externally observable events (though even these were conceded, in line with Weber's definition of action, to be socially meaningful). But in the hands of the functionalists, the paradigm made social values (the "structure" of society) the independent variable, the cause, and simply insisted on determining these by objective means.

The functionalists were aware, like all men of common sense, that thoughts, beliefs, emotions, feelings, and all the other aspects of human subjective experience, exist. They were even at times willing to grant them some importance. Parsons (1951), for example, argued that cognition and affect (i.e., thought and feeling) are both important aspects of an actor's orientation to any situation. However, the functionalists, like mechanists before them, were concerned with explaining the *patterns* of action, and they believed these patterns were the result of the third component of action orientation — evaluation. Values, or rules, were the fundamental independent, causal variables for the functionalists. As Durkheim (1951) put it: "Society is a moral phenomenon." Durkheim believed values must dominate and control human emotions or else society is destroyed (social disintegration results) or the individual himself is destroyed (suicide from egoism or anomie). Parsons (1951) went even further, arguing that the values of society determine whether affect is allowed to be relevant to the situation (values specify either "affective involvement" or "affective neutrality"). Parsons might have agreed that when feelings dominate values there is a failure of "boundary maintenance," but this was beyond the pale of relevance — almost inconceivable. For many functionalists society became synonymous with value patterns as social structure or social system was *defined* in terms of values.

The second major stream of sociological theory in America, the symbolic interactionism of Cooley and Mead, implicitly disagreed with the functionalists about the dominance of values, but agreed completely with the dominance of the cognitive, symbolic level of experience. The interactionists gave little direct consideration to ways in which social values determine social action, but they commonly assumed that values lie behind and determine or constrain the symbolic activity of actors.

The symbolic interactionists emphasized two aspects of human experience — symbols and social action. They saw symbols as the dominant factor, the cause of social action. As a result, their works commonly focused on symbolic activity, especially on the ways in which individuals construct and maintain self-images in terms of a shared universe of symbols (generally linguistic) through their interactions with other actors. The interactionists almost always emphasized the highly symbolic, highly shared aspects of social action. Even when they were concerned with the ways in which individuals construct self-images, they commonly dealt with the construction of highly shared, symbolic self-images (roles) out of a shared universe of symbols. Works in the tradition of Herbert Blumer were partial exceptions to this. Blumer's own work (1969) concentrated more on the choices of constructions than on the shared nature of action, but he gave little consideration to emotions or other less symbolic activity. Shared symbols were clearly the focus of Erving Goffman's writings on self-presentations and of the many works on what Becker et al. (1968) called group perspectives. Group perspectives are those ideas, such as "making the grade," that are shared by the members of a group and that tie together and, presumably, determine their group activities. These group perspectives were almost always named with linguistic symbols, so the focus of the work was on shared linguistic symbols and their determination of social action. Other writers commonly associated, however incorrectly, with the symbolic interactionists carried this emphasis on symbolic activity even further. For example, Kenneth Burke (1950, 1965) went to the extreme of considering linguistic symbolizations (rhetoric and grammar) independently of emotions, actions, or anything else.

The phenomenological philosophers and sociologists followed a similar line of development, but arrived at a different fundamental independent variable. Husserl's phenomenology was the philosophy of consciousness or intention — the meanings of things to the human mind (see Chapters 2 and 3). Explicitly it was a philosophy, not of the world out there ("being-in-itself"), but of how that presumed world is consciously experienced by man and how man experiences himself. But there was also an implicit assumption in this definition of purpose that proved of great importance in the development of the whole phenomenological tradition. This was the assumption that conscious, meaningful, intentional experience was the focus of phenomenology, the foundation of all that would ensue. Perhaps this assumption followed, as some have argued, from Husserl's commitment to shoring up, rather than abandoning, classical rationalism. Specifically, this focus on highly reflective experience seems to have been a result of the phenomenologists' primary concern with examining the properties of the "transcendental ego" (see later in this chapter). Regardless of its origin, it led phenomenologists to emphasize the conscious, cognitve, symbolically meaningful aspects of human experience. There are, of course, phenomenological analyses of perception and feeling, but these have commonly been seen as less fundamental and have been greatly affected by the supposedly more fundamental analyses of conscious, symbolic experience.

Nowhere is this assumption more clear or more important in the development of later social thought than in Alfred Schutz's theory of meaning and the central place this theory played in his social thought (see Chapter 4). Schutz (1967) started his analysis with the assumption that Weber was right in arguing that social experience must be defined as *meaningful* experience. The crucial points of his argument were that Weber had not really shown what meaning is or how we come to have meanings and that Weber's analysis of motivation was inadequate. Schutz agreed with Henri Bergson that there is a stream of human experience (the *durée*) which is the ground of all experience. But he did not see this stream of experience as constituting meaning. Rather, meaning was created when the *durée* was broken by reflection, by looking back upon earlier experience, or by projecting oneself from the present into the future. Schutz, then, defined meaning in terms of highly conscious, reflective experience.

Schutz did not define meaning in terms of feeling or emotion or simple perception, all of which may be subconscious or even conscious, but not reflective. (It is quite possible that Schutz saw all consciousness as reflective by definition, in which case unreflective, but conscious, feeling would be impossible by definition. If so, his definition is simply contrary to commonsense experience and the meanings of the term.)

The effects of this theory of meaning on Schutz's social theory are clear. His social theory was sharply focused on "typifications," or highly shared meaningful experiences, which are commonly associated with linguistic symbols (names). Although his social theory was only secondarily concerned with action, Schutz's theory implicitly assumed that in some way actions (such as work) followed from the typifications constructed for the situation. Moreover, the emphasis throughout most of his work was on the rational, planful nature of human thought and action, as seen, for example, in his basic concern with "projects."

Schutz's theory was carried to its logical conclusion by Berger and Luckmann (1967). These authors defined their work as a "sociology of knowledge" because they assumed that commonsense knowledge in everyday life is the basic focus and determinant of everyday social action. Their book was devoted to an analysis of the ways in which highly shared symbols are used to construct typified social presentations and patterns of action (roles), which are then objectified, largely as a result of a failure to remember (cognitively) that the constructions are indeed constructions. The purpose of the work appears to have been to provide a phenomenological foundation for the Durkheimian (functional) theory of social order. Berger and Luckmann assumed, with Durkheim, that the social world is indeed highly ordered and that this order is the direct result of social values. They emphasized the cognitive, symbolic, rational nature of society more than Durkheim did, as Durkheim was always at least aware of the existence of the "darker" side of human experience — emotions.

The ethnomethodologists took the same path, but frequently went to even greater extremes in considering only the highly symbolic and commonsensically rational forms of human experience (see Chapter 5). This is seen in the very definition of *ethnomethodology:* the study of "accounts" in everyday social life (Garfinkel, 1967). More specifically, this study of accounts focused on the ways in which the members of society show their actions to each other to be "rationally accountable." A huge realm of commonsense considerations was immediately shorn away by the definition of the term. The ethnomethodologist did not even recognize the legitimacy of asking whether the members themselves believe their own accounts (whether they are lying) or whether they are simply presenting "rational accounts" for public purposes, while knowing full well that they are doing something "because it feels good," or because they feel forced to act on the basis of "guesses" and "hope for the best," or "on faith," or for some other irrational reason.

The ethnomethodological concern with *indexicality* (the ways in which the situations of use are crucial in the interpretations of the meanings of symbolic accounts) could have led to a consideration of the unexpressed, even unexpressible, forms of human experience. In a few instances it did. But most ethnomethodologists moved steadily in the direction of considering only overtly expressed, linguistically symbolized accounts. At the ultimate extreme, as found in the writings of Harvey Sacks and his co-workers, this form of linguistic ethnomethodology imposed the further constraint that only those accounts that could be tape-recorded or videotaped could be studied. Ethnomethodology thus merged with linguistics. (This emphasis in ethnomethodology was probably due in large part to the implicit commitment of the ethnomethodologists to the search for the Husserlian transcendental ego; see later in this chapter.) Ethnomethodologists came to focus their work on symbolic, commonsensically rational, overtly expressed, linguistic accounts. As a result, the enterprise became a narrow one, with little or nothing to say, by self-imposed definition, about the experiences that concern human beings most in their everyday lives. Love, hate, anxiety, agony, order, disorder, deceit, lies, truth — all were supposedly irrelevant to the study of man and should, by definition, be ignored. They might be studied indirectly in terms of what linguistic statements suggested about them, but even this could not be assessed because assessment would involve answering such questions as whether those experiences exist and what their relations to linguistic statements might be. Any such questions were forbidden by the rationalist vow to study only accounts.

All of us who have contributed to this book on existential sociology began our sociological work within the confines of classical sociology. We early found that tradition inadequate to deal with the problems and truths we encountered in our everyday lives and in our research into a broad spectrum of American society. We thus used the phenomenological ideas to help us understand our social world. We came increasingly to see the limitations of that form of thought and then discovered that the existential philosophers had followed a similar line of development in moving beyond Husserl's phenomenology. All our work remains fundamentally grounded in our own experience and our ever-expanding research on American and European society, but we have found some of the basic ideas of existential literature and philosophy of great help in clarifying and systematizing our ideas, in building our theoretical foundations behind us as we move forward. Although we are committed to remaining open to new experience in the world, and thus to avoiding any permanent closures of thought about the world, it is helpful to start the presentation of our many findings and ideas with an overview of man in society. This is necessarily an elliptical overview, meant to stimulate insights, to be a general guide to understanding what comes later in this book, and to make more systematic what has already appeared in earlier works. The understanding is also necessarily changing, for we must continually rebuild our rational foundations as we gain new experience.

An existential view of man in society

All the traditional social science conceptions of man and society agree in seeing the individual as caused by something, though their conceptions of cause and how to infer it vary. Man and his actions are the dependent variables. Each theory recognizes the existence of other causes and may even accept them as in some undetermined way important; but each theory is fundamentally monocausal. The utilitarians in economics and sociology saw rational calculations of personal gain as the basic cause. The structural functionalists replaced these causes with values or norms.

The symbolic interactionists, the phenomenologists, and the ethnomethodologists replaced the idea of causality with a more complex view
of social processes, but remained largely in agreement that one basic
process of consciousness — symbol construction, rational accounting,
linguistic accounting — was the fundamental concern of social science.
Man remained monolithic, essentially symbolic, generally rational, and
in one way or another determined. Man was seen as the dependent variable that used its own reason to minimax that dependency. Indeed, the
ethnomethodologists have transcended man and his world by defining
their project as concerned only with the invariant (totally predetermined)
properties of symbolic accounts.

All of these monocausal theories involve some form of the rationalist
fallacy. The opposite strain of absolutist modern thought about man,
more common in the tyrannical Eastern societies, is Marxism. Rather
than viewing man as determined by values and cognitions, Marxism sees
him as determined by his external situation, primarily his economic interests and the modes of production in which he is enmeshed. Man, as
well as his values and cognitions, is the product of his physical situation.
Man becomes an irrational, almost unthinking, externally determined
puppet. This extreme form of the irrationalist, determinist model of
man has proved just as false and just as useless (except as political rhetoric
aimed at inflaming and justifying hatreds) as its opposite, the rationalist
model. Indeed, in its extreme form this irrationalist model is merely a
modern form of mechanism and possesses all the fallacies the functionalists saw in the earlier forms. Man can no more be grasped, understood,
and explained in terms of his external environment than in terms of his
symbolic universe (his rational accounts). Today, almost all intellectual
Marxists, such as the "critical sociologists" (Habermas, 1970), have
begun to look at man's interests in broad terms. These terms have become so broad that they have often merged the external puppet model
of man with the phenomenologists' internal consciousness model to produce a contorted phenomenological Marxism that retains nothing but
the name of Marxism and the weaknesses of the rationalist phenomenological model.

Between these two extremes of rationalism and external determinism
are the internal-determinist theories, primarily those of the biological
determinists and the unconsciousness determinists. The biological determinists have contributed much important knowledge about the
neurophysiological and hormonal substrata of some of man's feelings
and thoughts, but their attempts to explain man's actions in the world
have generally been so simplistic as to be ludicrous. (The new sociobiology of Edward Wilson, 1975, and others is a very important exception to this.) Only those ignorant of the vast complexities of man-in-the-

world pay any attention to them today, though their works were numerous earlier in this century. Those determinists, especially the psychoanalysts, who explain man's actions in the world in terms of unconscious forces, have also made important contributions to our understanding, especially of those forms of behavior that are rigid and unfree (i.e., neurotic). They have also shown how important, often vast, forms of social actions are at least partly inspired by such rigid, unconscious emotions. And they opened the way for the studies of nonneurotic sex and other vital forms of man's everyday emotional life. But the traditional forms of psychoanalysis, as distinct from the many forms of humanistic psychology, existential psychology, or *Daseinsanalysis*, remain too wedded to the study of neurotic behavior to offer a basic perspective in understanding man-in-the-world. At their worst, these theories are merely another form of irrationalist, monocausal determinism (e.g., using Oedipal conflicts to explain almost everything). The psychological theories that do not involve such assumptions (e.g., some personality theories) are more helpful, but are almost always concerned with personality structure cut off from the world and from man's concrete situations, and are more dedicated to scientific methods than to understanding man-in-the-world.

Commonsense concepts of man, as of most other things, are rarely monocausal, rationalistic, deterministic, or scientistic. Instead of being systematically wedded to one view of man, the commonsense actor uses many different views of man in different situations. In Western democracies, platitudes about human freedom and liberty abound; yet the same patriotic defender of individual freedom to choose one's own life can easily slide into economic determinism when he argues for capitalism as the only economic system that produces or sustains man's freedom. The same person who believes that each man makes his own bed commonly believes that each man must make his choices in accord with the iron laws of conscience. He may also believe that most people are sheep who conform to the dictates of society.

Men of common sense frequently appeal to reason or rationality, saying "Be reasonable, man . . . ," or "Rationality demands. . . ." Yet the one point about man that seems to pervade commonsense thought about human action is that reason is highly variable, undependable, and weak compared with emotions or feelings. There are many attitudes about the weaknesses of man, the inevitability of sin (generally related to sex and money), and the temptations of the world. Practical men commonly view the rhetoric of rationality with great suspicion: "Oh, yeah, what's in it for you?" Lust and greed, along with a host of lesser feelings, are assumed to be omnipresent and potent. Reason is seen largely as the handmaiden of these passions, the servant who caters to their interests, finding a way to fulfill them while hiding these realities from enemies. Morals were once thought to be powerful allies of reason, but today few men of common sense place much faith in morality as a dominating force in the world. Anyone who leaves his door unlocked is thought to be crazy, and people more commonly believe that everyone has his price (ultimately, everyone is greedy) than that the values on honesty will save his property and keep politicians honest. The man of practical wisdom is more likely to agree with Shakespeare that "morals are as straw in the wind to the fire in the blood" than to share the value determinism of most sociologists.

All our systematic observations of individuals in our own everyday lives and in our research settings (dealt with in our earlier works) have led us to believe that these complex, varied, and conflicting views of man are more true than the social science models of man. No mono-causal view of man can possibly capture more than the shadow cast by the vast and shifting mosiac of his realities. Man's existence is funda-mentally problematic, both for man as actor and for anyone who would understand his existence. Man is varied, changeable, uncertain, conflict-ful, and partially free to choose what he will do and what he will be-come, because he must be so to exist in a world that is varied, change-able, uncertain, and conflictful (or that seems so to him because he has never been able to cope with it successfully for any long period on any other basis). The only way man has been able to survive in his world, both the physical and social world, is by adapting himself to it. Man is necessarily open to his world, thrown into his worldly situations. Man is fundamentally grounded, situational — existential. His worldly exist-ence is fundamentally changeable and emergent (unpredictable, uncer-tain); so man, the most successful adapter and maker in the history of the animal world, is also fundamentally changeable and emergent. Man, is necessarily both situational and free. Yet to be situational is to be constrained by, at least indirectly determined by, the situation; to be free is to be the opposite, to be unconstrained and transistuational (transcendent). Man is both. Man is in basic conflict with himself and his world — determined and free, situational and transsituational. Try as they will, and there are many ancient religions dedicated to the at-tempt, most men can find no ultimate resolution to this necessary con-flict. Only small elites, living upon the struggling masses, but walled off from them, can realistically hope for that dreamy state of harmony, certainty, stasis, and lack of passion and individual selfhood — nirvana. The masses of men can only hope for it in a heavenly afterlife.

Practical wisdom is right in seeing man as fundamentally a feeling being. We live for feelings. Feelings lie behind, are the foundation of and the goal of, all thought. Feelings pervade thought, are fused with thought, inspire thought, and at the extreme, destroy thought. But feeling without thought is blind. Thought (reason, rationality) is the guide of feelings, the seeker and symbolic tester of ways to their expression, gratification, fulfillment, and growth. The primacy and ultimate dominance of feeling in our lives has led some existential philosophers, and many more men of practical action, to view man's life as ultimately irrational. They exult with Tertullian in their rebellion against reason: *"Credo quia absurdum"* ("I believe [it] *because* it is absurd"). Even the balanced Unamuno asserted: "Hegel made famous his aphorism that all the rational is real and all the real rational; but there are many of us who, unconvinced by Hegel, continue to believe that the real, the really real, is irrational, that reason builds upon irrationalities" (1954:5). William Barrett (1962) has even tried to capture the massive, multifaceted existential rebellion with the image of irrational man. But this supposed irrationalism of the existentialists is a gross exaggeration resulting from their angry, rebellious denunciations of the overrationalized concepts of classic, positivist, and scientific thinkers. William James was carried by this conflict to angry vituperations against reason, yet his own work (such as that on religious experience) retained and used all the strengths of Western reason. He simply wanted to right the balance, to assert the primacy of feeling, of the nonrational, not the irrational or the antirational, in human life. James was no more a man who thought with his blood, than Nietzsche was an intentional unleasher of the Nazi Superman or Merleau-Ponty a total devotée of unbridled passions and momentary feelings. As Barrett has rightly argued, existential thinkers (and all those whose thoughts we know of were precisely that — specialists in human thought and symbolic communication) were above all interested in reestablishing concern with the whole man as he lives in his world:

Both Marxism and Positivism are, intellectually speaking, relics of the nineteenth-century Enlightenment that have not yet come to terms with the shadow side of human life as grasped even by some of the nineteenth-century thinkers themselves. The Marxist and Positivist picture of man, consequently, is thin and oversimplified. Existential philosophy, as a revolt against such oversimplification, attempts to grasp the image of the whole man, even where this involves bringing to consciousness all that is dark and questionable in his existence. And in just this respect it is a much more authentic expression of our own contemporary experience. [Barrett, 1962:22]

To present the whole picture we must begin with the beginning, the foundation and the end of all else: feeling. We begin with what Merleau-Ponty called "brute being." But we must also see how necessary and valuable reason is to all human life, how reason guides feeling to expression, gratification, fulfillment, and growth. We must then see that reason can do this only by becoming fused with feeling, that it is inevit-

ably pervaded by feeling, and that reason in its most exalted form —
Absolute Truth — is commonly a masked and perverted form of man's
darkest, most dangerous passions.

Reason becomes a force, rather than merely a symbolic shadow or
memory device, by being invested with feeling, fused with feeling. It becomes fused with feeling by *succeeding* as a guide to the expression,
gratification, fulfillment, and growth of those feelings we have and
crave. Reason must ultimately meet the iron rule of practicality: It must
work to fulfill our ultimate desires. Man is not born with "categories of
thought" or "invariant cognitive procedures," though eons of evolution
have indeed endowed his newborn body with the neurophysiological
capacity quickly to learn the basic forms of reason. The newborn baby
does not know that he cannot have both x and non-x, cannot both have
his cake and eat it too. He must learn it the hard way, generally with
considerable pain. But all those who cannot so learn, and quickly and
thoroughly, soon die and disappear from the gene pool. It has taken an
immense history of such hard learning, of pain and death, for us to
achieve our present forms of reason. At some points, man learned to
generalize about reason, to see the general power of reason. Reason became an independent force in life, but only by remaining fused at its
foundations with feeling.

The lives of some part of society may even become primarily devoted
to reason, but this is a specialization of life that inevitably threatens to
become a perversion for such specialization is largely cut off from the
basic fact of life, the grounding of all our being in the world, in our existence, in feeling. Priests and intellectuals, men and women dedicated
to abstract (symbolic) ideals, may provide valuable services to life, but
they may also become the most terrible destroyers of life, for their very
strength in society (their symbolic abilities), may lead to their being cut
off from the basic force of life, to their using mythical symbolic forms
to oppress the masses, and even to their becoming destroyers of society.
For the man of practical wisdom, reason is for living, not living for
reason; for the intellectual and true believer, this basic priority may be
inverted and impassioned (neurotic) reason turned against the basic
forces of life. Presenting themselves as "idealistic lovers of abstract ideals
of justice," these "men of reason" can become impassioned haters of
those they see as the enemy. Men of unbridled physical passions — the
Genghis Khans — may rape, pillage, and destroy for brief periods. But
the men of passionate reason and abstract ideals — the Robespierres,
the Lenins, the Hitlers — are the builders of the world's absolutist tyrannies, which are sometimes destroyers of bodies, hearts, and minds for
centuries.

It is, of course, precisely the development of partially independent

symbolic thought that gave man his crucial adaptive advantage over all
other animals. It is this symbolic ability and its central integrating
mechanisms, especially of reason, or rationality, and creativity, that
allow man partially to stand back from, or transcend, his situation; to
imagine alternative paths of action in that situation; and to imagine new
situations and test out the consequences of his acts in the world before
commiting his body to those actions. It is their extensive development
of the symbolic abilities that gives certain cultures, especially the Western world in recent centuries, a crucial advantage in the international
struggle among cultures. From the standpoint of the struggle, of conflict and warfare, reason is indeed the glory of man. It is his crucial
weapon. Because of the central place of struggle and, thus, of weaponry
in all human civilization, this has led to a growing independence and official dominance of certain forms of rational thought in Western culture
and then in other nations as they sought to gain advantage against the
West.

This position of thought as a partially independent motivating force
was for centuries restricted to small elites of intellectuals, scientists,
technicians, businessmen, and government bureaucrats. But their suc-
cesses led to its spread throughout society, with the middle classes being its primary cultural carrier. They were able to impose pain and death
upon those who did not submit to their plans. For the first time large
segments of society were increasingly subjected to careful training (education), which had as its primary goals the learning of discipline, self-
control over the emotions, the ability to postpone gratifications, to
suffer in the short run for the long run. At first the recruits to this
rationalized segment of society were self-selected. But as that segment
of society succeeded and grew, submission to it became more and more
a necessity if one wanted to earn the money needed to buy the essentials
of life. But submission was not easy for adults or lightly accepted. Governments moved to force the young to learn the necessary discipline
through universal compulsory education. (Following such basic social
changes, and serving as a symbol of what exists, the value of universal
higher education became one of the official values in all Western societies, especially in the most rationalized.) As the success of the rationalization grew geometrically, the forced training increased and spread to
all groups in society. Most submitted enough to "get by" and "make
out." They put in their eight hours and developed fantasy lives, personal
relationships, and informal practices on the job to provide some means
of expressing, gratifying, and fulfilling their feelings. Those cultural
groups that would not submit to the early training necessary to learn
these painful internal repressions were supported at minimal levels by
massive government welfare programs to avoid massive revolt.

Because of the ultimate dominance of feeling in our animal lives, thought can become dominant in human action only if it is invested or fused with feeling ("cathected," in the terms of depth psychology). As soon as this is done, the individual suffers conflict within himself, for the primal animal feelings — those that constitute brute being — may be inhibited, or suppressed, by the learning of stronger feelings, especially learning the fear of expressing the primal feeling, but they can never be eliminated except through organic atrophy or death. Because of the great power of fear in the human animal, and the ease of eliciting it, fear has been the dominant feeling used to force children to learn to adapt to the rationalized society. This has produced great conflict within individuals, which has been partially alleviated by allowing (at least privately, behind the public fronts) some expression (but not gratification or fulfillment) of the primal feelings through massive fantasy life (pornography, drama, novels, comics, movies, TV viewer sports, daydreaming) and profuse escapism (modern leisure activities, tourism, participant sports). But the conflict has remained, has grown and spread as the rationalization grew and spread, has pervaded our lives with diffuse feelings of fear, anxiety, boredom, dullness, deadness of feeling, and even dread. But it is precisely these feelings, and the use of fear to produce trained internal conflict and the excessive dominance of abstract symbolic thought over feeling, that have led to the growing revolt of brute being throughout Western societies. The sexual revolution, the rage for spontaneity and feeling, sensitivity training (a rationalistic approach to derationalizing), humanistic psychology, Eastern religions, transcendental meditation, the many forms of existential thought (thought in the service of feeling), and a vast array of other modern individual and social movements express in complex and conflictful ways this revolt of our primal animal beings against the overrationalized and overfearful absolutist society that has been forced on us over the centuries. As our affluence and feeling of security have grown, our fears have waned and our positive feelings have grown — and we have revolted against inhibition of them. Our escapist activities (especially television watching, drug use, sports, and "action") have been reinforced by our pervasive anxiety and dread because they allow us to hide from those feelings, to deceive ourselves temporarily. Some of these feelings spring directly from the conflict between our rationalized (secularized) world view, which attacks our profound animal hunger, and our craving for immortality (or, at least, our desire not to die). Such anxieties and dreads can be overcome only by direct assertion of feelings over these absurdities of supposed reason. (I believe nothing could be more irrational than to deny our innermost beings and I believe

nothing is more basic to our beings than to live and to will to live.)
These conflicts with our overrationalized world are so deep and threatening, and so well hidden by convoluted forms of self-deception and
escapism, that we can hardly observe them except by probing within
ourselves and a few of our most trusted friends. These conflicts, then,
can hardly be dealt with by reason. Other conflicts are far more observable and far more amenable to rational (scientific) understanding and
partial resolution. These are especially the conflicts between some of
our ancient laws and our animal feelings, between our desire to live
freely and with personal integrity and the repressive giant bureaucracies
that needlessly herd us into abstract categories, and between the desire
to live our own lives and the demands of abstract Big Governments with
which we no longer identify — tyrannies. The power of the feelings
being unleashed, especially the feelings of rage and hatred that are
increasingly turned against those believed to be repressors, and by them
against those seen to be primitive revolutionaries, poses profound
dangers for social order. Only practical political reason can guide such
deep conflicts to a partial resolution and the specialized form of empirical reason known as social science can help us to resolve the complex
conflicts that make up the problem of social order in our society.

The problem of social order is central to civilized man's existence
and to all attempts to understand and deal with the problems of his
existence. It is a necessary problem flowing from the very nature of
man-in-the-world, especially of man-in-the-civilized-world. The vast
majority of mankind has always assumed that man is a social animal out
of simple necessity; that social life was always a basic adaptation of the
physically weak human animal to his harsh world. Man is thrown into
his social world at birth and can live only by being part of, within, and
pervaded by, society. Even those who revolt against a society use the
basic forms of social life they have inherited to rebuild society. (Indeed,
they often retain the basic forms and repress the emerging ones, so that
revolutionaries like Lenin unintentionally become the most extreme
reactionaries.) For men to live together, social order — some forms of
social patternings and agreements — is necessary. Social rules of many
different kinds have been universal tools used in attempting to construct
and maintain the social order necessary to social life. In their own private
lives, their face-to-face lives, men have almost always taken for granted
that the rules were made for living, not living for the rules; the rules and
the social order they were intended to further are in the direct and indirect service of our feelings, desires, motives in everyday life situations.
Because of the necessary uncertainties and freedoms of human beings,
conflicts within and among human beings are necessary, inevitable.

Thus, social order and the uses of rules are necessarily problematic and conflictful. But rules and ideas of social order, being abstract (symbolic), are subject to the same independence and perversions as any form of abstract thought: They may be invested with feelings themselves and presented as rightfully and necessarily dominant over all other feelings. The passion for rationality may even attack all feelings with hysterical emotion. When this happens within individuals, the result is individual conflicts (neuroses, guilt) and subtle and complex ways by which feelings circumvent the dictates of rules (repressions, evasions, rationalizations, self-deceptions). When it happens among individuals, the result is social conflict (arguments, fights, wars) and ways of circumventing the rules (rationalizations, evasions, deceits, lies, fronts) to express, gratify, fulfull, and increase our individual feelings. In massive, complex, pluralistic, and conflictful civilized societies, such as those of the Western world, and especially the United States, the rules may be invested with absolutist status, made to appear universal and objectlike, and entrusted to absolutist organizations (government bureaucracies, courts, police) presented as above individual feelings and thoughts (a "society of laws, not men"). These forms of official (bureaucratic) absolutism are largely attempts to deal with the enormous problems of social order in such societies. They have helped to do that at times, but the problems and conflicts have grown ever greater; circumventions have become massive from the bottom to the top of society; the absolutist forms are seen increasingly as political rhetoric; individual alienation from society and social disorder have grown. The alienated individual, whose social feelings of love, affiliation, and hope have been largely replaced with feelings of disgust, hatred, and anxiety, is increasingly common in Western societies. He is a real threat to social order. While many search for new, creative ways of rebuilding social order others look increasingly to the use of external force to support the absolutist forms of government or to supplant these with the tyrannies of idealistic rationalisms — the Central Plan of the Welfare State Bureaucracies.

New forms of man and society are emerging, partially constrained by the necessities of the world in which we must live, but partially chosen by men seeking to express, gratify, fulfill, and increase their innermost selves, their animal beings. Existential thought, from philosophy and literature to the social sciences, is grounded in and systematically analyzes the whole existence of man; it attempts to provide guides to the expression, gratification, fulfillment, and growth of these deep desires of men today. Existential sociology, by focusing on the vital realm of man's being in his social world, aims at making vital contributions to that more general understanding and practical action at both the individual and political levels.

The partial independence and dominance of feelings over thought

In dealing with such basics as the dominance of feeling over thinking and the complex fusions and interactions of thought and feeling, let me begin by noting that any decision about the independence and relative weights of feeling and thought is problematic in most concrete situations. Most of the activities of our everyday lives are a complex mosaic of external perceptions (visual images, sounds), thoughts, feelings, and actions. There is normally what John Johnson has rightly called a *fusion of thought and feeling* including a fusion of these with perceptions and actions). Perceptions, thoughts, and feelings run into, permeate, and pervade each other. As Johnson has also argued, this fact is well communicated by everyday language, which commonly uses "I think," "I see," and "I feel" ("in my opinion" and "my feeling") interchangeably. Even worse, for the social analyst, any concrete situation commonly involves a complex interplay of alternative, contending, and conflictful fusions of perceptions, thoughts, feelings, and actions. (To say, as Freudians do, that everyday actions are overdetermined, or determined by a number of motives interacting, is true, but an oversimplification. To say, as Parsons, Merton, and other functionalists do, that all action is motivated, is to recognize or assume that feelings always lie behind actions or ahead of them, but is grossly simplistic.) Consider even simple actions, such as a decision to go to the beach. Feelings of fatigue, exhilaration, love of the ocean, dislike of jellyfish or the cold water, fear of sunburn, the relative costs of gas, alternative pleasures that must be forgone — all these and many more may briefly intrude into conscious experience. In our everyday lives the resolutions of these complex interactions (or interfusions) are usually reasonably well patterned. We go to work even when we feel sleepy, tired, or bored as a matter of routine (custom). My argument is that this will happen only as long as these feelings are dominated by some greater feeling, such as the fear of losing a job, being embarrassed, starving. Routine or custom in human life is *not* the result of some principle of inertia or law of least effort. Man is a restless, nervous, emotional, striving primate, not an inert sloth. The argument is that we think of these possibilities and this triggers a feeling of fear that leads us to carry out the routine action of going to work in spite of the feelings against it. If the thought of losing the job does not trigger fear, but, instead, produces a shrug of the shoulders and a "so what," or, even more, if it triggers a feeling of joy, then we do not go to work. But my point here is that normally there is such a fusion of thoughts and feelings that we cannot be sure what is dominating what.

The worst problem involved in analyzing the complex flow of our everyday experience is that most of our experiences in everyday life are only semiconscious; the consciousness of them emerges as we do them; it does not precede and determine them. And the very act of thinking about them in order to observe them makes them highly conscious, so that the rationalist model of action appears justified (especially for intellectuals, who have been trained since childhood to take this view of man). Certainly some activities are carefully, consciously planned and then carried out as planned. But this is unusual. Even the supposedly rational, scientific planning called social planning is largely ex post facto rationalization of what is already being done or of what the planners wanted to do before they started planning. (As one high-level university planner told me about one of higher education's most important plans: "Naturally, I made sure it proposed that our campus should do exactly what we were already doing or wanted to do.") Social planning today is almost always a political deception. Normally, in our everyday lives we consciously plan our activities only when we are doing something problematic, when there are new aspects, uncertainities, conflicts, or dangers. Otherwise, symbolic consciousness of the activities emerges as we proceed, if at all. At the extreme, it is obvious that the degree of symbolic consciousness involved in the intellectual analysis we are doing here is relatively rare in human experience, made possible only by centuries of cultural development and by many years of intense individual efforts. Just as the ordinary language of the Oxford don is in no way the ordinary language of the East End of London, so is the ordinary internal experience of the intellectual not the ordinary internal experience of most people.

The nature of internal human experience can be observed without (basically) transforming it (i.e., without great uncertainty effects) only by a complex process of defocusing, grasping, self-observation, description, understanding, theoretical analysis and communication, in roughly that order. As I have dealt with the details and justifications of this process in another work (Douglas, 1976), I shall note only the major points here. First, the defocusing, or flowing with natural experience in natural situations, is crucial, especially for intellectuals. We have to immerse ourselves in a situation without thinking about it in any theoretical way before or during the experience. Otherwise, we determine our observations by our methods of theoretically experiencing the situation, and our findings end by being rationalistic. Second, we observe ourselves retrospectively. The phenomenologist introspects his experience; that is, he watches his own conscious experience of the world. The world thus becomes a highly conscious (symbolic) and intended experience. We become aware of how oversymbolized and overintentional such introspective experience is by retrospectively comparing it with our normal (defocused) experience. (This clearly makes the properties of human memory an important determinant of understanding. But, the fact (supported by all studies so far) that *conscious* memory retains symbolic experience more easily than nonsymbolic supports our conclusion from retrospective observation that defocused experience is not highly symbolic. Unlike introspection, which is almost always done in the armchair and in the library, self-observation is done initially in the natural setting. Third, our initial goal is to grasp the experience, to hold it in its natural form (largely unsymbolic) in our memories. Only later do we try to retrieve, describe symbolically, and then understand and theorize about our experience; and all these later stages are done as much as possible in the natural setting to fit the symbols to the natural experience so that others will grasp the natural experience. This involves not only fitting previously shared symbols, which is obviously necessary, but also creating new ones and, especially, using the old in new combinations and contexts to communicate new meanings. (I need hardly point out how problematic this is. It demands that the sociologist be poet first and scientist second, a combination that all our education has been aimed at destroying.) This kind of complex process, leads to my conclusion that feelings are the dominant independent force in our everyday lives.

In spite of the general problems involved, the relative independence of feelings in our experience is easily observed in certain ways. Everyone knows how important moods are in his life. On some days and in some situations, or even at some moments, an individual feels full of energy, optimistic, sure, confident, happy, exhilarated, ecstatic; or tired out, run down, used up, wasted, worn out, depressed, unsure, scared, anxious. A person can feel uneasy, feel that things are bound to turn out okay, have a sense of foreboding, feel in his bones that he will win. He can be irritated, at peace, mad at the world, happy with the world, benevolent, mean. We all know how important moods are in determining the things our friends, loved ones, enemies, and hated ones think and do. We know that some people in some situations are more moody and less moody. We watch for moods and, unless they rub our moods the wrong way at the wrong time, we are apt to take them into consideration in evaluating other people, the situation, and our best course of action. A statement such as, "Dad, Mom's tired today, so I wouldn't say that if I were you," is commonsensically wise. (It is the statement of a nine-year-old girl who has yet to learn much of human wisdom, but who already *grasps* the practical facts of human life — feeling.)

Moods are diffuse feelings that cannot be directly attributed to some external situation by the individuals involved. They come largely from within or from nowhere. Situational feelings are closely related to moods. Probably most situational feelings are so closely tied to everyday pat-

terns of thought, values, and actions that they appear (in our overrationalized society) to be merely the effects of values or thoughts. But there
are some that arise in situations in such a way that they seem to the individual to come from nowhere, to be inexplicable, or even to be so totally
foreign that they seem unrecognizable. He may even fight to deny them,
but they persist — mysteriously. Guilt is one of the most common feelings of this sort. An individual commonly provides all kinds of rational
accounts to himself for doing the action involved, both before and after
the event. He sometimes carefully constructs his rational case over a
period of years, even subconsciously manipulating others to get them to
act in such ways that he feels justified in doing what he does. He may
even subscribe to a whole ideology and social movement, or construct
his own rational system of ethics and act in the most rational manner
possible in carrying out his ideological commitments — only to find himself suffering a totally unexpected emotional conflict. After all the rationalizing, all the legalizing, all the justification, all the planning, and all
the arrangement of symbolic social definitions, the individual feels overwhelmed by guilt that comes from nowhere, wells up within him, racks
his body with bitter tears, fills his mind with the anguished or accusing
voices and faces of his victims, and may lead him to kill himself in remorse and repentance.

  This, for example, seems to be a common experience of women who
deliberately undergo abortions. They are often even deeply committed
to ideals of feminism, which lead them to believe as a matter of moral
principle that women have the right to control their own bodies, including the right to abortion "on demand." They make political demands
for abortion as natural and a right. But the feelings of their bodies often
astound them. We found this in the lives of two young women we studied over two years. The studies were long-term social biographical investigations done in natural settings. We were not relying only upon what
the individuals told us about themselves, as has been true in almost every
social biography done thus far and as is universally true in psychiatric
and personality studies. We knew these women, their friends, lovers,
enemies, and others in their natural settings. In the case of these two
women (though not in all the social biographical studies we have done),
we found that what they told us checked out with our own observations
and understandings of their lives. (This does not mean they did not
contradict themselves. Only simpleminded and overrationalized personality assessment questionnaires assume that noncontradiction is a test
of honesty. In fact, everyone is found to be self-contradictory in the
real world, simply because of the fundamentally situational and problematic nature of a person's understanding of himself and of his world.

Contradiction is often the best test of sincerity: The person is not well rehearsed.)

The first excerpt is taken from a taped discussion with Janine. We were not talking or thinking about abortions at the time. I had read that morning of a threatened suicide in which the threat was used by a young man to prevent his girl friend from getting an abortion. That led me to wonder if there were other such cases of profound feeling against abortion, besides those that seemed (at the time) to be clearly inspired by formal religious values. Although I had recognized the problem involved in defining abortion as victimless because of the death of the fetus, I had not previously thought of the woman as a possible victim. (Besides, such things are never discussed in the news accounts of the politics of abortion.) This discussion, then, came up by surprise, started me thinking about such surprising feelings, and led to surprising conclusions. We were talking about medical examinations when Janine introduced the subject of her abortion:

Janine: I had my sort of miniabortion yesterday . . . and I had to go into a separate room there . . . and there was a doctor and nurse there . . . and they were so nice . . . they were just the loveliest people . . . really good people . . . and it was really painful. I was surprised it was that painful. And in the beginning I had thought it would be nice if John could be with me 'cause it was his baby . . . also that we were killing it, you know . . . all this stuff was going through my head . . . really strange stuff.

J.D.: Yeah? Like, really upsetting emotionally?

Janine: Yeah . . . *especially* afterwards! Right afterwards, I was just *really* upset . . . 'cause, you know, at that time it was done and there was nothing I could do about it and that was it . . . it was over.

J.D.: That's one of those things you didn't anticipate? . . . that you feel that . . . well you felt depressed about it?

Janine: Yeah . . . I felt that I . . . that I had killed a baby . . . even though it was a, you know, a six-month — uh-h, a six-week old little thing that, you know . . . wouldn't mean . . .

J.D.: You hadn't felt that way about it at all before?

Janine: No! Not really . . . John had . . . John had been restless the night before. He couldn't sleep at all. He was really upset this morning.

[J.D. then mentioned the case of a man he had read about in the paper who had threatened to jump off the Golden Gate Bridge and had come down only when his girl friend promised not to abort their baby.]

J.D.: I certainly would have thought that . . . I mean I would have imagined . . . I can't remember your ever saying anything about it, but I would imagine that you know, like most young people today, and especially, you know, the liberated ideas or what . . . that you had bought the idea of abortion as everybody's right and all.

Janine: Yeah.

J.D.: And then it turns out different.

Janine: Yeah . . . it *really* surprised me . . . 'cause I *knew* there was no way I could possibly have a baby . . . I mean, I just couldn't . . . I just couldn't have a baby, 'cause I couldn't take care of it, especially 'cause I couldn't take care of it *with* John . . . 'cause John's not . . . not ready for a kid, I don't think, and I couldn't take care of it without John, 'cause I'm not ready . . . so there was, you know, only one answer, far as I was concerned . . . but it really surprised me when I got really upset about it anyway.

    J.D.: Yeah . . . [J.D. then told of an abortion he knew about of a "liberated" woman who felt the same. Janine then told about her roommate who had an abortion and felt the same *before* the abortion. Janine suggested her feelings might have been the result of the doctor's giving her Valium before the abortion, but doctors give tranquilizers precisely because they greatly *decrease* such feelings.]

    Janine: So, no matter what they say about . . . you know . . . what we say about, you know, women's lib and being able to . . . to realize what the best thing to do is, you know, is abortions, there's still feelings there . . . that surprise me . . . we put 'em down because we don't think we should have them, I think.

    [We then discussed the similarity of these feelings to those of women who put out their newborns for adoption.]

    [Janine left John weeks later and said at the time she did so because she couldn't stay with anyone who had made her go through the abortion. She later resumed their relation and married him.]

Fourteen days after the discussion with Janine, I was talking with Wendy (who is discussed later in this chapter) about her problems with her boy friend when I happened to mention Janine's abortion and how she felt unhappy afterward. I was using this as an example of how people commonly feel differently in a given situation from the way they think they will. As she was just sixteen at the time, I was quite surprised when Wendy responded (according to my detailed taped debriefing the next day):

    Wendy: Yeah . . . I've been on that trip before.

    J.D.: Oh, you've had an abortion?

    Wendy: Yeah, I guess it was inevitable.

    J.D.: Yeah? Did your abortion make you feel depressed?

    Wendy: Well, I guess I shouldn't say this, but I guess it really depends on my mood . . . I can really cut off my emotions if I want to, but . . . Sometimes I think about my baby . . . you know, I just felt certain that it would be a boy . . . I can just really feel that.

    [She smiled wanly, looked off dreamily, and seemed to me quite sad. I moved on to less sad things.]

A transcribed news interview with Sherri Finkbine Burrows, thirteen years after her highly publicized abortion in Sweden for a thalidomide-damaged fetus, revealed the same feelings, only more intense and dominating. She reported they had led her to start a workshop entitled "After Your Abortion" to deal with such anguished and surprising feelings:

"Many women after abortion suffer guilt feelings that need to be dealt with," said Mrs. Burrows.

    "Instead of tucking leftover feelings inside, pretending they don't exist, the idea is to bring them out in a rap session. An individual who has had an abortion doesn't just run around talking about it, but it is good to find others with the same feelings and to be able to release them. Like when you develop a bad back, all of a sudden you hear from lots of other people with the same problem.

"Women are coming to the workshop who have lived with a sense of guilt for years, who still keep thinking of how old that child would be now, what it would look like. It helps them to find other women who have had the same guilts, traumas, reliefs.

"And men, too, need this kind of counseling. Like the father who, with his wife, has agonized through the need for a daughter's abortion, or the young unmarried man whose girl friend has had to terminate a pregnancy. The aftermath of abortion, whatever the reason for the abortion — and there are many good ones — can have terribly destructive psychological effects.

"I know," Mrs. Burrows added, "because after 13 years I, too, have leftover feelings to conquer, even though I'm able to say mine wasn't a baby — it was an abnormal growth, a malformed fetus."
[*Los Angeles Times*, June 3, 1975]

The relative independence of feeling from thought is clear in these discussions of abortion. One can even see the feelings leading to important actions, such as a separating from a lover or starting a seminar workshop to deal with the feelings. (We have seen so many of the same contrasts between expected feeling and actual feeling in the concrete situations, especially in sexual and other matters that involve deep feelings, that our general rule of thumb, obviously not universal, is that things never feel as you expect them to feel.) But the champions of symbolism and rationalist accounts might still argue that these women went ahead with the abortions in spite of the feelings and the feelings appeared to come mainly after the events. I would reply that there were other feelings involved, such as the fear (and shame) of having the child with no father and the deep anguish over having a child who would live his life terribly deformed, but let us examine other cases where our general conclusion is even more clear.

Physical pain is one of the most interesting feelings to a sociologist because it is so relatively simple to analyze and so basic to life. Most physical pain can be assigned to some causal factor, and modern medicine can do something about it. This is a situational and temporary pain. But millions of people suffer continuing physical pain that cannot be attributed to a simple cause; many other millions suffer more problematic "mental" pains; and all of us who live into old age come to suffer the lesser physical and mental pains of old age. When these pains cannot be dealt with within the patterns of our everyday lives, we change those patterns. If those pains are great over long periods, they lead to great changes in our lives, our views of medicine, medicine itself, and even our body images (see Chapter 9). We all secretly build our lives upon our basic feelings: love and lust, hatred and resentment, desire for material gain and greed, fear and anxiety, boredom and depression, pain and agony, pleasure and ecstasy, foreboding and dread, hope and exhilaration. We reach out in some directions and constrain our lives in others in order to express, gratify, fulfill, and develop these feelings. We use our thinking, our massive symbolic universe, and our creativity to do this; and we use our previously established patterns of life to do this. Because of the once dominant cultural universe of symbols in the Western world, those of the Judeo-Christian religion and philosophical rationalism (which has become science and technology), we do this building largely behind the screens, the fronts, the rhetoric of rational accounts and value commitments. When we get close enough to the human animal to observe the building of his life, to distinguish, as he himself generally does, between his frontwork and his life building, and especially when we can see a new feeling (like persistent pain) introduced independently into his life, we can see how he builds to express, gratify, fulfill, and develop those feelings.

Unfortunately, it is precisely scientists, academics, intellectuals, theologians, and priests who are least capable of getting close enough to people-in-the-world to see how they are really building their lives; and it is precisely these people who have been trained since childhood and encouraged by their practical situations to invest their feelings in the rhetoric of rationality and value commitment, to look at themselves and present themselves in that rhetoric. They constitute that small minority of people Freud thought were really affected by the superego (value commitments, with rationality a major one), for they are the people whose feelings have become invested by those value commitments and rhetoric and by presenting oneself as so committed. They are the most symbolically conscious group, the most truly rational in the classic sense; but, even more, they are the small minority whose lusts, greeds, hatreds, and many other feelings are served by maintaining those fronts as realities. It is not difficult to see why the others, that vast majority of mankind (largely untrained in symbolic commitments) feels so uneasy when these symbol mongers come near; why they put on their best clothes for the priests, put on the best rational rhetoric for the social scientists studying them, and strive valiantly to keep them all out of the back regions where they do their living and life building. Nor is it difficult to see why those symbol mongers have been misled in their basic models of man. It is not even too hard to see why those scientists have commonly failed to grasp and understand how their own feelings were involved in their research on those others. This is precisely what John Johnson shows is true of social researchers (Chapter 7). Following the classic tradition of field research in the early part of his own research, he did not even note all the obvious emotional implications of his physical symptoms (bleeding nose, nausea, shaking knees). Looking back, he found that only one analyst of field research had directly mentioned feeling as important in determining his research and this one mentioned it as *"cognitive* love." Once he began to look at his own feelings, Johnson could see them pervading the research as one independent source. Insiders' reports on natural science research, such as James Watson's book, *The Double Helix*, also show feelings at work. This does not mean that reason is unimportant, or only a tiny voice, in scientific research. On the contrary, observation, self-criticism, and analysis are crucial in bringing reason to scientific research. But it does mean we must recognize that feelings are of pervasive and independent importance in science and that in the great world beyond scientific controls reason is normally only one voice amid the din of feelings.

Sex is one of the crucial areas in modern life in which we can see the independent working of animal feeling, the revolt of brute being. When we observe sexual feelings in many natural settings, we see that they not only inspire individuals to recreate their own selves and their personal lives, but also lead individuals to transform basic patterns of their everyday lives (social structures). It has long been a commonplace of theology and social science that sexual feeling was repressed in Western societies because of the values against it. Much recent history leads us increasingly to doubt that sexual feeling was so greatly repressed after all; rather, it was hidden behind the usual fronts, which were especially impenetrable to those who did the writing — the priests and their intellectual students. Moreover, all our general analysis of feeling thus far, and all our specific knowledge of individual sexual feeling from depth psychology, would lead us to reject such a theory. If sexual feeling was less expressed, gratified, fulfilled, and developed in earlier centuries, this was probably so only because there were far more situationally pressing feelings to express, gratify, and fulfill. It seems obvious that the demands of a world characterized by harsh scarcity that forced people to work intently just to stay alive were the primary constraint on sexual feeling and other joyful feelings. Those not so constrained by harsh necessities, the nobility, were not so constrained in their real sex lives. (It also seems likely the peasants were not very constrained during winter months.) As affluence, free time, and general freedom from physical constraints have spread in the modern world, sexual feeling has become an increasingly important force in building individual lives, social patterns, and whole societies. Sociologists and other social scientists have almost never tried to look closely at sex, except in the form of deviance, changing sexual mores, and changing family patterns (divorce). All these are in various ways the outcomes, or symptoms, of the revolt of sexual feeling, of the growing insistence on expressing, gratifying, fulfilling, and increasing sexual feeling. We have almost no sociology of sex, but a wasteland of the sociology of the pale reflections of sex. (Indeed, most of the sociology of marriage and the family is so rationally symbolic as to be ludicrous. There are literally basic textbooks in this field that include "indexes of marital compatibility.")

Any study of sex, any attempt to determine what is happening in this basic realm of modern life and why it is happening, must begin with and continually return to the study of sex as a complex mosiac of feelings. We must consider feelings first, perceptions (especially visual, olfactory, and auditory images, smells and sounds) second, thoughts third, and values last. Traditional sociological studies of activities like marriage and prostitution, which obviously have something to do with sexual feelings, did at times assume a tension-release model of sexual feeling. For example, Kingsley Davis has argued that prostitution is basically a tension release for individuals without adequate sexual relations in marriage and thus functions also as a tension release for society, so that the basic forms of marriage and the family are maintained. In sharp contrast to this, Rasmussen and Kuhn (1976) have found that tension release is only one of many motives for such new forms of sex for money as massage-parlor sex. Many other feelings are expressed and fulfilled, especially excitement in the new experience, in new sexual practices, and in violating rules and laws. The customers are not primarily acting to maintain some steady state or to eliminate feelings of tension. They are knowingly increasing disequilibrium, accepting considerable risks in their personal lives to experience new feelings. Feelings are not merely expressed, gratified, and fulfilled; feelings are purposefully increased, built up. Feeling is an end in itself. *More* feeling is craved, not less through some form of tension release. The same search for new sexual feeling, often mistakenly cast in the same traditional release or (Freudian) equilibrium metaphor, pervades and inspires our massive new social forms of marriage counseling, sex and marriage books, sensitivity training, humanistic psychology, pornography, quasi-pornography, sexual experimentation within and outside marriage, and all the casual sex scenes (see Douglas et al., 1977).

This explosion of feeling — of searching for, experimenting with, and rationally increasing feelings — and the long-term re-creation of social patterns are found in many other realms of our society, including the massive growth in the use of psychoactive drugs (drugs that alter states of feeling and mind) in all segments of society. Social scientists, doctors, politicians, and other would-be social reformers have done a huge amount of work and spent vast sums of money to discover why people use these drugs. They have almost always implicitly assumed such deviant behavior could be scientifically explained only by some negative factor, something wrong in the lives of the individual and groups using such drugs. This assumption has overlooked the most obvious of all explanations: The majority of the members of our society use psychoactive drugs

(which include alcohol and cigarettes), even though they know drug
use involves long-term dangers, because drugs make you feel better. As
we concluded in our study of street and prescription uses of psychoactive drugs:

> The belief in the magic potion that will transform our drab lives into a lovely fairy
> tale, or will at least enable us to "hold on," is probably more intense today than
> [was] the medieval belief in alchemy. The quest for "soma" is intense and massive.
> If we cannot find it in a "magic mushroom," then the "magic of science" will find
> it for us . . . The truth is that there is a great and growing demand for psychoactive
> drugs, a deep and restless search for organically and synthetically induced peaceful-
> ness, intoxication and mysterious highs, that is spreading to ever new groups in our
> society. [Douglas, 1974]

Once we understand that the human being at his very core is a feeling
animal, not a moral actor or a rational actor, and that the feeling animal
searches for and craves feeling, then our entire understanding of such
things as sex and drugs is transformed. What once seemed mysterious
and inexplicable is no longer so. And once our understanding is transformed this way, our entire approach to problems inspired by such
actions and our entire social policy for dealing with them are also transformed. We concluded from our study of drug problems:

> Given this deep, widespread, yet often secret craving for the psychoactive drugs
> from such large and growing segments of our society, *it is extremely unlikely that
> any general social policies will be adopted that control these drugs tightly enough
> to prevent drug problems.* All of our experience thus far has shown that even severe
> criminal penalties and vast social expenditures on official controls will not stop the
> flow of illegal drugs. A constitutional amendment and all the forces of prohibition
> did not stop alcohol consumption. The "new prohibition" against marijuana did
> not stop its spread to ever greater numbers of the young. Heroin replaced morphine;
> and methadone appears to be replacing heroin. This same persistence and ingenuity
> have been shown in the legal drug realm. If one drug is withdrawn, another will take
> its place; if one route is closed, another will be found. We must conclude, then, that
> the drug explosion will continue, even if new social policies enable us to control
> some of its more unrestrained dangers. [Douglas, 1974: 13]

This transformed understanding has led us to conclude that attempts to
control the use of psychoactive drugs that induce powerful pleasures,
such as heroin, lead almost inevitably to the discovery of alternative
paths to the same psychoactive state, so that new drug problems are
added to the old ones. Such a policy as a war on heroin produces the
opposite effect from that intended because it is based on a fundamental
misunderstanding of the human animal, the sometimes rational animal
who is always a feeling animal.

Although moods, body pains, body pleasures, and situated feelings
may precipitate lines of action that result in the most important consequences for individuals' lives, they are normally only continual per-
turbations in our everyday life patterns. The bursts of anger and love

quickly run their course. The fundamental importance of feelings generally, their ultimate dominance over thoughts, values, and actions, is most thoroughly revealed in precisely those feelings that change, disrupt, annihilate, transform, and re-create our normal patterns of life. In crisis situations we observe feelings to be the foundation, the ultimate core, of our being and, thus, the prime mover of the social world, the source and goal of all social structures. As long as our everyday patterns of life remain intact, it is easy to make the rationalist mistake, to see either thoughts or values as the prime movers of the social world; for in these steady-state situations (which were the only ones Parsons and other functionalists were explicitly concerned with) feelings, thoughts, values, and actions are highly fused. When the steady state is broken, when our individual and social lives are disrupted and transformed, we can see the human feelings in concrete situations dominating thoughts, values, and actions. Thoughts, values, and actions remain important, largely as expressions and reflections of the underlying feelings and established patterns of action, but feeling dominates all. Such crisis situations may build up slowly over many years, as we strive to express, gratify, fulfill, and build up our feelings within our previously established patterns of thought, value, and action. For most people basic feelings are the ambivalent fear and temptation of the unknown, of what will happen when we cast off, transform, or destroy those patterns. Others, even the adventuresome social entrepreneurs who crave uncertainity and creativity, must commonly fear retribution from the fearful and from the officials of the absolutist control bureaucracies. These fears restrain their other feelings. When we cannot find expression, gratification, and fulfillment, we eventually enter a crisis situation in which our patterns of everyday life, our selves, our societies, our world are destroyed and remade. Normally, of course, only some small segment of the pattern of life, such as a marital relationship, is remade; but there are times when the world goes berserk in a frenzy of hatred, when the world is remade over millions of bodies, or, possibly some day, when all is destroyed. And there are times, such as today, when large segments of societies are reconstructed by the burgeoning sexual feelings.

We have experienced and observed many situations over the years in which individuals have chosen, against vast opposition, at great cost, and often contrary to their own moral judgments, to recreate their lives in order to express, gratify, fulfill, and build up basic feelings such as sex. We have also seen lusts, anxieties, depressions, hatreds, and angers suddenly erupt in some of these situations, flooding out and sweeping away reason. One such case that I observed was the outcome of two years of slow buildup of sexual feeling, hatred, and many other emotions. It was part of a larger study of a casual sex scene, nude beaches, which I and a small team of researchers studied over several years:

I met Jon four years ago when he was twenty-six years old. I talked with him frequently as we strolled along the beach. It was almost two years before he was very willing to *talk* about what he was doing on the beach, because he distrusted everyone; but it was obvious what he was doing from watching him and from observing his body language. He was one of the most devoted "sexual hunters," always trying to pick up (or hustle) the women on the beach. His entire life, like that of quite a number of the people who came to the beach all the time, revolved around the casual sex scenes at the beach and elsewhere. He lived on a combination of part-time work, unemployment, and welfare, always making it clear that he did not want to work any more than was necessary to live. Money, success, greed — he had almost none of these common motives. Yet, as I eventually learned, he had worked for a number of years in Hawaii as a reasonably successful restaurant manager. He simply did not find work and success gratifying or fulfilling. They were "boring," especially in comparison with sex. Those who assume work and success to be the ultimate goals in life would no doubt call him a dropout, but neither he nor anyone who knew him well thought of him in such terms. He wasn't concerned with dropping out of anything and had almost no dislike of society, feelings of resentment against the rest of the world, or any of the ordinary feelings of rebels. (I probed for such feelings in various indirect ways, and about the most he ever said was, "Well, I guess I kind of wish I had some better place to live than my camper.") Jon was not dropping out, he was simply *getting into* something more exciting and fulfilling for him — casual sex.

Jon did not start out his adult life in the pursuit of casual sex. He grew up in a small town in southern Ohio. When he was eighteen, he and his girl friend left their town and eventually wound up in Hawaii. Though they did not get married until years later, they had two children and he supported the family with his managerial work. As his wife later told me, and as he indirectly confirmed in various ways, he was reasonably shy as a teenager and into his early twenties. His wife insisted unequivocally that she had only herself to blame for his getting into casual sex. She tried to convince him that he was really good at sex, partly as a simple matter of building his self-confidence. She insisted that he then started trying out his abilities, found himself successful at sex, and then became progressively devoted to it as an ego trip. Observing him closely, I always thought the motivation was more complex. Certainly there was the ego trip, the thrill of scoring, especially with the most sought-after women. But there was clearly the highly erotic aspect of it: When he talked about the body of a woman passing by, there was little of the "social prestige" or "ego trip" involved. The very possibility of his being successful at sex, of taking an ego trip, was built on his being erotic. Moreover, tied in with the ego trip was the excitement of the hunt. There are millions of men who devote much time and resources to hunting animals. Men like Jon find sexual hunting exciting in the same way — only far more so. Given all three powerful feelings, it is not hard to see how casual sex became a consuming passion with him.

After I had known Jon for two years (he was then 28), he introduced me to a sixteen-year-old he had met at the beach a few days earlier. Wendy was one of the most beautiful girls on the beach. Jon soon told me how exciting he found her. As I had never seen him with the same woman more than once or twice, I was quite surprised to see him with her whenever he came to the beach, for weeks, then months, then over two years. Though there were times when he would come without her and resume his sexual hunting briefly, these got rarer. He was increasingly devoted to her. She became even more devoted to him.

Wendy was much easier to learn about than Jon. She was friendly, extremely articulate, liked to talk about her problems, seemed very open, and proved to be honest in everything I was ever able to check out. When Jon was not there, or when she was looking for him, we would often talk about what she was doing: school, her life, and Jon. She was a junior in high school. Her father was a successful psychiatrist in town. Both her mother and father were highly liberal about sexual matters. They had even allowed one of her earliest boy friends to live with her in her home for some time. They knew very well that she came to the nude beach and thought it was fine. (But she felt even then that there were some limits to their liberality, as she kept her extensive drug experimentation and drug dealing secret from them.) She had started coming to the nude beach when she was fifteen. It was not easy for her to begin going nude. She had always felt "sort of unattractive, like a black sheep." She had wanted to get over this feeling, to gain confidence in her body. When I met her a year later, she was the only woman I knew on the beach who would walk alone totally nude, without any sign of uneasiness, past a hundred teenage male surfers in their wetsuits who were slowly turning their heads to follow her down the beach with their eyes.

When Jon started going to Wendy's home to pick her up, the parents made no protest. He stayed at their house a few times, but only when they were away. They never seemed to like him very much, perhaps because of his too obvious lack of devotion to work and success. I always thought they disliked him simply because they felt he would hurt their daughter. But Wendy and Jon always seemed not to understand why.

Jon was extremely careful to keep his other life a secret from Wendy and to keep Wendy a secret from his other life — his wife. Wendy began to suspect something was wrong after a number of months. Later she began to suspect specifically that he was married. Then one day she saw them together, completely by accident. She immediately went up to them, asked the woman if she was Jon's wife, and started crying uncontrollably when the answer was yes. Jon's wife, Nancy, was understanding and sympathetic. She had known that something more than his usual sex was going on and was not too surprised by the situation. She told Wendy how sorry she was and discussed the whole thing with her, telling her how it had been developing for years, that the name by which Wendy had known him for a year was not his name at all, that most of what he had told her about himself was false. Jon confirmed it all.

Wendy spent several days in deep depression and crying. As she told me through her tears, she was saddest of all over his lies, because she did not care if he was married. She could not even understand why he would lie and build a false life. Some time during this deep depression, probably because he insisted on knowing what was going on and because she expected consolation, she made the mistake of telling her father about it. He was furious at Jon. He got hold of Nancy (I do not remember how), and she agreed to insist that Jon come for a meeting of the four of them. I believe it was at this stage that Wendy's father first threatened Jon with legal action if he did not come. Jon went.

Jon's own view of the situation was mixed and conflictful. He wanted Wendy. But he was unwilling to give up his wife or he would probably have done so much sooner. He wanted the casual life without giving up his wife. (In fact, as became clear later, he was extremely possessive about his wife.) He thought he could protect his family life from his casual life and the other way around by building two identities. As far as I know, he was totally successful for years (except that I and a few others had guessed he was married), until the fateful accident of being discovered by

Wendy. Because he had so much to lose at home, and because Wendy's father's threats were so convincing, Jon and Wendy agreed to separate, to stay away from each other completely, and not to go to the nude beach at all.

A few days later I ran into Wendy at the nude beach. She was extremely sad and agitated. She wanted Jon and was looking for him. She found him and they were back together again. For months they spent much of their lives together on the beach, managing somehow, with considerable care and trepidation, to keep it secret from his wife and her father. Jon's conflict was obvious. Whenever I talked with Wendy alone about it, it was clear that she too suffered from the emotional conflict. But it was clear that the sexual attraction was too great for either of them to give up the relationship.

Nancy knew Jon too well. She went looking for him and discovered Wendy and Jon together on another nude beach. Rather than expressing sympathy this time, she came up from behind and attacked Wendy. She hit her three times very hard and screamed at her. She later got hold of Wendy's father, who made further threats. Once again Wendy and Jon agreed to a total separation and to stay away from the beach entirely. The threats were more intense now, the dangers more real. But only a few days later I ran into Wendy at the beach, still nursing her bruises, saying that she understood and could not blame Nancy for attacking her, but tearfully looking for Jon. She found him once again. (As the whole thing got more intense, I never gave any advice, but increasingly I expressed warnings and pointed out the dangers. I never expected this would have any effect, and I do not believe it did.)

Jon and Wendy now took great care not to be discovered together and came to the beach only occasionally when they felt safest. One way Wendy got away from her now very watchful father was to visit a girl friend's house overnight. Her father discovered one of these lies. He confronted her and, in great anger, demanded fiercely that she either give up Jon and continue living at home and attending college (where she now was) or leave home entirely. She walked out, thinking she had finally resolved her conflict.

The next day Jon and Wendy were working out at the university gymnasium when the police walked in and asked Jon to accompany them outside. He did and Wendy followed. Her father was outside. He insisted the police arrest Jon for unlawful sex with a minor, as Wendy's eighteenth birthday was one month away. The police asked Jon if he had had sexual relations with Wendy. He said yes. (Jon and Wendy both knew very well that he should not say anything at that point. Not only had they seen similar situations on television many times, but we had all talked on the beach about tickets the police gave for various things on the beach. In fact, Jon and Wendy had twice before given false names, addresses, phone numbers, etc., to the police in such situations. But, as they both said, Jon was simply "really scared" this time and could not think clearly.) The police arrested Jon and started taking him away. Wendy was now screaming, demanding that her father stop them, insisting she would never testify against Jon and would never talk to her parents again. Her father was also screaming and, for the first time Wendy could remember in her whole life, threatened to hit her. She felt he was "out of his mind." When the police took Jon away, Wendy returned home to plead for his release.

Jon spent a week in the felony lockup at county jail, thinking he faced years in prison. Being locked up, being with the convicts, the violence, the homosexual sex, the drugs all made a profound impression on him. He admitted he was "really scared." He wanted above all to stay out of prison. Wendy agreed to stay home at least until she was eighteen, only one month away. Her father dropped charges and

Jon was released. About a week later Wendy was back on the beach tearfully looking for Jon. He was not there, but they established an elaborate way of communicating through a friend. He started coming to the beach again a few days later, doing a little lackluster hunting (and being very cautious because he did not want
Wendy to know anything about this). It was unclear whether they could wait a
few weeks until her eighteenth birthday. (They did not. I came across them together a few days after writing this.) But it was completely clear to me that there
would be no quick end to these profoundly ecstatic and bitterly hateful conflicts.

We have also experienced and observed many situations in which built-
up hatred and anger became so intense that people went berserk, threatening their own lives and the lives of others. One social researcher inad-
vertently became involved in a near murder that resulted from a slow
buildup of resentments, hatreds, and many other feelings that erupted
in an instant, appearing almost totally to flood out conscious thought,
and were followed by deep feelings of guilt and remorse:

Bob and Chris were our next door neighbors for two years. We got to know them
and like them well by seeing them often, having dinner, exercising, playing bridge,
and eventually by serving as informal advisers for their problems. Bob is now thirty-
nine years old, an aggressive former hockey player with strong ideas about his masculinity. He is an insurance agent, which seems to reinforce his concern with approaching forty. Chris is an attractive twenty-eight, works as a secretary for an insurance firm, and is very concerned with her social status. They met three years ago
in a pickup bar. Both had recently been divorced and had begun the awkward task
of finding a new mate. They lived together for about a year with the understanding
that each could date others, but they became jealous of these dates and the agreement failed. They took this jealousy as proof that "this was it" and decided to get
married. They agreed to several conditions of marriage: Both would give up custody
of their children by their previous marriages; Bob would get a vasectomy to avoid
any pregnancy; they would work hard, save their money, and retire early. Although
they had the usual growing pains of any new relation, this worked well for the first
year. But then Bob decided to have his oldest son live with them. On the surface
this seemed inconsequential, as the son was fourteen, independent, and even able to
contribute financially from a paper route. However, Chris deeply resented this violation of their agreement. She knew her ex-huband would never give her custody of
their children and that Bob's vasectomy would prevent her having any more. She
expressed this resentment by making life difficult for the son, which led him to demand to return to his mother. This was patched up, but the situation remained
tense. It was during this period that Chris talked with my wife secretly about the
possibility of leaving: "What do we need with men anyhow? Let's both leave our
husbands and move in together." Twice Bob and Chris even agreed upon divorce,
but both times Bob persuaded Chris to stay. During one of these trial separations,
Chris was at our house. Bob appeared at midnight, slung Chris over his shoulder,
and carried her home.

    Shortly after this midnight adventure, Chris went on vacation to El Paso, sup-
posedly to visit her mother. What she was really planning was a week-long affair
with an old boy friend. Bob became suspicious, but Chris's mother covered for her,
so he did not know what she was really doing. (Chris had painted a very bad picture
of Bob to her mother, so she was willing to do anything to "get her little girl away
from the bastard.") When Chris returned, she again asked for a divorce and was

again talked out of it. It was now clear that she desperately wanted a divorce and was trying to create a situation in which Bob would agree. Having failed she told him about the affair in El Paso. He insisted he would forgive her "mistake," providing she did not do it again. She then said that the affair had taken place during her fertile period and she had taken no precautions, so she thought she must be pregnant. Bob was even willing to put up with this, providing she got an abortion. But she asserted she could not get an abortion for religious reasons. (This may have been true. She was Catholic, but had not been to a service for two years.) The dilemma was ended by the beginning of her period.

We all decided to get together to celebrate the "happy event." All was settled. They would live for the future, not think of the past, let bygones be bygones. We toasted the latest agreement with champagne. Shortly after this, on my thirtieth birthday, we had them over for dinner and celebration. We drank a good bit of wine during the evening, but no one got drunk. Bob and Chris went home about eleven. We settled down to watch some television movie. About midnight we heard screams from next door. At first we thought Bob and Chris were playing around, but as the shouts and screams got louder we realized they were having a serious fight. Though we didn't say anything, we were clearly in agreement that we didn't want to get involved. But it kept up. Finally my wife said, "Fuck it. I'm going over." I didn't like it at all, but I followed her. The screams were now terrible. We kept pounding at the door. Suddenly it flew open. Chris ran by us. Bob then picked up my wife and me in turn and threw each of us across the patio against the wall. He could not find Chris (who, we later learned, had fled to a neighbor's house to call the police). Bob seemed suddenly quiet, I went into the house with him to discuss what had happened. (My only serious injury was a badly cut knee.) He told me they had gone to bed and had started making love. Bob then asked Chris if she still cared for the boy friend. She said yes. He blew up and, after shouts and screams, tried to strangle her. (She had terrible bruises the next day.) The police car arrived, and Chris left under their protection for El Paso to return to her mother. I stayed close to Bob for the next few weeks because I was afraid he might commit suicide. He decided once again to forgive Chris. He said only, "You've got to sink to the bottom of your soul and existence to understand what is really important to you." She returned.

It seemed clear in this case that the slow buildup of resentment and anger was closely related to the deep threat Chris's sexual activities posed for Bob's existential self, his primal feeling of masculinity. His reaction of rage came in precisely the situation where this threat was total. Behind most feelings of deep hatred and rage is a threat to the core of the individual's being, his existential self. If the threat is manageable but persistent, the individual's hatred may be hidden for years, yet smolder behind his fronts of affability, even friendship, and lead him to attack his enemy secretly. If the threat is great, but manageable, he may be thrown into furious attack, a towering rage. If he cannot win in such a total war, he may sink into deep anxiety and lasting depression. Faced with any of these extreme situations that threaten his being and have triggered these extreme emotions, the individual enters an automatic response pattern. He is locked into, submerged in the immediate situation. He cannot think beyond the situation, cannot see that there is necessarily a brighter day ahead. He cannot be abstract, symbolic, rational; he is no longer a free man in any way. As one successful and brilliant businessman, who had succeeded against poverty and with tremendous effort, told me: "There are some situations which I cannot handle. When I come to them it is like falling off a precipice . . . I can't stop myself. I just fall. All I can do is try to avoid getting into those situations." He had spent a great deal of his adult, successful life trying to recognize the precipices and devising ways to avoid them. But the precipices are still there, in spite of all success, and there are times when they suddenly yawn before him -- and he falls. If an individual is carried to the ultimate extreme of deep, primal emotion, all symbolic thought may be swept away. Consciousness itself may be swept away, he may black out, yet continue to act furiously and appear completely conscious to others. He may even later regain a memory of what was blacked out and be overwhelmed by guilt feelings concerning it.

It is precisely such neurotic processes, as the existential psychoanalysts have argued (see especially May et al., 1958), which lie behind most homicides, manslaughters, assaults, and fights, and behind many suicides. The presence of this neurotic component is the reason the actions appear so irrational to those who observe their details and the reason all social policies based on theories of deterrence, which assume rational action, fail to affect them. As almost all his biographers agree, some such primal process lay behind the overwhelming hatreds and furies of Adolf Hitler, who would sometimes become so enraged with those who opposed him that he would fall to the floor biting the carpet (hence the name *Tappigfresser*, "carpet eater"). Sociologists search for the rational explanations and conflicts of interest to explain Hitler, the worldwide war he precipitated, and the worldwide social consequences of that war. There are some subsidiary ways in which those aspects are important; and they are of primary importance in understanding certain specific aspects of the conflict and their effects. But any truly rational man, any man who wishes to understand such terrible conflicts to avoid their devastating consequences, must understand that the primal rage of that one man, indirectly supported by the primal anxieties and rages of many of his countrymen, was the overwhelming fact. Such rational understanding may be of vital importance in avoiding that nuclear precipice over which the entire world could fall.

The partial independence and dominance of feelings over values

Many sociologists who would accept the general argument that feelings are an independent factor in life, that they are fused with, pervade, and ultimately dominate thought, would still argue that values are the basic determinants of social life, especially of patterned social life, such as we find in deviant and illegal activities and, above all, in bureaucratic organizations - the ideal model of rationalized, rule-governed social life. Indeed, some would argue this because they believe values are precisely those abstract principles to which the members of society have been trained to be committed, which involves an association of feeling to symbolic definitions. (As Parsons put it, values are introjected and cathected.) In fact, at least two major theories of deviance — those proposed by Robert Merton and by Howard Becker — have gone further to argue that feelings are important in some way in determining rule of value violations. However, all these views ultimately make feelings totally dependent on symbolic definitions of situations and on values as symbolic statements, and thereby, they fail to understand the nature of social rules, their uses, and their violations.

The most basic idea of structural-functional sociologies was that rules or values determine social actions and that values are shared (more or less universally) so that social actions are patterned: Shared values produce social order (structure). As Durkheim put it: "Social order is a moral order." There are many basic reasons, backed by massive evidence, for rejecting this theory as hopelessly simplistic and, worse, as an outcome of accepting official frontwork as reality. These have been presented many times (e.g., Douglas, 1971b). One of the first lines of argument leading sociologists to reject the simplistic structural view of rules and social action is that the theory has been unable to account for the ways in which rules are used to accomplish what people want in situations. As Becker (1963) argued in his theory of the entrepreneurial use of rules, and as ethnomethodologists argued in their works on rule uses (Zimmerman, 1970) society's members obviously choose when to invoke and how to interpret, use, and not use social rules. Most rules in a society become unused without being eliminated. They remain in code books but are forgotten. In some situations what everyone sees as a rule violation is overlooked, and in others the most minor violation is attacked. In some situations highly contorted interpretations are used to rationalize attacks on supposed rule violators.

But, though Becker and the ethnomethodologists saw the problem clearly, they failed to explain these choices of when and how to use rules. It is as if choices merely happen. (Parts of Becker's work tied these labeling choices to class interests, making his theory subject to all the weaknesses of the Marxist position.) In fact, the ethnomethodologists disowned any possibility of explanation by asserting that we should simply view rule uses as examples of presenting oneself as rational or rule-governed to one's fellow members of society. But, as Becker realized, there is almost always conflict over such presentations of rule-boundedness. One person says he is using the rule correctly, rationally; another person says he is not; and someone else takes another point of view (e.g., "I don't know if this is rational, rule-bound"). The ethno-methodologist has implicitly assumed that the rule use is accepted when in fact the rule use is almost always disputed. Rule uses in our society are problematic and conflictful. What determines the ways in which the problems are resolved?

Our previous argument leads us to expect that what lies behind the uses of rules in a concrete situation are a person's feelings in the situation. Carried to the extreme, the argument that feeling dominates rule use leads to the commonsense form of total cynicism, as exemplified in such clichés as, "It (i.e., what is right and wrong in a situation) all depends on whose ox is being gored" and "If it feels good, do it." Given the necessary conflicts among individual feelings (both within and among individuals), this argument suggests a "dog eat dog" or "war of all against all" social world. Such an anarchic state of total conflict never exists except in situations of total social breakdown and panic, if then. Instead, as our earlier argument leads us to expect, feeling is basic and the most independent factor, but is also partially fused with thought and guided by thought, including the social rules to which a person is truly (not merely publicly) committed. The crucial thing to recognize is that there is a continuum of feeling independence and dominance over social rules, ranging from the situation in which either profound feelings or (perceived) profound situational threats (to feelings in the short run) sweep away considerations of social rules (as in the near murder described above), to the situation in which the individual is a moral absolutist committed with profound feelings of fear (e.g., pangs of conscience) to the social rules. Most of us experience all degrees of this independence and dominance in our complex and changing lives, some of us going from moral absolutism to cynicism, some the other way around and back again, and all tending to be absolutist about a few things and totally cynical about many others. In general, however, our society seems to be progressing steadily in the direction of feelings increasingly dominating social rules. We are not moving, in general, toward adopting a new set of social rules, as many people like to assert in defense of their deviant activities; we are asserting our feelings over the traditional absolutist rules and casting off those rules in our private lives and thoughts, but hiding that fact behind elaborate self-deceptions and public frontworks and even using those fronts to attack others we want to hurt for reasons of personal feelings. (Such activities are rampant in politics and organizational life, including university life.) Let us consider some major forms of these developments and their implications.

Drug use once again offers a good example both because of its relative simplicity and because it covers the continuum from total feeling dominance to social definition and rule dominance. The most widely known and accepted sociological theory of drug use is Becker's theory of marihuana use. Becker has assumed that everyone who uses marihuana knows the social rules against it, which were quite strong and widely shared at the time he did the original work, in the 1950s. The question is: Why do they violate the rule? In simplest terms, his answer is that those who have others define marihuana use for them as pleasurable will continue to smoke it. The theory appears at first to make pleasure the determinant of rule violation. But the social definition of marihuana use as pleasurable is really crucial. The feeling of pleasure is assumed to be determined by the social definition, so definitions clearly dominate feelings in producing the rule violations.

There are two major objections to this theory, especially if it is extended to other drug-rule violations. First, why would anyone choose to define marihuana smoking as pleasurable for others? There are two obvious possibilities: (1) at the start of the whole process some individuals tried marihuana, found it pleasurable, told others about it and everyone who experienced the pleasure continued to smoke marihuana; thus pleasure dominates the whole process, and feeling totally dominates the drug-rule violations; (2) the individuals making the social definitions are using the marihuana-rule violations as a way of attacking those who make and accept the rules (the squares, the establishment); thus hatred or the desire to express hatred is the crucial determinant. I suggest that the explosion of marihuana use in the late 1960s in the United States was actually a result of both, but with the second factor playing the dominant role. Marihuana, especially the kind sold on the street in the United States, which has a low (1 percent) content of tetrahydrocannabinol, is a relatively weak drug: It has few measurable short-term effects on the central nervous system in ordinary doses. On the other hand, it does not appear to be a placebo whose effect on feelings is determined entirely by social definition. Marihuana is found pleasurable by a high percentage of users across very different cultures. But a "high percentage" of users is not all users. Most psychoactive drugs produce wide individual (and situational) variations in reactions, especially affective reactions. One of the failings of Becker's method of investigating marihuana use is that he studied only users and ignored those who had tried it and did not go on using it. There are individuals who try marihuana and find it has no effect on their feelings, even though experts have defined the experience for them as pleasurable. And, just as is true with alcohol, there are individuals who try marihuana, have it defined as pleasurable, find it unpleasant regardless, and do not continue using it — unless marihuana smoking is useful socially. It is probably the case that most individuals find marihuana pleasant when they use it in certain ways (learned or hit upon by accident). But surely this does not explain the great surge in the use of a drug that had been around for decades. The argument is especially weak when we remember that marihuana has affective effects very similar to those of alcohol and that, at the time of its greatest popularity, users had a realistic chance of being sentenced to years in prison for using marihuana rather than alcohol, to achieve the pleasant feelings. It is unlikely that marihuana's generally pleasurable, but small, effects led people to commit themselves to its continued use; rather, marihuana was probably being used as a means of expressing deep feelings of anger and hatred against the society that imposed the rule. Indeed, in retrospect this seems almost obvious. Marihuana has been widely used for decades by artists and other groups, probably also as a way of expressing feelings against the squares, but the increased use in the late 1960s was completely tied up with the counterculture movements of the young against the Vietnam draft and other establishment regulations. Once the war ended, the feelings of anger and hatred quickly subsided; the same young decreased their use of marihuana and started switching to alcohol precisely at the time the fear of legal consequences of marihuana smoking was realistically waning.

The second major argument against Becker's theory comes from the more general study of illegal drug use. The drugs most often used illegally and for deviant purposes are barbiturates, and tranquilizers. Heroin use, though not so widespread, is the most illegal form of drug use and one of the most hated and feared activities in our society. Our study (Douglas, 1974) of the uses of hard drugs (i.e., those that have powerful effects on the central nervous system) found that most were experienced as tremendously pleasurable without any social definition and, indeed, against widespread definitions of them as "just medicine." We concluded that most users had discovered the pleasure hard drugs induce and kept it secret so they would not be viewed as "dope addicts." Heroin produces more widely varied effects on individuals and often requires a period of use before its powerful pleasures are experienced (which suggests it is initially desired partly as an expression of other feelings, such as hatred); but it produces the most pleasurable feelings of all drugs. We also found that most people who have become addicted to hard drugs developed the craving without any social definition at all. Most did not even know the drugs would produce cravings and other addictive feelings. The psychoactive drugs act on the central nervous system to create profound feelings; as drug use continues, the feelings become an independent force (craving). These feelings are in some ways affected by social definitions, including rules, but these effects are largely restricted to the early stages before the profound pleasures are experienced and the cravings develop. Feelings are the dominant, but not the only, factor.

Now let us look at a different aspect of our social world — social class and the relations between class and deviance. It is commonly accepted by structural sociologists that individuals who achieve success in accord with the American value on success feel good (triumphantly elated), and those who do not feel bad (depressed). This idea, seems implicit in Merton's (1957) theory of anomie. Anomie appears to be a tension state that is produced in the individual by an inability to achieve success by legitimate means and that leads him to try to achieve the valued goal of success by illegitimate means. The success value, transmitted from generation to generation through education, and the external (class-determined) opportunities are the crucial causal variables; the tension (feeling) state is merely an intervening variable.

If Merton's theory is correct, the individual who achieves success, either legitimately or illegitimately, reduces anomie and, thus, reduces his striving. But in reality even when individuals achieve their expressed goals of success, they commonly go on striving in the same way. Indeed, the more successful they are, the harder they commonly work. As is well known, it is the executives, managers, investors, and entrepreneurs who work the long hours (from 50 to 100 percent more), not the workers. They are also the ones who work most intently, with the most tension and anxiety. There are many examples, and a good one is supplied by Mick Jagger, the most successful ("biggest") rock star. Commenting on the goal of being the "biggest star," he said:

It's the most futile goal I can imagine. But I can't put people down for wanting it. I know what it's like to be 14 and want more than anything to be like Little Richard up on the stage. But when you've done it, you say, "What's next?" There's never an end to it. [*Los Angeles Times*, June 22, 1975]

I believe a complex process is involved in this kind of overdriven striving that constitutes most of America's and other culture's struggle for success. It involves goal setting and changing perceptions and definitions of a person's self and his situation as he is caught up in the complex social processes involved in success. But behind the complex social processes are such deep feelings as basic insecurity, fears of inferiority, hatreds, and lust for power and prestige (dominance) over enemies. When such feelings are strong enough and, above all, when they are at the core of his being, his existential self, a major failure to dominate, to win, triggers a primal (core) anxiety. A major failure threatens a person's very being. His emotional reaction to anyone or anything that appears to threaten such failure is hatred. This hatred may lead to direct attacks on his enemies, but far more commonly it leads to a no-holds-barred struggle, a secret determination to win at all costs, to sweep aside all rules that stand in the way. Merton was trying to provide an explanation of the higher official rates of deviance for lower-class individuals. He simply did not realize that the middle and upper classes are involved in massive forms of unrecorded (unofficial) deviance (see Douglas, 1976) and that they commonly experience greater internal conflicts between what they want to achieve and what their legitimate opportunities seem to allow them to achieve.

But we must not conclude from this that the lower classes do not experience bad feelings of some sort as a result of their "failure." They do, in some important situations, but the feelings resulting from failure are not those of a tension state. The feelings are far more profound and the actions flowing from them more destructive than petty theft. Any analysis of the reactions of individuals and groups to their social situations must begin with a consideration of the partially situated nature of their lives. We cannot, as the Marxists and Merton believe we could, understand how the poor experience their situation by standing outside and looking in, imposing our own feelings about their situation upon them. One of the overwhelming facts about the poor in the United States has been their relative lack of general class consciousness and, thus, feelings about their general class situation as defined by social analysts. (It is precisely this overwhelming fact that has forced Marxist theories to assume false consciousness, that is, wrong definitions of their situation, by the poor.) But this lack of a general concept of themselves as sharing a class position does not mean they have not experienced feelings about being poor. They have often felt shame (over shabby shoes, a shacky house, shoddy clothes, a way of talking, parents) that is profound because it is more individual, more a person's own fault. Shame is a profound feeling, a deep haunting feeling that at the extreme literally weakens your knees, burns your face, ties your tongue, and returns in sudden waves for years. Shame is one of those primal feelings that threatens your very being. Shame pervades the lives of many of the poor in America. They normally manage it by hiding themselves: They live separately, they avoid school, they have numerous reasons why they cannot attend any setting where their poverty will be revealed to the better off. When they can, they hide the poverty at home by dressing up in public. Shame leads a person to avoid looking for a job, the very thing that could help end the basis of the shame. (Shame transcends and dominates reason. You cannot reason with great shame.) When forced into the shameful situation, a person may hang his head, shuffle, be vague, evasive, lie, mumble (for the overwhelming feeling and the withdrawal from it disrupts thought and produces an almost quaking voice), and feel and appear generally stupid. Anyone who cannot understand this feeling of shame the poor experience cannot begin to understand the poor, to deal with them effectively, to do anything to help them. Anyone who does understand it generally knows how to penetrate their frontwork, their evasions, their lies, their appearances of humility and stupidity. This is illustrated in an article, "The Shameful Cost of Dressing in Tatters," written by a black Los Angeles high school teacher who had lived the shame:

In the early '50's, I lived with my mother — a divorcee — my sister, and my brother in a housing project in Watts. We were "on the county." Yet my mother found it impossible to feed, house, and clothe three children and, so, in defiance of the rules then in effect, she went out on clandestine "day work" for five-six days a week.

We children never fully realized that we were poor; we never wore raggedy clothes. This was not so much because of any imagined wealth, as it was because of our mother's resourcefulness. She spent her weekends scouring second-hand stores, and managed to dress us in relative style.

Occasionally, we would wear something that was strange or different by our peers' standards, and each time they would ask: "Where did you get that?" . . . I lived in constant fear that our "terrible" secret would be discovered. Therefore I concocted stories of generous relatives who didn't exist, or else told my friends, "I've had these things a long time but I just haven't worn them to school." If I wore anything particularly "hip" my admirers would naturally want to know where they could get the same thing. That's when my answers turned curiously vague.

I suffered from this kind of anxiety until, as a sophomore in college, I got a job and was finally able to buy brand-new clothes of my very own. My shame about this aspect of my early life was so intense that I confessed the dreaded secret to my husband only a few years ago.

Now, twenty years later, I teach the children of my former classmates at the same junior high I once attended — and things have not changed all that much.

A woman I know has three children, one in junior high, the other two in elementary school. She receives $311 per month in welfare. Not long ago I invited her eldest to go to the movies, but he said he couldn't. He didn't have any good shoes, and his mother didn't have the money to buy him a pair.

His lack of clothing was no surprise. On rainy or cold days attendance at school drops to about 50% of total enrollment. When a staff worker calls home to check, the inevitable answer is: "He doesn't have a coat," or "She doesn't have decent shoes to wear" . . .

Among those who come to school despite a downpour or freezing cold — many are hatless and coatless and wear tennis shoes. In answer to incredulous questioning, the children say, simply, "It's not cold" or "Rain doesn't bother me."

The importance of good clothing, of course, transcends mere protection from the elements. In the ghetto as elsewhere, dressing well can impart immense stature. Last year a ninth-grader impressed the entire student body on several occasions by wearing flashy "super fly" suits. One of the suits, he said, had cost him $139 — money he had earned himself. [*Los Angeles Times*, July 14, 1975]

But shame is only one side of poverty. There is another side that is the opposite of shame. Shame is basic. Shame thus threatens one's existential self. This produces anxiety. If shame can be *blamed* on something, turned toward something one believes is the cause of the shame, then one hates. Hatred is also one of the most powerful human feelings. Just as fear is the powerful feeling that arouses the entire body for flight, so anger is the powerful feeling that arouses the entire body for fight, for attack. Just as anxiety is smoldering fear, cut loose from its original concrete situation and growing, pervading one's life, so hatred is smoldering anger, cut loose from its original concrete situation and growing, pervading one's life. Hatred can be an ever-present, pervasive, totally dominant feeling in an individual's life. It can lead him to lash out at those felt to be the threat to the self, in ways that cannot be explained or predicted by others or by the self, in ways that cannot be controlled. Hatred aroused is beyond reason, beyond the real situation even as the individual himself defines it. Hatred smolders within and lashes out. Hatred is long-burning and rarely transcended. The opposite side of shame is self-hatred, for shame is tied up with the inability to feel that someone else or some external situation is the cause of one's failure, one's poverty. Self-hatred is the first reaction of the poor to their situation and is generally found intermingled with later external hatreds. Self-hatred and the resulting self-destructiveness pervades the lives of the poor, but it is dominated by the direction of hatred externally. Hating externally can be a reasonable reaction to blaming one's situation, one's poverty, on external forces. It is that sometimes for the poor, though it tends to be individualized in the United States and thus to be turned against one's parents, so that it becomes another form of self-hatred. More commonly, external hatred is a defense against hating and destroying oneself; and the more one hates himself, the more he must hate externally.

Any outsider (non-poor person) who has a gut understanding of the American poor assumes implicitly that he must never do anything to offend them, to raise questions of their self-value, to impugn their manhood or womanhood. Indeed, I have always thought the truly wise person who must go through a poor area avoids all eye contact with the young men, for that alone may arouse shame. He knows that any arousal of the shame feeling, however unintended and irrational, is likely to unleash a violent reaction. Thousands of outsiders who did not understand that have died for what appeared to them the most trifling things. (Any sociologist who talked to the poor the way he talks to his colleagues every day would have a very short life expectancy.) Because shame and defensive hatred pervade the lives of the poor, violence pervades their lives. Honor and the duel have long passed out of the lives of the middle and upper classes. They live among the poor. The violence is generally random, at least from the standpoint of outsiders who do not know what situations arouse shame and thus hatred. Actually, it is simply situational. But it can be mobilized by providing the poor with a symbolic definition that seems plausible. When the poor can be convinced that their poverty is all the fault of someone else, then their hatred can be more systematically organized and directed against the enemy. When this happens, the force unleashed can be immense. America today is experiencing such an unleashing of hatred because some poor blacks were convinced by intellectuals and liberal politicians that they *should* hate the white man for their poverty. We now have politicized crimes of violence for the first time on a large scale. Those who purposely sought to arouse the poor by rubbing raw their hatreds intended to use these politicized hatreds for rational purposes of social reconstruction (though we must also wonder how much they were acting out their own hatreds). They misunderstood the hatreds of the poor and have, instead, merely added to the world's vast reservoirs of hatred and violence. Like the rational men who prepared the way for the horrors of hatred in the French Revolution and the tyrannical repression that followed, they will learn that such hatred is beyond reason.

Merton and those sociologists who followed him were right in thinking the poor steal. Theft is pervasive. He was wrong in thinking the rich do not. They simply do so in different (and much bigger) ways. He would have been right to believe that the poor are vastly more violent than the rich. That is the one great patterned difference in crime and deviance. He would be wholly wrong to think that any such pale feeling as anomie is responsible for this violence or that mere lack of legitimate opportunity can produce it. Once we recognize the powers of shame and hatred, we discover a whole new understanding of our society.

But let us take as the ultimate test of our idea of the dominance of feeling over rules the heartland of legal-rational rules — the modern bureaucracy. Sociological studies of bureaucracy began with Weber's highly abstract model of bureaucracy as governed by legal-rational rules and have moved progressively away from that model, but rarely to the point of seeing clearly what lies behind the rationalized fronts. The Weberian model, which could just as easily have been the Durkheimian functional model, focused upon the rational rules of bureaucracies that specified the rights and obligations of those performing the various roles of the organizations. The next fifty years of functionalist research and theory progressively complemented this emphasis on official rules with an emphasis on unofficial, so-called informal, rules of the subgroups created by the workers themselves. For example, instead of seeing the official rules on production rates as the sole determinant of action, the functionalists came increasingly to argue that the members form subgroups that set their own rules for rates of production and that set informal rewards and punishments to enforce those rules. The ethnomethodologists, in line with their general goal of replacing the functionalists' emphasis on values with the phenomenologists' emphasis on cognitive factors, later argued that any adequate understanding of rule uses must recognize that the group's members employ ideas of practicality in deciding how actually to put those rules into effect in their organizational routines. For example, in his study of the practicalities of rule use in a welfare organization, Zimmerman (1966) showed that the formally stated bureaucratic rules could not be applied without producing chaos. Instead, the secretaries had to create practical interpretations of how the rules were to be combined and applied to the concrete situations as they developed. The functionalists found their explanations in values, both formal and informal; the ethnomethodologists, in ideas. If feelings occurred in those organizations, we would not know it from reading these accounts. Even when the ethnomethodologists disagreed with the moralistic account of bureaucracies provided by functionalists, they did so only to rationalize the moralisms.

Almost any in-depth experience in the most formal of formal organizations makes obvious the importance of feeling, personal needs, personal desires, and personal aspirations. Indeed, they are so obvious that they are apt to be taken for granted as basic and other aspects examined for theoretical analyses. If, for example, one listens to the everyday discussions of sociologists or any other members of our bureaucratic centers of reason and science, the universities, he will hear them relying on the commonsense understanding of the basic importance of the personal and emotional to make sense out of what happens in their own experiences. Everyone knows that personal disputes, likes, and dislikes are basic determinants of what happens in faculty meetings. They forget such things, or take them for granted, only when they set out to conceive a formal theory of organizations.

David Altheide's study (Chapter 4) of television newsrooms looks directly at these personal and emotional aspects. One of the important aspects of newsroom work was the conflict and feelings of hatred that existed between many of the staff and the director of the news. Feelings of liking and disliking were also crucial in determining the teamwork necessary for doing the news. These same feelings were of basic importance in the formation and activities of the cliques that worked secretly for personal advancement.

Probably the most systematic and in-depth study ever done of the actual workings of whole bureaucratic organizations was Melville Dalton's (1959) analysis of four scientific and engineering organizations, *Men Who Manage*. Dalton's work was done from the inside and used many investigative social research methods, something Dalton saw as vital to getting at the behind-the-scenes truth about the organizations, especially at the higher levels. As he has said, his own "occupational involvements usually preceded questions and consciousness of problems to be studied" (p. 274). He began with experience, turned it into a subject of study, and worked up to his more general understanding of how the bureaucracies actually operated. (Because Dalton has drawn on the ideas of men throughout Western history, including sociologists, in developing and presenting this more general understanding, this existential basis for his understanding may not be apparent on first reading.)

Dalton's overriding, pervasive understanding of the ways the bureaucracies actually worked was clearly communicated by his subtitle: *Fusions of Feeling and Theory in Administration.* By feeling he meant the personal — all those biological, individual, and cultural needs, drives, desires, and motives of the concrete individuals. By theory he meant the complex sets of formal rules (and ideas, though the emphasis was on rules) that make up the organizations and within which they operate (laws). His basic idea was that there is a fusion of feelings and theories in the bureaucracies. The nature of these fusions (for there are many different forms) is complex and was only slowly revealed (and realized) by Dalton as he worked his way through the massive details of his findings and the many specific ways they made sense to the participants and to himself. For the sake of brevity, I present only a systematic and far simpler version of the understanding he arrived at.

Dalton concluded that, although man is necessarily social, he is also necessarily outside of and often in conflict with society and, thus, with the bureaucratic organizations in our society:

Santayana's observation that "society is like the air, necessary to breathe but insufficient to live on," essentially reflects the individual's condition in the rational organization, especially those of middle to large size. He lives from the firm, but some of its demands are contrary to his nature and inadequate for his impulses. He may feel so inhibited by it that he combines with others to elude it or to reshape part of it. In and out of industry, man against man, and man against the organization is a condition unlikely to end until our species evolves to something different. Perpetual harmony is alien to all life. [Dalton, 1959:241–2, 264]

There are also necessary, inescapable conflicts and contradictions among rules and, even more importantly, between the rules and the practical activities that must be undertaken to achieve the goals to which the rules are aimed as the means. Individuals inevitably suffer internal conflicts, and those who seek to achieve the practical goals of the organization and of their own advancement within the organization inevitably come into conflict with rules — if anyone invokes them. The executives, the men who seek to manage the firm and to get ahead, are above all the ones who necessarily encounter these conflicts and who must deal with them:

Daily the executive sails a "planned" course through a flood of mixed personal and impersonal alternatives and surprises. He must strike some kind of balance between rational and emotional behavior toward his juniors and associates. To survive the clash of logical and personal claims he "must appear to believe in the values of his company" but "be able to ignore them when it serves his purpose." When he decides in favor of the organization, contrary to demands of his group, he is immoral in their eyes. If he follows the group call, and the organization is damaged, he is immoral. Usually he shuns the route of "either-or" and follows the course of "either-and-or," which is compromise, or a third immoral choice to some. To take this path he must penetrate the inscrutable and seize what is useful for the occasion. He must know when and how to use clique ties. And he must improvise and match his departures and defenses and give both the right hue of dogma for powerful formalists who must be lived with. [Dalton, 1959:244—5]

As is implicit in his statement, Dalton believed that rationalized bureaucracy is instituted by the few to achieve their goals by rationally regulating or controlling the many. Bureaucracy thus inevitably creates more conflict between society and individual and involves more necessary conflicts of rules and between rules and achieving practical goals. These conflicts produce greater frustrations or sufferings within individuals, who develop massive "frontwork" and "prefigured justifications" (what ethnomethodologists would call "rational, reflexive accounts") for public presentation to protect their private, personal feelings and lives within the organizations. The frontwork and prefigured justifications allow the strong individuals to achieve personal goals without overtly rejecting or destroying the organizations (see Dalton, 1959:265, 267, 270).

All this must not be construed to mean that Dalton believed rules and rational planning have no effects in our society. On the contrary, there are all degrees of commitment to the rules and the literal meanings of rational planning. There are even some individuals within every organization (as John Johnson also found in his studies of welfare workers) who are rule-bound, formalists, absolutists about the rules and the rational plans. The point is that these individuals are, like the rules and rational plans themselves, inevitably out of step with reality. Dalton saw them as "the weak," those who lack the courage to go against the rules, the fear-ridden who cannot successfully adapt to the changing, ever-conflictful realities:

The weak are prone to lose sight of goals in concentrating on procedures. Hence in unstable situations not yet covered by the rules, or where rules are outdated or will never be detailed, they cannot improvise. Against this, the strong are so unconcerned with procedure — except when it is a clear aid or can be interpreted to their advantage or is a necessary symbol — and so accustomed to moving directly toward goals that they readily devise new methods in doubtful situations. [Dalton, 1959: 248]

In the end Dalton arrived at a thoroughgoing existential view of bureaucratic man striving courageously, artfully, evasively to fulfill his animal nature within an increasingly alien, conflictful social world:

The battle between impersonal organization and the personalizing individual is old. That does not sanctify the condition or mean that its recurrence is always the same, or say that the struggle cannot be constructively channeled in various ways. However, recognizing the timeless element allows a better appraisal of the individual's part in the conflict. Today's tempo is faster but the underlying process is the same. And it may be that the rapid pace is less painful than the strain between appearance and being for individuals who exhaust themselves maintaining unassailable fronts . . . Devised by the few to control the many, impersonal controls (of bureaucracy) provoke a condition of frustration and resistive intrigue that intellectuals have immemorially denounced in cries for a return to nature. . . .

With more resources to draw on and in more explicit language, demands are now made that the individual not flee but stand and assert himself in his daily life. These pleas — in various veins by H. F. Wilkie, W. H. Whyte, Jr., D. Riesman, and Orwell — are focussing too much on the visible. We have seen that the problem is less one of the individual's being himself than it is of his being free to show himself as he is. With higher managers approving departures that bow to the code, no commentary is needed on the volume of individual and collaborative "free-wheeling" existing at all levels.

Those who mistake surface conformity in organizations for *total* conformity and the death of originality, should refocus to concern themselves with the ethics of protective coloration among thinking animals. [Dalton, 1959:270—2; emphasis in original]

Love and hate, ecstasy and agony, pleasure and pain, lust and satiety, hope and despair, satisfaction and frustration, excitement and boredom, sympathy and spite, full and hungry, tasty and foul, comfort and discomfort. These and a vast number of other feelings, named and unnameable, are the core of our being, the stuff of our everyday lives. They are the foundations of all society. They come before symbolic meaning and value, lead us continually to reinterpret, hide from, evade, overthrow, and recreate thoughts and values. Feelings pervade all meanings and values. They inspire our practical uses of rules and they are the reasons behind our reasoned accounts. They are certainly not the whole of life. Without rules and ideas fused with feeling to inspire, shape, and control human passions and lesser feelings, we would not long exist, for social order is necessary to man's existence. But without feeling, without brute being, there would be no use for rules, ideas, or social structures; and there would be none. This fact is obvious to almost everyone in everyday life, including sociologists of all persuasions when they act in the practical world.

The transcendental ego, objectivity, and social order

The primary goal of classic theorists in sociology was to achieve absolutely objective knowledge of society. Their primary substantive concern, as Parsons and many others have argued, was the explanation of social order. Being so basic to their work, these two goals were intimately intertwined, each greatly affecting the other. The phenomenological sociologists were equally committed to these two goals, though they often did not recognize this.

The phenomenology of Husserl and his followers was primarily an attempt to rebuild the foundations of classic science and philosophy without radically altering the building constructed upon that foundation. Once it was recognized that the classic assumption of subject-object dualism could no longer be maintained, objectivity became the basic problem of the theory of knowledge. If knowledge was dependent upon the subjective being of the knower, it could not be objectlike. Was knowledge necessarily dependent upon the mind of any particular knower? And was knowledge thereby impossible, as the very word *knowledge* implied invariance, although dependence upon individuals seemed necessarily to imply variance? This was the primary stimulus to Husserlian phenomenology.

The Husserlian solution to the problem, like Kant's earlier solution to the epistemological problems posed by Hume's argument, was found in the nature of the knowing mind itself. If invariance could not be founded upon the nature of being itself, the external world of objects, or the perceptual relations existing between the world and the mind, then it could be founded upon some invariance in the nature of the knowing mind itself. These invariant properties of mind, of knowing, of conscious experience, are what Husserl and his followers called the *transcendental ego*. The discovery of this transcendental ego, or of its particular properties, was the primary goal of Husserlian phenomenology. Husserl seems to have believed that revealing the ways in which the mind *necessarily* knows the world would solve the problem of objectivity in a world of subject-object interdependence (see Chapters 2 and 3 for discussion of some complications of this argument). Subjectivity, or knowing, would thus be made absolutely invariant; and as invariance with respect to knowers and situations of knowing was the goal of absolutist scientific objectivity (as earlier of absolutist religious dogma), objectivity would be saved, if in a form not envisioned by the earlier epistemologists.

Two major points must be made about this argument. First, even if it were possible to discover such a transcendental ego, or a necessary set of properties of the knowing mind, Husserl and succeeding phenomenologists would not have saved absolute objectivity. Any such quest and any such argument would still be based on presuppositions that could in no way be *demonstrated* not to be presuppositions. This is true for at least two reasons. As others have pointed out, Husserl's argument presupposes the existence of an invariance in motives or values, specifically, of an invariant commitment to pursue such an argument and accept its results. To seek a presuppositionless knowledge and to take it seriously are to make value judgments that are not only not invariant but actually restricted to a few philosophers with significant influence on the actions of common men. Moreover, and most telling of all, the search for such a transcendental ego assumes that it exists and that it works to produce invariant (absolute) knowledge. The problem of infinite regress in this search for the ultimate basis of knowledge appears insoluble. The basic argument of the phenomenologists is aimed at rationalizing knowledge, but does not succeed in eliminating the ultimate mystery of knowing.

The second major point about the phenomenologists' search for the transcendental ego is that the quest has had the effect of reinstituting the absolutist view of the world. As Sartre argued about Husserl's search for the transcendental ego, the phenomenologists started with the announced intention of producing a philosophical revolution, of suspending all previous suppositions about the world; but, probably because of the implicit presupposition that their goal should be the discovery of necessary (invariant) knowledge, they wound up reinstituting or rebuilding the foundations of the absolutist, rationalist theory of knowledge, even to the brink of reinstituting idealism:

Now the cogito never gives out anything other than what we ask of it. Descartes questioned it concerning its functional aspect — "I doubt, I think." And because he wished to pass without a conducting thread from this functional aspect to existential dialectic, he fell into the error of substance. *Husserl, warned by his error, remained timidly on the plane of functional description. Due to this fact he never passed beyond the pure description of the appearance as such; he has shut himself up inside the cogito and deserves — in spite of his denial — to be called a phenomenalist rather than a phenomenologist.* His phenomenalism at every moment borders on Kantian idealism. [Sartre, 1960:73; emphasis added]

In this sense, phenomenology is merely a coup in the palace of rationalist philosophy. Some of the rationale and names change, but absolute objectivity remains and all is well with the traditional scientific enterprise.

The general effects of the epistemology of phenomenology have been twofold in sociology. First, the search for the transcendental ego has been the dominant, but usually implicit, goal of the phenomenological social thinkers in two ways. This quest for the transcendental ego, for the invariant properties of mind, lies behind the almost continual turning of the phenomenological social thinkers toward positivist methods of doing research and of "proving" their theories. The same sociologists, such as Aaron Cicóurel (1964), who have started their work with basic criticism of the positivist presuppositions of traditional sociological methods of survey research (e.g., statistical thought) have ended by imposing their own presuppositions upon the social world in the form of a whole technology of recording (recorders, videotapes) and of analyses based on actual or quasi-interview techniques (triangulations). They have also implied, if not stated, that by revealing the method of knowing (recording the research and then studying it) we are somehow able to produce objective results. This oversimplifies the problem of objectivity by assuming that reproducibility constitutes objectivity and that providing a record of research makes it possible to reproduce results.

There is even at least one striking instance, that of Thomas Wilson (1971), in which an ethnomethodologist has faced the problem of the infinite regress of knowledge. Having faced the problem, and without providing any solution, Wilson has simply asserted that ethnomethodologists must search for and find invariant properties in the social world (in accounts). Apparently he has not recognized that the infinite regress problem itself makes the idea of absolute objectivity involved in (absolutely) invariant properties absurd.

The second general effect of the phenomenological quest for the transcendental ego has been even more far reaching. Nothing is more basic to the absolutist perspective than the assumption that behind all the apparent flux of the world lies rational order (God, pure reason, laws of nature, social structure, social system) and that this order should or must be the primary goal of philosophical and scientific thought. In traditional sociology this assumption has led to a primary concern with discovering the (presumed) universally shared values. The same goal has been maintained in phenomenological social thought by the quest for the transcendental ego, both in the work on meanings and in that on social order.

The quest for the transcendental ego has been most apparent in the ethnomethodological work on social meanings, especially on language. The goal of this work is to discover the invariant properties of social meanings, language use, and cognitive structures. The invariant properties are thought to be various things, from the necessary conditions of status-degradation ceremonies or of establishing trust, to interpretive procedures (derived largely from Schutz), to invariance in the psychophysiology of perception. But the basic idea is always the same: Far behind the variability of everyday life situations lies a symbolic (cognitive) order that transcends all situations, that in some way enables us to explain all situated activities; and this symbolic order must constitute the primary goal of all sociological activity. These assumptions have obvious implications as well for the phenomenological study of social order.

Schutz himself was hardly concerned with social order as a problem. He seems to have assumed that social order exists and is the source of the symbolic typifications members use in constructing their paths through everyday life. Berger and Luckman, however, made the explanation of social order the central concern of their Schutzian work, *The Social Construction of Reality*. Their central question was: Given the social constructionist nature of social reality, how is it that there is order in the social world? They recognized, of course, that the shared meanings of society are products of human action rather than imposed from without by the will of God. But they took as a central fact of social life that there is a shared universe of social meanings (especially found in social roles) and, most importantly, that there is a high degree of order or structure in society that the members of society themselves take to be absolute — out there, relatively unchanging, and imposed upon them (see Chapters 2 and 4 for further discussion of their theory). The ethnomethodological treatment of social order has generally been only implicit. For example, Garfinkel, Cicourel, and Sacks have implicitly assumed, along with Schutz, that the social world is ordered and that their goal must be to discover the basis of this order — the transcendental ego in some form (e.g., commonsensically rational accounts, properties of meanings, deep rules of language use, invariant interpretive procedures). At the same time, the ordered nature of everyday activities has been used implicitly as a resource for analyzing (and possibly even explaining) the nature of accounts (see Chapter 5).

The one explicit attempt of the ethnomethodologists to deal with the problem of social order has been that of Zimmerman and Wieder (1970). Their essay was written as a critique of Denzin's (1970) essay, which tried to show that symbolic interactionism and ethnomethodology share a basic perspective on the problem of social order. Denzin argued that both theories see social order as a basic problem of sociological theory and that both attempt to explain social order in terms of the meanings that members of society construct in their on-going or emergent interactions. Zimmerman and Wieder began their critique of Denzin's interpretation of ethnomethodology by pointing out that this view of the problem of social order leaves social order as a reality discovered by the sociologists — a reality that may include some consideration of the constructions of meanings by the members of society, but one that is, nevertheless, independent of the members' own accounts of social order. They then pointed out that the ethnomethodologists are concerned only with the question of how the members of society render accounts or demonstrate to each other that a given social situation is rule-governed or ordered. The ethnomethodologists are concerned only with how a given situation appears to the members to be rule-governed or ordered or, even more correctly, how the members provide each other with the appearances of being rule-governed or ordered.

Thus, when the ethnomethodologists have dealt directly with the question of social order, they have merely reaffirmed their basic commitment to study the ways in which members render (rational) accounts of their actions to each other. They have not even purported to study the ways in which the members might construct what they themselves would define as social order. And certainly, given their presupposition that the sociologist cannot develop any knowledge that is more objective than that of the members of society, they did not believe the ethnomethodologist can provide any explanation of social order or provide any policies for altering, constructing, or destroying such order. Even more striking, ethnomethodologists have implicitly assumed that the members of society see their world as rule-governed at all times and that this accounting of it as being rule-governed is the same as (or constitutes) an accounting of it as being ordered. The ethnomethodologists, like the earlier phenomenological social thinkers, have implicitly assumed that there is a transcendental ego that leads the members of society to see their social world as highly meaningful, rationally accountable, justifiable (by typified accounts), ordered, and even homogeneous.

I have previously argued (Douglas, 1970a) that the research of the ethnomethodologists has been carried out almost entirely in the kinds of situations, such as public bureaucracies and scientific research organizations, which are the most highly rationalized, rule-governed, accountable, linguistically accounted for, authorized, homogeneous, stable, shared, and ordered in our society. Such settings are obviously the ones most apt to support any presuppositions about the existence and importance of a transcendental ego and about the rule-governed, accountable, ordered nature of members' understandings of their world. As I have argued above, the strong predisposition of the ethnomethodologists to use methods amenable to objective demonstration of their analysis also restricts their research to the most visible and most carefully controlled public presentations in the most highly public settings. Given their predefinitions of their subject matter, their philosophical and methodological presuppositions, and their research settings, it is not surprising that they "found" the transcendental ego and that their social actors took rational accounts so seriously. They have shown a relatively legalistic view of society that mistakes the code books for the social reality of the social actors. Although they started with a critique of positivist methods and absolutist theories of social rules and social order, they have ended by reinstituting those methods in a new form and partially reinstituting absolutism in the form of the transcendental ego and the assumption of the rationally accounted for social order.

The phenomenological neoabsolutism that follows from the presupposition of the existence of a transcendental ego involves both the assumption of a highly orderd, rational social world and the corollary assumption that the individual human being is the product of that social world. The phenomenologists freed man from the iron laws of necessity of the external (objective) world, but only to resubject him to the iron laws of the subjective world, the transcendental ego. The individual human being is no more free in phenomcnological thought than he is in traditional absolutist social thought. Indeed, he is even less free because his very being, his self, is assumed to be constituted by invariant interpretive procedures from which he cannot escape, whereas even in Durkheimian thought the individual was allowed to be secretly irrational and secretly deviant as long as he did not oppose the absolute social order. (If he did oppose the social order, then he was controlled and the boundaries were maintained.)

If we approach social experience without the presupposition of a transcendental ego, and without such positivist methodological assumptions and hardware, we find a very different social world. If we immerse ourselves in the situated experiences of everyday life in all kinds of settings, so that we can discover the unaccountable as well as the accountable experiences of the members of society, we find a vastly more complex social world. We find that there are many social settings, such as those of intimacy and the sacred, in which verbal accounts are almost forbidden or are highly restricted. Indeed, any situation recognized as involving great emotion is seen as demanding a nonrationality, nonaccountability. You may scream, shout, or cry; but to provide a rational account of those actions leads people to think you insane. We also find situations that are experienced as meaningless. There are even people, both philosophical and commonsense nihilists, who experience the entire universe as meaningless, empty, void, infinite nothingness. These everyday experiences of meaninglessness are of vital importance in understanding our social world. They must not be presumed nonexistent on grounds that sociology is concerned with meanings, not meaninglessness.

Far more commonly, we find that people experience some situations as highly accountable, some as totally unaccountable ("I can't explain it," "I simply don't know what to say," "I don't know what it's all about," "I don't know what's going on," "It's all Greek to me," "I don't know what to tell you," "It's better not to talk about it"), and most others in between. Many situations are experienced as suffocatingly ordered ("Nothing new ever happens around here!"), many as highly disordered ("My God, what a mess," "What the hell's going on?" "Doesn't anything ever go right around here?"), and most as a mixture of those. Many situations are experienced as highly rational and certainly rationally accountable, and many others are experienced as irrational ("crazy," "insane," "fantastic," "nonsense," "beyond me," "ridiculous," "absurd"). John Johnson, for example, has studied instances in which welfare workers involved in child-protection services explicitly define situations as "ridiculous" and "absurd." Moreover, in his work on welfare workers Johnson found numerous instances of "playing it by ear" or "flying by the seat of your pants" at precisely the same time the workers were carefully constructing and presenting rational accounts, even quantitative accounts, of their activities to superiors and to the government officials who audit the agencies. All our depth research into bureaucratic (rational-legal) organizations such as this have revealed that in the matters of greatest importance to the members, such as deciding on basic policies, there is almost always an important gap between what they consider to be the true situation and what they present as the rational accounts justifying their activities. Although it takes investigative research to discover how pervasive is the reliance on nonrationalizable forms of information and decision procedures, there are numerous insider accounts that present the basic truth and accept nonrationality as inevitable. Some of the finest of these have been written after the fact by the men who provided rational accounts while they were flying almost blindly through the bureaucratic haze of quasifacts and lies. Theodore Sorensen's work, *Watchmen in the Night*, was a recent example of this literature. Quoting others and relying on his own insider experience in both the Kennedy and Johnson administrations, he has reminded us how commonly insiders (even at the highest levels) see their own accounts as partly "bullshit" (the opposite of rational accounts) and has even ridiculed some of the official reports:

"I don't think people understand," said C. Jackson Grayson after his 1971—73 stint as Price Commissioner, "that really a lot of what's done at the central level is done on an awful lot of guesswork. . . [or] how many decisions we had to make where we did not really understand what was going to happen . . ." Those of us who had worked at the "central" level understood. I saw two Presidents required on more than one occasion by limits on their time, resources, and information to take actions or to make pronouncements which were one part improvisation, one part a response to headlines, and one part [expletive deleted]. Contrary to the prevailing view, life in the White House is not a series of dramatic crises but of unending daily efforts to keep the machinery of government running without too many break-downs or explosions. [Sorensen, 1975:67]

Everyone faces the same problem every day. Most of the time we deal with it without thinking in terms of putting a good front on our nonrational feelings: We just do it automatically. But every now and then people make an explicit search for a way to rationalize their non-rational feelings and actions. Students are notorious for this when they have decided not to take an exam (out of fear or laziness). It is so common in science that it is described in a cliché that is only half-joke: "I know it's true, now all I have to do is prove it." But one of my favorite examples is a letter to an advice column from a landlady perplexed by our world of bureaucratic legalisms and rationalisms:

Dear Mr. Campbell:
I have an 8-unit apartment complex and I am always at a loss whenever I turn down an applicant simply because I have a "feeling" about them. That they're going to mean trouble, or something. I've found that my feelings are usually right, but how do I make this sound legitimate without being embarrassed about it? — Mrs. R. W., Buffalo, N.Y.

These feelings, irrational and arational ideas have profound effects on the ordering and disordering or our social world. Millions of men have died in the twentieth century for love of country and fear of the firing squad faced by deserters. How many have died for commitment to a value such as equality? How many have died to uphold the rules of evidence forged by reason to provide justice? Who would doubt that these millions and the many millions more who fought with them had profound effects on the destruction and construction of social orders? Who would doubt that racial hatreds, ethnic hatreds, profound feelings of resentment by have-nots against haves, deep feelings of contempt and disgust by haves against have-nots are of greatest importance in overthrowing, maintaining, rigidifying, and transforming social orders? Who believes that all the evidence and reasoning about capitalist incentives and success will stop the attacks of those with profound resentments against the capitalist order, or that proof of the sufferings of the poor will persuade the rich to change that order? And who doubts that all the rational accounts by the two or more sides to these struggles are largely rationalizations of profound feelings? Each side, of course, insists that his arguments are rational, not emotional, and that the other side's are emotional, not rational. This is testimony to the importance of rationality as a public front, but does not convince us that a front is the primary reality and mover of the social world.

The importance and effects of reason and values on human life and social order are subtle and take a long time to develop. The importance and effects of feelings and nonrationalized ideas and experiences (including visual images unmediated by words) are clear, profound, and immediate. Reason and values are partly independent of these deep feelings and nonrationalized cognitive experiences, but they are largely inspired by, swayed by, and infused with such feelings and experiences. When these feelings change, the values and rational accounts commonly change also, though they may remain long in conflict and almost always engender a vast amount of deception and rationalization in public life to hide these conflicts, to allow us to do what we want to do because of secret feelings, while appearing to be doing it out of virtuous and rational reasons. Indeed, as I have argued before, public life in our vastly conflictful society is largely a front or, rather, a meshing, a conglomerate of many different fronts. Fronts are important. They are partly the means by which we try to arouse the feelings we want in other people and get others to act the way we want them to do; we persuade them that the front is reality or that it is in their best interest to act as if the front is reality. Fronts are also the screens behind which we can do what we want to do, if we are not found out and challenged. (The processes of creative deviance are examined in Douglas, 1977.) But to mistake the fronts for reality, the shadows for the realities casting the shadows, is to misunderstand reality and doom oneself to creating a pseudoscience. Goffman's (1959) argument that presentations are just as real as what lies behind them and, indeed, may be the only reality is another form of the phenomenological acceptance of symbols, accounts, as *the* reality. It almost always strikes the ordinary reader as bizarre, he knows from his own experience that there is an obvious difference between the front and the reality behind it and that the difference is important in understanding what really goes on.

Brute being, feelings, and conflicts of rationality with other thoughts and models of action we hold (see Scott and Douglas, 1972b) all contribute to the necessarily problematic nature of human experience, including the ordering of our social lives. But there are other reasons why we see experience as necessarily problematic, as necessarily free and situationally contingent. It is a basic fact of human life that, however much we strive to rationalize our world by restricting contingencies and programming all our responses to the situations we have so carefully controlled, we cannot anticipate all the events that will arise in concrete situations and we cannot totally program human experience and response to those situations even when we have total power and a total will to do so. Even the simplest of human activities, such as walking down the street, cannot be preprogrammed without danger of catastrophe, even when we have a vast amount of control over the environment in which the simple task is to be performed. Accidents will happen and the best laid plans often go awry. These truisms can be counted upon. They can even be taken into consideration, as they are in space shots under the rubric "unexpected uncertainties." But they cannot be eliminated. When we consider how vastly more complex our everyday experience is, and how vastly less control we have over the situations that arise for us independent of our will, it becomes ridiculous to think of most human experience in mathematical, deterministic terms. When we also consider the internally conflictful and contingent nature of human responses, such as the differences unpredictable moods can make and the insistence of human beings upon their own freedom and integrity, upon doing things their own ways and not according to some external program, it becomes utterly absurd to pretend that human experience is so ordered and produced from within or without that it can be analyzed and explained without taking into consideration the partially contingent and free nature of that experience.

It is obvious that the world, both the natural and the social world, is partially patterned, ordered, preprogrammed. If it were not, human life would be impossible and a science of that life ridiculous. But it is also clear that the world is partially unpatterned, disordered, not preprogrammable — that experience, internal response, and action are necessarily partly contingent and free. The question is not whether these things are true; they are obvious to any man of common sense. The crucial questions are: Which situations are ordered and contingent, in what ways, by whom, to what degrees, with what effects? How are human beings both constrained and free to create their situations and responses? How do they create them within such constraints and with such freedom? What effects do those creations have?

Given the necessity of pattern and order in human life, we can always expect to find pattern and order in human affairs. Human beings will find a way to create them or humans will not continue to exist to be studied. But, given the necessarily contingent and free nature of human experience, we can be equally sure that disorder, freedom, and disarray will arise. Given the highly complex, conflictful, contingent, free, necessarily problematic nature of our social lives, we can be sure that human beings will find the creation of social order highly problematic and that they will devote some of their most creative energies to solving those problems. We can be sure that all order will contain some disorder and the seeds of more disorder, and that disorder will be reordered. It is important that we not presume things to be ordered (or disordered) and that we try to find out how they are ordered and how disordered.

These truths and questions must concern us in the study of any society. They are especially important in studying our own society today, for our society is more complex, pluralistic conflictful, and rapidly changing than almost any other (see Douglas, 1971b). We know in our everyday lives that our values, beliefs, and feelings are commonly uncertain and often conflictful. We know that we often do not understand what is happening and that we do not know what to do or how to do it. We know that it is not uncommon for us to experience things as absurd, ridiculous, or meaningless. We know that we often must live with situations we ourselves consider evil and foul, while pretending they are acceptable; that we must often provide rational accounts of actions that seem irrational or unaccountable; that we must often hide the disorder of our lives or organizations behind a front of formal, planned, rationalized organiztion; that we must often struggle valiantly simply to maintain the appearances of order; that we are often playing it by ear or flying by the seat of our pants when we appear most rational and ordered. To fail to see the fundamental importance of these things in our society and to place them at the core of any understanding of our society, is to misunderstand our whole society.

This truth is damning enough for any phenomenological analysis of our society that is concerned primarily with symbolic experience, with rational accounts, with the quest for the transcendental ego, and that either assumes the existence of order or purports to explain that order by the properties of the transcendental ego. But, even more damning, all such analyses assume implicitly that the everyday social realm can be reduced to cognitive experience without losing the integrity of that realm, although their intermittent recognition of the situationally contingent nature of social life denies that very assumption.

We have argued that social experience is partly situational, that it is created and experienced by its members in significant part in terms of the concrete situation facing them at the time, and that it can be understood truthfully by the sociologist only if he takes into consideration that situational nature of the experience. This is an argument few phenomenological sociologists would deny, though they commonly have not seen it as so fundamental or sweeping as we have argued it is. Ethnomethodologists, for example, have stated that talk is "occasioned," that accounts in general are "irremediably indexical." Given this truth, it is ridiculous to expect that even a *total* knowledge of all those properties common to all human experience (i.e., supposedly, the transcendental ego) will allow us to understand situated experience. On the contrary, even a total knowledge of the properties of accounts, of deep rules, of interpretive procedures, of cognitive models, or of the transcendental ego in any other guise will not allow us to understand any situation completely. Even if human beings were not necessarily free, the contingent or problematic nature of situations would make it impossible for us to understand the relations between the universal prop-

erties of mind and the concrete, existing situations, For example, even
if ethnomethodology could discover all the interpretive procedures of
the human mind, and if these were a necessary and sufficient set of
rules for generating the inputs of the mind to any situation, they
would not allow us to understand the specific properties of the U.S.
Congress, of a political campaign, of a crime, of a mother's relation to
her child. They would allow us to understand only what is common to
all communications (*if* the assumption of necessary and sufficient held,
which I deny). Yet it is precisely what is different between situations,
what is different between prostitution and love, between love and hate,
between politics and science, that is of concern to us as practical human actors. In this sense the phenomenological sociologies are doomed
to irrelevance, and it is not surprising that they have never attempted
to contribute anything to our practical political understandings of the
social world.

An existential view of self and becoming

Even more striking is the fact that the phenomenological sociologies
have contributed so little to our understanding of ourselves. Any disci-
plined thought that takes conscious experience of the human mind as
its basic topic might be expected to enlighten us about ourselves, about
how we as human beings make our way through the world, about how
we experience our world and shape it, about how we see ourselves,
about our being. But the phenomenological sociologies have not done
so, for two reasons. First, as we have seen, the phenomenological sociologies have tended strongly to assume the existence of a high degree of
social order. In the process, they have reinstituted the structural-
functional view of the self as a set of functioning roles provided by the
society. Even Goffman, whose work has been specifically concerned
with the self more than anything else, has had little to say about the
self except as a "presenter" of predefined and learned social roles (see
Chapter 3). He has had almost no concern with the shadowy chooser
who must surely lurk behind these self-presentations to choose among
the vast array of conflicting role definitions in our immensely complex,
international, and changing society. The same fault is found com-
pounded in almost all other interactionist works, as they tend to assume that the self is a looking-glass self, a reflection of the socialization
practices of an absolutist society. Second, because the phenomenological sociologies have concentrated primarily upon the discovery and
analysis of the universal properties of meaningful communications, they
have said almost nothing about the concrete, substantive, self-reflective

being who uses these properties of meanings to achieve his goals in the world. The phenomenological self is a shadowy bundle of interpretive procedures, the product and subsequent constructor of a universe of symbolic social meanings. This pale shadow of man — man seen as the reflection of socialization or as universal properties of mind — belies the tumultuous reality of yearning, willing, struggling, excitement, content-ment, dreamy playfulness, and so many other experiences we all know from observing ourselves and other men- and women-of-flesh-and-bone.

I suspect that all men everywhere have, to varying degrees in differ-ent situations, felt some separation between themselves and the social world in which they lived and died. Perhaps most men in most societies have felt a relatively great sense of identification with their social world, a self-fulfillment through the roles it made available to them. But in our own society there can be little doubt that all men often feel keenly the sense of separation from the social world, of loneliness, of conflict, of alienation, of injustice, of the need to hide from that world, of the need to pretend and lie, of the need to escape, of the need to transcend, and even of the need to destroy and murder. It is a grave mistake to depict us all as strangers in the world, as some existential philosophers and writers have done. This is the opposite extreme, and our varied society is only distorted by extremes, as it contains all extremes and yet usually manages to hold them in shifting balance. And it is a distortion to see some particular group, such as the workers, as alienated, while seeing the rest of us as contented conformists and oppressors. In our society all groups and individuals feel some contentment and some alienation, and the rich and affluent are commonly as angry as or angrier than the poor and feel even more oppressed. (The so-called libertarian move-ment, inspired by rage against oppressive government, is fast growing in American society, but it is predominantly a movement by the middle-upper class.) Just as all simple pictures of our society belie the complex and conflictful realities, so do all simple pictures of our inner beings, of our selves.

Chapter 10 depicts the complex, shifting, and ever willful feelings, ideas, and strategies of selves among the members of two gay communi-ties and shows how different the realities of selves in this community are from those presented by interactionists and others who have been concerned with self. This is probably an extreme situation in some ways, as the members of the gay community are still stigmatizable in most of our society. Yet it may not be so extreme, for a large percent-age of Americans if potentially stigmatizable to the same extreme de-gree in some way from some source. Our society is now so fractionated, with such conflicting sets of values, ideas, feelings, and actions between and within groups and individuals that any person of experience knows that someone may "get him" at any time, either for something he has actually done or for something he cannot prove he did not do. Even the rich and powerful, even the men supposed to be running the system, including presidents, can suddenly find themselves stigmatized in numerous ways for innumerable things. Indeed, the more successful, influential, or simply active a person has been, the more certain it is that he has been involved in things that many or most people disapprove of in some way. The fact of success itself guarantees legions of enemies who profoundly *resent* a man's success and are looking for the chance to destroy his reputation or him. This situation, which is similar to that of the Italian cities in the Renaissance, led Dalton (1959) seriously to compare business today to the practices of Italians in the days of Guicciardini and led Lyman and Scott (1970) to see the relevance of Machiavelli's *Prince* to an existential analysis of our whole society.

In our society today most individuals must at some times in their lives create themselves and their social lives in a thoroughgoing manner. They do not simply present themselves, though they certainly do that pervasively and commonly with a great deal of cynicism. They must *choose* themselves. But this does not mean that they stand back from the tumultuous flow of their everyday lives and choose what they will become or even that they know what they want to become. On the contrary, our lives are so complex, conflictful, and changing that we commonly know very well that we cannot simply decide what to become and then carry out the decision. It even seems likely that the once strong feelings of individuality, of being this substantive thing or that, are fading; that our ideas of self are becoming more vague and more comingled with our ideas of the world external to ourselves. What it does mean is that the individual must himself decide upon his own path, upon the guises in which he will present himself to this part of the world and that part, and that he must do so wisely in terms of his own feelings, values, and ideas or he will experience feelings of guilt, self-betrayal, frustration, meaninglessness, even Sartre's feeling of nothingness. We have gone so far in this direction that people today are commonly very conscious of their self-creation and have complex theories about how to do it. Many people, for example, become their own therapists and decide what they should do in order to get over this hang-up, that feeling, that sense of guilt. Robert Gilmore (personal communication) has found good evidence of this in his studies of nudists. One of the clear motives for becoming a nudist is to overcome otherwise uncontrollable feelings of anxiety or guilt (hang-ups) about one's sex by putting oneself in a situation where his sex is taken matter-of-factly and where (eventually) no anxiety is experienced. This idea involves a complex understanding that what one feels and does is a complex result of experience in relevant concrete situations, rather than simply a matter of abstract choice or of talk with a therapist in an irrelevant situation or of simple self-presentation or verbal accounts.

Increasingly today, the members of our society know that we are not set, certain, irrevocable substantial selves. They recognize that we are commonly only vaguely defined, that we are often conflictfully defined, that sometimes we are terrifyingly unclear about who or what we are, even when others are able to give us a clear set of definitions in terms of our complex involvements in role play. They often recognize that we are able to re-create ourselves, but that doing so is a difficult, nonrationalizable activity with uncertain outcome. They increasingly recognize that who we are, what we are, is continually in the process of becoming and that we ourselves, though able to affect the outcomes of the process of becoming through our continual struggles, are not able to dictate the outcomes of this flux. We ourselves — our minds, our hearts, our society, our bodies — are in flux. That flux is crucial in our everyday lives. It is a cornerstone of existential sociology.

Truth, objectivity, and the practical involvements of sociology

There is another basic reason why phenomenological sociologists have offered no practical policies for dealing with problems of our societies or personal lives. This reason is their theory of truth and objectivity, which is largely implicit in their work, but has profound implications for it. Probably because they have almost never explicitly faced the questions of truth and objectivity, the ethnomethodologists have offered two conflicting perspectives on them. One view leads directly to solipsism; the other, which is growing and which we have already dealt with in our considerations of the search for the transcendental ego, leads to a reinstitution of the absolutist conceptions of objectivity.

The early ethnomethodological position concerning scientific objectivity is that associated with the work of Garfinkel, though it has been carried to its extreme in the more recent works of Blum and McHugh (1971) and Pollner (1970). It is based on the argument that we should study only accounts and that *all* human accounts, including all scientific communications, are "irremediably indexical." A great deal of their work has consisted of studying scientific activities precisely in order to demonstrate that they too are irremediably indexical. These ethnomethodologists have claimed that this necessarily indexical nature of scientific activity makes it simply another form of commonsense activity. This might be called the *radical ethnomethodological theory of objectivity*. Both the scientific activities and the commonsense activities have been viewed as interpretive. Instead of seeing commonsense activities as interpretive and scientific ones as literal or invariant across situations, these ethnomethodologists have rightly pointed out that scientific activities are also interpretive; that is, their meanings for the participants also depend on situational or occasioned properties, so that their meanings are subject to situational interpretations, hence variations. These ethnomethodologists have then insisted that there are no rational distinctions between common sense and science, at least not between common sense and sociology, and that it makes no sense at all to argue that sociology can ever be more objective or true than commonsense beliefs. They thus have excluded all consideration of objectivity from their work and have contended that they are simply studying the interpretive procedures of the members of society and that, indeed, theirs is the only rationally legitimate approach for a sociologist.

Some ethnomethodologists, such as Thomas Wilson (1971), have recently argued that there is no reason to accept this view of sociology as necessarily interpretive. They have proposed what might be called the *remedial ethnomethodological theory of objectivity*. Recognizing that the radical theory raises the danger of solipsism, of allowing everyone to do his own sociological thing, they have insisted that at least ethnomethodological accounts can be made quite literal; that is, that they can be freed from their dependence upon the situational understandings of common sense for their meanings and, thus, be made objective. In this view, ethnomethodological studies should be restricted, insofar as they are to be scientific studies, to the investigation of phenomena for which literal, invariant accounts can be given; that is, accounts for which universal agreement can be achieved, presumably because the phenomena under investigation are objectlike, or externally perceivable, and hence not subject to all the problematic, variable interpretations of common sense.

Both these ethnomethodological theories of objectivity believe that something is wrong with the traditional theory of absolute objectivity used by sociologists. The second, however, suggests that ethnomethodological studies can remedy these faults by making the scientific procedures themselves a subject of rationalized, systematic investigation and manipulation. It accepts the necessary indexicality of scientific activity, but seems to believe we can still get along with the classic, absolutist theory of objectivity and uses that theory in recommending that ethnomethodology be made a literal discipline. Although the proponents of this theory have not yet given us the examples of these literal, invariant social phenomena, I suspect that when they do, these phenomena will prove to be the externally perceivable, objectlike events of speech i.e., recorded talk or cognitive models or psychophysical laws. But their insistence on studying only externally perceivable events, rather than inferring from commonsense understandings the nature of experience to society's members, and thus their indulgence in interpretations, deny the necessarily problematic nature of social experience by excluding considerations of social experience. They become plainly and simply structural linguists or transformational grammarians and exclude from consideration the essential nature of social activity, its problematicness and situationalness.

The radical ethnomethodological theory of objectivity is quite correct in insisting that we include this problematicness and situationalness in our considerations and recognize that these are also properties of our own scientific activities because we necessarily ground those activities in commonsense understandings. This radical view is wrong only in insisting that our sole choice is between yes and no, between black and white, between objectivity and solipsism. I believe this is an unnecessary submission to the outworn absolutist world view. Our choice is not between solipsism and a retreat to the absolutist theory of objectivity. Rather, we are free to choose a middle road that offers many different degrees of invariability in our studies — and a new theory of scientific truth and objectivity.

We must begin our attempts to resolve some of these basic problems by distinguishing between truth and objectivity. Much of the confusion in philosophical and scientific discussions of scientific objectivity results from failure to make this distinction. Truth is the much broader concept and totally incorporates objective truth, but is not coterminous with it. We accept many things as true that can in no way be demonstrated objectively.

Any attempt to resolve the problems of truth must begin with a decision about where the criteria of truth are to be found. The traditional scientific and philosophical approach involves the assumption that we must impose criteria in an ad hoc fashion, based on the assumptions we wish to make in our philosophical or scientific work. This approach, however, actually uses our commonsense preconceptions about truth in a covert manner. It starts with some commonsense understandings of what truth is and how we determine truth, but then picks and chooses from among these commonsense ideas in terms of ad hoc purposes. I believe we can greatly improve our approach to the questions of truth by making this use of commonsense ideas of truth more explicit and thus making these decisions available for systematic consideration. Although a thorough examination of the nature of commonsense ideas of truth, and of their variability and invariability within and between cultures, remains to be carried out, certain basic ideas seem clear enough.

Through eons of interaction of our minds and bodies with the world, we have developed complex grasps and commonsense understandings of what we call truth. These feelings and ideas, far from being mere biases of common sense, are grounded in all of human existence. They grow out of our existence and are vital to our existence, because we cannot live without having a generally effective idea of what is true and what false, what exists and what does not, what works and what does not. Insofar as there is any transcendental ego, any necessary properties of thought arising from the universal interaction between the common human form and the common physical world, it will obviously be found by studying these commonsense concepts of truth. And insofar as there are culturally distinct ideas of truth, they will be found by studying what is universal and what is distinct in these ideas of truth.

A basic fault of the ethnomethodological attempts to study ideas of rationality is that they have implicitly assumed that all rationality is concerned with practical matters. This is not so. Any brief overview of Western history alone shows that many of the battles over truth have been concerned with precisely the problem of separating questions of practical truth from those concerning transcendental truth or sacred truth. Transcendental truths are those concerning religion and any matters involving predominantly the mentalistic (noumena) stuff of human experience. They overlap with the realm of practical thought (e.g., when we are concerned with how the word of God affects what we should do), but most men have distinguished between such sacred thought and everyday, practical thought. (It is important, however, to note that rarely has this distinction been as sharp and important as in our increasingly sensate or secular culture. Even today any fundamentalist would be deeply puzzled to hear that the sacred thought of Christianity or Judaism had no practical implications. What could be more practical than achieving eternal bliss?) The two have distinctly different, if overlapping, dimensions of meaning and feeling and are directed at different experiences. In general, transcendental truth is directed at internal concerns of man and is probably far more the direct product of the nature of our minds and bodies. Practical thought is directed at doing things, at being useful, in our relations with the physical and social world. Although a thorough analysis of either one must hinge on an analysis of both, we are concerned here only with practical thought, as sociology, like any other science, is directed toward the practical goal of doing things effectively in the social world.

There are a number of partially overlapping dimensions of meaning to practical truth. The two most general and important ideas seem to be existence and workability. An idea can be said to be true if it represents what exists (what really is, the way things are, the realities) or if it represents a relation believed to exist between two or more things that appears to work (to be useful, to work out).

Much of the confusion in the philosophy of scientific truth, and certainly in the sociological discussions of that truth, has resulted from a failure to distinguish between these two dimensions of meaning. The problem of objectivity is concerned predominantly, though not entirely, with establishing workable or useful, shareable truth (see Douglas, 1970b, 1971a). The question of existence is related to this, as it is useless to know about something that does not really exist; but many truths about existence, which greatly concern us and are important to us in everyday life because their existence is important in itself, cannot be demonstrated the way workable truths can, such as by independent retests. This has fundamental implications for all sociological understanding.

We use a number of major and subsidiary ideas in establishing for ourselves the truth (or falsehood) of anything in our everyday lives. But the two most important, found in some form in almost all ideas of truth in everyday experience, are direct experience and independent retest. Each is applicable to questions of both existence and workability.

Because of the highly situated, personal, and secret nature of much of our everyday lives, most of the things we consider to be true (or false) about our everyday lives are established by independent retest. This means that most of the things we consider true, especially the most important things (because they tend to be the most personal, situated, and secret), are not directly subject to retest and, therefore, are not subject to the test of workability or objectivity. Insofar as sociologists have insisted on treating any idea about social experience as true only if it can be made objective (i.e., established as true by independent retest), they have doomed themselves to irrelevance and, by imposing methods upon society as if the methods did not change what was being observed, they have also doomed themselves to studying a falsified or distorted set of experiences (see Douglas, 1976).

Consider an example to make this point clear. An individual, such as an Arthur Schlesinger, provides us with an account of his intimate involvements in a presidential decision that affects whole societies. It is sometimes the case that no one else has experienced this decision. The fate of nations is changed, but there are no independent retests. Is the decision, then, irrelevant to understanding the society scientifically? Should it be treated as nonexistent or necessarily unimportant because not subject to our puristic ideas of objective truth? The same questions affect our studies of the head of an organization or of any individual in everyday life, because we all make decisions like this.

Sociologists in the past have commonly relegated these phenomena to the realm of the scientifically unknowable and, thus beyond the realm of sociology. This arbitrary restriction of our studies to that which can be established by independent retest means that we miss the crucial matters of society and individual lives. We become a science of the irrelevant or the as if. Existential sociology insists on being relevant and dealing with the complete gamut of everyday experience, with all the truths and falsehoods of our lives.

But does this mean, as Garfinkel and others have implied through their arguments about the indexical nature of sociology, that we are doomed simply to study another form of common sense? I think the answer is no, for two reasons: (1) all experience is not irremediably indexical to the same degree; and (2) even when we cannot directly experience the same social phenomenon experienced by another sociologist, we can commonly find some experience that is similar. However, our findings about the truth of everyday experience definitely force us to transform our understandings of the nature of sociological knowledge.

Much of the ethnomethodological argument over objectivity and indexicality is the result of confusion over what is being referred to by the term indexicality. Indexicality has been used at various times in ethnomethodological works to refer to each of the following and to any combination of them, including all of them at one time:

1. The transcendental ego, or universal properties of mind
2. The properties of practical, commonsense accounts
3. The properties of linguistic accounts;
4. The necessarily situated nature of social accounts and activities in general
5. The unique situational aspects of any concrete account or activity
6. The unique, personal aspects of understanding of any account or activity

Insofar as the ethnomethodologists mean that any science is indexical in the first three senses of the term, I do not greatly disagree. We commonly presume those properties of communication in our work as scientists. But it is clear that we as sociologists can and do come to far more systematic, conscious, and controllable understandings of these things than do men of common sense. (Men of common sense must be told a great deal about philosophy and about phenomenological-existential sociologists before they even understand what the argument is about.) This does not deny that those considerations are themselves using the properties they are analyzing, as we saw earlier, and that, consequently, our understanding does rest ultimately upon a faith in the value or workability of the reasoning we are studying. But, given that faith, which I consider to be essential, our more systematic knowledge gives us a greater understanding even at this level than does unanalyzed common sense.

But in terms of the final three meanings of indexicality I cannot agree that all science is indexical. Some realms of social life are partially studiable by methods based on independent retests. These are mainly the highly public, eternally observable phenomena, such as population changes or orange-juice drinking. Sociological research about these is clearly far more rationalizable, far less necessarily indexical in these final three senses, than common sense. And that kind of investigation, when done honestly (without faking data, as is often the case in market research) really works better than common sense. In fact, censuses and polls are rapidly changing commonsense thought in some important realms of society — because they *work* better.

Insofar as we are referring to our sociological studies of the more intimate, secret realms of society, there is much more to the ethnomethodological argument. These are highly dependent on our personal feelings and thoughts in the concrete situations. And that, as we have insisted, is a vital fact that traditional sociology had continually tried to deny. That fact means that the sociology of the most vital realms of society is often based on direct, personal experience and is only partially or intermittently subject to independent retests. We must depend a great deal on direct experience of concrete situations, often secret, to establish truth, rather than on independent observations by many sociologists. But this too is subject to more rationalization than is usual in commonsense discourse. Such sociological accounts are done more systematically, more analytically, more often with the use of memory devices (notes), and more often with the aim of using independent retests or independent comparisons wherever possible.

It has been a mistake, largely resulting from the confused use of the complex term indexical or occasioned, to see sociology as necessarily another form of common sense. This mistake has been the opposite of the traditional, absolutist mistake of seeing sociology as totally distinct from commonsense experience. It is vital to avoid both extremes. Sociology is dependent primarily upon our commonsense experience of our everyday lives, especially for the truths about the most important realms of our social existence. We can change this to some degree, but not vastly. Our knowledge about society is not that of a social physics. It is only partially demonstrable and cannot be shared with those who insist on forcing society into a preconceived methodological mold, any more than with those who insist on forcing society into a preconceived mold of political dogma.

Our understandings of society inevitably remain uncertain. No matter how far we go in rationalizing that understanding, the necessary freedom of human thought and action assures that uncertainty. It is useful to all of us, at least within our present form of society, to reduce that uncertainty through sociological research and analysis and through the use of sociological knowledge in solving our problems. But the great uncertainties that will always remain are not to be denied or bemoaned. I suspect they are necessary facts of reality and a vital protection against the tyrannical trends in an age of bureaucratic technological collectivisms. They are a source of some of our worst human terrors, but they are also a source of creative vitality and joy.

PART II

The fundamental issues and
existential sociology

2

The emergence of existential thought: philosophical perspectives on positivist and humanist forms of social theory

RICHARD H. BROWN

It is widely acknowledged that social theory is in turmoil. More significantly, certain humanistic sociologists — neosymbolic interactionists and cognitive, phenomenological, and existential sociologists — have criticized currently dominant paradigms and attempted to forge new ways of understanding human conditions. In this context, whatever historical luggage the term humanistic carries, its core reference is to the person as a (potentially) conscious and intentional actor capable of exercising choice over his conduct and assuming responsibility for its consequences. In sociology a counterpart of this concept of moral agency is a theoretical approach that conceives of social actors as creators and organizers of cognitively and emotionally meaningful acts, and of social events as patterned according to commitments, intentions, and imagined consequences.[1] With such an assumption as a starting point, a humanistic sociology investigates the problematics of feeling and meaning, the social construction and use of moral definitions in specific settings, the role of power in such interactions, and how such conflictful negotiations of reality are constrained by the cultures, societies, and political economies in which they are embedded.

Such an approach seems one way of linking scientific to ethical concerns. One difficulty, however, is that the dominant notion of what constitutes a scientific explanation tends to exclude the type of existential analysis of reality construction suggested above: Analysis of meaning and construction and use requires an interpretation of feelings, actions, rules, and reasons; explanation in science has tended to speak in terms of causes and effects and to view behavior as *determined* by social forces.

I wish to thank Randall Collins, Jack D. Douglas, Stanford M. Lyman, Rudolf A. Makkreel, Herbert Marcuse, and Manfred Stanley for their critical comments on drafts of this chapter.

Does this apparent fundamental difference between scientific and humanistic thought mean that we can have the objective, practical knowledge of science or the moral and emotional sensitivity of humanism, but not both at once? More directly to our concern in this book, is it possible for humanistic thought to take a rigorous and practical form? The purpose of this chapter is to show that developments in philosophy over more than a century, and more recently in sociology proper, suggest that this combination is possible, but that the enterprise is far more problematic than previously envisaged.

Positivist epistemology and critiques of mechanical man

The absolutist metaphysic

The positivist perspective crystallized in the sixteenth and seventeenth centuries around certain protocols of reason that provided new definitions of the nature of knowledge and society.[2] The world had been rediscovered in the Renaissance revival of Greek science and by the great explorations, and it had been made rationally calculable through the use of Arabic mathematical techniques. Philosophers, scientists, and statesmen came to believe that the forces governing the world could be discovered and exploited. The aim of controlling a populace through an absolute state was paralleled by the hope of controlling nature through knowledge of absolute laws. The clear and distinct ideas of mathematical physics found their counterparts in the rise of clear and distinct individuals under Protestantism and in new statutes codified to replace traditional communal law. Discrete commodities arose in the market system, a linear perspective appeared in art and in history, the stained-glass windows were covered with the bourgeoisie's mechanical clock. The Cartesian notion of pure mathematical laws governing the universe, and the Baconian dictum that knowledge is power, together sum up the epistemology associated with these practical developments. Westerners had agreed that they could achieve mastery of their world by understanding the natural forces, the facts and laws, that existed out there apart from either God or man.[3]

In most expositions of the philosophical speculation of this period, two broad trends are seen as discrete and competing: the speculative, mathematical, logical-deductive tradition inspired by Descartes, as against the more empirical, inductive, research- and fact-oriented tradition heralded by Bacon. This distinction is useful for some purposes, but it is relatively trivial given that *both* these traditions are deterministic: Both sought absolute truth about reality. In this sense, early mod-

ern science and philosophy, despite their great achievements, still remained close to absolutist medieval concepts. As J. D. Douglas has put it:

All the basic ideas of "natural laws" (statements of necessary and immutable relations), "objectivity" (truth independent of the observer and the methods of observation), necessary and sufficient definitions, mathematical (logical) proofs, and so on,
were simply a secularized form of the old absolutist metaphysics [of the medieval
period] . . . This absolutist metaphysics . . . was most apparent in positivism, which
was both the most absolutist conception of man to be found in the social sciences
and *the* dominant theoretical perspective in the social sciences into the twentieth
century. [Douglas, 1970b:258, 266; emphasis in original]

The go-between for this marriage of medieval metaphysics and positivist sociology was the absolutist epistemology of early modern science,
as developed from Bacon and Descartes. Bacon (1561—1626) has been
criticized for his failure to appreciate the role of hypothetical-deductive
methods in science and his assumption that general laws somehow
spring forth from an aggregation of facts (Cohen, 1930, 1949). Yet he
may be called the first champion of empiricism for his stress on objectivity and on the need to overcome biases, or what he called "the idols
of the mind."

A younger contemporary of Bacon, Descartes (1596—1650) began
by doubting every possible presupposition, even his own existence. He
concluded that this process of doubting , even if it is in error, demonstrates that there must be someone doubting, thinking, or being in error:

While I wanted to think everything false, it must necessarily be that I who thought
was something; and remarking on this truth, *I think, therefore I am*, was so solid
and so certain that all the most extravagant suppositions of the sceptics were incapable of upsetting it, I judged that I could receive it without scruple as the first principle of . . . philosophy. [Descartes, 1912:117; emphasis in original]

Thus, thought, a feature solely of God and of human consciousness, is
the criterion of truth or being, and a radical distinction is thereby established between the soul or mind (and its expressions in logic and mathematics) and the body or the world of facts.[4] In asking what we can
know about the world, Descartes supposed that, as thought is knowable
by its clearness and distinctness, so ideas about the world are true to
the extent to which they also are clear and distinct. The physical "nature" or "factness" of things is the clear and distinct aspect of appearances that always recurs in the same manner and that, as such, admits
of being reduced to strict unbroken laws. The nature of truth of the
world is what we are able to extract as constant and abiding from the
sum total of phenomena known to us through the process of theoretical reflection. By disregarding the world of I and thou and instead
formulating objective scientific laws, man can become *"maître et pos-
sesseur de la nature."* The passage quoted above foretells much that

remained dominant in speculation after Descartes: the separation of mind and body; the epistemological priority of mental as opposed to existential experience and of *my* mind as opposed to other minds; and the tendency toward subjectivism in the search for objective knowledge on an absolute foundation.

As it was received by later generations, the positivist approach had two principal components: a Baconian one dealing with objective facts and a Cartesian principle of laws that explain them. Accordingly, we are enjoined to seek out the verifiable units of data hidden behind the surface meanings of events, to discard unverifiable (nonsensical) assertions, and to explain what is left as expressions of the operative factors, variables, causes, or laws (Ayers, 1966). Sociological *knowledge* in this perspective is constituted of explanations that are based on:

> "Objective data" — that is, observations free of the "biases" of the observer and verifiable by anyone at any time. The "facts themselves" have to speak independently of the particular voice of the observer or of the particularities of any observational setting. Moreover, such explanations must be expressed in terms of . . .
>
> "General laws" — that is, the variegated and contextually embedded world of lived experience must be abstracted into a controllable number of functions or variables that can be interpreted and codified into mathematical formulae or some similar law-like construction.

Positivist social theory

With respect to the human studies, these philosophical canons of natural science require that persons be redefined as objects. People become bodies, actions become motions, situations become events. Meanings are reduced to facts, choices to predictable effects. Cognition is separated into objective and subjective dimensions corresponding to the primary and secondary qualities of things in the external world. In sociological theory, the tension within positivism — between empiricism and idealism, object and subject, Bacon and Descartes — was reflected in the oscillation between pure speculation and theory-free research.

Statistical research appeared in the West during the Renaissance, when Italian city-states began using quantitative comparisons of social groups to assess political and military strength (Nef, 1960). In England, John Graunt's *Nature and Political Observations* (1662) and William Petty's *Several Essays in Political Arithmetic* (1682) initiated a tradition of statistical analysis of social rates that was inherited and continued by King, Davenant, Wallace, Derham, Maitland, Smart, Simpson, Hodgson, Short, and others. Government commissions and private reform groups also contributed to the gathering of social facts, especially after the inquiries into factory conditions in the 1830s. Even dialecticians such as Marx and Engels did not fully escape the deterministic imagery of positivism. Invoking the model of physics, Marx claimed to represent "the economic law of motion of modern society" as a "natural law." In the preface to the second edition of *Capital* he quoted with approval the methodological assessment of a Russian reviewer:

Marx seeks to demonstrate through precise scientific investigation the necessity of definite orders of social relations and to register as irreproachably as possible the facts that serve him as points of departure and confirmation . . . Marx considers the movement of society . . . as governed by laws that are not only independent of the will, consciousness, and intention of men but instead, and conversely, determine their will, consciousness, and intentions. [1946:VI:16—17] [5]

If such determination by natural law was the Cartesian side of positivism, other Germans were gathering facts in the manner of Bacon. Conring, Achenwall, and Süssmilch argued that statistical analysis must be *the* basic knowledge of the state. Such thinking, called *Staatswissenschaft* since the eighteenth century, became prominent after 1872 through the efforts of welfare oriented professors and administrators who grouped themselves into the *Verein für Socialpolitik*. In the French speaking world, La Place, De Geurry and Quételet undertook moral-statistical research that profoundly influenced Durkheim, whose study of suicide can be seen as a fusion of the Enlightenment tradition of social physics techniques of the moral statisticians.

In America it was not until the 1930s that the quasi-participative, interpretive style of the Chicago school was displaced by mathematical models and statistical methods after the image of physical science. In this approach, through the medium of operationization, abstract or ideal concepts are translated into discrete units of data. The subject and object both are collapsed into the operations of measurement. The recipe, in effect, defines the cake, regardless of who baked it and how it tastes (Lundberg, et al., 1954:34). Thus Binet defined intelligence as what is measured by intelligence tests. Similarly, group cohesion was measured in terms of rates of turnover in the membership of the group, rates of attendance at meetings, or rates of arrears in dues. Job satisfaction, anomie, or prejudice was defined in terms of the percentage of certain kinds of responses on questionnaires. Indeed, the questionnaire was particularly attractive as a measuring device because it standardizes responses, making them easily scalable and retrievable, in principle by anyone. The tabulation of these responses — assuming control for sampling errors, leading questions, and other sources of bias — constitutes objective data. In this manner Chapin (1939) operationally defined social status in terms of a social status scale. Riley et al. (1954:7) saw scales as providing "empirical representations of certain sociological concepts." Similar operational instruments are Bogardus's social distance scale, Thurstone's social attitude scale, Guttman's scalogram analysis, and the various ordinal measuring devices invented by Stevens and Coombs, Guttman, and Lazarsfeld (Gabaglio, 1888:1—36; Thurstone and Chave, 1929; Sjoberg, 1959:606; Douglas, 1971b; Collins and Makowsky, 1972:219).

Positivist and neopositivist self-criticism

This approach has been criticized by positivist sociologists and philosophers themselves. One line of their commentary has sought to clarify traditional canons of evidence and to chastise those who do not adhere to them strictly. For example, Park (1969) has shown how even numerically and experimentally oriented researchers tend to sneak mentalistic concepts into their theories. He noted that anomie and other such concepts are used as explanatory variables by Durkheim but are not defined as independent from that which they are supposed to explain. To solve similar problems with such pseudovariables as relative deprivation, social status, esteem, prestige, and disintegration, Park has called for greater operationalization and experimental controls. Along the same lines is Deming's essay, "Errors in Surveys," an inventory of ways in which questionnaire research can go wrong. Similar warnings are to be found in numerous texts and articles on research methods by Chapin, Lundberg, Hyman, Festinger, Zetterberg, and Lazarsfeld.

A more pungent line of self-criticism is that of neopositivist philosophers, who have modified some of the foundational assumptions of earlier positivist thought. For example, the idea of causality has been qualified by theories of probability; the canons of proof and verifiability have largely been replaced by those of disproof and falsifiability. Carnap (1953:195) has limited the task of inductive logic to testing hypotheses rather than discovering them. Similarly, Feigl has warned that "If some of the extremely tough-minded psychologists relegate questions such as those concerning the instincts, the unconscious, or the relative roles of constitution and environment to the limbo of metaphysics, then they cut with Ockham's razor far into the flesh of knowledge instead of merely shaving away the metaphysical whiskers" (1943:371—417).

By narrowing the domain of metaphysics, Feigl has expanded the concept of rationality of early positivism. Other neopositivists were even more liberal. For example, Weyl (1949) noted that only the subjective is absolute, the objective being relative to rules of observation and verification, which, as rules, presuppose a shared community of discourse. Similarly, Karl Popper allowed that the foundations of science are less bedrock than swamp:

> The empirical basis of objective science has thus nothing "absolute" about it. Science does not rest upon rock-bottom. The bold structure of its theories arise, as it were, above a swamp. It is like a building erected on piles. The piles are driven down from above into the swamp, but not down to any natural or "given" base; and when we cease our attempts to drive our piles into a deeper layer, it is not because we have reached firm ground. We simply stop when we are satisfied that they are firm enough to carry the structure, at least for the time being. [Popper, 1959: 111]

In a similar vein, Thomas Kuhn distinguished the neopositivist position from the traditional one:

> [While we] both insist that scientists may properly aim to invent theories that *explain* observed phenomena and that do so in terms of *real* objects, Sir Karl and I are united in opposition to a number of classical positivism's most characteristic theses. We both emphasize, for example, the intimate and inevitable intanglement of scientific observation with scientific theory; we are correspondingly skeptical of efforts to produce any neutral language of observation. [Kuhn, 1970:2; emphasis in original]

This view that science is not an exact copy of reality, but rather an instrument for explaining it, also appears in the writings of social scientists themselves. Kroeber and Kluckhohn noted that "patterns of implicit culture [are] purely inferential constructs" (1952:161–2). Schumpeter stated that "the very work of constructing the schema or picture will add further relations and concepts to, and in general also eliminate others from, the original stock" (1954:42). Similarly, Tolman distinguished "immediate experience as the actually given, rich, qualified, diffuse matrix" from those logical constructs "by which the psychologist attempts to explain it — to help in predicting and controlling it" (1961:97). Archpositivist Ferdinand Lundberg made this point even more firmly: "All propositions or postulates regarding the more ultimate 'realities' must always consist of inference, generalizations, or abstractions from these symbols and responses which they represent" (1964:8–9). But all these are predominantly rationalist criticisms of empiricism.

Criticisms from a humanistic perspective

Such circumspection about their own methods would seem to safeguard positivists against criticism from nonpositivist points of view. Yet the assumption of Park, Deming, Feigl, Popper, and others is that the biases noted can in principle be corrected and the limitations overcome, so that the positivist approach to knowledge can be made to work. In contrast, other thinkers have challenged the basic assumptions of the positivist method and metaphysics. They have argued that the subject matter of sociology — human conduct — cannot as such be known through purely objectivist methods and that, in fact, the more objective our observation becomes, the further we are removed from what we want to know. The views of humans as objects, and of statistical experimentalism or deductive functionalism as an explanatory ideal, according to these critics, begs the very questions the human studies should address.

At stake is the basic model of the nature of social action and of knowledge about it. The early positivists not only wanted explanatory laws to which everyone must agree, but also insisted that these laws corresponded to a purely material world (out there). They denied all subjective reality, even that of their own theories. Then neopositivists modified this: They still sought law-like generalizations about real objects, but they allowed that these objects could never be directly known and that their theories could never be justified absolutely either by physical facts or by mathematical truths. In contrast to both early and later positivism, however, some humanist critics have suggested that if we conceive of the actor as conscious *agent*, rather than as object, we seek, not causes of behavioral events, but *reasons* for meaningfully intended *conduct*. This, of course, means imputing feelings, awareness, and choice to the actors and imaginatively reconstructing the meanings they experience in and give to their situations. Thus, where the positivist seeks causes — independent and dependent variables generalized into law-like constructs — the humanist seeks the grounds and consequences that emerge in existential situatons. For the one, the explanatory terms are external forces; for the other, they are the actors' concepts of meaning and value (Fite, 1930:34).

Robert MacIver (1937) illustrated this nonobjective character of conduct by pointing out the "essential difference between a paper flying before the wind and a man flying before a crowd." Both occurrences may be studied in terms of forces and motions, causes and effects. But with the man flying before a crowd there clearly is another element present: "The paper knows no fear and the wind no hate, but without fear and hate the man would not fly nor the crowd pursue." Unless we can understand these emotions and purposes, we cannot explain the phenomenon or predict what the man and crowd will do. Indeed, we cannot even know what is going on. One positivist, George Lundberg, responded explicitly to just this point: "I do not declare MacIver's analysis of the man and the crowd to be *false*, I merely point out that possibly I could analyze the situation in a frame of reference not involving the words fear or hate but in operationally defined terms" (1964: 13).

We thus appear to have a pluralism of methods, each with its own definition of the subject matter and its own canons of evidence. More sophisticated spokesmen of both positivism and humanism acknowledge this, at least insofar as they allow that their respective models of the self and society are intellectual constructs, symbolic mediations of a reality that cannot be directly known. There is, however, a critique of positivism that is more radical than such a pluralism seems to permit. This critique is advanced by the new theorists who insist that the sociologist must be concerned not only with his *own* construction of categories, but also with that of the persons whom he studies. It is not a matter of the sociologist's *symbolic* constructs as against a concrete social reality; rather, his typifications are typifications of what the *actor* has typified. Moreover, his self-reflection on his own process of concept formation, instead of removing bias should remain in dialectical tension with his study of the actor's formation of concepts in everyday life.

This position may be illustrated by contrasting it to Lazarsfeld and Barton's account of how the commonsense, subjective categories of actors are to be transformed into objective data. First, the positivists' view:

Suppose we want to classify the reasons why women buy a certain kind of cosmetics. Women have a great many comments on their reasons which are hard to group if one takes them at face value. But visualize a woman buying and using cosmetics. She gets advice from people she knows, from advertising, and from articles in mass media; in addition, she has her own past experiences to go on . . . All the woman's comments might be related to the following scheme: "channels of information," "desired appearance values," "prospective audience," "bad consequences," "technical qualities," "application problems," and "cost."

The reason the comments would fit is that the scheme of classification matches the actual processes involved in buying and using cosmetics. These are the processes from which the respondent herself has derived her comments; the classification, so to speak, puts the comments back where they came from. [Lazarsfeld and Barton, 1951:160]

By this procedure, so it would appear, responses that for the women are subjective become objective data or indicators of general concepts when gathered through survey procedures. Assuming that we control for bias of sample, interviewer, and so on, the data yielded can be analyzed to make possible the creation or testing of general formal theories, preferably, expressed in mathematical form.

As Cicourel (1964) and others have noted, there are a number of contradictory assumptions built into this practice. The data obtainable through Lazarsfeld and Barton's method are tautological. By first visualizing what the real causes of women's behavior *must* be, they then are able to allocate women's *actual* accounts of their behavior into categories of their schema. So allocated, the data obtained confirm the correctness of the reified categories. Analysis of such data may reveal unsuspected statistical relationships between categories, but such data or categories in themselves constitute no evidence that they are descriptively or analytically relevant to the processes under study. Rather, the commonsense notions of sociologists are substituted for the commonsense notions of women, and there is nothing in the manipulations the sociologists' notions are undergoing that establishes their epistemological superiority to the notions of the women. On the contrary, it is likely that women have a better understanding of the world of cosmetics than male sociologists who have not existentially entered this world and who, rather than accepting members' reports about it, substitute a different world that they visualize as matching the actual processes involved. The accuracy of the sociologists' predictions is a reflection, not of the sophistication of their methods, but of the chance congruity of their commonsense assumptions and those of women who buy cosmetics.

By taking the measurability of social facts as unproblematic, positivist sociologists overlook the more fundamental questions that the human studies must answer: How are facts socially constructed? How do some materials get defined as cosmetics, or as the best buy in cosmetics, or as anything else? Such processes of reality construction, it has been argued, slip through the positivist net. As F. A. Hayek has put it:

A "word" or a "sentence," a "crime" or a "punishment" are of course not objective facts in the sense that they can be defined without referring to our knowledge of people's conscious intention with regard to them. And the same is quite generally true wherever we have to explain human behavior towards things; these things must then not be defined in terms of what we might find out about them by objective methods of science, but in terms of what the person acting thinks about them. Cosmetics, e.g., for the purposes of social study, are not what improves a person's looks, but what the person acting thinks about them. [Hayek, 1955:30]

A prime obstacle to understanding processes of reality construction may be the assumption that our apparatus for defining and measuring social facts is scientific. Instead, suppose we imagine that crime is the end product of police procedures, or that mental illness is a label that emerges from what psychiatrists do. From this perspective (suggested by Znaneicki, 1968, and revived by Garfinkel, 1967), the question, What is the crime rate? turns our gaze away from the more basic question of how these rates are created in the first place. This type of inquiry takes Pandora's box down from the positivists' attic. Yet to act as though there were no box is arbitrarily to impose our own common-sense categories onto the subject matter and then, in turn, to impose onto these categories the formal logic of mathematics. The common-sense of the sociologist has no necessary relation to that of the actor; nor is the structure of mathematics necessarily isomorphic with that of the actor's worlds.

Such a critique bristles with problems of its own, of course, even seems to call for a new epistemology and a new form of social science. To these we attend in the sections that follow.

Philosophical perspectives of humanist social thought

Positivism provided a legitimizing theory of knowledge and of society for the scientific and industrial era. Yet, at least since Marx, many have thought that the very success of the industrial system would undermine its own ideational foundations. In advanced industrial societies such as America, the belief in progress through positive science appears to be diminishing, and there has emerged concurrently a new relativity of perspectives, a new awareness of the possibility of orchestrating one's own world view. As the forms and products of industrial civilization come to seem increasingly meaningless or irrelevant, there has arisen a belief that meaning is something people can create, that relevance is an on-going human achievement.

The philosophical justification for such a humanistic or existential view can be said to have begun with Vico's rebuttal to Descartes. Today, such a theory of knowledge and action is expressed in three major philosophical schools: pragmatism, the analysis of ordinary language, and existential phenomenology. The respective American, British, and Continental practitioners of these schools generally are not on speaking terms. Yet the ways in which they complement each other are important for the creation of a human-centered science of society.

The most striking similarity of these thinkers is a negative one: their revolt against Bacon and Descartes. In his articles of 1868, for example, Peirce launched a systematic attack on the basic tenets of this positivist framework: the ontological duality of mind and body, the subjectivism implicit in the ultimate appeal to direct personal verification, the belief that language is nonsymbolic — a mere vehicle or ornament of thought, the doctrine of clear and distinct ideas and the unreality of that which is vague, the belief that language can be sidestepped in favor of a direct intuition of objects, and the method of doubt and the elimination of bias as a path to an absolute foundation for knowledge.[6]

A similar attack on intuitionism, subjectivism, and the givenness of facts is found in Wittgenstein's (1953) analysis of ordinary language. Indeed, Wittgenstein's idea of "language games" presupposes that meaning and truth are dependent on rules, intentional action, and intersubjectivity; by contrast, in the Cartesian framework knowledge is wholly contemplative, grounded in logical absolutes, and discoverable only through personal intuition.

A critique of positivism is also a main theme in existential phenomenology. The primary dependence of knowledge on either ideas or perceptions was challenged by Kant's notion of knowledge as mediated by the categories of the mind. Fichte and Hegel dialecticized inquiry, making truth and reality, subject and object, two moments in the same process. Then Kierkegaard, Dilthey, Heidegger, Merleau-Ponty, and Sartre once again grounded knowledge and understanding in the practical realities of the individual's existence.

In addition to their critical similarities, these schools overlap in the ideas they put forward to replace the positivist model. The pragmatists speak of conduct; analytic philosophers have recently shown great interest in action; existential phenomenologists use the terms praxis, experience, or existence. Though the histories, nuances, and emphases of these terms are different, each presupposes humans to be feeling, conscious, and intentional actors. Each school conceives formal knowledge — whether in the sciences or the arts — as presupposing the experience and understanding of social life: Scientific knowledge is necessarily based on shared experience and commonsense understanding, and is itself a problematic construction.

Philosophers as diverse as James, Dewey, Dilthey, Husserl, and Wittgenstein agreed that the commonsense understanding of everyday life experience is the framework within which all inquiry must begin and to which it must return. Dewey spoke of this framework as the "social matrix" within which emerge "unclarified situations" that may then be transformed by science into "justifiable assertions." Wittgenstein referred to knowledge as a "form of life." Husserl wrote of the "life-world" within which all scientific and even logical concepts originate. Alfred Schutz, speaking of the basic subject matter of sociology, summed up a perspective common to all these thinkers:

Any knowledge of the world, in common-sense thinking as well as in science, involves mental constructs, syntheses, generalizations, formalizations, idealizations specific to the respective level of thought organization. The concept of Nature, for instance, with which the natural sciences have to deal is, as Husserl has shown, an idealizing abstraction from the *Lebenswelt*, an abstraction which, on principle and of course legitimately, excludes persons with their personal life and all objects of culture which originate as such in practical human activity. [Schutz, 1970b:272]

He then drew the inference of such thinking for the social sciences:

Exactly this layer of the *Lebenswelt*, however, from which the natural sciences have to abstract, is the social reality which the social sciences have to investigate. [Schutz, 1970:272]

Yet what is the nature of this layer of the *Lebenswelt*, and by what methods can it be known? In the rest of this section we trace three lines of speculation on these questions — pragmatism, ordinary-language analysis, and existential phenomenology — toward the vanishing point at which they converge.

The pragmatism of Charles Sanders Peirce

Peirce's main contribution to an epistemology of human existence lies in his attempt to articulate the relationship of action to meaning, the properties and functioning that experience must assume in order to acquire the status of knowledge. The result of this attempt is a theory of symbols — a semiotics of knowledge, conduct, and reality. In developing this theory Peirce first attacked the notion of knowledge as having an absolute foundation and of the knower as a passive, isolated observer. In the positivist view, knowledge must be founded on some absolute and indubitable basis, whether it be sense impressions, simple facts, operationalized measures, universal laws, or a priori or self-evident truth. From this perspective the job of the philosopher is to identify the foundation, show how it can be made to yield more complex knowledge, and derive criteria for distinguishing falsehood and truth. In this view, also, knowers are spectators. Rather than participating in life, they sit in the grandstand as it parades before them.

In contrast, Peirce sought to avoid the Charybdis of transcendental idealism and the Scylla of unmediated facts. Knowledge for Peirce cannot be grounded in the pregiven categories of Kant or in Comte's world of concrete facts (1960:VII:322; VIII:16). Instead, Peirce believed knowledge emerges only in the context of action and experience, where the process of inquiry serves specific pragmatic functions: the settlement of arguments, the elimination of paradox, the avoidance of surprises, the fulfillment of expectations, and the fixation of belief (V:197). Thus, there exists an "inseparable connection between rational cognition and rational purpose" as socially enacted (V:412). Peirce's theory was based

upon a study of that experience of the phenomena of self-control which is common to all grown men and women; and it seems evident that to some extent, at least, it must always be so based. For it is to conceptions of deliberate conduct that pragmatism would trace the intellectual purport of symbols; and deliberate conduct is self-controlled conduct. [Peirce, 1960:V:442]

Peirce did allow that "all instruction given or received by way of argument proceeds from pre-existent knowledge." In this limited sense he accepted the truth of the foundation metaphor as given by Aristotle. But it does not follow that there are absolute starting and ending points to inquiry that can be grasped through some direct intuition. It is here, indeed, that Peirce differs from both early and modern positivism. For he aimed not to clarify the logical structure of scientific theories, but to elucidate the logic of the procedure by which such theories are obtained (Habermas, 1970:91). Our claims to knowledge, said Peirce, are legitimized not by their origins, but by the norms and rules of inquiry itself. These norms and rules form a sign system that is itself subject to the feedback of experience — not scientific experience in the narrow sense, but experience in life, in the confrontation of situations that have become problematic or paradoxical.[7] The fallibility of all knowledge is not a deficiency, but a necessary feature. Every claim to knowledge has meaning only in terms of a system of signs that is open to further interpretation and has consequences that are to be publicly tested and confirmed. According to Bernstein: "In opposition to the subjectivistic turn in philosophy implicit in the Cartesian framework, Peirce argues that all language, signification, and consequently all inquiry and its end product, knowledge, are essentially social in character. The very meaning of our concepts depends on the role that they play in a social context of rules and norms" (1971:176). And according to Peirce himself: "The very origin of the conception of reality shows that this conception essentially involves the notion of a COMMUNITY, without definite limits, and capable of a definite increase in knowledge" (1960: V:311; emphasis in original).

This community, or collective world of life and action, is constituted of symbolic interaction. Peirce made this clear by linking sign processes with processes that involve mediation (thirdness), that is, social processes between persons:

It is important to understand what I mean by *semiosis.* All dynamic action, or action of brute force, physical or psychical, either takes place between two subjects . . . or at any rate is a resultant of such actions between pairs. But by "semiosis" I mean, on the contrary, an action, or influence, which is, or involves, a cooperation of *three* subjects, such as a sign, its object, and its interpretant, this tri-relative influence not being in any way resolvable into actions between pairs. My definition confers on anything that so acts the title of a "sign." [Peirce, 1960:V:484; emphasis in original]

One example of such a relationship is "giving," which does not occur unless the event of transfer of an object from one hand to another is mediated by the intentions of both parties. Because of this mediation, the event becomes an act, the motion becomes conduct.

Peirce then developed this formulation to show that reality, mind, and indeed man himself, are symbolic. A sign, which is "essentially triadic," is defined "as anything which is so determined by something else . . . and so determines an effect upon a person . . . that the latter is thereby mediately determined by the former." Then Peirce added a telling remark: "My insertion of 'upon a person' is a sop to Cerberus, because I despair of making my own broader conception understood." As interpreted by Morris (1932:284), this "broader conception" is tied directly to Peirce's generalization of the symbolic process from epistemology to ontology. The "effect" (interpretant) or meaning of a sign itself becomes "in turn a sign, and so on *ad infinitum.*" Instead of the sign being for a person,

the word or sign which man uses *is* the man himself: Man makes the word, and the word means nothing which the man has not made it mean, and that only to some man. But since man can think only by means of words or other external symbols, these might turn around and say: "You mean nothing which we have not taught you, and then only so far as you address some words as the interpretant of your thought." In fact, therefore, men and words reciprocally educate each other; each increase in man's information involves and is involved by, a corresponding increase of a word's information [Peirce, 1960:V:313] . . . That every thought is an external sign, proves than *man* is an external sign. [II, 156, emphasis added]

Ordinary language and the new teleology

Ordinary language philosophy, like pragmatism and existential phenomenology, takes as its starting point the clash between the scientific or mechanistic image of persons and the image that is manifested in everyday life (Sellars, 1963). This manifest image is expressed most directly when we observe accounts of behavior in ordinary language: "Why do you study hard?" "Because I *want* to get into college." "Why does she walk that way?" "She's *trying* to get picked up" (cf. Lyman and Scott, 1970:111–44). Even positivist writers, in their everyday lives, act on the assumption that we are feeling, conscious, intentional agents. Thus Carnap wrote books that deny occult concepts such as consciousness or intention, yet the very fact that he wrote such books presupposes a conscious and intentional author and audience (Schutz, 1970b:266).

In the positivist view, however, accounts of behavior couched in ordinary language can never be granted the status of knowledge. Because they refer to mentalistic concepts (e.g., wanting, trying), they represent an obstacle to the acquisition of empirically grounded explanations. The job of philosophy thus is to purge language, or at least scientific language, of such usage. Language must be made objective, the word must refer to the thing or to the specifiable relation between things, preferably in an operationalized form.

A host of difficulties emerges when attempts are made to put this

principle into effect. The basic problem is that positivists have confused motion with act, reflex with conduct (Urmson, 1956). For example, a woman holding her arm out, palm forward, might be directing traffic, warding off an attacker, drying her nail polish, or admiring a ring. But if mind is reduced to body, there is no way to distinguish these actions. The purport of this example, for the ordinary language philosopher, is that the above instances are acts, not motions, and hence they cannot be explained in terms of causes. Indeed, in terms of the thing-world of cause and effect, we cannot even know what these actions are and mean. Rather, it is argued, because behavior is essentially normative and bounded by rules in contexts, it is logically impossible to explain human conduct if we restrict ourselves to the vocabulary of physical science. There is no way of deducing from physiology that an extended arm, palm forward, is a sign for traffic to halt, or that a clenched fist is a sign of political solidarity. Instead of having the character of self-evident physical facts (whatever these may be), action must be understood in terms of reasons, rules, and projects. Thus the very possibility of a social *science*, at least on the model of the physical sciences, is called into question (Skinner, 1953:14—22; Winch, 1958; Louch, 1966).

In contrast, neopositivists such as Paul Feyerabend have insisted that even if we grant the presence and structure of the purposive image of humans, such an image is not necessarily true. None would deny that a persistent strain in philosophy since Kant has sought to identify the basic categories of thought. Yet all these efforts have focused on the purposive or manifest image of persons. This image, they have agreed, is radically different from and not reducible to, the scientific image of man. Instead of ensuring the truth of the purposive model, these differences guarantee its falsity. The purposive image — though perhaps an accurate account of our beliefs — is a false picture of the way things really are.

This dualism between explanation by reason or intention and explanation by cause echoes the debate between ideographic and nomothetic explanation in nineteenth-century historicism. R. S. Peters, for example, has distinguished two characteristic theses concerning the concept of action. There is the traditional nomothetic thesis stemming from Descartes, Bacon, and Hobbes, which states "that there can be an all-inclusive theory of human behavior from whose basic postulates answers to all forms of questions, 'why does Jones do X?' will be eventually deduced" (Peters, 1960:148). The second, ideographic, thesis is not causal and law-like, but teleological and contextual. In terms of this latter thesis, the woman raises her hand in order to stop traffic; yet her intention to stop traffic is not a cause of her raising her hand in the traditional sense

(C. Taylor, 1964:33; R. Taylor, 1966:39). Instead of being an ante-
cedent cause, the intention itself is known retrospectively in terms of
the consequences and context of the act. That is to say, even the simple
act of raising one's hand, or the simple intention "in order to stop
traffic," makes no sense unless there are social rules constituting normal
driving procedure. There are other actions, (e.g., dancing, playing) that
might be called *autotelic*, in that they appear to have no end outside
themselves. Yet even these activities are bounded by rules about how to
dance, when to dance, and that dancing should be for the fun of it
(rather than just to show off). In contrast to the causal thesis, Peters
has posited a "rule-following" purposive model (1960:5 ff; c.f. Simmel,
1950; Moore and Anderson, 1965).

On the basis of this distinction between reason explanations and causal explanations, Peters (1960) has gone on to make several other claims:

> 1. The two forms of explanation are "logically different and
> sometimes logically exclusive" (p. 148)
> 2. "Most of our explanations are couched in terms of this
> [intentional] model and our predictions of people's behavior
> presuppose it" (pp. 6—7)
> 3. This rule-following purposive model shows "that human
> actions cannot be sufficiently explained in terms of causal con-
> cepts like 'colorless movements'" (p. 8)

The last point is a direct challenge to Hull, who has argued that
"even so-called purposive behavior ought . . . to begin with colorless
movement and mere receptor impulses as such, and from these build
up . . . behavior" (1943:25). But Hull is only one instance of the more
general way of thinking that Peters criticized:

If we are in fact confronted with a case of genuine action (i.e., an act of doing
something as opposed to suffering something), then causal explanations are *ipso
facto* inappropriate as sufficient explanations . . . There cannot therefore be a sufficient explanation of actions in causal terms because . . . there is a logical gap between nature and convention. [Peters, 1960:12, 14]

Stephan Strasser has made a similar point, adding that a sufficient explanation of conduct must include an "intentional description."

What is essential is the . . . notion of consciousness in the sense of intentionality. To
speak of an "intentional description" of something is to speak not just of any description which this thing bears, but of the description which it bears for a certain
person, the description under which it is subsumed by him. Now the notion of an
action as directed behavior involves that of an intentional description. [Strasser,
1964:58]

If we accept intentional description as essential to the understanding
of action, it becomes questionable whether behaviorists are able to ac-

count for human conduct at all. Whether we put ourselves into the role of the spectator or of the agent, what an event is, *as an act*, only emerges from "the description which it bears for a certain person, the description under which it is subsumed by him." For example, whether a death is suicide or accidental depends upon the attributions of intention and other meanings (Douglas, 1967).

The debate surrounding the new teleology can be characterized as a dualism and antithesis between teleological and causal-mechanical explanations. Each of these views claims priority over the other. Peters has stated that "human actions cannot be sufficiently explained in terms of causal concepts," and Louch has insisted that in their efforts to imitate the natural sciences, "most of psychological and sociological inquiry . . . has been vitiated by methodological concerns that have no bearing upon the puzzles and problems that arise within a view of man as an agent" (1966:237—8).

Existential phenomenology

Like the other two schools discussed, existential phenomenology launches a concerted attack on the two tenets at the heart of the positivist paradigm: the assumption of objectlike facts and the postulate of explanation by causal or mathematical laws. The basis of this critique is as follows. The naturalistic fact-world is not in itself a finding of science; it is a presupposition or assertion about the nature of Being in general. As such, it is a metaphysical proposition, and its acceptability depends on its philosophical justification. It is true that the Cartesian Baconism of positive science gives procedures for identifying shared attributes and temporal correlations of entities (e.g., the acceleration of bodies falling through space in time). Yet, as even the logical positivists discovered, these procedures offer no help in knowing either the nature of the entities themselves or the meaning or relevance of the attributed causes, probabilities, or laws. Such questions, it is argued, are not ones of objective observation or mathematical correlation, for which positive science accounts. They are questions of meaning and interpretation. And, insofar as they have been assumed but not accounted for, these questions constitute the basis for an existential phenomenological critique that at the same time helps provide a foundation for a new science of conduct.

The development of this critique began with Kant (1724—1804), who tried to find his way between two apparently opposite theories of knowledge: Hume's empiricism and Descartes's idealism. The one asserted that, because all knowledge is based on perception and experi-

ence — which vary from person to person and are notoriously untrustworthy — sure knowledge is impossible. The other agreed that the
senses are untrustworthy, but instead of denying the possibility of certainty, sought it in self-evident propositions or mathematical laws that
are independent of the senses or imagination. As he saw it, Kant's task
was to defend reason from Hume's skeptical empiricism and at the same
time save it from Descartes's mathematical determinism.

In pursuing this problem Kant demonstrated that there are certain
transcendental categories that are neither derived from experience (this
table is green) nor self-contained truths (2 + 2 = 4). These transcendental categories (e.g., space, time, causality) refer to the phenomena of
experience but are not induced from them. Nor are they innate ideas or
metaphysical beings. According to Kant, the transcendental categories
are immanent in the structure of consciousness itself. One proof of this
is that no phenomenon can be apprehended outside space and time.
Yet these intuitions of space and time are not phenomenal sensations
themselves. They are norms of perception and reasoning that are distinct from both empirical phenomena and from purely metaphysical
concepts. They refer neither to the content of experience (sensa) nor to
some ultimate reality beyond experience; they represent the structures
of judgement, the forms of mental life by which our subjective sensations are ordered into a phenomenal, intersubjective, external world.
Thus, the reductive empiricism and idealism of both Hume and Descartes are combated. Knowledge based on perception is possible, but
only as mediated by mind.

If Kant established the categories of reason as independent of nature,
yet indispensable to understanding it, Hegel (1770—1831) radicalized
this notion by asserting that the world is an *expression of* the process of
reason itself. In traditional logic, according to Hegel, the contradictory
of any *A* is always treated as *not A*, and the opposite of *not A* (i.e., *not,
not A*) is again *A*. For Hegel, however, this static logic was inappropriate to understanding the immanent nature of reality. Nothing that
"is" can be grasped except in terms of the "is not" that it is becoming
in time. In a basic sense, subject and object, logic and ontology, are
one. The subject may be said to "constitute" the object; its objectivity
or "thingness" is constructed by the mind. Because phenomena are
integrated through thought, comprehension of experience must begin in
the examination of the entirety of that which presents itself in consciousness. In the objective world of science and common sense, events
are ordered into fixed categories from which generalizations are syllo-
gistically drawn. This world, however, is a false one to the extent that it
is assumed to exist independent of mind. Dialectical thought, in contrast, denies the objectivity of the here and the now on the grounds

that both disappear when considered in time. Yet the very alienation of mind from false objectivity, the very negativity of this "other" world, provides just the antithesis against which mind can reestablish its freedom.

In applying this dialectic to the development of society, Hegel was not concerned merely with ascertaining the bare facts or events of history. He focused on the problem of why the events happened as they did. History is not merely a congeries of processes or a temporal evolutionary sequence. History is a logical (i.e., dialectical) development in which subject and object are fused in the self-realization of the spirit that animates them both. Caesar, for example, did not *merely* cross the Rubicon; he crossed it for a purpose; that purpose could not be realized unless he *had* crossed the Rubicon; yet neither the purpose nor the act can be *understood* except as an expression of the spirit of the age, which Caesar, in turn, helped to create. Hence, unlike the natural world of science, which presents us with a succession of events, history is a series of purposive acts that are objectifications of reason. Knowledge of human conduct is not arrived at by induction from the facts of the historical record. Instead, the historical record itself can exist only if conceived as an intentional, dialectical product of Mind.

For the existentialist Kierkegaard (1813—1855), Hegel's notion of Mind realizing itself in history was an *obstacle* to a more complete understanding of one's own existence. Kierkegaard accepted Hegel's critique of traditional Aristotelian logic, but he saw Hegel's transcendental dialectic as putting the individual even further out of contact with his life. Kierkegaard rejected Hegel's "objective spirit" as an ontological mystification that distracts men from facing the only reality with which they must deal — their own existence. Reality is not objective, but neither can it be known through the manipulation of abstract laws or systems, even dialectical ones. Knowledge must begin in direct intuitions of oneself. Because he believed the dimensions of the self are more readily brought to light in periods of acute inner tension, Kierkegaard tended to focus on extreme or abnormal states of feeling and consciousness and on the processes by which they can be subjectively understood.

Another step in developing the critique of positivist science is the work of Wilhelm Dilthey (1833—1911). Unlike Kant, Dilthey did not recognize a priori mental categories that impose order on our phenomenal experience. In sympathy with Kierkegaard, he suggested that the pre-predicative structure of mental life is made explicit and becomes logical only through interaction with and in the world. Moreover, although he criticized Hegel's spiritualization of history, Dilthey embraced and elaborated the notion that history, society, and all human products are objectifications of the mind. His central concern was neither with explanations of the cause and motion of objects nor with intuitive knowledge of personal existence; rather, he asked how we can understand the meaning and significance of human works.

The positivist methodology of the natural sciences, according to Dilthey, is inadequate to the understanding of human phenomena except in their aspect as natural objects, and to apply such causal logic to human expressions by definition obviates their essential meaning. Instead of induction and generalization, or a priori positing of Cartesian laws, knowledge of persons must be through a hermeneutical (interpretive) procedure grounded in the possibility of our imaginatively recreating the inner experience of others. We know that other minds exist by analogy to our own mental life. We *understand* other minds by immersing ourselves in the interpretive study of their external objectifications as found in concrete cultural-historical expressions: "Exactly because a real transposition can take place, because affinity and universality of thought . . . can imagine forth and form a *social-historical* world, the inner events and processes in man can be distinguished from those of animals" (Dilthey, 1957—1960:V:250; emphasis in original).

Dilthey saw this "real transposition" of minds not as the I—it objectivity of the natural sciences, but as an intersubjective relationship between I and you or I and thou. Understanding (*Verstehen*) thus refers to one mind's engaging another mind. This process involves the interpretation of the lived experience of that other mind which we have imaginatively recreated in our own mind upon the presentness of the other's objectified expression. Hence, knowledge of others (and thereby, of ourselves), is not gained through introspection on our own subjective feelings, nor as an objective comprehension of abstract relationships between things, nor as some mysterious direct communication of spirits. Knowledge of the human world is achieved through an apprehension of the inner meaning of works, through the interpretive study of the expressions of other minds, expressions that make up the total "social-historical world," the world of language and gesture, art, law, religion, and politics, the shared community of human experience in its living, and hence historical, aspect.

Edmund Husserl (1859—1938) saw his goal as the establishment of an essential basis for knowledge of experience that would be free of all unjustified philosophical assumptions. In this project he differed from positivists by arguing that only phenomena are given, and that *in* these phenomena are the essences of that which is. Husserl's concern was not *whether* things exist in either an ultimate (Cartesian) or a naturalistic (Baconian) sense; instead he focused on the *what* — the essential necessary properties — of phenomena as they are given to us in conscious experience.

Moreover, whereas in Descartes and Kant the subject remains within a purely cognitive universe, for Husserl the subject "intends" a world. The subject does not coincide with being, as in Descartes's *cogito sum*, but is intentionally directed toward a world which it is not, but of which it is the lived experience (Edie, 1967:242). This intentionality of lived experience, according to Husserl, is incompatible with the traditional concept of an external world independent of our immediate awareness. All our conscious acts and sentiments exist within a field that is related with and receptive to any objects that appear in it. Everything we sense or feel or understand has its place within the horizon of this *Lebenswelt*. This intentional, horizon structure of experience converts all seeing into construing. The scientific universe, which is abstracted from the life-world, has no ultimate claims; instead, it is a special form of perception and constitution (Strasser, 1962:251—6).

At this point a question arises: How do we grasp this life-world as a whole? How do we get at the essential whatness of the phenomena of consciousness? To do this, according to Husserl, we first must hold aside the commonsense constructed notions of the natural standpoint and then reflect on the phenomena of consciousness through a series of purifying and distilling "reductions." Husserl described this holding off or "bracketing" of the natural standpoint:

Instead of remaining at this [thesis of the natural] *standpoint . . . we set it as it were "out of action." We "disconnect it," "bracket it."* It still remains there like the bracketed in the bracket, like the disconnected outside the connexional system . . . *but we make "no use" of it.* Thus *all sciences which relate to this natural world . . .* though I am far from any thought of objecting to them in the least degree, *I disconnect them all, I make absolutely no use of their standards . . .* as a truth *concerning the realities* of this world. [Husserl, 1931:I, Sec. 27—32; emphasis in original]

Since Husserl, most phenomenologists have abandoned the goal of establishing a formal presuppositionless philosophy (Farber, 1940). Instead, they have applied the technique of bracketing to psychological and cultural phenomena as well as to the more mathematical or purely logical phenomena that Husserl stressed. Moreover, instead of remaining strictly true to the method of phenomenological reduction, many of Husserl's followers have sought to reintegrate the dialectical and interpretive methods of Hegel and Dilthey. Further, in exploring the preconscious levels of experience, these interpreters have stressed people's intersubjectivity and being in the world, as opposed to Husserl's focus on the unique consciousness and knowing. This, above all, is the contribution of the existentialists that makes them most relevant to sociological studies.

Heidegger (1899—), for example, has stated that there is a primordial level of human Be-ing (*Dasein*), prior to any cognitive reflection, in

which man already understands himself to be fundamentally related to
the world in a manner that precedes the split between subject and object. In contrast to Husserl's reduction, Heidegger has proposed a "her-
meneutic of facticity" to get at this strata of existence that underlies all
formal thought. Where Dilthey conceived of hermeneutics as the
methodology of the human studies, and particularly of history, Heidegger has asserted that both hermeneutics and history are the method
and process of understanding itself. And instead of focusing on the
structural properties of consciousness in stages, Heidegger's hermeneutics is meant to decode consciousness as a historical and developmental
process.

In a similar modification of Husserl, Maurice Merleau-Ponty (1908—
1961) quoted Jean Waehl, who said that Husserl "separates the essences
from existence." "What Waehl means is that Husserl sees the essences as
absolute points in the fluid world of the phenomenal and that he separates these absolute points from the flowing stream" (1964c, ix—xii).
Merleau-Ponty rejected this notion of absolute insights or essences that
are valid for all phenomena. Instead of searching for invariant properties of a transcendental ego (see Chapter 3), he viewed the entire order
of essences as merely a provisional conceptual fixation, imposed on us
by the character of language and by the ultimate inaccessibility of preconscious experience through purely cognitive means. Thus, Merleau-
Ponty introduced the notion of the "body-subject" or brute being,
which he used to interpret all experience (Kwant, 1963:153—68).

Like Heidegger and Merleau-Ponty, Jean-Paul Sartre (1905—) has also
focused on man's being-in-the-world, but he carried the notion beyond
Heidegger (and back to Hegel) by giving it a dialectical twist: "But it
would be necessary to complete the [Heidegger's] definition and formulate it more like this: consciousness is a being such that in its Being, its
Being is in question insofar as this Being implies a being other than
itself . . . It is . . . the Being of the world which is implied in consciousness" (Sartre, 1956a:lxii). That is, we know our own Being only by
contrast to that which we are not. In dialectical fashion, freedom of
consciousness is known and affirmed only in its positing its own non-
being, or its negation, in the world of things. Consciousness grasps
itself as uniquely conscious by negating the in-itself of its own Being.
Thus man is revealed as not a thing, as no-thing-ness in the realm of
Being. Man is not yet determined; he is necessarily free to make himself.

In sum, then, we have seen the marshaling of a phenomenological
existential critique of positive science and the natural standpoint. First
Kant established a transcendental mind as autonomous of nature and
experience. Hegel then asserted that history and society are objectifications of Absolute Mind and that dialectic is the mode of knowledge and

of Being. Kierkegaard and Dilthey conceived of history as the objectification of *human* rather than absolute or transcendental consciousness and developed the hermeneutical method for understanding history and society. Husserl showed how all concepts, those of history and of nature, are objectifications of consciousness. Heidegger and Merleau-Ponty expanded this notion and integrated it with Dilthey's interpretive method of understanding. Sartre reintroduced Hegel's dialectic and restored human freedom to the center of the philosophical stage, but shorn of any idea of absolute spirit. These ideas, together with those of pragmatists and ordinary language philosophers, advance a radical critique of the facticity and determinism of positive science and invite us to a more existential approach to the study of society.

To carry all these perspectives to their point of convergence is the task of a whole generation of scholars. But from that vanishing point we hope to see a human-centered science of conduct that is at once objective and subjective, at once valid and scientifically and significantly humane.

3

The existential thought of Jean-Paul Sartre and Maurice Merleau-Ponty

ANDREA FONTANA AND RICHARD VAN DE WATER

The analysis of the basic developments in Western thought about scientific knowledge (Chapter 2) leads us to see the necessity of rejecting the idea of subject-object dualism. This rejection of subject-object dualism means that any attempts to get at truth, to rationalize our thoughts about the world, to make them more objective inevitably depends in significant part upon an analysis of the knowing mind itself and, most likely, of the preconscious aspects of the human knower as well. More specifically, once the rhetoric about treating thought and meaning as an object or "like a thing" (as Durkheim put it) is seen as impossible, we recognize that the truth of any study of the social world depends in part upon the mind's knowing itself — upon some form of systematic introspection and rational analysis. As is true of all other forms of knowledge, sociological knowledge depends in part upon the introspective understanding that is the social strength of philosophical thought. Sociology ultimately rests upon philosophical foundations.

The traditional scientist who accepts this argument and the conclusion that all knowledge ultimately depends in part on introspective analysis might easily conclude that all objectivity is impossible and that, therefore, we are cast into a world of solipsistic experience, a do-your-own-thing world in which anything is true if someone asserts that his own experience proves it to be true. This is, indeed, a conclusion often asserted by those who accept the argument that knowledge is ultimately partially dependent upon introspective understanding and, thus, on personal experiences and situations; and sometimes this assertion is made in the name of existentialism. (This use of existentialism as the banner for solipsism is largely the result of the excesses of Sartre's ideas of absolute freedom in his early works, the frequent use by existential writers of unique experiences to "prove" general points, a good deal of misunderstanding, and a desperate desire to find some legitimacy for patently absurd ideas.) Introspection, however, poses the threat of solipsism only for those who do not understand it or for extremists who insist on having either absolute objectivity or no objectivity.

If it were true that human subjective experience is always, or even generally, unique or relatively disorganized, then it would be reasonable to expect that introspection would lead to disorganized concepts of the world, to unique concepts of what human experience itself is, and possibly to Hobbe's "war of all against all." But the prima facie evidence against this assumption of the uniqueness and disorganized nature of subjective experience seems overwhelming. Except possibly for those with extreme forms of insanity (and probably only where there is some organic damage), all human beings seem to share some common, general perspective in their understandings of the world — some common, general forms of subjective experience. At the least consciousness and meaning seem to be universal aspects of human experience, regardless of the vast variability in their specific content. These are the necessary aspects of mind itself (though they must not be confused with Husserl's transcendental ego). But there are also far more specific ways in which human subjective experience is common, if not universal. The human body, with its many basic needs and desires, and the world in which that body must exist are basically the same the world over. The excesses of cultural relativism during this century, which have focused social scientists' attention almost exclusively on the specific variations in cultural expressions of these shared needs and desires, have obscured the obvious facts of the sharedness in human experience stemming from this fact that we share a common human body in a roughly common physical world. Most obviously, all human beings can confidently assume and take for granted that all human beings will eat, sleep, drink, excrete, be born, die, think symbolically, have feelings of pleasure and pain, and so on. Specifically, it is obvious that this common "horizon of experience," as phenomenologists have sometimes called it, is wide enough to enable all human beings to understand each other sufficiently to translate most of the experiences of one group into the symbolic forms of another group so that the latter can adequately understand (for practical purposes) the experiences of the former. The potential shareability of human understanding based on such basic needs and desires is so great that complex systems of exchange can be constructed by groups who share no language (e.g., the Kula's exchange system described by Malinowski), and nations that use many different languages can effectively take part in a complex system of diplomatic relations, even when many of those nations hate each other and even when they are at war with each other. And all this, of course, is done without any objectified scientific knowledge about such matters.

It is equally obvious that within one universe of cultural experience, even a pluralistic and partly amorphous universe, such as has existed within the Western world among educated groups for centuries, the outcomes of introspective, subjective thought are far more shareable and ordered than thought around the world. The philosophical thought of Western philosophers may have been too variable and uncertain for the scientists and even for most of the philosophers, but their introspective, rational analyses of experience and the world have never produced an anomic state of affairs. In fact, the philosophical arenas have commonly been the public stage upon which a relatively few major sides have contended in any one period, within the confines of many agreed-upon rules of reason and fact, over a relatively few basic questions. Even in our own day, when representatives of every major cultural tradition can be found contending upon the Western philosophical stage, and when representatives of total subjectivism or solipsism are trying to seize the stage with their purposely distorted (surrealistic) pictures of the world, there is still a great realm of agreement about reason and human experience based on introspective, philosophical thought. Indeed, a set of agreements in Western philosophy, if no universal consensus, seems to be emerging (Chapter 2). Even those who try mightily to suspend or destroy their own reason and that of others, to turn themselves and our world into drunken boats, are generally forced to use powerful drugs, such as the psychedelics, to achieve their goal — and even then they commonly recognize that the visions of their trips are surrealistic. They know what is real and what is not; they simply want to transcend this dull, all-too-ordered reality of ours. The scientific rage for absolute certainty must not be allowed to obscure the orderliness that does exist in nonobjectified thought, any more than it should be allowed to obscure the disorderliness of our social world.

We have argued that all thought, including objective scientific thought, is necessarily grounded in a foundation of introspective, rational thought, and that this introspective thought does not lead to a chaos of competing ideas about the social world. That is an essentially negativist approach, arguing from the standpoint of what we have to do and that this necessity is not ruinous. It is a biased approach that fits well with the empiricist rhetoric of traditional science. But we think there are clearly greater, more positive values to such philosophical analysis in sociology. Anyone who knows much about the history of Western thought is aware that the *systematic* introspection and rational analysis of philosophy, as distinct from the more situational, disjointed thought of common sense, have been of tremendous importance in the advancement of thought, including scientific thought. Although one can well argue that the part played by Platonic thought in the origins of mathematical physics was largely a historical accident, and that for each such happy accident there are as many or more unhappy effects of abstract philosophical thought upon scientific thought (such as the imposition of the Aristotelian philosophy of substances upon physical observations), it is equally clear that only philosophical thought can provide an understanding of such basic ideas as the nature of concepts or definitions or the relations between eidetic images and linguistic symbols. Moreover, only systematic philosophical analysis of sociological works and theories — such as Schutz's (1967) analysis of Weber's theory of motivation, Parson's (1937) analysis of the structuralists, Altheide's analysis of Schutz's theory of typifications (Chapter 4), or Douglas's (1967) analysis of Durkheim's theory of suicide — allows us to see basic weaknesses in these works. If sociologists had done more systematic, critical analysis of Durkheim's work earlier in this century, instead of holding it up for students to worship as a paradigm of research methods, we might have been spared decades of irrelevant analyses of suicide that covertly imposed meanings upon suicidal acts. And if we had earlier taken seriously the works of linguistic analysts, phenomenologists, and existentialists, we might have saved many years of painstaking work that eventually has led us to converge with some of their basic ideas.

In these ways existential philosophy and analytical literature generally serve as a vital, but partial, foundation for existential sociology. We have not started our work with an assumption that the existentialists are right about our social world. We started with our experience and our research, but now we find the philosophers and writers useful in building our more systematic understanding of that experience and research. Although we have drawn upon many different existentialists in our many different works, we have consistently found Jean-Paul Sartre and Maurice Merleau-Ponty the most truthful and useful philosophers of social experience. For these purposes and with these cautions we present the basic ideas of their social philosophies.

Sartre and man

A comprehensive review of Sartre's works would be a massive undertaking beyond the scope of this chapter. Moreover, it would probably become so abstract as to commit the rationalist fallacy we are trying to displace. We examine here only those segments of his work that are directly relevant to our understanding of man in society. Sartre was himself a man-in-the-world, a man of both thought and practical action. We should not forget that his disenchantment with the superficiality of society and his quest for an existential understanding of man stemmed from the fluid and insecure times of Europe between two world wars.

The "heroes" of *Nausea* and *The Wall* presented the absurdity of this human experience. In these works Sartre portrayed the daily existence of squalor, loneliness, and uninvolvement of human beings — a life with nothing in sight. He later attempted to systematize his views of existentialism in his philosophical treatise, *Being and Nothingness*. But it is in the novels that Sartre has given us his feelings and ideas about his concrete existence. His lucid prose transmits powerful images and ideas of man that are strangled by a maze of logical arguments in his abstract philosophy. Sartre's being-in-the-world later lifted him out of despair. The outside world closed in on Sartre: the rise of fascism, war, being captured, and ill health. Finally, released and back in Paris, he realized that we are involved in a tangible world, and commitment to a cause, any cause, became the ladder that led him out of the nothingness that pervaded his early works. In his trilogy, *Roads to Freedom*, this outlook on the world achieved full realization.

This is the Sartre we examine here. The Sartre-of-flesh-and-bone.

Existential man in Nausea

Let us begin with the novel in which Sartre's art and philosophy were first fused in a great expressive work, *Nausea*. It is the diary of an intellectual, Antoine Roquentin, who describes the boredom that seems to penetrate him to the marrow:

I held the book I was reading tightly in my hands: but the most violent sensation went dead. Nothing seemed true; I felt surrounded by cardboard scenery which could quickly be removed. The world was waiting, holding its breath, making itself small — it was waiting for its convulsion, its *Nausea* [Sartre, 1964b:76—7]

Roquentin in his solitude is willing to talk to anyone, even to the Self-Taught Man. This character represents the things rejected by Sartre. He has no critical judgment and deludes himself intellectually just like the bourgeoisie, which Sartre hates so much for its pat values and superficial justification of life. The Self-Taught Man is reading all the books in the library in alphabetical order, with no discrimination and an almost comical naiveté about the nature and acquisition of knowledge:

He has passed brutally from the study of coleopterae to quantum theory . . . he has never been disconcerted for an instant. He has read everything . . . And the day is approaching when closing the last book on the last shelf on the far left: he will say to himself "Now what?" [Sartre, 1964b:30]

Apart from the Self-Taught Man we see only a few peripheral characters around Roquentin. They are all engrossed in the concerns and rewards of their daily lives. Roquentin becomes aware of the pettiness of this existence, this day-to-day, squalid, hypocritical existence, for which he no longer finds any justification, and is suddenly overcome by nausea:

Monday, 29 January 1932:
Something has happened to me, I can't doubt it any more. It came as an illness does, not like anything evident. It came cunningly, little by little; I felt a little strange, a little put out, that's all. Once established it never moved, it stayed quiet, and I was able to persuade myself that it was a false alarm. And now, it's blossoming. [Sartre, 1964b:4]

For Roquentin anguish no longer comes and goes in temporary flashes; it is here to stay as an integral part of his life. This world is losing its familiar face for Roquentin; he no longer can rely on the comforting feeling of security in a world that suddenly appears strange to him:

This thing I'm sitting on, leaning my hand on, is called a seat . . . I murmur "It's a seat," a little like an exorcism. But the word stays on my lips: it refuses to go and put itself on the thing . . . This enormous belly turned upward, bleeding, inflated . . . is not a seat . . . It could just as well be a dead donkey . . . things are divorced from their names . . . I am in the midst of things, nameless things [Sartre, 1964b:25]

Things have lost their daily features and nomenclature, and the nausea keeps spreading. It reaches a state of absurdity. Roquentin's own body becomes strange to him: "I see my hand spread on the table. It lives — it's me . . . It shows me its flat belly. It looks like an animal turned upside down" (1964b:98). This absurdity that has grown to reign around Roquentin makes him realize that our lives have no intrinsic meaning, that we are in this world gratuitously.

In *Nausea*, Sartre came face to face with existence in a negative context: Existence is what causes nausea, what is disgusting in itself, expressed by the daily humdrum of a shallow existence. As Roquentin experiences nausea, he becomes able to interpret the world in different ways; he can see things in a different reality because he has done away with his shell of a self, and what is left is "consciousness of":

Now when I say "I," it seems hollow to me. I can't manage to feel myself very well . . . And just what is Antoine Roquentin . . . and suddenly the "I" pales, pales and fades out . . . Consciousness . . . is consciousness of being superfluous . . . But it never forgets itself. [Sartre, 1964b:170]

Roquentin is experiencing a Husserlian *epoché*, without the long preparation involved in Husserl, but occurring suddenly, by accident, and resulting in a vacuum feeling of terror, not one of reassurance, as in Husserl. This feeling that overcomes him in the face of the absurdity of conventional life is the proof of his existence, as he is committing an act in the very process of negating a way of life.

Sartre saw in Roquentin that the self is a constructed image, that if one steps back from his previous recollections, interpretations, accounts of his self, he is left, not with a transcendental ego, but with a vague "consciousness of." Hence, the self is not a being but a becoming, as one becomes through his choices what he wants and chooses to be.

Being and nothingness

Sartre (1956a) explored the relation of things to consciousness in his philosophical treatise, *Being and Nothingness* and more systematically developed many ideas present in *Nausea*. In particular he examined two concepts closely. The first deals with the dualism between an opaque, self-contained being-in-itself and a being-for-itself that represents conscious existence.

Being-in-itself (*l'être-en soi*) represents things in themselves, in their act of being what they are. Being-for-itself (*l'être-pour-soi*) exists within the realm of consciousness. My thought is in a state of continual flux, either projecting itself in the future or looking back in the past; I am never able to freeze thought in the here-and-now moment, so I can never say "I am" but I can look either at my past self in terms of reconstructed accounts or at my future self in terms of my yet-unrealized and future choices of projects.

Consciousness is transcendental and in its conscious actions creates a self, which is ever changing. But man seeks to rid himself of the anxieties caused by the uncertainty of this continuous transcendent process: Man seeks to be a thing-in-itself. But this is impossible, as man's consciousness carries him continually *beyond* himself. This gives rise to a paradox. Man's gift of transcendence is also the very thing that causes man's anxieties, as it never lets him stand still. Man cannot become an absolute being, a thing-in-itself and for-itself, because this is a contradiction in terms; one is a thing *as it is* and the other *as it becomes*. This absurd quest to be an absolute being, to be and to become simultaneously, in other words to be God, is Sartre's second important point in *Being and Nothingness*. This point led him to see life as "a useless passion," bound to fail in this futile human attempt to reach an impossible state.

From being Sartre passed on to consciousness, which he saw as the negation of being, a negation introducing meaning into the meaningless world of being. This negational aspect of consciousness is what gives us our freedom to negate alternatives, to choose our own projects within a given situation. In *Being and Nothingness* Sartre defined consciousness as "that which is what is not, and is not what it is" (1956a:20).

The above statement was perhaps better explicated in *Nausea* by the actions of Roquetin. In the novel Sartre showed that people live in a world in which things take on the meaning that is given them. Hence, if consciousness were of a positive nature, it would itself be a thing, it would become static and solidified. Instead, in its negative state consciousness confers meaning to that which it has chosen to the exclusion of others.

For Sartre, consciousness is always consciousness of something. In a Husserlian fashion, it is intentional, it emerges in the world, and it can be observed only in the everyday world: "My consciousness never exists in the abstract but only because it thinks of a tree or of Pierre's face; it manifests itself only by imagining something other than itself. It is born of something other than itself; it is born of something which is not." (1956a:28). Sartre's concept of consciousness allows for a dimension of temporality, which would not be possible without consciousness. Man is seen as a projection of his future and not-yet-realized being, while at the same time man is escaping his past essences, which he no longer is.

Sartre's Heideggerian description of consciousness in terms of "not yet" and "no longer" indicates the existence of consciousness before our existence as beings, in that we are definable, not at any given time, but in terms of past or future. Sartre's ideas in regard to consciousness were close to those of Heidegger and Husserl, but with important differences.

They were close to Heidegger's for their concept of being and temporality, but although the German philosopher used time as the main component of being, Sartre's use of time led to the negation of being rather than to its aid — to nothingness, from which experiential possibilities become actualized.

Sartre's use of consciousness also differed from Heidegger's in its Cartesian proposition and was closer to Husserl's phenomenology. Sartre used an encompassing *epoché* in his works, which acts as a pervasive experience allowing man to bracket his belief in the world, while a thin, veiled consciousness exists a priori and independently of the outside world (although it can only find expression in this world).

Sartre differed from Husserl because he viewed consciousness as the "noetic" or transcendental element and the ego as "noematic" or transcendent. For Sartre, consciousness is the subjective pole of the relationship; it is created by an act of consciousness. For Husserl, the ego is transcendental; it is a part of the stream of consciousness.

Thus Sartre was Cartesian, but of a different brand than Husserl. Sartre kicked the ego downstairs from a Cartesian cogito and a Husserlian transcendental ego to a transcendent one. The ego is in this world; all that is left on the transcendental side is a feeling of nothingness, which is consciousness. Consequently, for Sartre, existence or individual consciousness precedes essence to the point that "to exist" becomes a transitive verb and is used in this fashion: "existing-one's-body."

Sartrian existence has great implications for man in this world because, given Sartre's tenets, man chooses himself and his projects; he becomes fully responsible for his actions. This is the heart of Sartre's social philosophy: Man must become what he wants to be; he must commit himself to a choice:

I am nothing, I have nothing. As inseparable from the world as light and yet exiled, like light, sliding along the surface of stones and of the water, and nothing ever grapples me or causes me to run aground. Outside. Outside. Outside the world, outside the past, outside myself. Freedom is exile, I am condemned to be free. [Sartre, 1945a:286—7]

The others

Life in its perpetual becoming state proves difficult for man, who must create his own world at every instant. This responsibility is a heavy burden for man, and man attempts to escape it. Sartre called this attempt to escape "bad faith," which is the self-deception derived from deluding oneself, fiom routinizing one's exterior world into preestablished patterns, from accepting premolded roles in which to present oneself to others, from reducing one's intellectual life to a superficial one allowing for little constructive and analytical thinking, as one accepts others' definitions of reality unquestioningly. Men are seen as turning to others in their attempt to be, to feel reassured by being recognized as a self by others: "Thus we escape anguish by trying to apprehend ourselves *from without* as we would the Others or a thing" (1956a: 81; emphasis in original).

Sartre expressed his concern about the others in *The Wall* and *No Exit*. In these novels he showed man attempting to establish his own personality by relying on the definitions of others. In *No Exit* one of the characters seeks to see himself through mirrors: "There were six big mirrors in my bedroom. Whenever I talked, I would be in a position where I could watch myself in one of them. As I talked I could see myself talking. I saw myself as other people see me, and that kept me awake" (1947:136).

In *Nausea* Sartre referred to the others as *salauds* ("swine"). They live a smug existence, feel no anguish, and easily find meaning and justification in their lives. Roquentin feels disgusted when confronted by *salauds*:

I glance around the room. What a comedy! All the people are sitting there, looking serious and eating. No, they are not eating; they are recuperating in order to successfully finish their task. Each of them has his little personal difficulty which keeps him from noticing that he exists; there isn't one of them who *doesn't* believe him-self indispensable to something or someone. [Sartre, 1964b:111; emphasis in original]

Man in his willful ignorance has built a fortress around himself in which he lives secure, buttressed by his solid values.

It is in this concept of the others that Sartre's social philosophy assumes great importance for a sociological discipline. If man, in order to come to see his unfolding consciousness, stopped in a static picture, a reconstructed self, turns to others, then a social relationship is established. But how do I know the others? I become aware of the presence of others around me, of other consciousnesses vainly trying to be beings-in-themselves and for-themselves, through their gaze. This comes to me in a shocking revelation when I realize that I am reduced to an object in the others' gaze.

Sartre, Mead, Goffman

Sartre's reliance on the other to know oneself bears comparison with the sociology of George Herbert Mead. As Sartre's man literally creates himself through the opinion of others, so does Mead's "me," by making use of the "generalized other" in order to act properly in the world. But although for Mead "acting satisfactorily" for others seems to be a successful goal in itself, for Sartre it would be an instance of bad faith because man is attempting to take the easy way by fitting himself to ready-made roles and taking on preestablished values to please others.

Meadian man presents a picture of himself to the others, a picture he wants them to accept. But in Sartre's view, man by doing this, hopes to escape the continual flux of analyzing, rejecting, deciding. In order to be secure, he gives up his own freedom; he becomes a mask; he plays at being someone:

Take the bartender. A moment ago he had been smoking a cigarette, as indifferent and poetic as a bindweed; now he had roused himself and was a little too much the bartender; he rattled the shaker, opened it, poured a foaming yellow liquid into the glasses with movements which were just a little too precise. He was playing at being a bartender. [Sartre, 1945c:181]

One could argue that Mead also considered an existential I as a part of the self. This, however, does not change the fact that even the I gives me, in Meadian terms, a freedom that takes place and is directed toward a social order that is defined for me by the "generalized other."

A better comparison can be established between Sartre and Erving Goffman, the American sociologist, because Goffman's model of the actor is more clearly developed and because Goffman made use of Sartrian notions, although not correctly.

Goffman (1959) quoted Sartre in order to support his model of the actor:

Consider the waiter. His movements are quick and sure, a little too precise, a little too fast. He comes toward the customers a little too quickly, bends over a little too eagerly; his voice, his eyes express a little too much concern over the client's order; finally we see him coming back, trying to imitate in his walk the inflexible rigidity of some imaginary automaton and carrying his platter with the daring of a funambulist, continuously throwing it off-balance and continuously restoring its delicate equilibrium with the slight movement of his arm and hand . . . His is playing a role, having a good time. But what role is he playing? It is not necessary to observe him long to realize that he is *playing at being a waiter*. [Sartre, 1956a:98—9; emphasis in original]

However, Goffman's implications for playing a role are very different from Sartre's. The Goffmanian actor presents his own interpretation of the play; he skillfully manipulates roles to present a specific impression to a certain audience; he may change his presentation as required by different audiences. We have the impression that the actor knows what repertoire to use in various circumstances, as a consummate actor who uses a certain script, a certain way of performing, a certain mannerism, to please an audience, an audience the actor knows will be likely to accept and perhaps even enjoy his performance.

The Goffmanian man is acting according to a predetermined, largely problematic script, which we all attempt to play, with different success according to our qualities: "The cultural values of an establishment will determine in details how the participants are to feel about many matters and at the same time establish a framework of appearances that must be maintained, whether or not there is feeling behind the appearances" (1959:241—2). Man is seen as playing a part for others, for society at large, so that by the part played one can be measured by the others and categorized.

This is what Sartre would call self-deception because man plays a role so that he can avoid the anguish of being himself or constructing life anew. It matters not for Goffman whether his actor believes in the part or maintains role distance; what matters is successful performance within a paramount reality.

Sartre, it must be remembered, was presenting, in the waiter and similar characters, the others, the *salauds*, hypocritical men who are playing a part for themselves to ease their own consciences from the burden of freedom; they use the approval of the others to appease themselves, but they are not, as Goffman believed, playing for the benefit of the others.

But Sartre's existential man is not this kind of man. Sartrian man has no paramount reality, no predetermined text; he creates his own reality as he goes along. He is a Roquentin, who says: "I am in the midst of things, nameless things. Alone, without words, defenseless, they surround me, are beneath me, behind me, along me. They demand nothing, they don't impose themselves: they are there" (1946:25).

The emphasis should not be on attempting to freeze myself in a picture but on constantly choosing my course and *becoming* in the freedom of my choices. The others, after all, are not my allies, they may reject my presentation of self, they may not support my claim to reality, and then, as Sartre put it: "No brimstone is necessary; hell is other people" (1947:182).

Sartre's social philosophy can be seen as a moral one because man is morally committed to choose and become himself continually; Goffman's sociology is, on the contrary, an amoral sociology:

But, *qua* performers, individuals are concerned not with the moral issue of realizing these standards, but with the amoral issue of engineering a convincing impression that these standards are being realized. Our activity, then, is largely concerned with moral matters, but as performers we do not have a moral concern with them. As performers we are merchants of morality. [Goffman, 1959:251]

For Goffman one can become "a merchant of morality" in order to succeed, but this success would be seen as tragicomical by Sartre. Comical because man's performance shows the paradoxical situations in which man places himself in order to perform in front of others. In *The Wall* Sartre (1939) parodied what could be the Goffmanian idea of "front stage," by looking at men while they are performing from a rather curious backstage position, by looking down on them from a balcony on the sixth floor. From up there, men, who take extreme care to present a front for spectators of average height, are seen as ridiculous, as something to be laughed about. Men forget to protect their shoulders and head with vivid colors and good-quality cloth, thus appearing to the Sartrian viewer as "squashed on the sidewalk, and two long legs half-rampant came out from underneath their shoulders" (1939:77).

Man is tragic for Sartre because of the extremes he will reach in attempting to seek and maintain conformity. Sartre's (1947) most poignant example of this extreme comes from a play about a town in the American South, *The Respectful Prostitute*.

Lizzie, the prostitute, is placed in a position to accuse an innocent black man, whom the town believes guilty of having raped her, in order to protect the guilty party who is an influential white man; Lizzie listens to the frighteningly compelling logic of the Senator, who is a close relation of the guilty man; the Senator confronts Lizzie with the social worth and utility of the two men:

Senator: He is one hundred per cent American, the scion of one of our oldest families, a Harvard graduate, an officer . . . he has the duty to live . . .
Senator: Lizzie, what good is this Negro that you protect? He was born by chance,

> God knows where . . . He was nourished (by the Nation), and in exchange,
> what has he done? Absolutely nothing . . .
> Senator: Do you believe that a whole town could be wrong? [Sartre, 1947:299—300]

Lizzie does not believe it, and she gives in to the Senator, letting the
Negro be lynched in the name of social order.

Commitment to a cause

Sartre later added an important element to his social philosophy that
was absent in his earlier and perhaps more famous works: commitment
within one's situation in the world. The war probably brought this point
home to Sartre. The "heroes" of his prewar works were lonely figures
who found nothing but aesthetic outlets for their freedom and creativity,
reflecting the loneliness and disillusionment of Europe in a changing
phase. But times changed and World War II struck France. Sartre came
to believe that finding an outlet in music and book writing is not enough.
Man must commit himself to something else, he must take responsibility
by embracing a cause. The nature of this cause appeared at first tentative in Sartre's works.

In *The Flies* (1947) we can see this change in Sartre's thought:
Roquentin's main concern is to repudiate ready-made ways of life, but
Oreste enters the everyday world, he commits himself to an enterprise
of his own (the avenging of his father), and he assumes the risk and responsibility of this task, no matter what the consequences may be.

The trilogy, *Roads to Freedom* (1945b), shows Sartre's changing
thought in the various degrees of commitment by the main character,
Mathieu Delarue. The first of the three volumes, *The Age of Reason*,
shows Delarue as a man aware of his freedom but hesitant to committing
it, for fear of losing it: "Thirty-four. Thirty-four and I taste myself and
I'm old. I've worked, I've waited, I've had what I wanted: Marcelle,
Paris, independence; it's all over. I expect nothing more" (1945c:53).

Delarue is a weak person, afraid of committing himself, and the presence of his friends, who have made such a commitment, causes jealousy
in him. One of his friends is Gomez, a fighter in the Spanish war, upon
whom Delarue looks with envy:

> The steaks are on the table; one for him, one for me. He has the right to relish his,
> he has the right to tear into it with his beautiful white teeth, he has the right to
> look at that pretty girl on his left and to think, "a nice piece." I don't have. If I eat,
> a hundred dead Spaniards will jump at my throat. I haven't paid. [Sartre, 1945a:219]

In *The Reprieve* Mathieu Delarue is shown as unable to avoid commitment; external forces and the situation influence man's individual freedom. Mathieu is not personally involved in the war, but he cannot be

outside it either, as he is caught in the vortex of events around him. Man is still free, but his freedom is situationally bound.

In *Troubled Sleep*, the last volume of the trilogy, Mathieu becomes involved. As the Germans approach Mathieu and the demoralized soldiers around him, he realizes that to be really free he must commit himself fully. He joins the relief troops and, armed with a rifle, fires at the advancing German forces:

He fired, and the commandments flew through the air — Thou shalt love thy neighbor as thyself — bang! right in the mug — Thou shalt not kill — bang! right in the bastard's face. He fired on Man, on Virtue, on Freedom, on the World: Freedom is terror. A fire raged in the town hall, raged in his head. [Sartre, 1949:193]

This period of Sartre's writing is important to a consideration of his social philosophy. Although all the previous facets of man still hold, man has changed from lucid isolation, finding escape in aesthetic enterprises, to seeking full commitment in social involvement. Man is no longer an isolated being; he becomes situationally bound. His freedom depends upon the circumstances he is in:

We must regard this freedom neither as metaphysical power inherent in human nature, nor as a license to do as we please, nor as some unidentified inner refuge which we would have even in bondage. We do not do as we please, yet we are responsible for what we are: that is the brute fact. [Sartre, 1965:26—7]

Man also comes to depend more on others, who are no longer seen as "hell," but as fellow beings who carve their existence around me, in the same situation and setting; I cannot ignore them, but I am morally committed to them and they to me, because what I do affects them and what they do affects me. Sartrian man has come down from his Nietzschean mountain into the everyday world and sees the constraints around him, the "brute facts," and decides to throw his lot in with his fellow men.

This view of man harnesses the almost unlimited freedom of man in Sartre's earlier works and binds him to the social world in which he lives. This is perhaps the best picture of existential man in Sartre: man bound to the hard facts that surround him, yet without relinquishing his inner understanding and freedom to determine in earnest commitment his own course of action.

The committed period: political involvement

Sartre decided to commit himself to others; he no longer was the lonely individual of the thirties and forties, but had joined mankind:

We are sorry for them [the uncommitted writers], for there was something that they missed forever. We would miss nothing in our era: it may not be the best, but it is ours; we have but this life to live, right in the middle of this war, this revolution perhaps. [Sartre, 1965:12—13]

After 1946 Sartre's work took a turn toward politics; the artistic creation of Roquentin gave way to the social commitment and the struggle to free the proletariat, who are the less free elements of our society. Sartre (1960) felt that only under Marxism, when class structure will be done away with, will existentialism be truly possible, as the restraints on man's freedom present in the capitalist system will be eliminated.

Sartre advocated a social revolution, not necessarily violent, in order to change the order of private property and institutions; the workers must be educated, giving rise to a proletarian culture. Finally, Sartre envisioned a social democracy controlled, not from the top, but from the lower ranks.

The journal *Les Temps Modernes*, of which he became editor, allowed him to direct his social philosophy to the benefit of political and social analysis. Sartre was obviously not an impartial analyst, but he supported the side of his choice: Like his character, Mathieu, in *Troubled Sleep*, he fully committed himself.

All Sartre's work ceased to pursue his earlier model of existential man. Instead, it was aimed at the support of his political cause. No longer were Sartre's characters individuals. They became mere devices manipulated by the author to propagandize a political ideology (Sartre, 1951, 1956b, 1965).

But Sartre did not throw away his philosophy of existentialism for dialectic materialism. In *Criticism of Dialectic Reasoning*, he attempted to reconcile a doctrine based on collectivity and factors external to the individual with his individualistic tenets: "There would be no trace of even partial totalization if the individual were not himself totalizing. *The whole structure of the historical dialectic rests on individual praxis insofar as it is already dialectic*" (1960:165; emphasis in original).

Sartre held on to his individual. But he emphasized the need to become committed, to take on responsibility in the world. Sartre reconciled existentialism and Marxism by passing from the individual to a group of individuals living within a situation, who give rise to a collectivity.

Has Sartre been guilty of bad faith in channeling his ultimate freedom to the service of a political cause and toward other beings? Perhaps his nausea became so strong that he had to find an outlet for it in the everyday world. But by so doing, his choice of freedom became contingent upon his political commitment; thus personal choice became intertwined with a predetermined cause, limiting the freedom of choosing.

Perhaps the greatest paradox in Sartre's philosophy is his own life: By committing himself to a cause, he limited his own freedom and fell into the very pit he had been trying to avoid. He tried to be someone, a sociopolitical analyst, thus perpetuating man's futile attempt to be a being-in-itself as well as a being-for-itself.

Understanding Sartre

It is paradoxical, in true Sartrian fashion, that Sartre's writings ceased to be sociologically relevant just when they become sociologically oriented. It is through his novels and his plays that Sartre came closer to existential sociology, as these works present, in quasi-empirical fashion, man in action, man involved in his beliefs and his problems, man becoming what he chooses.

We have, as readers, become painfully aware of the nausea created by seeing through a pat reality, a world in which the script and the parts are written in advance. We have realized, through the insights of the Sartrian characters, that it need not be so, that we need not live in bad faith, that we have the freedom to deny all this, that it is our moral responsibility to choose a path.

Sartre's guidance has given us insight. But if one wants systematic methodological prescriptions on how to analyse man, Sartre is the wrong person to look to. One should look instead to the works of his compatriot and sometime friend, Maurice Merleau-Ponty, who has approached man systematically and theoretically, with primary consideration of how we are to know about man.

Sartre dichotomized the world into a Cartesian subject-object dualism. He turned the screw once too much with his penchant for absurd paradoxes. He made too much of man's freedom by brushing aside the obvious situational constraints we face, until his own political commitments led him to leap too far to the opposite extreme. Maurice Merleau-Ponty brought us back to the world by grounding man in this world and making him and his actions interdependent with his milieu, instead of giving man complete freedom of choice, as the early Sartre did, or almost total structural constraint, as the later, Marxist Sartre did.

Sartre can undoubtedly be faulted on these and other counts, but to do so would be to misunderstand his fundamental message. Sartre tried to create in his reader the feeling that pervades his writings, a feeling of absurdity, because this is the stuff of which he found the world to be made.

A comprehensive analysis of Sartre would have stifled the feeling emerging from the pages of his work as phantoms haunting the reader, as reflections of dark halls that mirror an empty reality. Indeed, Merleau-Ponty brought man back in this world and his approach to man is perhaps more valuable to the social sciences seeking to understand man in the world. But has Merleau-Ponty captured modern man in an absurd world and revealed him in his writings as Sartre did? We think not.

Merleau-Ponty prescribed an approach to the understanding of man that ties man to the contingencies of the world, but no one has been able to express the inner anguish of modern man better than Sartre. He showed us man faced with the task of making sense out of a world in which taken-for-granted values have suddenly collapsed, leaving him nauseated, facing the whole world in its nothingness. Man is forced to be free, to choose what he will become, to recreate his own society and his world. It is an anguished vision, but a heroic one, inspiring creation, not destruction. It is not the whole truth, but it is a vital one for man today.

Husserl and Merleau-Ponty

Husserl (see Chapter 2) conceived his phenomenological philosophy to be both a resumption and a critique of the Cartesian search for indubitable foundations of knowledge and experience. Descartes had erred by supposing that the subject is enclosed within itself, that experience is a matter of "I think." Whereas philosophers in the Greek tradition had granted the realm of external reality an autonomous existence Descartes's fundamental error was to delegate this autonomy to subjectivity. For Husserl, neither position was justifiable. Although subscribing to Descartes's critique of the objectivist ontology, Husserl refused to accept his thesis that the subject is enclosed within itself, that subjectivity pure and simple holds the key to worldly experience. What was primary for Husserl (1970a) was not the thinking subject (ego cogito) but the subject who thinks a world (ego cogito cogitatum). Consciousness is always consciousness "of" something. And this something is no less a self-evident datum than is the act of thinking. As Joseph Kockelmans observed: "Husserl does not see the ultimate root, the radical and absolute starting point of philosophy, in any single basic concept, in any single fundamental principle, in one simple cogito, but in an entire field of original experiences" (1967:29).

Consequently, Husserl proposed, if we are to be truly vigilant in our search for the indubitable grounds of all possible knowledge, it is imperative that we return to the analysis of the phenomena given to us in lived experience, making no claims whatever concerning their status as real existents. Husserl argued: "The whole concrete surrounding life-world is for me, from now on, a phenomenon of being, instead of something that is" (1970a:19). The methodological dictum "to the things themselves" constitutes the central tenet of phenomenological inquiry and provides the vital link between the philosophies of Husserl and Merleau-Ponty. For both, the uniqueness and the radical character of phenomenology derives from its intense preoccupation with the problem of methodological purity. As Quentin Lauer (1965:47, 58) has suggested, phenomenology constitutes above all a theory of evidence. Both being and truth are functions of evidence; not only does the phenomenal world — the world of experience — constitute the original field of human experience, it is also the high court to which all our claims to knowledge make their final appeal.

Phenomenology as a philosophical method seeks a return to the things, the phenomena of experience, in themselves. Merleau-Ponty argued:

To return to things themselves is to return to that world which precedes knowledge, of which knowledge always speaks . . . It is not a question of confining ourselves to phenomena, or imprisoning consciousness in its own states [as does the phenomenalism of Hume and Ayer,] while retaining the possibility of another being beyond apparent being . . . but of defining being as that which appears. [Merleau-Ponty, 1962:397]

Phenomenology seeks the origin, the ground of meaning in the manner in which the world becomes known to us or is presented to us. The origins of truth and reality must be sought in the particularities of the relationship that binds the subject and his world; and the essential characteristics of this relationship are to be determined by an explication of the logos of the phenomenal world, the world not as an existent in-itself but as an in-itself-for-us.

The phenomenological method is essentially descriptive. Instead of feigning to adopt the position of the omnipotent observer, detached from the world, both Husserl and Merleau-Ponty examined the essentials of the bond between the subject and his world in a more organic and fundamental fashion: by embracing the data of lived, immediate experience in all its worldliness and meaningfulness. The real has to be described, not constructed or formed . . . The world is not an object such that I have in my possession the law of its making; it is the natural setting of, and field for, all my thoughts and all my explicit perceptions" (Merleau-Ponty, 1962:x, xi). To purport to explain the world and the structures of experience with reference to a set of "conditions of possibility" (as did Leibnitz and Kant) is to presuppose that which is to be explained. Merleau-Ponty argued:

To be sure, a perceived world would not appear to a man if these conditions were not given . . . but it is not they that *explain* the world . . . The Kantian subject [a conglomeration of conditions of possibility] posits a world, but, in order to be able to assert a truth, the actual subject must in the first place have a world or be in the world. [Merleau-Ponty, 1968:22; emphasis in original]

The fundamental error (or, shortsightedness) of the objectivist or positive apprehension — whether couched in terms of idealism or empiricism — is its tendency to "treat everything as though it were an object-in-general — as though it meant nothing to us and yet was predestined for our own use" (Merleau-Ponty, 1964:159). The world to which we have immediate access is neither a conglomeration of simple facts (empiricism realism) nor a system of ideas (intellectualism idealism). Merleau-Ponty said: "All we must do is situate ourselves within the being we are dealing with, instead of looking at it from the outside" (1968: 117). For instance, we shall never understand the multitudinous ways of expressing sexuality if we confine ourselves solely to an examination of its physiological chemical antecedents. Indeed, in this case "the question is not so much whether human life does or does not rest on sexuality, as of knowing what is to be understood by sexuality" (Merleau-Ponty, 1962:158).

Phenomenological description involves a return to the preobjective, pretheoretical field of experience of which positive thought is the second-order expression and in which it finds its relative justification. Neither Husserl nor Merleau-Ponty conceived of phenomenology as a refutation of positive (i.e., scientific) thought. According to Merleau-Ponty: "There will be found no *refutation*, but only an effort to understand the difficulties peculiar to causal [i.e., positive] thinking . . . in order to make its meaning quite clear and assign to it its proper place in the body of truth" (1962:7). "We seek not to restrict or discredit the initiatives of science but to situate science as an intentional system in the total field of our relationships to Being" (1964a:152). Both were convinced, however, that phenomenology is a necessary prolegomenon for any discipline that aspires to comprehend fully the significance of its activity. The alleged (metaphysical) neutrality of scientific methodology propounded in the positivist tradition has been faulted on many counts. As Burtt observed: "Even the attempt to escape metaphysics is no sooner put in the form of a proposition than it is seen to involve highly significant metaphysical postulates" (1954:6). In this vein, Merleau-Ponty notes:

> It was no use denying any ontological value to the principles of science and leaving them with only a methodical value, for this reservation made no essential change . . . since the sole conceivable being remained defined by scientific method . . . Science must nevertheless understand itself; it must see itself as a construction based on a brute, existent world . . . [It] must return to the "there is" which underlies it. [Merleau-Ponty, 1962:55]

From the phenomenology of pure consciousness to the phenomenology of perception

Although both Husserl and Merleau-Ponty embraced the phenomenological method, the rigorous description of the phenomena of experience, as the sole conceivable means by which to apprehend the world as it actually is-for-us — and thereby to discover that which is indubitable in our experience — their respective philosophies found quite different expressions. It is important to note the essential difference between indubitable and exact. *Exactness* pertains to expressional form and is not conceived to be a necessary feature of a philosophy that aims at the explication of the grounds of knowledge. *Indubitability* is a function of evidence and entails the prescription that all our claims to knowledge be submitted to the kind of verification each demands. Although Merleau-Ponty (1964:159—81) was adamant in his insistence that he was merely carrying out the full implications of Husserl's own work, references exist in many of his writings that indicate a number of subtle, yet profound, points on which his thought diverges significantly from Husserl's.

Throughout the course of his philosophical career, it was Husserl's aim to formulate a "systematic egological science," a description of cognitive experience that would "constantly glance back from the side of the object to the side of consciousness and pursue . . . [their] general existing connections" (1970a:16). The theory of intentionality that constitutes the cornerstone of Husserl's phenomenology was conceived as an attempt to explicate the cognitive aspects of the relationship between the subject and object poles of conscious existence. In focusing upon existence as a relationship of knowledge, Husserl tended to idealize both the subject and the object poles of experience. On the side of the subject, Husserl's theory of intentionality maintains that consciousness *intends* its object: It gives meaning to that which is presented to it. In so stressing the intending aspect of consciousness, Husserl came close to committing the Kantian error of positing an idealized structure of consciousness. In order to avoid the intellectualism of the Kantian concept, Husserl attempted to give equal weight to the noematic or object pole of conscious act. But, again, he tended to deal with the problem in idealized terms. Husserl sought to elucidate, through the phenomenological reduction, the essential or necessary nucleus of meaning that makes each particular object of consciousness (cogitatum) what it is, to discover that which is basic and unique to each intentional object. On the side of the object, also, Husserl sought explication through idealized structures.

The fact that consciousness is purely intentional, that it is always consciousness "of" something, demands an explanation of why consciousness intends *this* something and not another. What, in other words, assumes the directive function in consciousness? Husserl posited a transcendental ego as fulfilling this function: "As ego, I have a surrounding world, which is continually 'existing for me'; and, in it, objects as 'existing for me' " (1970b:68). The transcendental ego, for

Husserl, functions as the I-referent of all conscious acts. Here again is a concept of existence as a relationship of cognition pure and simple.

The ideal of a systematic egological science devoted to the explication of the intentional structures of conscious existence guided all Husserl's investigations, even though his many excellent analyses of experiential phenomena involved circularities that seem to indicate that the realization of this ideal was, in principle, impossible. For Merleau-Ponty, the circularities that plagued Husserl's search for some absolute foundational features of cognition served as an important lesson:

> This senseless effort to submit everything to the properties of "consciousness" (to the limpid play of its attitudes, intentions, and impositions of meaning) was necessary — the picture of a well-behaved world left to us by classical philosophy had to be pushed to the limit — in order to reveal all that was left over. [Merleau-Ponty, 1964a:180]

The absurdity of characterizing existence as a polarization of subject and object points to the unjustifiability of further maintaining the point of view of pure consciousness, of forcing existence into the dual categories of subject and object:

> The relationship of subject and object is no longer that cognitive relationship in which the object always appears as constructed by the subject, but is an ontological relationship, through which, to use a paradox, the subject *is* his body, his world, his situation, and in a certain sense enters into interaction with it. [Merleau-Ponty, 1964c:72]

For Merleau-Ponty, the Husserlian ideal of an "objective science of subjectivity" represented an attempt at the absolutization of knowledge — a form of knowledge that would be capable of the total explication of the world. The possibility of a system of absolute knowledge, in turn, presupposes the ability to detach oneself from the world that constitutes the field of the subject's experience. Husserl's concept of the relationship between consciousness and the world was a horizontal one (i.e., a relationship of cognition); he concerned himself with the structures through which consciousness gives meaning to the world. Moreover, the act of conferring meaning upon the world had, for Husserl, a fully conscious character. And it was by laying bare these conscious structures of intentionality that Husserl proposed to advance an objective science of subjectivity and meaning. But for Merleau-Ponty, the scientific universe of absolute, objective knowledge was not a self-contained one but was a derivative of a more original mode of experience. All the tenets of the sciences that strive for some form of absolute knowledge — and this includes Husserl's phenomenological psychology — are grounded ultimately in the primordial field of perceptual (i.e., phenomenal) experience. Our behavior and our thought cannot be considered as events occurring in the universe of science; rather, the universe of science is but an imperfect and incomplete formalization of the events occurring in our perceptual universe, the pretheoretical field of experience.

Merleau-Ponty refused to accept the horizontal nature of the relationship Husserl posited as existing between consciousness and its world. Neither (1) the polarization of subject and object nor (2) the claim to the absolute are justified in the light of phenomenological descriptions of concrete, immediate experience (as the circularity and in principle incompleteness of Husserl's own analyses attest). First, according to Merleau-Ponty, the weakness of the parallelism or dichotomization of subject and object "is that it provides itself with correspondences between the two orders and conceals the operations which produced these correspondences by encroachment to begin with" (1964c:18). Perhaps we do not have to think of ourselves and the world in terms of the bifurcation of subject and object. The task of phenomenology, radically conceived, is to "unveil a third dimension in which this distinction becomes problematic . . . to unveil the pre-theoretical layer on which . . . these idealizations find their relative justification" (1964c:162, 165).

Second, the possibility of attaining the Husserlian ideal of absolute evidence (indubitable and precisely formulable) and, subsequently, absolute knowledge is not guaranteed by even Husserl's own phenomenological descriptions of experience. His ideal has a certain a priori character to it. As Quentin Lauer (1965:133) has noted, it is not at all clear that the world of phenomenal experience is or necessarily should be susceptible to the sort of completely rational explication Husserl sought.

In an effort to elude the a priori tendencies of Husserl's concept of absolute consciousness, Merleau-Ponty took the notion of gestalt as his starting point, suggesting that man receives meaning from his world in addition to giving it. Meaning is both conferred upon the world and derived from it. The origin or genesis of meaning is to be sought by uncovering, as it were, the vertically constituted world — the world as experientially derived meaning. Meaning is not simply the product of a transcendental consciousness that maintains a distance between itself and its world of intended objects; it is a product of our experience, an experience that is prior to the idealistic dichotomization of subject and object.

In taking this position with respect to Husserl's philosophy, Merleau-Ponty effectively advanced his thought from the realm of epistemology (horizontal constitution) to ontology (vertical constitution). By subscribing to the gestaltist notion of meaning as an experiential totality, he simultaneously disavowed the tenability of the Husserlian point of view of pure and transcendental consciousness.

In the place of a phenomenology of pure consciousness, Merleau-Ponty substituted a *phenomenology of perception.* The world of perception constitutes our primary reality. The simple act of perception, moreover, does not necessarily have a conscious or intellectual character. On the contrary, many of the meanings that pervade our perceptual experience are rarely subjected to perusal by conscious intellect. We rarely question ourselves, for example, about the phenomenon of time as it is apprehended or, more precisely, lived by us in the course of everyday experience, even though anthropological investigations have informed us that the Western concepts of time and historicity by no means have a monopoly on cultural experience. In this fashion, many of the elements comprising our perceptual reality are essentially non-conceptual and preconscious.

We can grasp the nonintellectual character of the perceptual field of experience in yet another way: When we perceive something (consciously or otherwise), we see it on a ground; the figure to which our attention is directed is surrounded by an environment that contributes to the meaning of that figure, although we often are not explicitly aware of this coreferential aspect of the single perception. It may be well to speak of our perceptual world as a field of experience that is sedimented with meaning, much of which is simply taken for granted; it exists, it is, and it is real.

In that this primordial field of perceptual experience constitutes our primary reality, Merleau-Ponty echoed Husserl's claim that the rationality we commonly discover in our experience of the world is "aesthesiological" (i.e., sense-ical). The perceived world, moreover, provides the ultimate ground for the absolutized rationality that acts as the foundation for the scientific disciplines as we commonly tend to conceive them. The pure logic of mathematics and the intellectual activities is but a formalization of the nascent logos of the field of our perceptual experience:

The perceived world is the always presupposed foundation of all rationality, all value and all existence. This thesis does not destroy either rationality or the absolute. It only tries to bring them down to earth . . . Scepticism begins if we conclude from this that our ideas are always false. But this can happen only with reference to some idol of absolute knowledge . . . (again,) there is no destruction of the absolute or rationality here, only of the absolute and the rationality separated from experience. [Merleau-Ponty, 1964c:13, 21]

Merleau-Ponty and existentialism: existence made incarnate

As pointed out above, Husserl intended the subject of phenomenology to be consciousness, pure and simple. In the process of constructing a phenomenology of perception, Merleau-Ponty effectively divorced himself from the Husserlian form of phenomenology, although he retained the phenomenological method. A phenomenology of perception necessarily meant that Merleau-Ponty considered it impossible to divorce consciousness from the world in which it was involved without succumbing to either idealism or realism. By postulating such a communion between the subject and the object, he denied the validity of Husserl's noetic-noematic, subject-object distinction: Consciousness is simply too bound up in its world.

Merleau-Ponty's concern turned from a concept of consciousness as "consciousness *of* the world" (Husserl's intentionality) to one of "consciousness *in* the world" (*Dasein*), implying a greater emphasis upon the organic or existential facets of lived experience. It is reasonable to assume that Merleau-Ponty received some direction or initiative in this respect from Heidegger, the first and (possibly) foremost of the existentialist philosophers (although Heidegger rejected the existentialist label as applied to himself).

For Heidegger, the fundamental weakness of Western philosophy was its total ignorance of the problem of Being — the problem that should be the pivotal point of all philosophies. According to Heidegger, the Western philosophers (with the exception of a few pre-Socratic Greeks) tended to treat Being as an a priori fact, as the null point of all philosophical investigations. Being was a first assumption, the basis and the implications of which were never explicitly made objects of investigation. Heidegger insisted that the very condition which is Being radically affects the entire realm of subject-object relationships that has been the traditional concern of Western philosophy.

Being, Heidegger contended, conditions the world that is present to beings. Man is not just present to the world, as an autonomous and non-involved subject; he is totally involved in it. He is Being-in-the-world (*Dasein*). The world, moreover, is that field or region which is my concern or care. The world has a character of "mineness"; not because of the I-pole of some transcendental ego, but because the world that is present to me (with me) is my concern, the field of my involvement. There is no place in Heidegger's philosophy for the Cartesian subject-object dichotomy. Subject and object are a copresent unity. Being is the context in which all individual beings come to be known.

The vital link between the philosophies of Merleau-Ponty and Heidegger is found in the way they construe the Husserlian concept of intentionality. For Husserl, intentionality was the basic structure or condition of consciousness and described the cognitive relationship between subject and object. The Cartesian origin of such a concept is clearly evident insofar as it retains the language form of the subject-object dichotomy. Both Heidegger and Merleau-Ponty, on the contrary, tended to view intentionality as a preconscious and ontological relationship. Intentionality is the primordial and preconceptual awareness through which consciousness or the perceiving subject understands itself as fundamentally related to its world. As Merleau-Ponty observed:

The relationship of subject and object is no longer that cognitive relationship in which the object always appears as constructed by the subject, but is a relationship of being, through which, to use a paradox, the subject *is* his body, his world, his situation, and in a certain sense enters into interaction with it. [Merleau-Ponty, 1964b:72]

The primary datum then is not the conscious, thinking subject or the Cartesian cogito, but the act or fact of existing. Any epistemology, therefore, must be preceded by and founded upon an adequate ontology. In this respect, Husserl's philosophy is an epistemology that, owing to the traditional dualistic language in which it is expressed, tends to remain ignorant of its ontological foundations.

Although the emphasis upon intentionality as an ontological relationship characterized both Heidegger's and Merleau-Ponty's phenomenological philosophies, it had radically different implications for the subsequent development of their respective systems of thought. For Merleau-Ponty, consciousness was not a matter of "I think" (Husserl) or simply "I feel" or "I sense" (quasi Heidegger). It is more adequately characterized as "I am able," implying bodily presence to the world as a determining factor of the existential relationship between consciousness and its world. This is evident in Merleau-Ponty's thesis of the primacy of perception. For Heidegger, the question of the Being of beings constituted the primary reality. Merleau-Ponty, on the other hand, maintained that the world of perceptual experience is the primary reality and gives us the first and truest sense of the real. At this point the ultimate uniqueness of Merleau-Ponty's phenomenology is clear: the concept of the corporeal or incarnate cogito as an "I can."

The radical aspect of Merleau-Ponty's thesis of the primacy of perceptual experience derives ultimately from the notion of corporeality: Consciousness is literally and metaphysically embodied in the world. It is even somewhat misleading to speak of consciousness in this light, as the term has commonly been used to distinguish certain mental functions or processes from the profanity of the sensual body. One of Heidegger's shortcomings, from Merleau-Ponty's standpoint, lies in the fact that his notion of existential involvement in the world does not account for the ramifications of corporeal presence in the world. Indeed, in (purposely) avoiding recourse to such traditional philosophical terms as consciousness and man and relying totally on the concept of Being, Heidegger paradoxically reduced Merleau-Ponty's man-of-flesh to man-of-consciousness, thereby reentering the very impasse he was trying to avoid. For Merleau-Ponty, consciousness was basically the anonymous, prepersonal life of the body-subject. We do not simply feel, sense, or know our history, our temporality, our Being, our reality; we are bodily immersed in them. The body is the ultimate and primary source of all distances, time, and meanings. The body is the measurant of its world.

The body of which Merleau-Ponty spoke is not merely the subject pole of the conscious world. To prevent such a misinterpretation, he referred not simply to the body, but to the flesh. The flesh, in this sense, is the sensible sentient, the exemplar sensible. It is that which is both seer and seen, that which touches and which is touched. The body as the self-awareness of an "I am able to" (re: motor power) provides the intersection between the perceiving and the perceived. My carnal being forms the anchorage of my world.

In this light, how are we to describe the relationship between this body-subject and its world of objects? In that the body is an object among objects — and is that object by which other objects come to exist "for me" — it is not really proper to separate subject and object. The body as perceived in self-awareness and the body as perceiving motor power are linked in coexistence or "compresence." There is an intertwining, a chiasma, of consciousness, body, and world; this is the preobjective order of the flesh. Nor is it proper to speak of an identity of the body-subject and the world. The relationship is more correctly understood as one of reversibility; the one is not without the other, they are simultaneous aspects of the same phenomenon.

Such a relationship is not only difficult to comprehend, but difficult to express in the usual terminology with which the history of philosophy has endowed us. This is quite obvious in Merleau-Ponty's last, unfinished, and posthumously published work, *The Visible and the Invisible.* Here he avoided many of the traditional forms of Western philosophical expression in favor of a more metaphorical language that bends to fit the "in-directions and allusive logic" of the world of pretheoretic experience (i.e., the world as we live it prior to any systematic thematization). This is virtually inevitable because language is geared primarily to the realm of the natural attitude where an (assumed) closed universe prevails, where the subject-object, immanent-transcendent dichotomies are invoked as means for dealing with the reality that confronts us.

But philosophical interrogation need not, and must not, entail the mythical stance of detachment from the world. The origin of meaning and the nature of our organic relation with the world can be rediscovered or explored by embracing our pursuit of meaning in its totality. Such a method of interrogation will reveal that the primary characteristic of brute being, the not-yet-rationalized and preconstituted being of

the sensible world, "is not opacity but dimensionality . . . Perception is
not first perception of things, but perception of elements . . . of rays of
the world, things which are dimensions, which are worlds" (Merleau-
Ponty, 1968:xlix). Regarding being as opacity was the fallacy of Western philosophy and is the a priori of the natural attitude. For Merleau-
Ponty, on the contrary, brute being is not revealed by penetrating the
opacity of objects in search of their essence, but by conceiving of them
as latent pregnancies of possibilities. The dimensionality of brute being
reveals "every color [to be] a level, every point a pivot, every line a
vector, every plane a horizon by transparency, every fact a category"
(1968:l). Brute being is the "proliferation of generating axes for visibili-
ty." The flesh, finally, is also dimensional; it is the prototype of the
sensible in that it is the sensible thing that senses. In the flesh is accomplished the

equivalence of sensibility and sensible thing . . . My body is to the greatest extent
what everything is: a dimensional this . . . a sensible that is dimensional of itself.
But while the things become dimensions only insofar as they are received in a field,
my body is this field itself . . . It is the universal thing . . . the universal measurant.
It is in this elemental being of the flesh that the secret of sensibility is to be sought.
[Merleau-Ponty, 1968:liv, 260]

In retrospect, Merleau-Ponty's concept of brute being and the manner of its representation in the perceptual world of the body-subject is
quite similar to Heidegger's concept of Being as a field. Merleau-Ponty,
however, has radically twisted the Heideggerian notion by introducing
the thesis of the primacy of (bodily) perception and the notion of corporeality. He has made Being incarnate.

Merleau-Ponty and understanding the world

How, then, are we to proceed in our efforts to submit existence to our
demands for knowledge?

We must, at the beginning, eschew notions such as "acts of consciousness," "states
of consciousness," "matter," "form," and even "image" and "perception" . . . Not
that these distinctions are definitively meaningless, but because if we were to admit
them from the start, we would re-enter the impasses we are trying to avoid . . . We
are not implicating in "our experience" any reference to an ego or to a certain type
of intellectual relation with being . . . We do not even know in advance what our
interrogation itself and our method will be. The manner of questioning prescribes a
certain kind of response and to fix it now would be to decide our solution . . . We
do indeed first have to fix our gaze on what is apparently *given* to us. It is in this
entirely methodic and provisional sense that the subdivisions we will presently use
are to be understood . . . The resolution to confine ourselves to the experience of
what is in the originating or fundamental or inaugural sense presupposes nothing
more than an encounter between "us" and "what is" — these words being taken as

simple indexes of a meaning to be specified. [Merleau-Ponty, 1968:178—9; emphasis in original]

Understanding the world in this manner demands a thoroughgoing reconceptualization of our usual notions of truth and progress in knowledge. The preceding formulation suggests that we are no longer justified in believing either (1) that there exists some absolute ground from which our investigations may proceed or toward which they may seek to culminate in any sort of a finalistic sense, or (2) that there is some form or order of existence (and knowledge) that can be circumscribed once and for all. Instead, truths are elaborated from within the thickness of some particular social and historical situation. This same world provides the background for the scientist's investigations. Merleau-Ponty said:

The philosopher thinks about his experience and his world. Except by decree, how could he be given the right to forget what science says about this same experience and world? Under the collective noun "science" there is nothing other than a systematic handling and a methodical use — narrower and broader, more or less discerning — of this same experience. [Merleau-Ponty, 1964b:102]

The philosopher always thinks about something, is always oriented to some realm of empirical facticity (thereness); and "the sociologist philosophizes every time he is required to not only record but comprehend the facts" (Merleau-Ponty, 1964b:401). The attempt to effect a rigid separation between science and philosphy and their respective modes of inquiry is unforgivably naive. If any distinction must be made, we should perhaps say that science strives for effective knowledge and that philosophy is not a particular body of knowledge, but the vigilance that does not let us forget the source of all knowledge, which is the field of preconscious, pretheoretical existence. The following conclusion seems justified:

When it seems that methodology has incontestably established that all induction is baseless in the absolute sense of the word and that all reflection always carries with it whole vistas of experience which tacitly cooperate to produce the purest of our evidence, it will undoubtedly be in order to revise the classical distinction between induction and reflection and to ask ourselves if two kinds of knowing are really involved or if there is not rather one single way of knowing, with different degrees of naiveté or explicitness. [Merleau-Ponty, 1964b:98]

For Merleau-Ponty, the existential enterprise was irremediably reflexive, and rightly so if we are to understand ourselves as beings-in-the-world. If the products of our theorizing activity — whether philosophical or sociological — are to have any truth value, we must explicate the sense of that activity itself. An insistence upon the necessary reflexivity of our theorizing activity is the key to its integrity. The essential nature of reflexivity guarantees that it will not be overcome or bracketed out of our investigations through the introduction of new methodological techniques. What is required, instead are new forms of understanding and of expression that will allow us more adequately to apprehend, appreciate, and verbally render the sociological nuances and implications of this fundamental phenomenon.

What Maurice Natanson said about the use of the phenomenological method may be applicable to the method of existential sociology as well: "Use is bound at one end to a philosophy of perceptual experience and at the other to pragmatic considerations of what is being sought, what a problem calls for, and what level of clarification is appropriate to the goals of the inquiry" (1970a:110).

PART III

The phenomenological sociologies and existential sociology

4

The sociology of Alfred Schutz

DAVID L. ALTHEIDE

Alfred Schutz (1899—1959) has greatly influenced recent sociology.
His work forges links between the phenomenological philosophy of
Edmund Husserl, the theories of other philosophers of his day, and the
sociology of Max Weber. It has influence on the phenomenological sociologies, especially the social constructionist theory of Berger and
Luckmann and the ethnomethodology of Garfinkel and Cicourel. His
work is a crucial part of the foundations of phenomenological sociology
and shows many of the strengths and weaknesses of this approach.

Schutz's philosophy of the social world

Schutz's philosophy was influenced by William James, Henri Bergson,
and Max Weber, but the overriding influence was the phenomenological
philosophy of Edmund Husserl. Husserl's work was an attempt to solve
the crisis of philosophy and science precipitated by the controversy
over subjectivism and objectivity begun by Hume and Kant. Schutz
sought to develop an approach to the social world that was grounded in
existing philosophical knowledge about human consciousness and the
part this played in making experience meaningful.

Husserl and other phenomenologists saw consciousness as the genera-
tor of reality (see Chapter 3). Schutz built on this foundation. He set
out to clarify how understanding of consciousness can be useful for
understanding the social world. His task was to build a social science on
the fundamentals, or invariants, of social existence; to show how daily
life is built on perceptions, experience, and shared understandings.
Schutz was concerned with clarifying the nature of the social world so
that social scientists would not mistakenly treat situations as though
they were objects. He set forth a basic theory of the social world to direct sociological investigations.

Schutz wanted social science to rest on the phenomenological foundations outlined by Husserl. But he disagreed with his former teacher and others about the origins of social life, shared meanings. He insisted that the understandings essential for communication in social life are not constituted by the individual ego. Schutz argued that this problem cannot be solved

within the transcendental sphere, but is rather a datum of the life-world. It is the fundamental ontological category of human existence in the world and therefore of all philosophical anthropology. As long as man is born of woman, insubjectivity and the we-relationship will be the foundation for all other categories of human existence. It can, however, be said with certainty that only such an ontology of the life-world, not a transcendental constitutional analysis, can clarify that essential relationship of intersubjectivity which is the basis of all social science — even though, as a rule, it is there taken for granted and accepted without question as a simple datum. [Schutz, 1966:82]

Providing an "ontology of the life-world" needs more than a theory of consciousness and intentionality.[1] Social scientists, Schutz maintained, also require an explanation of order within and between people. The former is essential in understanding how two solitary egos can share meanings and communicate. Schutz developed an elaborate explanation of the process, grounded in an individual's capacity to order experience in space and time. But he had to clarify how people can make transitions from one situation to another, from one problem to a solution, and from one moment to the next. Henri Bergson's writings about how individuals experience the temporal flow of their lives and William James's work on the discrete but continuous nature of human consciousness provided important insights for Schutz on these questions.

Husserl, Bergson, and James provided the philosophical foundation for a theory of the social world, one that was thought to be constructed by individual intentions. Unlike activists who claimed that social order was external to people, a phenomenologically based social science located social organization in consciousness. But it was Max Weber who provided a model of social *behavior* that essentially preserved this idea. Weber's understanding of social action further propelled Schutz's efforts to establish the basic principles of social life.

Max Weber (1947, 1949) recognized the importance of a theory of meaning for sociology. He was one of the first social scientists to grapple with the methodological and philosophical issues involved in this. Philosophers like Hume, Kant, Husserl, and Bergson were trying to solve once and for all the problems of how anything can be known for certain. Their quest was highly philosophical and uninformed by an interest in empirical social research. Weber provided an understanding of the major methodological tasks to be settled before a science of society would be possible. Schutz's opinion of Weber's work is evident:

Never before had the project of reducing the "world of objective mind" to the "behavior of individuals" been so radically carried out as it was in Max Weber's initial statement of the goal of interpretive sociology. This science is to study social behavior by interpreting its subjective meaning as found in the intentions of individuals. The aim, then, is to interpret the actions of individuals in the social world and the ways in which individuals give meaning to social phenomena. [Schutz, 1967:6]

Weber's interpretive sociology (*verstehen*) attempted to articulate situations as typical actors would see them. His definition of social action was consistent with this. For Weber, sociology was the science that uses interpretive understanding of social action to explain its course and effects:

In action is included all human behavior when and in so far as the acting individual attaches a subjective meaning to it . . . action is social insofar, as, by virtue of the subjective meanings attached to it by the acting individual (or individuals), it takes account of the behavior of others and is thereby oriented in its course. [Weber, 1947:88]

Schutz lauded Weber for establishing subjectively meaningful and goal-directed activity as sociology's subject matter. This was to be studied by the interpretation of the actor's subjective state and intentions for his behavior. This approach was essential to the study of social life, but it was not enough. As not all action is the same, Weber developed the "ideal type" as a way of generalizing about discrete courses of action. For example, Weber (1958) maintained that generalizations about specific types of religion can be established, and then these can provide a general definition and theory of religious behavior. The task of the sociologist is twofold: to develop ideal types and then to examine the empirical relationships of one to another.[2] In this way sociology can be grounded in actors' meanings, but still provide general principles of social and historical relationships.

Schutz (1967) accepted most of Weber's groundwork, but noted several problems. Schutz found Weber's writings ambiguous about the nature of meanings. Weber had confused meaning for the observer and meaning for the actor. Schutz (1967:3—44) analyzed this discrepancy and emphasized Weber's failure to articulate a theory of meaning and the importance of its interpretation. Schutz also found an inconsistency regarding the relationship of motives and meanings. Schutz contended that the latter underlie the former; a person cannot be motivated to do something unless it is meaningful to him. He felt these problems stood in the way of developing an adequate basis for social science. So he sought to overcome Weber's misunderstanding about consciousness, intentions, and domains of interest.

Phenomenological sociology

Schutz wanted to develop a new perspective for understanding the social world, one with more respectable epistemological foundations. He believed that an adequate understanding of the social world must consider the meanings actions have for the actors. This calls for a general theory of meaning to explain the relationship between an act, an actor, and a situation. The problem is to articulate explicitly the process by which a person selects one meaning over another, how two or more persons share meanings, understand each other, and engage in concerted (ordered) social action. This entails a closer look at the natural attitude of daily life. By drawing on my observations and experiences during a lengthy field research investigation of television newsworkers conducted between 1970 and 1973 (Altheide, 1974), I will illustrate with substantive examples the relevance of Schutz's theoretical ideas about these social processes. I will show how they apply to enhance our understanding of TV newswork and, later, some of the problems they raise.

The life-world as taken for granted

Schutz believed that the key to social life is what people take for granted. Several terms clarify the relationship between commonsense understandings and social organization: natural attitude, stock of knowledge, recipe knowledge and typification. The *natural attitude* is the presymbolic awareness of all competent persons. It consists of a *stock of knowledge* about social reality. This is cultural experience ordered in such a way as to permit a person's realization that one situation is different from another, that changes have occurred, or more commonly, that one situation is like another. The sharing of a stock of knowledge is, therefore, essential for day-to-day routines. This is acquired through social learning.[3] It provides *recipes* for all varieties of activities, such as turning on a light, recognizing hunger pangs, or knowing when to come in out of the rain. Society is possible because all members share this commonsense awareness of order. But, Schutz insisted, it is their taken-for-granted acceptance of this perspective that actually promotes order, as reality is recreated each day. To the extent recipes are held in common, much social experience is routinized, normalized, taken for granted, or *typified*.[4] To act as though these routines are arbitrary or illegitimate is to be thought incompetent, maybe insane.

Social competence rests on the capacity to operate within the natural attitude. The shared knowledge and assumptions that constitute the natural attitude provide the recipe knowledge for elementary social competence. As a person's purpose becomes more specified, his stock of knowledge also becomes more diversified. This process makes shared meanings more problematic. Many examples of this can be found in the news business.[5] TV newsworkers share many understandings, terms, and problems not available to their audience. This awareness is a sign of membership and distinguishes them from outsiders. News personnel are often baffled by viewers' questions, complaints, and criticisms, because "anyone who knows anything" about news would never make such comments. For example, a viewer sometimes calls and asks to speak with the anchorman he is watching on his television set. The viewer seems unaware that delivering the news prevents the anchorman from talking on the telephone. Sometimes a viewer asks to speak with the network anchorman, not realizing he is actually thousands of miles away. Such a viewer is not "competent" as a news watcher, from a newsworker's point of view. In one man's words: "People who don't understand what we're trying to do are just plain stupid." These examples support Schutz's contention that people must have similar stocks of knowledge to share meanings.

Newsworkers and audience often misunderstand each other because they have different purposes: newsmen present news, the audience views it. Different purposes may preclude a spontaneous understanding of the other's activity because each party interprets the actions through a particular frame of reference. This is the difference between members and outsiders. For example, cameramen are upset when people smile for the camera. Would-be subjects for the nightly news are often unaware that cameramen are concerned that the camera will disrupt the naturalness of an event, especially if people want an opportunity to perform. The subjects regard the camera in certain terms; cameramen define it in others. For most people cameras signify an occasion to present oneself favorably by smiling. But this is not the appropriate interpretation for cameramen whose work it is to capture social reality, not atypical grins. TV cameramen are like their nonprofessional peers in other situations, however. The most serious TV cameraman will frolic and perform with his children when making home movies. On-camera behavior has different meanings to those unfamiliar with the newsworkers' project. With increased familiarity, however, the project becomes taken for granted. Rookie reporters, inquisitive and uncertain about why some things are done, learn the ropes and eventually become bored with the questions of newcomers. In short, the more often we perform certain tasks and draw on an ever-expanding stock of knowledge, the more likely we are to type the experience and establish recipes to make it unproblematic.

The examples of newsworkers' perceptions illustrate how occupational tasks can contribute to interpretations of otherwise ordinary acts, like smiling. Schutz was not interested in the manufacture of news, of course. But he did seek to clarify how shared understandings like those of newsworkers are possible. His task was aided by concepts such as stock of knowledge, recipe knowledge, and typification. These illustrate how meanings and communication are tied to common experiences. Recipe knowledge is the product of sharing experience in particular times and places; it leads to common frameworks for seeing the world. Just as coworkers are brought closer together through their projects and typical courses of action, so are an individual's ties with others. Schutz listed four historical and experimental degrees of social nearness that constitute a range of our temporal, social, and spatial distance from others: contemporaries, consociates, predecessors, and successors.

Contemporaries share our historical period and are familiar with the general knowledge common to our culture. Societal members are also aware of a range of variations, of the problems and concerns of persons in different age or other social categories. Palm readers and other lay social scientists make use of these social understandings in predicting the future (e.g., "you will decide which boy you like best"). And their clients are often convinced there is really something to palm reading or other social forecasts. The reason one's future can be predicted in a general sense by someone who knows very little about one's personal life and aspirations is that normal people are presumed to fit certain patterns. There exist commonsense cultural criteria of relevance about one's biography that make such predictions possible.

Consociates are contemporaries with whom we are personally involved. We know more specifically about their plans and problems than about the plans and problems of those who merely live during the same time span we do. Consociates are intimates with whom we share personal knowledge; we can take more for granted with them. This is why a palm reader, who is a contemporary, can make a mistake a consociate would rarely make — for example, telling a lesbian she will have a nice husband and children. What is generally acceptable for normal young women is not likely to be true of a lesbian. We have more shared experience with consociates and are able more accurately to interpret and typify situations (e.g., "I know what you're thinking when you look that way").

The final categories of social nearness are socially present but physically absent. *Predecessors* are now dead and *successors* have not yet arrived. Nevertheless, we have a sense of both and orient our lives accordingly, by adhering to tradition even as we plan for the future and our successors. This is how the meanings that constitute culture are transmitted from one generation to the next and take on an aura of realness and necessity. This knowledge is our basic mode of orientation and it is so common that many people cannot otherwise imagine life. It is not surprising, then, that as each generation more or less alters previous definitions and adopts new meanings, others trumpet the decline of society, the end of an age, or the impending apocalypse.

Schutz's interest in social nearness is that common experience provides a stock of knowledge from which to draw in certain situations. This facilitates communication, which in turn expands one's stock of knowledge. For consociates, the process may eventually preclude explicit communication in favor of implicit nuances embedded in interactional contexts.

Meanings and motives

Schutz began his analysis with the *natural attitude* because most people take it for granted as common sense. This common sense, however, is grounded in shared experience that is meaningful because it serves various practical purposes. A person's competence is assessed partly by how well he chooses among courses of action. For newsmen this means that good newswork requires certain activities. This is so widely known among newsmen that competent and incompetent filmwork is obvious to all members. A newsman occasionally rebels against a poor assignment by purposely violating the criteria of good work, although he admits that the work is poor only when he feels confident that co-workers are already convinced of his ability and will agree that he screwed up intentionally and regard it as an exception to his typically competent work.

Schutz devoted considerable effort to clarifying the relationship between a person's goal (*act*) and the specific steps (*action*) essential in fulfilling it.[6] The act provides the context within which each action is regarded as sensible. Schutz specified how every action is tied to an awareness of how it fulfills some future project, the act, although each particular act and action is understood as part of a more general context of meaning. Thus, each action entails an understanding of the intended act; the latter gives meaning to the former.

This complex procedure is best illustrated in cases where common-sense reasoning is not shared and projects are not understood. Emphasizing instances where sharedness is absent is useful for demonstrating how essential intersubjective understanding is in our daily affairs. Examples abound in the world of newswork. When a cameraman speaks of "shooting a talking head" (his act), it is understood that certain procedures or actions will be required. He will gather various pieces of equipment, load them in a car, talk with a reporter for directions, locate the setting, set up equipment, and check out his power source and lighting arrangement. All this is common knowledge to a newsman, but it is not understood by many who are on the news. Because some interviewees have little experience with the specifics (the action) that constitute the news interview (the act) they are unaware of the amount of time it takes to set up equipment or plan the interview. They are especially confused when the cameraman shoots cutaways, segments where the reporter asks questions already recorded on film. This technique is important for editing purposes, but seems strange to outsiders. Even though interviewees are instructed not to answer such cutaway questions, novice news subjects elaborate their previously recorded responses. The important message is that newsmen have a unique way of relating particular action to complete the act that provides a meaning context (Altheide, 1976). Unless one shares their stock of knowledge sufficiently well to recognize how "shooting a talking head" is a typification that enables newsmen to routinize their work, one misapprehends what each specific stage of the interview means. This shared experience then facilitates communication and intersubjective understanding. If news subjects do not have this practical knowledge, they do not understand what news interviews are really about. On occasion, they voice displeasure at what they see on the evening news; the news product as constituted by the newsmen's project may be interpreted from another point of view.

Schutz spelled out the importance of shared experience for the commonsense understandings that underlie all social order. But he was keenly aware that shared meanings are not the same as motivation. For concerted action to occur, meanings have to be shared sufficiently well to inform one actor about another's motives. The questions, then, are: How do people share perspectives in specific situations? How are the appropriate typifications and recipes recognized? In further dissecting the natural attitude, Schutz distinguished two kinds of motives: *in-order-to motives* and *because motives*. When one's stock of knowledge at hand typifies another's behavior as an action for an encompassing act or project, the groundwork is laid for understanding why the other person had selected this behavior.

The *reciprocity of perspectives* is an essential procedure for interactional routine. Encounters between newsmen and interviewees illustrate the misunderstandings that may occur when perspectives are not shared. Some interviewees are puzzled when a reporter repeats a question he asked moments before and are more perplexed when their comment is cut off. The disjunction is easily traced to the incongruity of their perspectives. The reporter has the newsman's perspective, or the projected act of doing a new interview for unifying specific action. This includes understandings about editing techniques, how cutaways fit into this, and why editing is essential to reduce a five-minute interview to a minute. The cameraman shares this perspective. But the interviewees operate from the background of their own commonsense experience: namely, when asked a question, you provide an answer. We saw earlier that purpose gives an action its meaning. The purpose becomes the context of meaning. In our example, the reporter's in-order-to motive is to facilitate editing; if the interviewee shared his perspective, he would not answer the question *because* it is irrelevant for the practical task of editing. It would detract from the news purpose and would label him (in the newsmen's eyes) as inept. Newsmen are quick to recognize a news novice by his general uncomfortableness in interviewing. The common stock of knowledge of the interviewee does not include the particular typifications of the newsmen. The news novice is incapable of the correct interpretation of the action within the context of news-work and is thereby prevented from joining in the reciprocity of perspectives. The question still remains why one thing is intended rather than another. This is what Schutz termed the problem of relevance.

Relevance

Schutz saw the life-world as the embodiment of numerous pragmatic purposes. Individuals and shared courses of action make up daily experience. Schutz (1962:227) believed that all pragmatic considerations grow from the "fundamental anxiety," our knowledge and fear of death. Even though death is the most relevant concern, most of us must wait for death and realize other pragmatic purposes involving sleeping, eating, work, and leisure. This is the source of the problem of relevance: Given the large number of alternatives, why are some chosen over others? Schutz answered that we intend tasks that are believed important for the purpose at hand, whatever it may be.

Schutz (1964:125; 1970) discussed four regions of relevance: (1) that part of the world within our reach which can be immediately observed is *primarily relevant*; (2) *mediately relevant* domains are areas not open to our domination but related to the primary focus (e.g., tools for achieving a project); (3) the *relatively irrelevant* seem to have no important connection with our immediate interests; and (4) the *absolutely irrelevant* are believed to exert no influence whatsoever on our practical affairs.[7] What is relevant depends on the particular project, which provides a context of meaning. Particulars that seem central to our task are *thematic*; others are on the *horizons*. The crucial matter is what we intend. Newsmen again provide useful examples. The inept interviewee discussed above is likely to act on the basis of his project: namely, to get his point across. However, newsmen have their own priorities and can get the point across *after* the interview has been filmed, reduced, edited, and packaged. Their project provides its own relevances or contexts of meaning. A problem only alluded to by Schutz is the source of these meaning contexts. In newswork these are seldom shared by those soliciting news coverage and those doing newswork.

Newswork is enmeshed in interweaving relevances, which in turn provide meaning contexts in which news must be accomplished, regardless of the story. First, there are considerations of a local station's network affiliation, the community, and what competing news media are presenting. Secondly, there is the relation of the news to the overall station operation, including sales, production, and programming. Next comes the commercial consideration of capturing the largest share of the audience. This is followed by the various political and organizational influences of management. Then there is the news director, who contributes to the work of the producer, and the assignment editor, who schedules, selects, and assigns stories to cameramen and reporters. All these, plus problems of working with sophisticated equipment, greatly influence what cameramen and reporters do on any story. In other words, each of these considerations is relevant, but some more than others; they pervade the everyday world of television news.

Newsmen establish routines for their work load. Most reflect the constraints of scheduling and making it interesting, but occasionally other matters become relevant. Consider the problem of editorializing. The station management is responsible for making explicit editorial comments. Cameramen and reporters, who are supposed to follow prescribed story patterns as they transform reality into news, occasionally usurp the managerial prerogative and offer their own subtle contributions. They occasionally dig or get back at an individual or group by the way they film the story, edit it, and write it. In these instances, they choose to make such evaluations more thematic, although their editorial comments are more subtle and often recognizable only by them. Their subtle editorial gibes are seldom detected by management. More importantly, seldom do superiors examine programs in terms of "finding out if those guys are sneaking anything in." The work of reporters, and especially cameramen, is viewed with management's understanding of the overall news act and not the particular pieces of action. This suggests that interpretations of experience are informed by particular contexts of background meanings. What is selected as relevant is itself a piece of a broader understanding and our stock of knowledge. The problem of relevance is a pivotal point for existential sociology's departure from the Schutzian perspective. But it is important to recognize that Schutz acknowledged the existence of plural realms of meaning, although he insisted that the natural attitude is a common base for interpreting these.

Multiple realities

Schutz believed that the natural attitude is similar for everyone, although he was aware that the world of everyday life is only one of many realities.[8] Schutz (1962:207—59) included among the diverse realms of experience the worlds of dreams, imageries and fantasy, art, religious experience, scientific contemplation, and play. He referred to these distinctive domains as "finite provinces of meaning" because "it is the meaning of our experiences and not the ontological structure of the object which constitutes reality." These experiences have significance, however, precisely because they are recognized as departing from the orientational perspective of the natural attitude of everyday, common-sense, practical activities. We know we have had a dream or viewed a play as opposed to more routine endeavors, and we are able to recognize such diverse experiences by reflectively comparing them with the world we take for granted.

This brief mention of multiple realities rounds out Schutz's analysis of the natural attitude and the structure of the life-world. A discussion of Schutz's methods further clarifies what phenomenological sociology is and how existential sociology differs.

Schutz's method

The method Schutz proposed was aimed at providing general knowledge of social life. Even though he never conducted formal research, he clarified the procedures to be followed if social scientists were to understand their subject matter. First, Schutz (1967:241) believed that all scientific knowledge of the world is indirect and that people can be best understood as types and not as individuals. This position is consistent with his views on the relationship between typical motives, projects of action, and communication. A second and related point for his methodological guidelines is that social science, and especially sociology should be interpretive. "The primary task of this science is to describe the process of meaning-establishment and meaning-interpretation as these are carried out by individuals living in the social world" (1967: 248). These two points led him to employ abstract types as a research technique.

Schutz (1962:34—7) utilized the ideal type as a method that permitted objective classification of acts. It is clear that he focused more on procedures for analysis than on methods of observation, data collection, and the like. Like Weber, Schutz saw the ideal type as a means of contrasting possible courses of action.

The ideal type can be viewed in two ways: (1) the personal ideal type, which consists of a model of an actor who expresses himself in a certain way; (2) the course-of-action type, which refers to the expressive process, or the outward results we define as signs of this process. The first is derived, but the second can be considered independently as a purely objective context of meaning. Schutz stated the relationship between the two:

> In the process of understanding a given performance via an ideal type, the interpreter must start with his own perceptions of someone else's manifest act. His goal is to discover the in-order-to or because motive (whichever is convenient) behind that act. He does this by interpreting the act within an objective context of meaning in the sense that the same motive is postulated as constant for the act regardless of who performs the act or what his subjective experiences are at the time. For a personal ideal type, therefore, there is one and only one typical motive for a typical act. [Schutz, 1967:187]

An individual's motives, and presumably the meaning for his action, are deduced from a course-of-action model that is oriented to a context of meaning. Schutz did not base these course-of-action types on the experiences of individuals in real situations. "The social scientist replaces the thought objects of common-sense thought relating to unique events and occurrences by constructing a model of a section of the social world within which merely those typified events occur that are relevant to the scientist's particular problem under scrutiny" (1962:36).

Schutz instructed social scientists to delineate what might be relevant to a course of action independently of the actors: "The scientific problem, once established, determines alone the structure of relevances." The scientist's first task is to "construct typical course-of-action patterns corresponding to the observed events" (1962:39). But how does the scientist determine what is typical independently of the actor's frame of reference? Is it merely the frequency of an action, or is it what the actors say they are doing? Schutz did not deal with these questions. He proposed that a model of an actor, or a personal ideal type, can be derived from the rational course-of-action types:

> [The scientist] ascribes, thus, to this fictitious consciousness a set of typical in-order-to motives corresponding to the goals of the observed course-of-action patterns and typical because motives upon which the in-order-to motives are founded. Both types of motives are assumed to be *invariant* in the mind of the imaginary actor-model. [Schutz, 1962:40. emphasis added]

A concrete illustration clarifies this idea of invariance. An observer can understand a cameraman's actions by locating the setting up of a tripod within the context of camerawork. One learns that a tripod is used to steady a camera so the picture will not be jumpy. The action of setting up the tripod is part of the act of filming. All that remains is postulating an agent — the personal ideal type — who typically intends this activity. The motive of anyone who sets up a tripod can then be typified as following this procedure in order to have a steady picture. The actor's subjective meaning is thereby deduced from an objective meaning. The implications of such an analysis are not comforting, however.

Schutz's commitments led him away from the world of everyday experience to a model of the social world based on purely rational acts, the uncomplicated world of a "puppet and his artificial consciousness."

Thus the concept of rationality in the strict sense already defined does not refer to actions within the common-sense experience of everyday life in the social world; it is the expression for a *particular* type of constructs of *certain specific* models of the social world made by the social scientist for certain specific methodological purposes. [Schutz, 1962:42; emphasis in original]

Schutz tried to solve the riddle of objectivity studying subjective meanings by giving the social scientist an omniscient privilege of assuming what is relevant for a course of action. The model works or represents what actually occurs if the person who carries out this typified action

had a perfectly clear and distinct knowledge of all the elements, and only of the elements, assumed by the social scientist as being relevant to this action and the constant tendency to use the most appropriate means assumed to be at this disposal for achieving the ends defined by the construct itself. [Schutz, 1962:44]

Schutz's preoccupation with rational model building led him to see the social world through a certain method rather than developing an adequate method after the life-world and its structure of relevancies were understood. Thus we are left with models of rational actions, but not the actions of people who define actual situations. Schutz has offered insightful interpretations of the complexity of the life-world, but his writings seem strangely at odds with his method of analysis.

The presumption of a shared social world lies at the core of Schutz's interpretive sociology. Consider his interest in and use of the natural attitude. He assumed that he knew how this attitude is manifested by actors in everyday life, that they take many of the same things for granted. How did he know this? We can assume that actors have the ability to take things for granted, but it does not follow that they view these things the same way. We must discover through careful observation the actor's first-order constructs. For example, Schutz said that one pragmatic orientation to the life-world is avoiding death, "the fundamental anxiety":

It is the primordial anticipation from which all the others originate. From the fundamental anxiety spring the many systems of hopes and fears, of wants and satisfactions, of chances and risks which incite man within the natural attitude to attempt the mastery of the world, to overcome obstacles, to draft projects and to realize them. [Schutz, 1962:228]

Do most people view death this way? Available research suggests they do not. Jack Douglas's (1967) study of suicide shows that some suicides are motivated by a meaningful interpretation that death will establish their credibility. Others kill themselves as a way of becoming something in the next world. These people seem not to fear death, but to welcome it.

The view that the social world is constructed through concerted efforts and is perceived in the same way enabled Schutz to typify contexts of meaning in order to explain behavior. The social world is produced through actors interpreting essentially similar stocks of knowledge, which, over a period of time, become taken for granted. Schutz said very little about the contribution of the actor in a given situation, including the options to choose among several relevant courses of action. But such a model of the life-world and its actors is not derived from careful research and observation.

It is clear that Schutz was trying to cement social science to a method that was insensitive to the complexity and variability of everyday life. However, he did leave the way open for revising his course-of-action models. He set forth three postulates that should be met:

1. The postulate of logical consistency demands that scientific constructs be clear and distinct, compatible with the principles of formal logic. Schutz argued that their "strictly logical character" lends objective validity and distinguishes them from commonsense thinking (1962:42—4).

2. The postulate of subjective interpretation requires a scientist to construct a model of an individual mind that is capable of handling the specific actions entailed by the rational course of action. This means we "refer to the activities of the subjects within the social world and their interpretation by the actors in terms of systems of projects, available means, motives, relevances, and so on" (1962:35).

3. The postulate of adequacy cautions the social scientist to make certain that each term in the rational course-of-action model will be "understandable for the actor himself as well as

for his fellow-men in terms of common-sense interpretation of
everyday life" (1962:44). This postulate was intended to keep
the social scientist's eye on the commonsense constructs of experience.

The second and third postulates provide an important check on
Schutz's proposed method. Both require that actors be able to recognize what the social scientist is saying about them. However, Schutz did
not tell us what to do if the actors disagree with the course-of-action
types, if they insist there is more to it than was included as relevant.
Thus, although Schutz previously argued that the scientist decides what
is relevant, he seems here to call for the societal members to serve as a
validity check. There is a further problem. The postulates were intended to evaluate the course-of-action types indirectly by comparing these
models with actors' constructs. If there is consistency between an actor
model and the action type, then we have more confidence that the objectivity of the former reflects the subjectivity of the latter. If this is
not true, then how do we improve the model? Where do we get additional data to build generalizations? Schutz was silent on this matter.
But one answer lies in studying the members' actual perspectives.

Existential sociology calls for a return to the life-world for insights
about what is relevant and important for social behavior. This is the
surest way to orient our claims about social reality. From Schutz and
other abstract phenomenological thinkers, we are directed to return to
the world of everyday life, where people and not "homonuculi" come
to grips with their situations and each other. This is the only way to
comply with Schutz's postulates of subjective interpretation and adequacy. This is the only check on a scientist's arbitrary classifications,
which may have no empirical linkage to the life-world. This is also
where existential sociology diverges from phenomenological sociology.

A return to social life and personal experience

We have seen in the examples drawn from research on television news
that Schutz's ideals are useful in directing a researcher's understandings. The elements of social life discussed thus far constitute Schutz's
ideas about the basic and invariant properties of meaning, understanding, and the life-world. Chapter 6 shows how these ideas dominate
ethnomethodology, a sociological approach that investigates how persons interpret situations and rules. Ethnomethodologists focus on the
procedures for interpreting reality. But social science will remain incomplete if it examines only the how of social behavior and not the

why. These two are not easy to separate, as the actor's purpose always shapes its completion. Ethnomethodologists claim to be aware of the linkage between the *variant* properties of biography, situation, and practical task. But their methods and research decontextualize these features to focus on *invariant* procedures for processing information. This orientation turns the sociological eye from the actual context of meaning. The failure to address the juxtaposition of variant properties of action with invariant procedures has virtually obliterated their interest in social life. Ethnomethodology has turned inward toward the techniques of social life and thus misses most of what is crucially important to our lives. To this extent ethnomethodologists have learned too well from Schutz; they insist the people they study, their "reality constructors," are not real people, but can be simulated by machines programmed to employ the invariant procedures required for presenting a sense of reality (Mehan and Wood, 1975:114).

Existential sociology purposes to start from actual life experiences and decipher what is relevant and worthy of further inquiry. Unlike phenomenological sociology, which is mostly concerned with the invariant features of cognitive processes, existential sociology also considers creative and relatively unusual features of specific acts. This allows us to understand both continuity and divergence in social life, including feelings and situated motives. A meaningful social science must be able to make sense out of what is important to actual people, and not merely reduce them to actors who "do" social life. Existential sociology seeks to articulate the way action becomes relevant in certain contexts. Knowledge of the invariant procedures cannot tell us why one man kills and another loves. But this is precisely the kind of thing we desire to know in our daily lives. We want to understand, for example, how a context of meaning, such as newswork, can influence and be influenced by motives, feelings, and ambiguity.

Feeling your way through a newsroom

The world of television news hardly approximates the routine and shared life-world envisioned by Schutz and his students. On the contrary, newsworkers direct their lives through existential moments in conflict. There are routines, to be sure, but these are entered into and sometimes experienced with degrees of fear and trembling. Even seemingly mundane tasks like producing a film story are pregnant with feelings of suspicion, fear, revenge, joy, obligation, resentment, and politics. Feelings such as these cannot be adequately understood if one thinks they develop after the participants have already made some rational decision about their acts. Indeed, it typically occurs in just the opposite fashion: The feelings motivating the *action* are the prime movers of the events, and what is sometimes asserted to be the intended act comes very much after the fact.

Newsworkers understand the common elements of the news process, but not all those in a particular job carry out their tasks in the same way or for the same purpose. Nevertheless, their actions are informed by the daily project of putting on a newscast. This context of meaning provides newsmen with the routines for producing the news. These tasks become taken for granted as sedimented knowledge for the members, although an outsider, such as a researcher, is at first confused because he does not share this knowledge. Typifications, however, do not account for crucial aspects of the newsworkers' activities. Describing these types would contribute only a portion of all that is relevant in making news. Instead of shared perspectives, it is common to discover great conflicts about the nature of news, the quality of work, and the best way to present a story. We noted earlier how a reporter, cameraman, and assignment editor look at stories with different perspectives. The same is true for ideas like professionalism, objectivity, and efforts to influence the shape a story takes. Each member of the news team brings a biography and interest(s) in news to the events the team covers. Not surprisingly, there are different ways of doing the news. Some of these differences involve feelings, including the widespread dislike of the news director, personal jealousies, and fears that others are trying to use the newsworkers for unacceptable purposes.

Newsworkers do not merely follow routines; they also commonly view their activities strategically. My research showed that on numerous occasions they performed so as to get back at the news director, who was hated by many. They often elected to do a poor job on a story if the boss requested it. He was constantly harassing one or more of them, cutting back their overtime, ridiculing them in front of coworkers, and making their work more anxious than enjoyable. One example is a story the news director suggested about the mayor's attendance at a Big Brother's banquet. It was well known by all that the news director had been a long-time supporter of the mayor. He often provided freebies to give him more publicity. The cameraman refused to shoot any film of this story, saying it was not an important news story. One reason for this was the lack of visual interest; namely, that chewing and eating are not exciting. However, on other occasions, similar stories had been covered. In short, the cameraman evaluated his assignment in terms of objective criteria of news quality with which most colleagues may agree, but he was also cognizant of the reasons behind the story. This capacity for news personnel to act on the basis of what they see as relevant calls for careful study.

Occasionally an experienced cameraman butchered a story by poor filming techniques and imprecise editing. This occurred if the camera operator was not feeling well or if he felt the event was a publicity stunt. His reaction was informed by work experience and feelings about his job.

News procedures can be typified, but the situated course of action cannot be divorced from the workers' immediate relevancies and feelings. Moreover, although many of these understandings and feelings are situationally shared, they are seldom spoken about. One reason is that verbalization of the feelings that motivate one's work may be used as evidence by those with different feelings. This is why the world of newswork can never be fully understood by relying only on written and spoken documents. On many occasions, my efforts to obtain spoken proof of another's intentions were met with: "You've been around here long enough to know what I mean."

Newsworkers avoid making explicit what is implicitly understood. For example, it is understood that cameramen and reporters will do the nuts and bolts of television news and leave editorial commentary to station management. This division of tasks is typified as an element of the stock of knowledge, but it does not dissuade some from editorializing. In the example noted earlier, a cameraman intentionally included film showing politicians managing a film story. Any competent cameraman knows that such film should not be included. This cameraman included it because he felt he had been used for another's personal gain at the expense of his personal integrity. He set out to "get the bastards." The decision to get back is not part of the typifications that make news possible, but it is involved in the way the news gets done. Under these circumstances, it does not matter that a subtle rebuttal may be understood by not more than one or two co-workers.

The prevalence and primary motivational importance of feelings are evident to all newsroom insiders. The dislike for the news director and some of his lieutenants led a few employees informally to challenge some policies. Crime reporting is a good example. It was well known that two cameramen were reserve police officers who occasionally put down their cameras to aid the police. They also tended to film the police view of crime. This included providing unsubpoenaed film about civil disturbances to be used as evidence. Co-workers often resisted such assignments. One reason was that there is nothing challenging about shooting film of the scene of a crime. Another reason was the suspicion that the station was "promoting the damn police department." The context of meaning was the same, but other criteria of relevance were invoked. By the same token, those sensitive to the self-serving intentions of others, in rare instances promoted causes they felt committed to. In one case, a cameraman's daughter had been frightened by violence at her high school. A reporter recommended that they reopen an investigation. He felt publicity would overcome the doubletalk the newsman father had received from school officials. This was one way of showing them. The investigation was cut short because the superintendent of schools, a personal friend of the news director, would have been embarrassed. But such caution was not evident during an award-winning investigative report of border corruption that led to the indictment of several immigration officials. This corruption was worth exposing because it was further removed from the personal lives of the news personnel.

Feelings played a primary role in many activities in addition to covering news stories. The news director was the target of much scheming by his subordinates. The object was to get rid of him, to wipe him out. Several newsworkers felt that any scientific research about news should be an exposé of his dastardly deeds in order to force him out. Their feelings had become such an integral part of their work that they felt any research should be directed toward specifying names, dates, and places. Some newsworkers were so intent on changing regimes that they also sought to get rid of his lieutenants including the assignment editor and producer. The rank and file could not openly make these suggestions because they lacked power and could have been fired. They could operate within the dominant context of meaning that provided typifications for their work. They could carry out assignments with the minimal amount of work, but do nothing extra. As one worker put it: "We do the lousy kind of job these assignments deserve." The workers felt their efforts reflected the "kind of leadership we have around here" and eventually would lead to the dismissal of their bosses. As one worker put it: "The sooner things get really bad, the sooner they'll be out." And they were right. Their motives were informed by the typifications and recipes of news production. But more importantly, they were sharply aimed at interpretations top management would probably make about their actions, including the belief that those in charge are responsible for how well the new department is doing. Instead of the meanings stemming from these contexts, as Schutz's analysis would lead us to expect, these contexts were *used* for other meaningful purposes.

This brief look at one segment of the social world — a television newsroom — shows that tasks are done not only to complete work assignments but also to earn personal satisfaction. When this involves a desire to do a professional job of filming a story, it will be done. By the same token, if newsworkers seek to do a job on someone who is trying to hurt them, the professional feelings are subordinated to something more relevant, such as getting even, fighting back, and playing it cool. Each action is meaningless outside the context of purpose.

Conclusion

Understanding our social existence is more complicated than just delineating the cognitive structures of the life-world, as Schutz suggested. We must also clarify how and why anything becomes relevant in a situation. We gain by being aware of the intersubjective foundations of common sense and the operations of reciprocity or perspectives and typifications. But we gain even more when first-hand research experiences illuminate the sentimental and motivational sources of such cognitive processes. The sentiments come before the cognitive operations and last beyond them. To understand the cognitive rationality out of its sentimental context is to misapprehend most of what is important to us in our daily lives.

5

Ethnomethodology and existential sociology

JOHN M. JOHNSON

Phenomenology and existentialism, as noted in previous chapters, partially owe their emergence to the feelings generated by the great moral
and political crises of the twentieth century. Many of the thinkers mentioned earlier were among those who became profoundly distressed by
the failure of the conventional wisdom of their times, whether theolog-
ical, scientific, or political. Men such as Husserl, Schutz, Sartre, and
Merleau-Ponty felt inspired to reexamine the basic foundations and
assumptions of the existing conventions, to build a more realistic or
better understanding. It cannot be said that any particular set of social
conditions is responsible for generating any particular type of social
knowledge; to do this would be to formulate what the philosopher
Abraham Kaplan referred to as a "malicious philosophy of science."
But it can be said that personal perceptions and experiences of grave
social crises are commonly the precursors of basic intellectual change.
And so it is today. Increasing numbers of our respected scholars have
advanced claims, on various grounds, that our existing bodies of theoretical knowledge fail to provide us with an adequate understanding of
ourselves, our social situations, the broader social world into which we
have been thrown, our likely futures. And in recent years many have
called for a fundamental reexamination of the established theories.

In the present context of crisis, reexamination, and intellectual renaissance, the term *ethnomethodology* is often heard. Ethnomethodologists, as well as some of those who have written about this emerging
intellectual development, have claimed it represents a radical break
from the existing sociological conventions; radical, that is, in an etymological sense, meaning a fundamental or root change in scientific per-

I am greatly indebted to the contributions and assistance of C. Robert Freeman to
earlier drafts of this chapter. I also wish to express my gratitude to David Altheide,
Jack Douglas, and Peter Manning for their helpful comments and criticism.

spective. Much confusion surrounds the term itself, some of this caused directly by failure to distinguish the etymological sense of the word radical from the conventional political sense. Ethnomethodology has been, on various occasions, associated with a distinctive theoretical perspective, a methodological stance, a body of findings, its political implications, a research style, a cult, a sect, a world view, a style of exposition. Some of these associations result from misunderstandings about ethnomethodology, but others result from the failure to appreciate the intellectual diversity subsumed by the term. On certain matters those who practice ethnomethodology appear to be of one mind, and so for discussions of these matters the term can be used discriminately. But such agreed-upon subjects are very few. On most issues of actual or potential relevance, ethnomethodologists differ significantly, and so for discussions of these subjects only the plural, ethnomethod-olog*ies*, can remain true to all the diversities.

Ethnomethodologists have asserted for their work a radical character so fundamentally different from the traditional concept of scientific conduct that the questions they pose are naive to the established traditions. On the basic nature of this difference, Pollner wrote:

As is obvious, perhaps, such questions are possessed of peculiar properties. They are "radical" questions in the sense that they cannot be resolved by an appeal to the normal operating procedure of the discipline to which they are put. Whether or not sociology's phenomenon ought to be A or B and whether or not its foundational methodology ought to be X or Y is not amenable to answer or solution in the same way that questions formulated within the confines of sociology's "normal paradigm" are resolved. They cannot be answered within the normal paradigm because it is precisely the normal paradigm which is under our consideration. "Radical questions" are radical in that they question the foundations of the discipline from within which they are asked. Because radical questions are directed to the very foundations of the discipline, they cannot be resolved by procedures indigenous to the discipline. They must be resolved in ways which may be quite alien to the discipline and even to the entire intellectual tradition of and in which the discipline flourishes.

The primordial questions of "What is the phenomenon?" and "How is it to be approached?" are asked on a bridge unsecured at either end. A bridge, moreover, which traverses an abyss whose walls are sheer paradox. A limited example of the perplexities that can be encountered by "radical" questioning is furnished by considering the peculiar consequences of a global polemic against sociology's phenomenon, and the method through which it is investigated. In one sense there is an "argument" or critique; and yet in another there is none. The conventional sense of critique dissipates when an entire discipline is comprehensively challenged — from its conception of its subject matter to the conception of its method — because then one is not so much offering a challenge as formulating an alternative discipline. [Pollner, 1970:2—4]

These comments reflect several important points on which virtually all enthnomethodologists have agreed: a specific critique of how Western social sciences have conceived of their subject matter and the appropriate methods of investigating it. Historically, the social sciences have defined their objects of interest, human activities, as similar in principle to the objects studied by the natural and physical sciences. The fundamental features of the scientific enterprise, ethnomethodologists have argued, consist of a set of methodological procedures that intend the empirical investigation of these other realities. This accepted version of appropriate scientific conduct is usually known as the hypothetical-deductive model (sometimes as the hypothetical-statistical model). It demands of scientific observers the specification of empirically testable propositions, commonly deduced from more general theoretical statements, prior to the conduct of a research project. Such propositions should be stated in causal terms and should meet the demands of formal logic. Operational definitions of the key elements of the propositions are then made, and methodological techniques of various kinds are used to direct the empirical observations of the phenomenon of interest. The observational results are then compared with the earlier hypothetical predictions, and the more general (or theoretical) understandings are confirmed, denied, or further modified. When these general ideas first appeared in the late eighteenth and early nineteenth centuries, they represented a radical challenge to the established religious and philosophical ways of knowledge. But today, many of us learned about the scientific method at a young age, and many societal members think of it as the only appropriate means of investigation.

All ethnomethodologists have agreed that using the methodological approach described above results in a basic distortion of social reality. There have been different arguments concerning this, but the common claim has asserted that this approach entails an imposition of the cognitive rules of science on the everyday social realities of those whose lives are the topic of a given study. Various arguments have explained how such an imposition of the scientific reality produces a basic distortion. Some have said the distortion results from the requirement that observers specify hypothetically the meanings of the relevant phenomena prior to conducting research, thus making it impossible, or at least difficult, to determine whether these are indeed the relevant meanings. Others have said it results from the requirement to phrase scientific propositions in causal terms, necessarily one step removed from the actual empirical realities of daily life. Still others have derided the use of formal logic, which according to them is not one of the actual features of (nonscientific) daily life. And some have faulted the traditional approach for promising but never delivering literal measurement of the things studied. And there have been other arguments as well, all of a more complicated nature than can be depicted here. At this point it suffices to say that ethnomethodologists have not shared the traditional conceit about the priviledged position of scientific knowledge, that the rationality of science is superior to the rationality of common sense. By contrast, ethnomethodologists have regarded scientific conduct as just another topic worthy of study, equal to any other, but certainly not a better or superior one. This is one of the important reasons why Pollner said, in the remarks quoted above, that in one sense ethnomethodology represents a challenge to or critique of conventional social science, but in another it represents the formulation of an alternative to it.

This chapter further examines the nature of ethnomethodology, its commonly shared critique of social science, and the diverse alternatives proposed by its practitioners. This information will give the reader an understanding of this emerging intellectual development and how it differs from existential sociology.

The early ethnomethodological critique and program

All ethnomethodologists have been critical of what has heretofore passed as social science. According to them, the objects of social scientific inquiries are different from the material objects studied by the natural and physical sciences. Thus, to treat the two kinds of objects as if they were similar is to introduce a fundamental distortion in the understanding produced by the studies.

By contrast, ethnomethodology locates the distinctive nature of its investigations by taking the everyday life-world as a phenomenon in its own right. Instead of seeing the perceptions, definitions, interpretations, and understandings of a society's commonsense members as epiphenomenal to some social structure presumed to determine them, ethnomethodologists have sought to understand the rationality of common sense on its own terms. This goal of ethnomethodological studies has been characterized in several ways: taking the theoretical as opposed to the natural stance toward common sense (Garfinkel, 1967; Douglas, 1970a); remaining true to the phenomenon, human action (Douglas, 1970b); carefully distinguishing common sense as the topic as opposed to the resource of an inquiry (Bittner, 1965; Garfinkel, 1967; Zimmerman and Wieder, 1970); and conceptually and empirically clarifying the observer's (or researcher's) reliance on the basic as opposed to the normative rules of interpretation (Cicourel, 1964, 1970a, 1974). In the writing of some ethnomethodologists, these distinctions have been used rhetorically, to distinguish their work from that of the professional practitioners of the various traditional sociologies. Others have used them to indicate their goal of understanding the realities of daily life on their own terms instead of translating those realities into terms that fit the presuppositions of positivist science. Chapters 2, 3, and 4 discuss this distinction and the theoretical alternatives proposed by various phenomenologists and existentialists to the traditional absolutist ideas of the Western social sciences.

Whereas in the past the social sciences have drawn upon common-sense definitions, perceptions, and interpretations as resources for studies, ethnomethodologists have commonly regarded common sense itself as the focus of inquiry. An example of this confusion of common sense as topic with common sense as resource is supplied by a field research study of college students by Becker et al. (1968). Of their study of students at the University of Kansas in the early 1960s, the authors commented:

> We use the concept of perspective to analyze the collective actions of relatively homogeneous groups — homogeneous with respect to their social position within an institution . . . Perspectives, though, as they are used by the individual to organize his activity, are a group phenomenon, coming into being when the members of a group find themselves sharing common or similar goals in a common situation. [Becker et al., 1968:5]

These remarks fail to make clear whether "perspective" is one of the analytical concepts of the authors, or the students, or both. On this point, the authors further stated:

> The perspective students develop on their academic work — we can call it the *grade point average perspective* — reflects the environmental emphasis on grades. It describes the situation in which students see themselves working, the rewards they should expect from their academic work, the appropriate actions to take in various circumstances, the criteria by which people should be judged, and relevant conflicts in goals. [Becker et al., 1968:33]

These remarks stress that the grade point average perspective is (1) produced by the college environment, (2) used by students to solve the practical problems encountered in their situation, and (3) descriptive of an *actual situation* (instead of something used by students to *create* one). The authors also stated:

> Because the several points of the perspective seem, both to students and to us, to form a coherent and understandable unity, we can think of the perspective as furnishing the underlying basis for many diverse, and seemingly unrelated items of student thought and behavior. For this reason, we regard evidence about any one aspect of the perspective as evidence for the existence of the perspective in its entirety. [Becker et al., 1968:41]

This study is a good example of sociologists using the commonsense ideas of those in the setting to describe what was observed about them. Specifically, the authors assumed that those in the setting share a set of meanings, in this case the grade point average perspective, and then used this assumption to clarify the relationship between this sanctionable (or moral) order and the students' actual behaviors — the actions observed during the research. But the assumption that all members of a particular setting share common meanings, ethnomethodologists would argue, can be used to account for stable social actions only if it can be demonstrated that the meanings possess a stable operational content applicable to a variety of similar situations; that the meanings are trans-situational or objective. But Becker et al. indicated this was not so:

The generalized goal students have on entering, then, may be no more than an idea that they are going to take their academic work seriously, work hard, do well. That goal, broadened and its connections to other areas of college life made specific, exerts an influence on the perspective students develop on their academic work. *It does not tell the student how to act while he is in college; it only points the direction in which an answer must be sought and specifies a criterion against which any solutions to the problems of college life will have to be measured.* The generalized goal does not tell students the precise perspective they should adopt toward their academic work; many perspectives might satisfy its requirements. But the generaliz-ed goal does stand ready to tell students when a potential perspective is not in keep-ing with their long range aims. [Becker et al., 1968:32—33; emphasis added]

These comments raise some serious questions. If the Kansas college students involved in this study do share the social meanings of the grade point average perspective — and, indeed, this sharing is a morally sanc-tionable condition of competent membership in the community, according to the authors — but if the meanings do not prescribe specific situational behaviors for the students, then in what sense are the shared social meanings relevant and meaningful for the actual things students do in their daily lives? What are the actual features of the college stu-dents' commonsense judgment and decision making? How is the rele-vance of the so-called generalized goals interpreted on actual occasions? How do the students reconcile these goals with actual conduct on a day-to-day basis? How do the students develop a sense that their actual conduct was accomplished in accordance with a given rule (of the grade point average perspective) or other social meaning? These questions remain unanswered. Becker et al. adopted the students' concept of social order and treated it as a determinant condition of the setting, rather than as a contingent, problematic, situational accomplishment of students.

The study raises another important issue. If the Kansas students share a common perspective, but if the perspective is of so generalized a nature as to preclude immediate relevance in terms of specific, con-crete actions, then how is it possible for the observers to investigate negative cases (students who do not share the grade point average per-spective)? Is it not the assumption of shared meanings that alone pro-vides the possibility of interpreting some cases as negative? (Even if it can be shown that *most* of the Kansas students believe in the grade point average perspective, does this provide a plausible justification for saying that those who do not share it are negative cases?) Put in different terms, what are presented as deviations from the shared meanings are explained in terms of the authors' assumption that the meanings are in fact shared. In this study there has been a serious confusion of commonsense interpretation as the resource with common sense as the topic of the study; the existence and nature of social order, at the University of Kansas in the early 1960s, has been assumed instead of investigated.

If an ethnomethodologist conducted a study similar to that reported by Becker et al., the research would probably be focused not on using the subject's commonsense interpretations (e.g., the grade point average perspective), but on examining commonsense interpretation as a phenomenon. In the early stages of the development of ethnomethodology, this would have been done by focusing on the manner by which individual actors construct particular social scenes so as to provide one another evidence of an objective, taken-for-granted reality. The goal would have been to specify the sense-making processes used by those in a given setting, not just the normative rules involved (e.g., the grade point average perspective). Early ethnomethodology reflected an interest in *how* commonsense interpretations are done, as opposed to the substantive issue of *what* those interpretations are. And because of this emphasis, according to Paul Attewell (1974), early ethnomethodology represented an extension of Erving Goffman's sociological studies of how social interaction is done.

How can one conduct a sociological study wherein common sense is only the topic of the research, and not one of the implicit, taken-for-granted resources used by the observer? In any absolute sense, this is, of course, impossible, as one must necessarily use words commonsensically to discuss anything, even common sense. But with this caveat in mind, Zimmerman and Wieder (1970:288–89) proposed three steps to assist a researcher who wishes to study commonsense interpretations as a topic: (1) suspend the belief that social action is rule-governed or normative in nature; (2) begin to notice that the orderliness and rationality of social life are described and explained in just such (normative) terms; and (3) treat these orderly and rational appearances of social order as appearances produced by those in the setting. Put differently, one should not just accept the commonsense interpretations as describing an orderly or rational situation, as Becker et al. accepted the students' notions of the grade point average perspective; rather, one should study actual situations to discover how the people in them see and report social structures thought to be orderly and rational. The purpose of an ethnomethodological study so conceived would be to spell out the interpretive practices by which the taken-for-granted world is made visible in daily life. Harold Garfinkel, the sociologist responsible for the early formulations of ethnomethology, believed one should not assume that the members of a setting share meanings or common understandings, but should study the methodical ways people claim (or "account for") these common meanings and understandings. According to Aaron Cicourel, one of Garfinkel's earliest co-workers and now the most prolific of the ethnomethodologists, the objective should be to articulate the basic or invariant rules of commonsense interpretation, those rules presumed to be so universal and natural that they transcend all social and cultural relativity. And, according to Cicourel, these basic rules are distinct from normative ones, those subject to social, cultural, and historical variations in their meanings.

Ethnomethodology shares with some other sociological and linguistic approaches a focal concern with socially meaningful activity. But it is distinct in its emphasis on the singular importance of an individual's talk for any adequate understanding of how such meanings are constructed. Meaningful action and talk are considered by ethnomethodologists to be of an indexical nature. *Indexicality* refers to the essential importance of the context (or situation) of communication for determining the meaning (or sense) of particular utterances or gestures occuring in it (see Bar-Hillel, 1954; Garfinkel, 1967; Cicourel, 1970a). One of Garfinkel's (1967:4—7) major criticisms of traditional sociology centered around its attempts to substitute objective (or context-free) for indexical expressions in what he argued was a premature attempt to transsituationalize knowledge. Indeed, Garfinkel and Sacks (1970) defined the treatment of indexical expressions as a definitive distinction between ethnomethodology and other sociological approaches. Whereas the other approaches seek to remedy the connections between indexical and objective expressions, ethnomethodology seeks to investigate and describe "the rational properties of indexical expressions and other practical actions as contingent ongoing accomplishments" (Garfinkel, 1967:11). By concentrating on the indexicality and the social world's situated construction, such studies seek to reduce, if not eliminate, the introduction of shared (commonsensical) meanings as implicit resources of their inquiries.

The emphasis on indexicality is evident in Zimmerman's discussions (1966, 1969, 1970) of the uses of social rules. A rule, he argued, can be used to account for social action only if one assumes that its content transcends the specific occasions of its use. An actor's orientation to and compliance with rules assumes that they possess a stable operational meaning across situations. Thought of in this manner, rules become a resource for sociological studies rather than their topics, as in the study by Becker et al. (1968). Instead of relating behavior to rules, Zimmerman argued, ethnomethodologists try to clarify how individuals continually develop the sense of rules as applicable to them when they treat actual cases. Each situation should be thought of as unique, and thus the relation between a rule and the setting in which it is applied is a feature of the actor's accounting practices. A rule's sense is elaborated so that the actor's behavior appears consistent and rational. By radicalizing contextuality to the point where each situation is seen to possess essentially unique elements, ethnomethodologists claim to have eliminated the use of shared rules as a resource in their observations.

This radical contextuality can be seen in Zimmerman and Wieder's (1970) rejection of traditional sociology's belief in the problematic nature of the social world. They have argued that the assumption is not that the world is unproblematic, but that it is beyond problematic. The term *problematic* implies that the relations between situated elements and intentional states are, though complex and difficult to ascertain, potentially knowable. Believing this, sociologists have generally sought to uncover the real nature of their phenomena (i.e., the actor's intentional state and its relation to the world). In line with this, some sociologists have argued that meanings are unimportant, others that they are crucial; some have argued that meanings are stable and unambiguous, others that they are emergent and situated; all assumed that there was indeed something to get at: "Whether 'problematic,' 'negotiated,' or 'processual,' whether couched in the language of norms, as in the case of the structural functionalists, or in emergent meanings, as in the case of the interactionists, the end result is the same" (Zimmerman and Wieder, 1970:288). The ethnomethodologists rejected sociology that seeks to account for social order in terms of a shared universe of symbols that, whether located normatively or in terms of functional imperatives, necessitates a reliance on intersubjective or transitional elements.

This extreme situationalism is perhaps best illustrated in Zimmerman and Pollner's (1970) discussion of the *occasioned corpus*. They used this term as an expressive device to highlight certain features unique to ethnomethodology: "We underscore the occasional character of the corpus in contrast to a corpus of member's knowledge, skill and belief standing prior to and independent of any occasion in which such knowledge, skill, or belief is displayed or recognized" (1970:94). In describing the implications involved in the concept, Zimmerman and Pollner listed six major points. First, the corpus is to be viewed as a corpus with no regular elements. The term *element* is defined as "those features of the situation members rely on, attend to, and use as the basis for action" (1970:96). Second, the situation is important; the study of a social setting's construction should be emphasized. They suggested two new terms, corpusing and decorpusing, which underscore the concept's refusal to impose an order on an otherwise irregular set of elements. This is opposed to the act of treating the elements as members of a subset, something implied by traditional sociologists when assuming either the sharedness or transsituationality of a setting's features. Third, the uniqueness of the situation and the impropriety involved in generalizing its aspects to other settings is reemphasized. Note that in affirming each situation's essential uniqueness, Zimmerman and Pollner left the situation's temporal structure unspecified. Is the relevant duration in describing a member's assemblage of a particular scene the length of the encounter, or is it something less? If each succeeding moment is seen to constitute a new situation (as implied by the use of such terms as "for the moment" and "here and now"), then it seems impossible to talk of a setting's on-going accomplishment. Members cannot "assemble" a setting, because "to assemble" is a process and implies a temporal bond relating sequentially situated activities. Making the occurrences in one moment either distinct from or ungeneralizable to other moments appears to place the sociologist in a precarious position. Even the act of looking to a group's accounting practices assumes that successive phrases, even successive words, stand in some relation to one another. To deny this results in solipsism and makes any kind of social understanding impossible.

The next three points in Zimmerman and Pollner's essay sought to remedy this problem by providing for the "immense generality of members' procedures for assembling and employing the features of a particular setting so as to recognize and account for . . . those scenes within an 'objective societal context' " (1970:99). This introduces the notion of a "family of practices and their properties" by which social settings are constructed (i.e., made accountable) so as to appear ordered and rational. This, they argued, reduces the multitude of features in everyday settings (the occasioned corpus) to that group of practices by which they are assembled. They asserted that the appearance of an ordered world (a corpus with regular elements) is an achievement of the work involved in assembling the corpus. They concluded:

The typicality of the world, its historical continuity, its order, its furnishings, and the rest, are preserved. The members of that world, lay and professional alike, may continue to address it in the same way and to deliver their ordinary accounts of its features. What is changed by recourse to the notion of an occasioned corpus is the status accorded the features of that world, and the accounts, explanations, and stories accompanying encounters with it. They are made available as phenomena in their own right. [Zimmerman and Pollner, 1970:98—9]

These points raise several questions about the occasioned corpus and the methodology involved in examining its construction. Zimmerman and Pollner implied that the occasioned corpus is used as a sensitizing concept by which the "obstinately familiar world can be detected." Before accepting such an explanation, let us examine this concept in reference to the problems it seems to have introduced. The first three points result in a highly situationalized concept of the corpus, a concept that precludes both understanding of and knowledge about the social world. How do the last three points surmount this difficulty? By relating the appearance of an ordered world to a family of practices by which this world is assumed to be assembled, Zimmerman and Pollner suggested that though it is unjustified to conceive of the social world as shared, it is necessary to hypothesize a set of practices that allows this appearance. If the goal of ethnomethodology is the search and explication of the fundamental properties of common sense, and if this goal is coupled with the assumption that these properties are universal, then ethnomethodology seems to take on the character of an eidetic search.

Granting for the moment that the interpretive practices are invariant and universal, several methodological problems arise. As previously mentioned, Garfinkel argued that traditional sociologies use common-sense knowledge of social structure as both a topic and a resource of inquiry, and that ethnomethodology's strength lies in its topicalization of common sense. By conceiving of society as an occasioned corpus and emphasizing the practices by which regular elements of the corpus are made to appear, all recourse to shared understandings is presumably eliminated. But this argument seems correct on only one level. If the argument is valid, then indeed common sense becomes in one sense a topic, and the goal of the study is to understand its constituents. Yet if the discovery of these constituents is the goal of the analysis, are not the constituents also the means by which this analysis can take place and, hence, its primary resource? In other words, does one not have to assume the existence of these properties and their status as intersubjective before one can proceed to interpret anything? If nothing is transsituational or shared (or at least cannot be assumed to be), the sociologist has no basis on which to examine anything, certainly not something as complex as a social world. These practices seem to be a necessary resource for their own discovery. If the mechanism by which the world is produced is the same mechanism by which this production is described, ethnomethodologists seem caught in a circularity at least as great as that of which they accuse other sociologists.

Ethnomethodologists have given the impression that these properties are derived empirically, gleaned from the members' accounting practices. By a variety of methodological tools, such as disruptive tactics and quasi-experimental interviews, ethnomethodologists claimed to have begun the search for them. They claimed to have done so without the use of such resources as sharedness and transitionality. Yet these practices, being a necessarily shared feature underlying any form of common sense, are discoverable without recourse to an empirical world. Surrounding us, these practices need only to be uncovered, not discovered. The social analyst need not search at all, but merely penetrate that which he has already seen before. These practices are uncovered not empirically, but phenomenologically. In other words, instead of being derived solely in accord with the rigor of empirical analysis and experimental acumen, the outside world becomes a resource for a phenomenological reduction, bracketed and systematically reduced. This yields an image resembling Schutz's (1967) effort. Schutz studied meaning by use of a phenomenological reduction intending progressively to reveal the structure of consciousness. It was primarily an intellectual operation, accomplished without a rigorous analysis of the particular meanings available in the social world. And though Schutz chose to explicate his findings by using illustrative scenes from everyday life, the scenes were themselves merely interchangeable expressive devices. Do ethnomethodologists do the same thing? Their methodological procedures seem to indicate a strong reliance on the visible world; yet their findings seem and are claimed to be generalizable to other scenes. Is the sole reason for examining various scenes the fact that no one scene contains all these properties? If this is so, are these properties derived empirically, from careful observation, or phenomenologically, with the scene itself a mere resource for an intellectual reduction?

If ethnomethodology is an empirical science seeking to reveal the underlying practices by which the world is produced, is this all a sociologist might wish to study? Often writing polemically, ethnomethodologists have accused traditional sociologists of providing a professional folklore and have presented ethnomethodology as an alternative to, rather than a supplement for, these absolutist sociologies. Yet it seems, at least on the surface, that ethnomethodology is unable to deal with many highly relevant and studiable features of the social world. If in fact all accounts are necessarily constructed from the same family of practices, this, in itself, does not reveal anything about the variable status of these accounts in particular milieux. It is clear that some things are seen as natural and normal, but others are experienced as warranting justification. Furthermore, it appears commonsensically obvious that some justifications (or accounts) are accepted, but others are judged unacceptable. Accounts honored in a hippie community may find little currency in a court of law, and vice versa. If the only topic worthy of study is the primordial makeup of commonsense interpretation, how can one explain the differential status accorded various accounts within a given society?

These comments suggest how early ethnomethodologists would likely have criticized a traditional sociological research and describe alternative programs some have proposed to remedy these deficiencies. We now turn to a consideration of some of the actual empirical researches done by ethnomethodologists to see how they satisfy the criteria specified in the criticism of the scholarly work of others. As one moves from the abstract criticism of traditional social science to the empirical researches of ethnomethodologists, it is easy to see that, although some researches are in some ways distinctive, and several are very competently done, they fail to justify the abstract claims of a categorical difference between the two research traditions. The ethnomethodological studies indicate, just as do those of traditional social science, an inevitable and necessary reliance on commonsense interpretations as a resource for an observer's inquiries.

Ethnomethodological researches on social rules

Most of the empirical researches done by ethnomethodologists have been either directly or indirectly concerned with the uses of social rules in everyday life. *Social rules*, in this context, is a generic phrase, referring to the cognitive criteria used by societal members to organize their daily affairs. Such rules may be highly formalized and codified, as in legal and bureaucratic settings. Or they may be relatively uncodified, as taken-for-granted features of commonsense knowledge within a given culture, such as the appropriate rules for being a man, woman, parent, and so forth. Ethnomethodological interest in the uses of social rules in daily life is best understood by contrasting it with the traditional sociological theories of which ethnomethodologists are critical. Previous social theories — whether called structuralism, functionalism, symbolic interactionism, behaviorism, exchange, or Marxism — have been seen by ethnomethodologists to embody a normative concept of social action. According to Thomas Wilson (1970b), this concept is articulated by or implied by all existent social science theories. And Douglas (1971b) has claimed the assumption of a direct relationship between social rules and social order to be the major recurring theme of Western thought. The ethnomethodological interest in social rules, then, amounts to nothing less than an effort to formulate an alternative to existing social science theories.

Three central elements characterize the normative concept of social activity; actors, social situations, and rules. In general terms, actors are seen to follow rules in situations, with *rules* in this sense commonly termed values, norms, interests, anticipations, expectations, mores, folkways, and motives. The rules themselves have often been regarded by traditional sociologists as external to and transcendent of social actors, but determinative of the individual's behavior nevertheless. They were seen as Durkheimian social facts. Ethnomethodology has rejected this normative perspective in favor of an interpretive perspective that emphasizes the situational determination of the meaning of a rule, the on-going interrelationships of actors, rules, and situations which continually inform each other and are never absolute. Ethnomethodological studies of how the members of society actually use rules in daily life have included investigations of prosecuting and defense attorneys (Sudnow, 1965), policemen on the beat (Bittner, 1967a,b), juvenile officers (Cicourel, 1968), juvenile courts (Emerson, 1969), traffic courts (Pollner, 1970), halfway houses (Wieder, 1973), welfare officials (Zimmerman, 1966, 1969), schools (Cicourel and Kitsuse, 1963; Mehan, 1974; Cicourel et al., 1975), medical practices (Garfinkel, 1967), mental hospitals (Wood, 1968), and social scientific situations (Garfinkel, 1967). A closer look at some examples of actual ethnomethodological research gives us a better understanding of the alternative perspective proposed by ethnomethodologists and a sense of how their researches differ from those they have criticized.

Zimmerman's (1966, 1969, 1970) empirical studies of the uses of rules illustrate ethnomethodology's theoretical stance toward common sense. His empirical problem centered on how an organization's formal program or rules is used by welfare workers to deal with the practical problems they encounter in their daily lives. He focused upon the intake receptionists in a bureau of public assistance. The job of the receptionists involved, among other things, the assignment of persons applying for aid to one of several intake caseworkers. The procedure by which the applicants were assigned was governed by a formal rule, which designated the order in which intake workers were to be given applicants. When followed routinely, the rule was said to have been applied literally. The literal application of a rule was distinguished from an interpretive application, which involved situational considerations. In observing the receptionists, Zimmerman noticed several nonliteral assignments and sought to discover the reasons for the breaches in formality. In one case, the deviation resulted from a backup in applicants caused by a particularly long interview; in another, the switch was prompted by a specific request on the part of an applicant for assignment to a particular caseworker. In a third, a difficult applicant was turned over to a worker reputed to have a special talent for such matters. The procedural transgressions were accounted for in terms of the particular situation in which they had occurred. In his discussion, Zimmerman referred to the receptionists' orientation to the intent of the rule, "its intent being formulable on a particular occasion by situationally relevant reference to the 'usual' course of affairs its routine or precedented use typically reproduces" (1970:232). In noting the receptionists' concern with the *appearance* of an ordered flow of activities, Zimmerman argued that "the routine character of the process will be seen to be one of its most salient features, onto which receptionists orient and, by their management of work activities, seek to preserve" (1970:227). In relating the receptionists' behavior to the organization's rules, Zimmerman commented:

Receptionist (and other personnel as well) orient to the management of the day's work so as to provide for the defensible claim that it was accomplished in sufficient-for-all-practical-purposes accord with rule and policy . . . based on both tacit and explicit understandings of such matters in light of "what anyone knows" about the practical circumstances of work in general and on particular occasions. [Zimmerman, 1970:227]

Zimmerman's study illustrates the problems an armchair sociologist would have in doing an abstract study of organizational rules by delineating meaning in terms of the rules' literal significance. It demonstrates that the application of a rule is an interpretive process depending to a large extent on the context of its application. The study does not show that the meaning of a rule is completely dependent on the situation; indeed, it does the opposite. Zimmerman made it clear that the receptionists had a clear notion of what constituted a "usual course of affairs" and used this concept as a precedent for interpreting a rule's intent. Furthermore, the receptionists possessed a sophisticated, albeit unarticulated, understanding of what transgressions could be accounted for by reference to "what anyone knows." These common understandings were not only simply revealed by Zimmerman; they were an important feature of his own commonsense understandings of what had occurred. As is clear in the several passages quoted above, they constituted a shared understanding by reference to which the receptionists' actions were related to typical mental states.

Zimmerman was confronted with the problem discussed earlier in this chapter: In order to locate the practices by which the world is constructed, one must already know them. If the only manner the empirical world can be approached cannot extend beyond these practices, and if these practices are, at least initially, unknown, how does an investigator use his original, uninformed observations of the world? It appears as if he cannot. Surely, as argued previously, the practices are not derivable in accord with a presuppositionless empiricism, as the question of what constitutes a presupposition can only be answered in terms of the practices. The only other alternative is to conceive of the search in terms of a strategy of a progressively transsituationalized understanding in which an investigator seeks increasingly to penetrate common sense to reveal its primordial structure. This alternative, in fact, has already been formulated by Douglas (1970a,b). Note that this concept implies that the ethnomethodologists must necessarily start with data that can be characterized as profane because it involves the use of shared understandings as a reductive starting point (presumably gained from the observer's own commonsense experiences as a member of society). To admit this point would break down the radical distinction ethnomethodologists have drawn between their investigations and those accomplished by the practitioners of other phenomenological and/or existential sociologies.

Another well-known ethnomethodological inquiry is Harold Garfinkel's (1967:116—85, 285—8) study of Agnes, a transsexual for whom acting female was a managed rather than a taken-for-granted activity. Agnes was one of those rare persons who possess both a well-developed female body and the normal external genitalia of a male. The situation was further complicated by the fact that, until she was seventeen, Agnes was raised as a male; then she left home and assumed a female identity. Shortly thereafter, she came into contact with Garfinkel when seeking an operation for her condition. Garfinkel, realizing the difficulty of examining something as taken for granted as sexual identity, usually sought persons for whom this topic was problematic. He began interviewing Agnes in the hope of elucidating how she coped with her variable status. The essay these interviews generated was organized around four basic topics. First, Garfinkel was interested in what he termed the "natural, normal female," and what the members of society and Agnes felt were its salient features. Second, he sought to uncover how Agnes went about the task of managing her everyday activities so as to appear a "natural, normal female" and what, if any, problems arose for her in this respect. Third, he tried to discover how Agnes reacted to these problems in terms of a potential discovery of her status. This led to a discussion of the methods and techniques by which Agnes sought to maintain her identity as a female in the face of situated disclosure. Fourth, Garfinkel was interested in Agnes's problems in assuming an identity for which she was improperly trained and how she went about the task of acting female. The natural emphasis of the study was on the discovery of the social meaning(s) of acting female.

One of the most interesting aspects of this investigation was Garfinkel's concern with the truthfulness of Agnes's responses, a concern that was well justified. It was not clear, he mentioned on several occasions, whether Agnes was answering his questions honestly or using them as an index of which answers would do. He termed this situation one of "secret apprenticeship" and described it in terms of Agnes's tendency to call on the environment to furnish answers to its own questions. He noted.

> This occurred, I regret to say, with disconcerting frequency in my conversations with her. When I read over the transcripts and listened again to the taped interviews while preparing this paper I was appalled by the number of occasions on which I was unable to decide whether she was answering my questions or whether she had learned from my questions, and more importantly from subtle cues both prior to and after the questions, which answers would do. [Garfinkel, 1967:147]

By comparing Agnes's answers to both current and previous questions, Garfinkel apparently hoped to discover the extent to which these answers could be taken at face value. In doing so, Garfinkel was engaged in what is termed *documentary interpretation*. Following Karl Mannheim (1952), this term refers to the mutual implications of a series of appearances and the underlying pattern they are taken to describe. Typically applied only to lay sociologists or members of society, it often constitutes an accurate description of what ethnomethodologists do, namely, search the elements of an interaction for clues to the nature of the interaction. This observation would be trivial if it were not for the claim advanced by many ethnomethodologists that their enterprise is unconcerned with interpretation (presumably meaning, in this context, that they do not seek to rationalize or remedy the members' interpretations). Note, though, that the very act of engaging in a documentary interpretation presupposes that the various indexical particulars stand in at least some relation to one another.

Garfinkel's central recommendation for ethnomethodological inquiries was "that the activities whereby members produce and manage settings of organized everyday affairs are identical with members' procedures for making these settings accountable" (1967:1). In other words, Garfinkel said that ethnomethodology advises us to view human experience as equivalent to the words we use to describe and understand it. But, to refer back to the study of Agnes's managed achievement of sexual status, it is clear that Garfinkel expressed a concern with the truthfulness of Agnes's responses to his questioning. It seems obvious that Garfinkel was using his (commonsense) cultural wisdom to investigate the actual or potential discrepancies between Agnes's verbal accounts and her actions, just as we often do in everyday life, and that Garfinkel himself did not follow the central recommendation of his own program. Thus, one of the differences between the early ethnomethodological statements and the later developments is that the earlier studies were still committed to some (taken-for-granted, unexamined) idea of scientific objectivity, whereas the later ethnomethodological works were not (see Pollner, 1970; Mehan and Wood, 1975).

Several of the best ethnomethodological studies of rule use have been conducted in settings where the criminal justice institution operates. Egon Bittner (1967:699—715) studied how police perform on their skid-row beats. His research observations indicated that police rarely if ever use a literal interpretation of the formal rules, the legal codes, which they are charged with enforcing. Instead, their use of the legal codes is at all times informed by their commonsense knowledge of the community context of their work, the specific individuals on skid row with whom they work, and their general purposes of keeping the peace in this area of town. The police do not invoke formal rules, according to Bittner, when they encounter violations as such, but only when they see using the rules as useful for their immediate purposes at hand. The knowledge police use to organize their tasks is largely taken for granted during their daily routines. Asked to articulate these commonsense and contextual understandings, most of the policemen were unable to do so. Nevertheless, their commonsense knowledge about types of people, types of situations, and appropriate forms of social interaction, and their contextual understandings of the community and the immediate situation continually guided and informed them in their legal work.

Another research that supports these general points is Aaron Cicourel's (1968) study of juvenile police officers. He also found community, contextual, commonsense, and situational factors to be the determinant features of the routine decision making of juvenile police officers. When asked to explain why they did one thing rather than another, within the context, they invariably referred to these implicit and taken-for-granted understandings rather than to an understanding of the legal code's literal interpretation.

Two excellent studies of courtroom decision making are Emerson's (1969) study of juvenile courts and Pollner's (1970) study of traffic courts. These researches showed formal rules such as legal codes to be incomplete when operationalized in the courts and demonstrated the necessity and inevitability for the participants to fill in the particulars on the basis of their commonsense and situational knowledge. Emerson's study nicely illustrated the fact that the courtroom participants usually have access to the same information, such as that contained in the juvenile's dossier, but may reach contrary judgments about what it means, such as whether the juvenile is a bad boy or a good one. Such a situation leads the participants to propose alternative courses of action about what should be done in a given case. Pollner found much the same situation to obtain in traffic courts, where participants (e.g., a motorist and an arresting police officer) appealed to the same events which occurred on the highway, but insisted on different meanings for them. According to Pollner's analysis of the traffic court setting, all participants involved were oriented to and made use of mundane reasoning, defined by the assumption that the meanings of things are what they appear to be, that they remain stable and unchanging over time, and that they are not subject to (legitimate) different interpretations. (Pollner's research is an especially apt illustration of the shortcomings of the ethnomethodological approach. The verbal accounts proffered in a traffic court rarely if ever correspond to the human experience and the subjective feelings.)

The ethnomethodological studies cited above illustrate the ethnomethodological critique of social science and the general nature of the proposed alternative(s) to it. They provide a foundation for assessing how ethnomethodology and existential sociology differ.

Ethnomethodology and existential sociology

The ethnomethodologists have gone off in many different directions since Garfinkel (1967:1) formulated the first definition of the enterprise. But all still share a similar critique of the existing absolutism of Western social science. In one way or another the point is taken that social scientists have imposed their own criteria on the realities of daily life, thereby distorting their real nature. Ethnomethodologists seek to counter this absolutism with radically relativistic alternatives, each of which intends a faithfulness to the unique, situated, contextual, occasional, reflexive nature of daily actions.

As one moves from the abstract critique of Western social science to the actual ethnomethodological studies, readers are left confused about how the empirical studies differ from earlier ethnographic researches and how they resolved the problems of earlier theories mentioned in the critique. The ethnomethodological studies of the uses of social rules in everyday life have shown that rules are interdependent with actors and situations, that these three continually interact with one another, that actors are not judgmental dopes, and that actors must continually assess a rule's relevance in terms of emergent situations. But most of these general points can also be found in the earlier writings of the symbolic interactionists in sociology. On the other hand, the ethnomethodological studies have *not* shown that they achieve a literal description of the phenomenon of interest, which Sacks (1963) and Cicourel (1964) said is necessary for a scientific understanding. Nor have they shown that ethnomethodological studies avoid the use of commonsensical (undefined, taken-for-granted, unexamined) uses of the language. Neither have they unambiguously demonstrated the utility of following Garfinkel's recommendation to view all human experience as equivalent to the practices used to talk about or describe it. And they have not shown, as Zimmerman and Wieder argued, that social life is primarily or even generally situational or without shared meanings. And the ethnographic research reports by ethnomethodologists have not commonly spelled out how the interpretive practices or operations or rules or procedures relate to what are presented as the findings of the research.

The ethnomethodological models proposed as alternatives to existing social science methods represent attempts to deal (theoretically) with the problems of indexicality and/or reflexivity. Indexicality refers to the crucial importance of the situation or context for understanding the meaning of any communication, and reflexivity refers to the mutual interdependence of observer or knower to what is seen or known. The ethnomethodologists' faith in the realities of indexicality and reflexivity led them to propose alternatives that are consistent with it. We have already mentioned Zimmerman and Wieder's concept of the occasioned corpus, one that presumably remains true to the indexicality of daily communications. This proposal represents a radical situationalism. Much opposed to this are the proposals of Sacks and Cicourel. They have suggested ignoring the indexical nature of daily communications in order to focus on the deep structures or basic rules or invariant properties from which the indexicals of daily communications stem. This alternative represents a radical structuralist resolution to the problems of indexicality and reflexivity. Whereas both these alternatives assert a loyalty to the goals of scientific generalization, others eschew such goals. As scientific generalization must necessarily distort the contextualized nature of everyday realities, Blum and McHugh (1970) have proposed a version of ethnomethodological inquiry that conceives of all analysis and theorizing as nothing more than the analyst's "display of mind," bearing no relationship to any external reality. Mehan and Wood (1975) have proposed a similar alternative; they viewed ethnomethodology as a "way of life," with one of its objectives the articulation and explication of the individual's sense-making processes. Both these represent radical idealist alternatives and tend toward solipsism.

The proposed ethnomethodological resolutions to the problems of indexicality and reflexivity clearly indicate exclusive concerns with purely philosophical issues, cognitive models, and the processual forms of interpretation. The various ethnomethodologies largely represent a reaction against the subject-object dualism implicit in positivist social science. Whereas positivist social science claimed to "speak on behalf of

Nature," the external world, and objective facts independent of the observer, the ethnomethodologies have sought to speak for themselves. Ethnomethodological studies are increasingly being done by those who desire to display their own commitments to indexicality and/or reflexivity, and few ethnomethodologists remain committed to the study of sociological questions or express concern with substantive issues. Even though ethnomethodology and existential sociology stem from similar intellectual traditions (see Chapter 2), this represents an important difference between the two. Existential sociology remains committed to substantive questions; to meaning rather than form; to giving us a better understanding of the world in which we live and create our lives, not just an understanding of what a theorist has had to assume in order to do his work. Ethnomethodological studies are increasingly being conceived of as merely demonstrations of their own definitions of themselves (cf. McHugh et al., 1974; Mehan and Wood, 1975). Insofar as this is so, ethnomethodological inquiries will be increasingly irrelevant to the social sciences and our own self-understandings.

Existential sociology owes allegiance to the whole of human experience, in all its variety, in all its forms. The relevance of language and linguistic accounts to human experience remains to be ascertained, for particular activities; it is not something to be settled by fiat at the beginning of inquiry. One can commonsensically suspect that linguistic accounts are more important for some things, less so for others; but the important point is that one cannot presume this as a matter of preferred definition. Even with respect to the relative importance of the affective versus the cognitive features of given activities (see Chapter 1), the position of existential sociology is not absolutist; it may well be that the cognitive features are predominant for some kinds of activities and the affective for others. Again, the point is that such relations should not be presumed in advance of the experiences or observations. Any sociology that seeks to remain faithful to the entire gamut of human experiences must eschew narrowly conceived definitions of its enterprise; only in this way will we be stimulated to search out the creative self-understandings that are appropriate for our times.

6

Practical reasoning in action

JOHN P. ANDERSON

This chapter reports on observational field research conducted by the author at the San Diego County Community Mental Health Center screening unit between July 1970 and December 1971. The purposes of the study were to explicate the methods staff members used to go about their work at CMH screening and to examine the factors (of whatever nature) that influenced patterns of patient referral from the screening unit. Two lines of thought (epistemologies, concepts of social order) are involved in the research report: (1) elements of what is commonly called ethnomethodology and (2) elements from a variant of more conventional sociology.

As is true of conventional sociology, ethnomethodology has displayed a concern with the problem of order. However, instead of seeing order in purportedly objective patterns of stable interaction between people, ethnomethodology sees order (a familiar social world) as created in the accounts (talk) members exchange with one another. Instead of treating orderly social life as a fact, something in the world out there, ethnomethodology views order as an accomplishment of members' practical reasoning processes — a constructed appearance (Zimmerman and Wieder, 1970). *Practical reasoning* means reasoning oriented to a world "that is presumed to exist independently of the mode and manner in which it is explicated" (paraphrased from Pollner, 1970), and this characterizes both the commonsense reasoning done by members in the course of their everyday lives and the reasoning done by practitioners of science (for detailed consideration of the properties of practical reasoning, see Pollner, 1970).

Thus, though the word *order* remains the same, the substantive topic of concern is actually quite different for the two lines of thought. The same is true concerning what is conceived of as the basis of order. In conventional sociology, the basis of order is assumed to be some set of values held in common by the members. In line with ethnomethodol-

174

ogy's differing orientation on this question, Garfinkel gave the sociological concept of *sharedness* an ethnomethodological formulation and
in this way tried to demonstrate what he saw as the root difference between the two brands of thought: "'Shared agreement' refers to the
various methods for accomplishing the members' recognition that something was said-according-to-a-rule and not the demonstrable matching
of substantive matters. The appropriate image of a common understanding is therefore an operation rather than a common intersection of
overlapping sets" (Garfinkel, 1967:30). The conventional idea of
sharedness as described by overlapping sets (i.e., the set of ideas held by
person A is the same as those held by person B) is replaced by operations people go through to produce the appearance of sharedness (or
anything else). "The mode and manner in which [the world] is explicated" by members is the subject matter for ethnomethodological
study.

The other element of this research report (from more conventional
sociology) is the idea of intentionality: the idea that staff members
intend things by asking the patterns of questions they do and suggesting
referrals for further treatment. Staff members try to find out what the
patient's problem is and make a meaningful referral on that basis. They
also try to find out what the patient intends by coming to CMH:
whether he is there for what they see as a legitimate purpose (i.e., to get
psychiatric help for his psychic problem) or whether he is trying to
make what they see as illegitimate use of the facility (e.g., cut the expense of his habit, escape criminal prosecution). Members of the CMH
screening staff engage in practical reasoning to carry out their intentions with the patients they encounter.

The status of these comments about intentionality should be made
clear at this point. There were obviously always two sides to the interaction at CMH (patients and staff), but in the position of observer, the
author was able to observe only one of the sides (staff) consistently,
when patients were present and when they were not, day in and day
out. The comments made here about patients' intentions are, therefore,
the staff's interpretation. Also, obviously, intention is being treated
both as a topic of investigation (i.e., a members' category) and as a resource for conducting the investigation (i.e., and observer's category).

The aim of this chapter is to examine, in an empirical case, the extent to which the practical reasoning approach is adequate to deal with
the activities people perform in the course of their everyday lives. It
should be noted at the outset that the everyday activities under scrutiny occurred in the context of a formal bureaucracy. Additionally,
these particular activities were probably the most formalized and routinized activities in which staff members commonly engaged. Practically

speaking, this means the investigative approach was used in the context in which it was first developed.

The research report (and argument) are developed in eight sections:

1. An outline of the legal, financial, and organizational context in which screening workers operate, matters having direct bearing on the handling of patients

2. An explanation of the term *constructing treatment problems*, first by providing a contrasting view of screening work (that of finding problems) and then by making and illustrating the distinctions between presenting, real, and treatment problems

3. A fairly detailed examination of the formal methods staff members use in the construction of treatment problems

4. A report on the essentially cooperative nature of the screening interview

5. An explanation of how these formal methods fit into the normal course of the screening interview

6. A report on the typifications about patients that staff members have and the importance of such typifications in constructing treatment problems

7. A demonstration of how these matters impinge on what the members see as the sense of their activities

8. A summary of the major points made in the preceding sections about the nature of constructing treatment problems

Constructing treatment problems

Overview of setting and process

With the passage and implementation of the Lanterman-Petris-Short Act, the Community Mental Health Center in San Diego became the primary public psychiatric evaluation and treatment facility for an area with a population of something over 1 million. All persons seeking public psychiatric aid voluntarily, or referred by some other agency, must first pass through CMH screening, which is where the decision about whether and how to intervene are initially made.

The screening unit operates twenty-four hours a day, seven days a week. The normal complement on the day shift (the only shift observed during the course of the research) was, at the time the research was conducted, two psychiatrists, two social workers, a psychiatric nurse, a clerk-receptionist, and a financial eligibility worker from the Department of Public Welfare, who was attached to the unit but not part of it.

Formally, almost none of the services offered by the CMH screening unit (or by CMH in general) are considered free, and an accounting of all monies owed for services is kept by the county. If persons wish, total payment may be deferred indefinitely, though should they acquire or transfer property some time in the future (transactions that are monitored by the county), the county can demand payment in full. Usually, an agreement is made whereby the patient makes partial payment and the county forgives the remainder of the debt. Ability to pay for them is not a requirement for receiving services, but having too much money may disqualify one from receiving extended services (outpatient or inpatient) at or through CMH. This is to say, anyone can get a screening interview, but only the nonrich can qualify for further care at CMH. All others are referred to a private facility and are billed for the referral.

The center occupies a number of fairly modern one-story buildings adjacent to the new high-rise University Hospital. The screening unit is located in the newest of these buildings, which also holds the superior court psychiatric courtroom, admissions personnel and facilities, and the two locked wards for adults. The outpatient department, most administrative and all financial offices, the children's ward, and the open ward are located in other buildings.

Although there are literally hundreds of possible referral resources available to CMH screening personnel, only a few are used with any regularity. During the time this research was conducted, the overwhelming majority of referrals were to a relatively small number of treatment agencies:

Inpatient
1. In the CMH Center itself, two locked wards for adults (Ward 100 for women, Ward 200 for men) and an open ward (Ward 300) handling both men and women
2. Patton State Hospital, mainly for the mentally ill, but also for alcoholics
3. The Viejas Rehabilitation Center, for the treatment of alcoholics and drug addicts

Outpatient
1. The CMH outpatient department, where patients can come for weekly therapy sessions, and also a number of satellite outpatient clinics located around the county, where patients can be sent for regular therapy sessions near their places of residence and to get their medication prescriptions refilled
2. The CMH Day Center, which operates from 8:30 A.M. to 4:30 P.M. on weekdays
3. The CMH Crisis Group, an open-ended on-going group run

weekday mornings by the outpatient department, to which
patients may be referred without first going through an eligibility interview

4. The University of California's fifth and University Clinic
5. The County—University Hospital Methadone Maintenance
Program

These agencies define the boundaries of possibility within which CMH
screening workers must work. Patients may be referred to these facilities with a high degree of assurance that they will be accepted for
treatment, not shunted back to screening as unsuitable. Indeed, some of
these facilities are required to take anyone screening sends them, and
that is certainly not the case with the far more numerous private treatment agencies. Alcoholics Anonymous' Twelfth Step House, for instance, can and does refuse to accept some of the patients screening
tries to place there.

This list does not include all the referral facilities CMH has used; it
may be impossible to compile such a list. New services are being opened
all the time, and others are being closed (e.g., the Crisis Group was a
relatively new development, and the Viejas facility closed and opened
several times over the course of the research). However, the facilities
listed were the most frequently used during the course of the fieldwork
in response to the diverse problems for which some 2,000 persons per
month seek aid through CMH: alcoholism, drug addiction, family fighting, age and infirmity, unwanted pregnancy, suicide attempt, drug
overdose, sex problems (homosexuality, exhibitionism, child molesting,
incest), anxiety attack, bad trip.

Usually, the screening process begins when the prospective patient
comes to the reception area in the lobby, and the receptionist fills out
an emergency visit form (also called a face sheet). Once this initial information is gathered (name, address, telephone number, religion,
spouse's name and address, employment, name and address of any person accompanying patient) has been gathered, the receptionist checks
her card file for a record of previous visits. The face sheet and card (if
there is one) are then given to or picked up by a social worker. If the
person is brought in by the police or by ambulance, he is taken directly
to a locked admissions lobby and seen by a psychiatrist, without the
intermediate step of an interview with a social worker.

Once the social worker has the form and card, she reads the account
of the previous visit(s) and then calls the person into her office to begin
the interview. During the screening interview, the social worker first
tries to determine what is troubling the patient, and then makes some
recommendation for action. If the recommendation is outpatient therapy, she sends the patient to the eligibility worker, and the responsibil-

ity of the screening unit is at an end. However, if the problem is more serious, and the recommendation entails either administration of psychiatric medication or admission to an inpatient facility, the patient is sent on to see one of the screening psychiatrists.

To do this, the social worker sends the patient back into the lobby and then writes an account of the visit on the screening card. She then takes the card and face sheet to one of the psychiatrists. Occasionally, a social worker makes a verbal presentation of the case to a psychiatrist, especially if she wishes to push some given disposition. More often, however, the psychiatrist just reads the social worker's account of the visit and calls the patient in. The psychiatrist then interviews the patient again and makes recommendations for action. From the psychiatrist, the patient is sent out onto the street or into the wards or referred to the eligibility social worker. With the referral, the formal responsibility of the screening unit for the patient ends.

The work of constructing

The question addressed in this section here is: How do staff members go about transforming the account of personal troubles presented by a patient into the basis for a meaningful referral? There are no doubt many ways to look at the work done by members of the CMH screening unit, but the term *constructing* has deliberately been chosen to emphasize certain aspects of their work. To elaborate on the meanings glossed by this term, it is perhaps best to begin by contrasting it with what may be called the conventional psychiatric view of screening work.

In this conventional perspective the patient is seen as having some sort of illness that manifests itself in certain patterns of behavior, affect, and perception. The job of the screening worker is to discover the nature of this underlying problem during the course of the interview (make a diagnosis) on the basis of the information available (patient's behavior, patient's accounts of his feelings, others' accounts of his behavior). On the basis of this assessment of the problem, the patient is referred to an appropriate treatment facility. It is understood that the underlying problem dictates the type of solution or recommendation made by the screening worker (e.g., schizophrenia and organic brain syndrome require different patterns of treatment).

Constructing a treatment problem is somewhat more complicated. Before examining the process, it is necessary to differentiate among presenting, real, and treatment problems.

The social worker takes that face sheet and screening card into the lobby and calls the patient's name. The patient responds, and they walk down the hall to the social worker's office, where the social worker closes the door and introduces herself (or himself) as "Mrs. (or Mr.) _____ , a psychiatric social worker," and the author as "Mr. Anderson, a sociologist on our staff." With everyone seated, the social worker begins with something like: "What brings you here today?"

The patient responds, however haltingly and inarticulately, with an account of his troubles. This account is the *presenting problem*, the things the patient says are bothering him, and from this account the social worker tries to find out what is psychiatrically wrong with the patient. This "what is psychiatrically wrong with the patient" may be conceived of as the *real problem*, that which is (professionally speaking) at the root of the patient's troubles. To refer back to earlier comments on the conventional psychiatric view of screening work, this is the trouble that is to be found by the staff in the course of the interview.

If the presenting problem is what the patient says his troubles are, and the real problem is what a professional sees the problem as, the *treatment problem* includes those aspects of a patient's troubles the screening staff can do something about (i.e., that is treatable). The treatment problem is the part of the patient's difficulties that can become the basis for a meaningful referral. The presenting problem, the real problem, and the treatment problem are thus not necessarily the same thing, though they are not necessarily discontinuous, either.

To illustrate the difference among them take the case of a divorced white woman of thirty-five, unemployed and receiving payments of aid to families with dependent children, with three children: a son of fifteen who is in a juvenile reformatory, a daughter of thirteen who is in some sort of unspecified trouble (her caseworker accompanies the mother to CMH), and a son of six who is retarded (Down's syndrome). The woman reports feeling nervous, depressed, and unhappy; that she finds herself crying a lot, and is afraid some agency will take her little boy away from her because she is an unfit mother. She is afraid she will be considered an unfit mother because she cannot control her two older children.

From the point of view of the screening social worker, the woman's real problems are legion, but most of them are untreatable. CMH can do nothing about the son's or daughter's legal troubles, or the little boy's retardation, or the possibility that he may be taken from his mother and placed in a state facility. All they can do is prescribe drugs to combat the nervousness and depression and suggest that she begin outpatient therapy in the hope of eventually becoming better able to deal with her fears. The patient outlines a formidable array of real problems, but it is only the problems that CMH has a referral for that are treated, and the screening interview is designed to reveal the treatable aspects of patient's problems.

Of course, the social worker's or psychiatrist's evaluation of the real problem does not necessarily coincide with the presenting problem, even though it did in the above example. A seventy-three-year-old divorced white woman was brought to CMH by the operators of the convalescent hospital where she had been residing for several months. The operators reported that her bills were being paid by Medicare, Medi-Cal, and Social Security, and that she was generally a good patient, one they wanted to keep. But lately she had been demanding to be released, complaining that the operators were brutalizing her and stealing her money. The operators of the hospital were not legally empowered to hold her against her will, though she had been placed there by the Adult Protective Services of the County Welfare Department and though they wanted to keep her.

For her part, the old woman told the psychiatrist that she wanted to leave the hospital, that she wanted to get out on her own and "make some plans." She also asserted that the operators of the hospital were brutal to her, were stealing her money, and were in league with people in the Post Office, who were intercepting and destroying the letters that she wrote to her daughter, actress Jane Powell, asking for aid. The operators told the psychiatrist that the old woman had gotten into trouble with Jane Powell's lawyers over the letters, and the old woman replied that that was "the other Jane Powell, the wrong one," but she had the right one this time.

In this case, the psychiatrist's assessment of the real problem and treatment problem diverged considerably from the patient's presenting problem. Her account was, in fact, treated as something to be taken not as fact, but as evidence of what the real and treatment problems were (senile psychosis).

Consider the case of a twenty-one-year-old divorced white woman. Before bringing her into the office, the social worker read the author screening card account of her previous visit. At that time the patient had reported having approach-avoidance problems and wondered why she was unable to love and keep on loving someone. She was employed as a waitress and at the time of the previous visit had reported that she was planning to get married. The screening worker who had seen the patient had recommended she begin outpatient therapy, and there was a notation on the card to the effect that the patient had begun therapy, but had not continued.

The social worker brought the patient into the office and began asking her questions regarding her discontinued therapy program, to which the patient tersely replied that she just plain did not like group therapy, and that was that. When the social worker asked her about the approach-avoidance problem, the patient cut her off by saying that she did not want to talk about that. She said she wanted help for the real bad problem she had now, which was that she was one month along and just could not be. The social worker said, "Oh, then you're not getting married?" and the patient responded, "That's sure as hell right I'm not getting married and I just *can't* be pregnant." Arrangements for a therapeutic abortion were made in short order. In this case, the presenting, real and treatment problems were the same: unwanted pregnancy.

From these examples, it is possible to begin drawing some inferences about the work done by screening workers and the process that has been referred to as constructing treatment problems. One inference is that not everything a patient says is troubling him can necessarily become the basis for a meaningful referral. There are some troubles CMH can do nothing about. In the case of the divorced white woman with three children cited above, CMH had no capacity whatsoever to deal with the legal problems the two older children were facing, and the social worker consequently did not ask questions about these legal problems, even though they probably had something to do with the woman's depression.

Another inference is that not everything a patient says is necessarily believed by the screening worker. The elderly patient's claim to being the mother of a famous actress was discounted by the psychiatrist and seen instead as a manifestation of the woman's underlying psychiatric problem — senile psychosis. Her claim was not supported by the context in which it was made. This aspect of constructing is more commonly seen in interviews with narcotics addicts and others seeking admission to the closed wards; in these cases, claims to serious psychiatric illness are sometimes very carefully scrutinized.

To show more clearly the importance of context, take the case of a thirty-eight-year-old divorced white woman, who was brought to CMH from the board and care home she had been living in by a worker from the Community Services Division (CSD). The woman insisted that she would no longer remain in the home, that she was active and liked to move around, whereas all the inmates were elderly and bedridden, and that she needed a special diet that the manager of the facility could not provide. The CSD worker backed up her account of her living conditions, and said that she should be readmitted to Ward 100.

The social worker asked if the patient really needed hospitalization or just a place to stay temporarily. The CSD worker told the social worker that the patient was really ill and asked the patient to tell about the voices she had been hearing "again." The patient thereupon claimed to be hearing voices "again." The screening worker pressed them both about the voices, then passed them on to one of the psychiatrists to see about admission to Ward 300 (the open ward). After they left the social worker told the author she did not believe the voices story and thought they just wanted to get the patient admitted because the CSD worker

could not think of anything else to do with her. The background problem (finding a place to live) had made the claim to serious psychiatric
illness unbelievable. Although they had obviously hoped that the woman would be diagnosed as schizophrenic and admitted to one of the
wards, it was clear to the social worker that the real problem prompting
the visit was lack of a place to live; and it was also clear that the social
worker thought this an improper use of CMH facilities (it costs about
$90 per day to keep someone on the closed wards).

Formal aspects of constructing: asking questions

The patient is made the locus of a routine treatment problem during
the course of the screening interview, which is patterned to provide information that is useful to the screening worker. The account a patient
provides may have many dimensions and ramifications, but the staff
brings these problems down to routine proportions by asking only certain patterns of questions, by seeking only certain kinds of information
about certain problems, and leaving many possible areas of inquiry
unexplored. This shaping of a problem as part of the construction process is illustrated in the case of the depressed woman with three children, cited previously. The screening worker did not ask questions
about the children's troubles with the law or how long the son was likely to be incarcerated: These were matters out of the control of CMH.

Several other things about this process should be made clear. One
point, exemplified by the case of the girl seeking an abortion, is that
the screening worker need not always go through a pattern of shaping
questions to find out what the patient's problem is. The unwanted pregnancy was a direct statement of a problem that required no further
elaboration for a referral to be effected. There is thus a difference between the statements "I am pregnant" and "I am feeling depressed."
The screening worker does not ask, "How are you pregnant," but does
need to ask questions about the depression, as shown later in this chapter. Another point, also expanded upon later, is that although methods
exist for bringing problems down to routine proportions, the methods
do not always work.

One implication of what has been said so far is that staff's questions
tend to fall into patterns (e.g., schizophrenia patterns, narcotics addiction patterns), and these patterns of questions are used by the staff to
elicit information that can be used to document various aspects of the
patient's psychiatric condition. If a social worker thinks the patient is
an alcoholic, she asks different questions than she would ask of someone she thought to be schizophrenic.

The kinds of questions asked appears to be heavily influenced by the information available to the screening worker before the interview begins (this information may come from screening card accounts of previous visits or from the report of a person accompanying the patient), as well as by what the patient says during the interview. For instance, a woman brought her son to CMH, complaining that he was disoriented and she suspected he was back on drugs (he was supposedly being treated through the Youth Drug Program at CMH). The social worker began the interview with a series of questions about the date, month, year, day of the week, place, state, and governor (which the patient was able to answer to the worker's satisfaction). In all the months of the research project at CMH, no other interview began with this pattern of questions, though similar patterns appeared in the course of other interviews.

A patient who comes to ask for a refill of his medication prescription is usually treated quite perfunctorily by the social workers. Commonly, only the name of the doctor, the type of medication and dose, the length of hospitalization or therapy, and financial questions are asked, and the patient is sent directly to a psychiatrist. No other problem-finding or problem-shaping questions are asked. Some psychiatrists take an extensive history on even this sort of case, although others issue tranquilizers almost on the social worker's say-so. This pattern is fairly constant among social workers also, though occasionally a social worker tries to sell the patient outpatient therapy.

Some characteristic patterns of questions are:

> *General orientation pattern:* Asking the patient to give the date, day of the week, month, year, city, state, governor, president.
>
> *Schizophrenia pattern:* Asking the patient if he hears voices; if he feels someone is putting ideas into his head; if he feels his thoughts and actions are not his own, that he is a puppet and someone else is pulling the strings; if he feels he has so many thoughts running through his head so fast that he cannot think straight; if he sees things other people do not see; asking him to interpret a common proverb (e.g., "people who live in glass houses shouldn't throw stones")
>
> *Depressive pattern:* Asking the patient if there are long periods when he feels very down; if he feels lacking in pep and energy; if he has ever thought about how he would go about attempting suicide; if he has ever tried to commit suicide; if he cries for no apparent reason; if he can think of any reason he should feel so badly; how long he has felt this way; if he has

ever felt this way in the past; how he is sleeping and eating; if he feels nervous or anxious

Alcoholic pattern: Asking the patient how long he has been drinking "this time"; what he has been drinking and how much per day; where he gets the money to buy liquor; what the alcohol does for him, if he is trying to get rid of some other problem or what; if he has ever been hospitalized before, when, where, for how long, and how many times; if he has ever quit drinking for any length of time; if he has ever had delirium tremens

Narcotics pattern: Asking the patient what he has been using; how much his habit costs; when he had his last fix; how long he has been using; if he has ever kicked before, when, where, and how many times; if he is on probation and who his probation officer is; if he is awaiting trial or under any other legal restraints

There are also more or less general questions that are asked at the beginning of the interview and that can lead to an outpatient referral if the case is not thought to be sufficiently serious to warrant an inpatient referral. Examples of these unstructured questions are the opening lines commonly used by screening workers ("How are you troubled?" "What brings you here today?") as well as probes of various types ("Could you say more about that?" "Why do you think you feel that way?" "What's happening at home?" "Do you get along with everyone there?" "How long has this been going on?"). In the course of these interviews, screening workers occasionally ask one or two questions from the schizophrenia or depressive pattern, but do not pursue that pattern if the patient's responses indicate he is not schizophrenic or depressed.

In addition, there are two types of questions that are asked of almost every patient: those having to do with finances (employment, insurance, income) and those having to do with previous psychiatric experience. The first is asked to screen out persons not financially eligible for extended care through CMH. The second is asked because the information is considered relevant to the formulation of the problem and negotiation of the disposition.

The screening interview as a cooperative venture

On the basis of the patient's answers to these patterns of questions, the staff determines the patient's problem and makes a disposition. This is fairly easy if the patient is moderately knowledgeable and cooperative; it can be extremely difficult if he is not. Nothing demonstrates the problematic nature of this process better than the contrast between interviewing a patient who knows how to be interviewed and answer questions and interviewing one who does not.

To make the screening interview a smooth-running interaction, the patient has to be able to talk about the topics the screening worker thinks are important. He must be able to construct verbal accounts of his activities, thought, and emotions for the worker, and refrain from talking about psychiatrically irrelevant matters (e.g., telling the social worker she is pretty and trying to date her). The psychiatrically inexperienced person may be inarticulate about his troubles and unwilling to open up, so that he fails to give the screening worker enough information. A person who has been in therapy for a while, by contrast, often presents the screening worker with the opposite problem: getting the patient to shut up.

An example of the former is the case of a twenty-seven-year-old black man, who was separated from his wife. After introducing herself and the investigator, the social worker asked, "What brings you here today?" The man replied that his brother said he should come. The social worker asked why his brother had said he should come to CMH. The patient shrugged. The social worker asked the patient if he was having problems. The patient said, "Yeah." The social worker asked what sort of problems he was having. The patient replied that he was unhappy and "didn't feel good."

This interview lasted fully forty-five minutes, during which the social worker did most of the talking (she asked questions) and seldom received more than a monosyllabic response from the patient. She eventually extracted the information that the patient was unhappy because he was separated from his wife, had been living with his brother for the past several months, and was unable to work (he was an unskilled laborer) because he was so upset about the separation. He did "nothin'" all day but maybe watch television, and his brother was getting worried about him. After the patient left (his problem assessed as "situational depression"), the social worker commented that the patient "really made me work."

At the opposite extreme, this same social worker interviewed a divorced white woman in her mid-twenties, who had been brought by a friend to CMH from the family care home in which she had been living. The patient said, in response to, "What brings you here today?" that she wanted to be hospitalized because she was beginning to feel like she did when she'd had to go in before — nervous, depressed, and unhappy, like the world was too much for her to deal with and was going to swallow her up, she was always afraid and confused and couldn't remember things. She said that the medication she was taking was doing this to her, she did not want to take it and had been doing well up until the time the doctor had said she had to start taking it. In response to the social worker's questions, she supplied the names of the drugs she was taking, the places and dates she had been hospitalized before (seven times since 1963).

This was a rather short interview (about ten minutes), partly because the social worker was not going to try to negotiate a disposition with the patient, just send her on to a psychiatrist, but also because she did not have to ask many questions or do much digging. The patient readily supplied all the necessary information, and the social worker had only to write it down; indeed, it was only because of the mass of information to be recorded that the interview lasted as long as it did. There were periods of silence when the social worker just sat and wrote; the patient filled these in with statements about how unhappy she was and by crying.

The difference between these two cases is instructive. Though the black man was able to produce responses recognizable as answers to the social worker's questions, they were not good answers because they provided only minimal information about his problems. The interactional situation in this case was obviously uncomfortable for both parties (though illuminating for the author). It is unclear how any set of purely formal criteria can account for the fact that not every answer recognizable as an answer is interactionally appropriate and helpful. Making a problem visible and amenable to treatment is essentially a cooperative venture. Not only does the social worker have to know what questions to ask and how to ask them, but the patient must know how to answer these questions and talk about his feelings. People who have been in therapy prior to coming to CMH know how to anticipate what the social worker or psychiatrist is going to want to know and can provide this information almost before it is asked for (the sets overlap). The social worker had to do a lot more work to provide treatment in the case of the black man than in the case of the white woman. It takes substantive knowledge to be a good patient, just as it takes knowledge to be a good screening worker.

The normal course of the interview

The screening interview has a normal and predictable course. During the first part of the interview, the social worker or psychiatrist focuses questions on the patient's past and present activities and feelings. When the worker feels that a sufficient amount of appropriate information has been gathered to formulate a treatment problem, she begins to make suggestions for referral to the patient (these are meant as suggestions, even though they may be formed as questions; e.g., "Wouldn't you like to have someone to talk to about your problems on a regular basis?"). Once the social worker or psychiatrist begins asking these kinds of questions, no further informational or problem-shaping questions are usually asked, and the emphasis lies instead on getting the patient to agree to some course of action. This orderly aspect of the interview is perhaps revealed most clearly when it is naturally disrupted; that is, when something happens to throw off the original routine and cause the institution of a new routine.

Consider the example of the young man mentioned above whose mother brought him to CMH because she thought he was disoriented and might be back on drugs (marihuana). The social worker began the interview with a number of orientation questions that the patient was able to answer satisfactorily. Seeing that the patient was not disoriented the social worker then asked him if he was back on drugs; the patient denied he was. The social worker asked him how he had been feeling lately and what he had been doing with himself, and the patient replied that he had been feeling pretty good and spent most of his time watching television. In response to a question about whether he had any plans, the patient shrugged and said no.

The social worker then stated that the records indicated he had been assigned to the day center and asked the patient if he had ever gone. The patient replied that he had gone a few times (three times in two weeks) and then had quit going. The social worker asked him if he would like to try going to the day center again, and the patient said no, he thought the day center was a total loss and would not go back there again. The social worker then asked him if he would be interested in having therapy in some other form, if he would like to have someone to talk with about his problems on an hour-a-week basis. The patient was rather diffident, but shrugged and allowed as how it might be all right.

The social worker told the patient it would be very useful for him to have someone to work on his problem with, but also that it would take work to change himself, and the patient said that he thought something like this might do him some good. While filling out the outpatient referral form (the last bit of paperwork before the patient leaves), the social worker again commented that the patient would really be helped by working with someone on his problems. The patient replied that he'd had lots of courses like that in junior college -- government, psychology, lots of courses like that.

This comment had a rather marked effect on the course of the interview. The social worker stopped writing and looked at the patient, then asked him what he thought the proverb, "People who live in glass houses shouldn't throw stones," meant. The patient laughed slightly, shrugged, and finally came back with an inappropriate response. The social worker then asked him what he thought the expression, "When the cat is away, the mice will play," meant. The patient mumbled something about cows in the field. The social worker then asked him if he ever heard voices, and the patient said he did. In response to questions, he said that the voices came from the television set, that they told him to kill himself, and that so far he had not been paying any attention to them. The social worker then asked him if he would like to go to the state hospital for a while and let the doctors there look him over.

This interview demonstrates a number of things about screening work, in addition to the normal course of a screening interview. The shaping of problems according to the patterns of questions that are asked is quite easily visible. The social worker began the interview with a number of orientation pattern questions, asked a drug pattern question, then negotiated a disposition with the patient. However, after the patient's inappropriate (for the context) comment about the courses he'd had, the social worker launched into a full-scale pattern of schizophrenia questions. The patient's problem had initially been defined as an adjustment reaction, and the referral was to the outpatient department. After the second round of questions, the patient was diagnosed as schizophrenic and agreed to go to the state hospital. The social worker moved from one set of problem-shaping questions to another after the interview had almost completed its normal course.

This brings up an important point, in light of our concern with ethnomethodology. Although treatment problems are undeniably shaped by the patterns of questions asked in the course of the interview, they are also undeniably influenced by the specific answers given to the specific questions. Put differently, the initial diagnosis in this case (adjustment reaction) would be commonsensically viewed as an error: The patient's actual problem was not adjustment reaction, but schizophrenia, and the screening worker simply did not ask the right questions the first time around to bring this out.

Types of patients, problems, and motivations

In the course of formulating treatment problems and effecting meaningful referrals, screening workers use some shared ideas about patients and dimensions of their problems (these might be called typifications of the type of patient who went with the type of problem) to guide both the problem-formulating process and the negotiation of a referral.

A report on the latter is far beyond the scope of this paper. In regard to the former, it can be said that some of the elements of these typifications can be seen in frozen form in the patterns of questions examined above. These patterns are designed to cover those areas of behavior, affect, and perception the staff believes to be involved in the various psychiatric problems. These typifications are usually most elaborately developed for those classes of patients who are seen as having serious (i.e., hospitalizable) problems and who are encountered frequently by the staff. These include alcoholics, heroin addicts and users of other drugs (e.g., barbiturates, amphetamines, glue, paint), and the seriously mentally ill (depressives and schizophrenics).

Included in these typifications are certain assertions about the behavior of patients. Commonly, it is thought that there is a hospitalization-release-readmission cycle for alcoholics, heroin addicts, and the chronically mentally ill (this appears to be the defining criterion for chronicity). Patients are admitted to a hospital or some other facility for a period of drying out (kicking the habit, getting settled down), then go back on the outside for a while, where they sooner or later take up their old habits (alcohol or drugs) or begin to feel the pressure of a less-structured environment, and eventually are brought back in.

That the staff assumes this cyclic behavior for alcoholics, addicts, and the chronically mentally ill does not mean that the staff views all such patients the same way. Several characteristics are imputed by the staff that distinguish these types from one another. For instance, the alcoholic and heroin addict are seen as somehow more blameworthy for their problems than the chronically mentally ill; they are seen as people who should have greater voluntary control over their behavior, whereas the mentally ill person is seen as more helpless. This is manifested in the staff's taking a generally harder line with alcoholics and addicts than with the chronically mentally ill.

Furthermore, addicts and alcoholics are seen as often quite blatantly manipulative in their relations with the staff and services at CMH; the mentally ill are sometimes seen this way too, but less censure appears to be attached to their manipulativeness. For example, a twenty-three-year-old white male narcotics addict came in seeking admission to the closed ward for initial detoxification and then transfer to the open ward (300) for continued treatment. He said he had been detoxified on ward 200 three months ago, and the ward psychiatrist had recommended that he go on to Ward 300 for continued treatment. He said that he hadn't wanted to stay in the hospital at that time because his wife was thinking of leaving him, and when she finally did, he went all to pieces and back on heroin. The social worker asked how much he was using, and the man replied "three or four spoons" (he was a fairly heavy user).

He said that since his wife and he had split up, he'd been doing a lot of thinking about the things the psychiatrist had said to him while he was on the wards, and had come to understand some things about himself. He said he realized that the heroin was just symptomatic of his dependence on his wife, as the doctor had said, and now he was really ready to start working on these problems and overcome them. His face fell a foot when the social worker told him that Viejas Rehabilitation Center was the only place he could get in, that he would have to sign himself in for from three to six months. The man said he heard as much, but thought he might as well try to get into CMH anyway. After he left, the social worker commented that he was just trying to talk his way onto the wards to cut the expense of his habit and that he would have found some other excuse to avoid going onto Ward 300 this time. If he had been really serious about trying to kick the habit, the social worker thought he would have taken the Viejas offer.

This attitude of distrust is caused by what the staff sees as the motivations people have for coming to CMH; thus, inquiry into patients' motives becomes an important part of screening work. But staff members do not make such inquiries directly; they assess a patient's motivations or intentions by attending to certain contextual features of the patient's situation, as these are reported to them, that influence the believability of the patient's assertions (e.g., of illness, of a desire to rehabilitate himself). The narcotics addict just cited and the woman seeking admission who claimed to be hearing voices "again" are cases in point.

Thus, whereas the mentally ill patient is thought to be seeking help, the addict is suspected of attempting to use the facility for his own ends (to cut the expense of his habit). Also addicts are thought to use admission to CMH as a means of avoiding arrest or prosecution for their illegal activities or of impressing probation officers or judges with the sincerity of their efforts to rehabilitate themselves. For this reason, questions are always asked about an addict's legal status, and if he is in legal trouble, CMH will not touch him. The attitude toward alcoholics is apparently somewhat more ambivalent.

Whereas the addict and alcoholic are seen as persons who should be able voluntarily to control their problems, the mentally ill are spoken of as almost helplessly unregulated. They are seen as people who need to have some structuring imposed upon them from without, and this is what admission to the wards of CMH or to the state hospital is said to provide. Admission to one of these facilities is spoken of as something to "settle them down," "impose some regulation on them," with the aim of eventually "stabilizing them at some level of functioning," which prepares them for release. The same terminology is used in speaking of the effects of psychiatric drugs: They are said to have a stabilizing influence on the person and allow him to make some level of adjustment on the outside.

However, to say that the staff views the mentally ill differently from the alcoholic or drug addict is not to say that the staff does not see them as manipulative also. The chronically mentally ill patient has had extensive experience with psychiatry, usually reaching back many years and involving more than one psychiatric facility. It is thought that when life gets too rough on the outside, the patient develops his symptoms again (the degree of conscious deliberation attributed to the patient is ambiguous) and tries to get, as one psychiatrist put it, "back to the womb." Thus, though the mentally ill patient is likely to be admitted if he asks to be and can demonstrate his symptoms, there is some prejudice on the part of psychiatrists toward changing or adding to his medications (e.g., adding chloral hydrate for sleeping, increasing the dose of tranquilizers), and sending him back home for a few days "to see how you will be able to do with this new regimen."

Finally, the staff members seem to be rather pessimistic about the chances of curing the people they see, so much so that it is rare for them to say anything to the effect that some patient has a good prognosis. For instance, after interviewing a patient, a social worker commented to the author that the patient seemed "motivated for therapy," but then acknowledged hating to say things like that, because patients "so often disappoint you." Similarly, after sitting in on an interview with a chronically schizophrenic white woman of twenty-three the author commented (in response to the social worker's question) that he was surprised to see a chronically mentally ill person with that much "personality" — mobility and facial expression, wit, vocabulary (considering she had only a tenth-grade education). The social worker said yes, and that she probably had a file a foot thick up at the hospital, reporting people's attempts to help her. In ten years the file would be two feet thick, and in another ten they'd quit trying. Repeated disappointment takes its toll.

The sense of screening work

Earlier in this chapter reference was made to the methods staff members utilize for standardizing and characterizing the troubles patients report to them. It was also asserted that although methods exist for bringing problems down to routine proportions, the methods do not always work. Whether or not the methods work can be judged only in terms of an understanding of the way staff members view the purpose of their work with the patients.

One might categorize the work done by members of the screening unit as people shuffling. A person comes to them with a sad story and a request for help, and they always respond by sending him to see someone else. Given the general sense of pessimism expressed by staff members about their patients' chances for cure or substantial improvement, it might be thought that the staff could well see their work as a form of people shuffling. However, they do not.

The sense of screening work is that they, as therapeutic agents, are providing the patient with short-term therapeutic help and giving him a meaningful referral. This does not imply that staff members see a referral as a solution to the patient's problem in any absolute sense; it only means that the patient may get help for his problems if he faithfully follows through the course of action decided upon in the screening interview. In other words, a *meaningful referral* is one that the staff believes holds out the hope of betterment to the patient, if he does his part. To the staff, doing screening work usually means more than just people shuffling. The fact that we have examined meaningful referrals and asserted that the methods do not always work clearly implies that screening workers do make nonmeaningful referrals. Some patients have legitimate psychiatric problems that CMH screening can simply do nothing about, and screening workers know quite well that the referrals they give hold out no hope of help for these patients. An examination of some of the highly problematic cases where this has occurred illustrates the contingencies faced by screening workers.

Take, for example, the case of a married white woman in her middle thirties who came in one afternoon for an emergency interview. She complained to the social worker that she had been experiencing a long series of epileptic seizures and wanted help for this. She reported having been on Ward 300 for a period and was still in therapy with one of the doctors there, but had been unable to reach him when she needed help "this time." She said she had been talking and ventilating as she had been taught to do by her therapist, but this had had no influence on the rate at which she had been having the seizures. She reported being so depressed by this condition that she was thinking of killing herself. The social worker asked her what medications she was taking, and she said none -- she was allergic to all the anticonvulsant drugs used to treat epilepsy.

The social worker told the woman she would have to see one of the screening psychiatrists and asked her to wait in the lobby. The social worker then presented the case to one of the psychiatrists. On finding that the woman was allergic to the medications, the psychiatrist's reaction was, "Oh, no, you're not shoving her off on me." The social worker reported having no idea what to do with her either. The psychiatrist found out who the woman's therapist was and stayed on the phone until the doctor could be located and someone was sent over from the ward to accompany her there.

A number of points can be made about this case. It can be said that the sets evidently overlapped quite well, in that the woman was able to present her account well, and the social worker had to ask very few questions. The patient knew how to speak the psychiatric language and appeared to be highly motivated for treatment, but her presence and predicament were highly distressing to the staff involved.

The fact that her case could be written up for the records as a rationally accountable referral appeared to mean nothing to the staff members who had to deal with her, as far as their emotional response to the situation was concerned. Staff commitment appeared to be toward making the system really work, and there was no way to get around the fact that hers was an untreatable problem. People shuffling was thus the meaning that case handling had in this instance. Neither of the staff members was able to maintain the sense of short-term help and meaningful referral in the face of what was seen as a totally intractable problem: the woman's allergy to anticonvulsant drugs. They could not help her, so they got rid of her as soon as possible.

Another example is the case of a twenty-five-year-old male Chicano. In response to the social worker's "What brings you here today?" he replied that he was tired of hustling for a living, wanted to quit that life, and had heard he could get help at CMH for his problem. The social worker asked him what his problem was, and the patient replied, "Heroin." The social worker asked him how long he had been using and how much he was using. The patient replied that he'd been on and off since he was twenty and used whenever he could score.

The social worker told him the only thing they had was the Methadone Maintenance Program at County-University Hospital, and the patient responded that he'd been on it and quit. He asked about going up to the Honor Camp (Viejas), and the social worker told him that Viejas was no longer accepting narcotics users and that the methadone program was all they had. The patient said that he didn't want to go back to that and expressed the belief that they wouldn't take him back anyway. The social worker again said, "That's all we have," and wrote out the phone number of the program on a slip of paper. The patient rather disgustedly took the paper and walked out, terminating the interview. After the patient left the room, the social worker commented to the author that "the guy is probably right" that the methadone maintenance program would not take him back and stated that their waiting list was "months long" anyhow. It thus appeared that the screening worker knew quite well that the referral given the patient was in fact no referral at all and had been given only because there was nothing else to do with the patient. At that time, with Viejas closed to addicts, heroin addiction was de facto an untreatable problem.

The course and outcome of this interview reinforce the point that not every legitimate real problem brought to CMH is a treatable problem. In addition, they demonstrate that what is a treatable problem can vary over time. For example, at no time in the past did CMH have a meaningful referral for the epileptic woman who was allergic to anti-convulsant drugs, and it is perhaps doubtful that they will have one soon. However, had the addict appeared at CMH one month earlier, when Viejas was still accepting addicts, or some time later, when Viejas was again accepting addicts, his problem would have been a treatable one. In other words, whether a problem can be made into a treatment problem is entirely a matter of what referral resources are available, and these resources vary over time. When referral resources are unavailable, or when the ones available are not meaningful, screening workers ex-perience difficulties maintaining the sense of their activities. For these patients, their methods do not work.

Summary

The preceding discussion examines in some detail the ways in which staff members of the San Diego CMH Center screening unit go about transforming the account of personal troubles presented by a patient into the basis for a meaningful referral. The features of the convention-al psychiatric view of screening work are briefly elaborated, to provide a comparison with the constructionist account of screening work devel-oped later.

The distinction is made among presenting problems (what the patient says is troubling him), real problems (the professional view of what his problem is), and treatment problem (those aspects of patients' prob-lems that are treatable). Several cases are reviewed to illustrate the general proposition that the three problems are not necessarily the same, but are not necessarily discontinuous. The cases presented illus-trate (1) that not everything a patient says is troubling him is part of the treatment problem ultimately formulated, and (2) that not all of the symptoms a patient reports are necessarily believed by the screening staff.

In examining some of the formal aspects of problem construction, we report on the patterns of questions used by the staff to elicit certain kinds of information necessary to formulate a routine treatment problem. It is noted that some problems require extensive elaboration (many questions are needed to assess the problem), and some others require almost no elaboration at all. It is also suggested that although methods exist for formulating problems along routine lines, these methods (i.e., asking these standard patterns of questions) do not always result in the formulation of a treatable problem.

The features of the screening interview as a cooperative venture are examined, and the point is made that not only does the screening worker have to know what questions to ask and how to ask them, but the patient must know how to answer such questions. A good patient knows what features of his activities, perceptions, and emotions the staff member is interested in and is able to report on such matters; the psychiatrically inexperienced patient presents difficulties to the screening worker. Illustrative cases are given in support of this major point.

We then review the normal course of the screening interview and illustrate that normal course with a case in which it was disrupted. In light of our concern with ethnomethodology, the shaping of treatment problems according to the questions asked is reviewed, and the point is made that the specific utterance of the patient disrupted the interview, not the question asked. The point is therefore strongly emphasized that the treatment problem ultimately formulated depends not only on the questions asked, but also on the substantive answers given.

Next, we report on certain typifications staff members held regarding patients and link these typifications both to the patterns of questions asked by the staff during the course of the interview and the staff's concern when imputing motives to their patients. The point is made that staff members are generally pessimistic about patients' chances for cure or permanent improvement.

Finally, and in light of all this, we examine the sense that screening work makes to its practitioners. We suggest that members define the purpose of screening work in terms of making a referral that holds out the hope of betterment to the patient, if he follows through on it. Having already outlined a case where only part of a patient's real troubles is treatable, we examine two cases where *no* part of the real troubles is treatable and suggest that staff members cannot maintain the sense of their activities under these conditions. The final point is made that what constitutes a treatable problem can vary over time, as the availability of treatment varies.

Screening work thus appears as a highly contingent pattern of social interaction. The screening worker seeks to provide short-term therapeutic help and meaningful referral to the patient, but, according to the specific problem the patient has and the availability of treatment resources, he may fail in this endeavor. Substantive matters, therefore, seem to be involved in every phase of constructing treatment problems.

Discussion

One of the elements of this study is intentionality: the intentions of the staff members in asking questions of the patients and suggesting referrals and the intentions imputed to the patients for coming to CMH. Staff members carry out their intentions in the situation initially by asking questions of the patient, but the specific problem that is formulated (even whether a treatment problem is formulated at all) depends on the substance of the response. An assessment of the patient's intention in seeking aid at CMH is made in the same fashion.

Staff members and patient both receive opportunities to demonstrate their skills at practical reasoning in each encounter, but practical reasoning is only a part of action. Action must also be seen as guided in its course by substantive matters. Staff members have to know which problems they may take as self-evident and needing very little elaboration, what questions to ask to develop the features of certain types of problems, which background features may be seen as crucial in assessing the patient's intention and suitability for treatment.

Members of the CMH screening staff are engaged in practical reasoning when they are asking questions of patients, when they are trying to construct familiar problems and effect familiar solutions. Practical reasoning as done in the CMH Center is just that: practical. Reasoning practices are not given free play to make something out of nothing: The context places restraints on what can and cannot be done. A meaningful referral can sometimes be made easily and as a matter of course, but it can also be impossible, and no amount of interpretive work will allow the worker to maintain the normal sense of his activities.

In fact, it appears that the only place where practical reasoning procedures can make something out of nothing is in the formal records, made after the fact — as in the case of the epileptic woman. In the recorded account, her visit appears normal in its course and outcome to anyone reading it, but her visit was anything but normal to the staff members who experienced it. Limiting one's investigations to formal records means that most of the human aspects of situated interaction cannot be approached.

In making this implicit comparison of the normative and interpretive paradigms and in criticizing the latter, one must also touch on the matter of the researcher's analytic intent. It is no doubt possible to subject transcriptions of screening interviews to the same sort of analysis to which one might subject any other instance of story telling. But, although such an analysis might reveal the invariant features of all social interaction (in terms of the features of practical reasoning, the sequencing of talk), it will tell an investigator precious little about what elements influence the sort of problem formulated and the sort of disposition made. Both these issues are critical if one wishes to say something about why certain patients are given one type of referral (e.g., inpatient) and other patients given another (e.g., outpatient). Story telling in the context of a psychiatric interview has features that differ (e.g., in consequences) from story telling at home or in a work group.

The author has been critical of ethnomethodolgy from a position on the outside, in that he is unwilling to deny science the special and privileged position it enjoys as something more than and better than common sense, though it must be recognized that science and common sense share some initial assumptions and formal properties (see Garfinkel, 1967). At the same time, it must be recognized that the ethnomethodological critique has profound implications not only for how we should go about sociology, but for the nature of the scientific endeavor itself.

All representations of the world — scientific, ethnomethodological, or common sense — are of necessity glosses. They can be expanded indefinitely. However, the inference one can draw from this can be different from what some ethnomethodologists apparently want to draw, but always stop short of (i.e., that science is impossible). One can equally infer that scientists must penetrate (or elaborate) the gloss enough to accomplish their purposes. Sociologists have for too long been content with merely the gloss of order and so have expended large amounts of intellectual energy and uncounted hours of computer time for precious little result. They have assumed common meanings, not investigated them; they have assumed order, not investigated its production. By making us aware of these matters and by raising these possibilities, ethnomethodology may help make us better sociologists.

PART IV

Beyond the rational frontwork

7

Behind the rational appearances: fusion of thinking and feeling in sociological research

JOHN M. JOHNSON

It is difficult to remember the exact details of our personal experiences, and those of our friends, when we took the first sociology class at the university. One need not know all the intricacies of physiological or cognitive psychology to recognize the difficulty. Indeed, it is entirely possible that some of the most pervasive features of our personal lives at that time have been altogether forgotten.

What were some of those personal thoughts and feelings so crucial for understanding our actions and those of our friends? Feelings of infatuation for the attractive individual sitting in the second row? Boredom? The tug and pull of those sexual fantasies that seem inevitably to intrude on one's concentration on the distinctions between patrilineal, matrilineal, exogamy, endogamy, conjugal, and consanguine? Sympathy for the neophyte instructor who did not have it all together? Resentment toward that arrogant professor at the lectern? Fears of not making the grades, of being drafted, of being rejected as a pledge to your mother's sorority? Fears of being caught using Jacob's term paper or having Dale take one of the exams for you? A sense of fascination upon learning that suicides are caused by conditions about which the suicidal individuals are not aware? Or was it that first sense of cultural vertigo upon learning of the sexual customs of Eskimos, the exchange rituals of the Kula, the medical practices of the Azande (and perhaps the American Medical Association), the mortification rituals of the BaMbuti, the business practices of the men who manage, the political activities of those in a small town of a mass society, the nature of the tearoom trade, pederasty, prison homosexuality, and all those other exotic topics somehow overlooked in the civics class at the Warren Harding—Eugene Debs consolidated high school in Indianapolis? A confusing bewilderment with the implicit suggestion that *everything*

201

about human living could be some other way? Was that the semester when one began to develop a lust, or perhaps disgust, for organized bodies of knowledge? And ditto for poetry. Was that the "lost semester" when Jack left school with thirty bucks and a copy of Kerouac's *On the Road* in his pocket, to seek adventure as a dishwasher in Florida? Or was that the one when we went 27-0 during the season, but lost the first round of the play-offs? Was that when Stuart was killed in the accident? Was that when Mom and Dad got a divorce? When one pauses to reflect, it is difficult to recall all those complexities of our personal lives and how they affected us at the time.

Whatever else may have been involved in our lives during our participation in the introductory sociology class, one can observe all these were unimportant. At any rate, they were not on the exams. But all of us intuitively recognize the pervasiveness and importance of such features and many others not mentioned. Such thoughts and feelings, from the big ones to the little ones, are invariably related to our daily conduct. They are the important, meaningful stuff of our personal lives. When viewed in this context, our written answers on the sociology exams are little more than a facade of rational studentry.

Some of us may have been motivated to take the first sociology class by the hope that sociology had something to tell us about the many complexities of our personal lives. Even more importantly, perhaps it could tell us how our lives relate to our contemporaries making up that mysterious entity called society. This kind of natural interest and curiosity accounts for some of the existing good fortune of academic sociology. But the chances are great we waded through a considerable amount of material either unrelated or only tangentially related to our natural curiosities. Our instruction was to think of sociology as both a profession and science. One of the venerable sociological traditions, so we learned, consists of making distinctions between scientific knowledge and our commonsense knowledge of daily affairs. These distinctions were claimed as the grounds not only for considering the two forms of reasoning as fundamentally distinct, but for judging the former as superior. On the high authority of this tradition, we learned, for example, that commonsense knowledge is often incompatible and inconsistent, whereas scientific knowledge exhibits logical relations among its propositions. This appears plausible as long as one is not too diligent in comparing the logical propositions in sociology with those in anthropology, psychology, humanities, business, political science, or history.

Claims of the superiority of scientific knowledge are based on several grounds. The most important concerns the methodology of scientifically conducted research. Those who do science claim the possession of a set of formally rational cognitive criteria, called the *scientific method*, which is systematically used to assess critically the probative sense of the evidence about a given problem. The purpose of the formally rational criteria is to exercise control over all empirical observations so that the observational records of an investigation are not affected in any significant manner by the subjective or personal characteristics of the observer. This presumably excludes such features as the observer's religious, political, or ethical values from the observations. The argument is that when one sincerely uses these criteria, the observations are actually or potentially capable of independent verification by others. Put differently, the factual character of scientific observations is considered warranted to the extent competent investigators use the formally rational criteria of the scientific method. In the introductory sociology class, we were instructed to conceive of the dual principles of controlled observation and independent verification as definitive of the *essence* of scientific conduct. All other distinctions, such as those commonly made between quantitative and qualitative methods or hard and soft data were to be viewed as different strategies to effect the common goal of all scientists. This goal was the development of an apodictic (absolutely objective) body of knowledge purged of all the subjective elements of common sense.

When one is concerned with the methods used to establish certain claims to scientific truth, presumably the relevant questions are those asking *how* the claims were generated or *how* the research was accomplished. These are the important issues if the research is to be independently verified by other observers. For a given investigation, the observer may have been personally motivated by the hope that the research would be a step toward the realization of some abstract ideal concerning the ultimate purposes of the research. This might include abstract ideals like advancing knowledge, bettering mankind, alleviating human suffering, solving social problems. But such teleological justifications are methodologically irrelevant. For methodological purposes, the important ones are the how questions, not the why questions. When we recall the intimate linkages between what are considered scientific facts and the methods used to produce them, it is easier to understand why introductory sociology classes devote so much time to this topic and why a course in methodology is usually required for all sociology students.

As we reflect on our understanding of the intricate fusions of thinking and feeling in our personal lives and compare this with what the traditional methodological literature tells us about the conduct of scientific research, we are confronted with a paradox. All of us recognize, on the one hand, the importance of our private feelings for how we act in our daily lives. There is a vast range of human feelings, and only a few of them have been mentioned here. But the relevance of feelings of sexual desire, resentment, infatuation, competition, fear, and all the rest is unmistakable for understanding what we do in our practical affairs. On the other hand, the traditional methodological literature of the social sciences instructs us to believe that *none* of these features is present in the conduct of an actual research investigation.

If we review the methodological writings with an eye to discovering how scientists conceive of their actual conduct as scientists (i.e., the implied model of rational scientific practice), we discover an idealization that is unrecognizable as any actual person in our everyday lives. With only a few exceptions, there are no appreciable differences between the hypothetical-statistical (quantitative) and analytical-inductive (qualitative) approaches in terms of the implicit model of rational scientific conduct. This idealized model of competent scientific inquiry implies a Rational Observational Boob. For pedagogical purposes, we can personalize the model with the name "Rob." What kind of man is Rob?

Rob is, first and foremost, a man of absolute intellectual principles. When selecting his problem for scientific research, he chooses to investigate only that which ties in with some abstract body of general theory. And he does that only after a thoroughgoing review of all the literature with any conceivable relevance to the problem. He bears little resemblance to the graduate students we knew in school. Those people studied suicide because of a seething incomprehension of why a brother shot himself; studied homosexuality because they were homosexual; studied old age homes because there was a grant available to do it; studied welfare agencies, hospitals, or banks because their spouses were social workers, nurses, or tellers; studied some criminally inclined juvenile gang because they wanted to make some intelligible sense out of their biography; or studied the linguistic minutiae of commissary conversations in a factory because that was the chief interest of the chairman of the thesis committee. Rob has, and will have, none of this. He is an intellectual's intellectual, unconcerned with and restrained by any such worldly practicalities.

Second, Rob is a man with an absolutely singular purpose. Having chosen his scientific problem and rigorously designed the investigation, his daily living embodies the resolute commitment to the research. He is not like the rest of us who must continually balance and manage our multiple practical involvements in our families, jobs, love affairs, friendships, recreational activities, and politics. For Rob, such multiple involvements never include conflicts among them, playing one off against another, doing less than one might otherwise desire. The literature asks us to believe, for example, that a researcher doggedly puts in a sixteen-hour work day for a period in excess of several years (Blau, 1963:269–305). And not once, so we are told, is this maddening ritual interrupted to help a friend in need, repair the toilet, renew a driver's license, fight a peripheral struggle at work, partake of an afternoon tryst, or just plain loaf on a bad day.

Third, Rob is a man of formal rationality. Unlike the rest of us, who sometimes do things and then figure out reasons for them after the fact, Rob always knows, for example, what course of action he will elect in order to effect the most beneficial results for the research prior to engaging in any course of actual conduct. As our information is always incomplete, Rob's preselected course of action may be subsequently altered, of course, as additional information becomes available. But these alterations of research practice are also always made on rational grounds.

Finally, Rob is an unimpeachable utilitarian. Having selected the problem, designed the research, and charted a formally rational observational protocol, he weighs all subsequent actions in terms of their utility for yielding efficacious research results. The implicit imagery of the sociological researcher is an iron-willed, steel-nerved, cunning Machiavellian manipulator of the tools of everyday discourse.— all in consideration of research utility. The traditional methodological literature instructs us never to discuss politics, ethics, or sex with the societal members from whom we solicit information. This is likely to turn them off for purposes of the research. The traditional program advises against using the language to judge, evaluate, criticize, argue, cajole, or make fun of others. Conspicuously absent from the literature is any mention of using our social competencies for expressive purposes. Indeed, although the insightful analyses of Erving Goffman are usually credited with enhancing our understandings of the expressive meanings of everyday communications, the methodological literature cites Goffman's works to recommend an investigative policy of using these understandings for more useful research results (Scott, 1959). It is not too farfetched to speculate that Rob might even follow Balzac's advice about retaining the semen to effect more lucid expositions of one's ideas. Clearly, the idealized model of scientific practice depicted here is a rational boob rather than a robot; if we ever encountered a jerk such as this in our everyday lives, we would not give him the time of day. For Rob, the taken-for-granted world view is solely that of traditional (or Continental) rationalism. Apparently one must share this perspective to play the scientific research game.

Constructing an idealized model possesses the advantage of highlighting certain unexamined features of many writings, in this instance

the model of rationality implied throughout the methodological literature. But it possesses the fault of ignoring all the qualifications and
equivocations. It is not entirely correct to assert that the topic of personal feelings has gone wholly unnoticed by researchers. There are some
exceptions to the idealized model here personalized as Rob. But they
are few. More importantly, when personal feelings are noted, they are
not accorded serious consideration. One example is William Whyte's
(1955) expression of embarrassment, and even fear, upon being threatened with physical harm as a result of an inappropriate advance toward
one of the girls in a street-corner tavern. Another example is Rosalie
Wax's (1952) reflection that getting drunk on sake decreases one's
ability to record field notes. A third example is Donald Roy's (1970)
partial explanation of why he has continued his research studies with
labor union organizing campaigns for several decades: "I must admit
that conversing with working stiffs is for me a matter of taking the line
of least resistance." And there are additional exceptions to the idealized
model.

The traditional literature on sociological field research is relatively
clear in its emphasis on the crucial importance of establishing relations
of trust with those in the setting where the research is conducted. Given
this emphasis, perhaps it is not entirely unexpected that certain ties of
intimacy might result from such endeavors. There is, in fact, one author
who glosses such intimacies in a three-page journal article on the problems of overrapport (Miller, 1953). The phrase explains why so few sociologists win Pulitzer prizes. What is more surprising is that so few have
mentioned this, whether by the name of overrapport or some other. So,
although there are some exceptions and qualifications to the idealized
model, on the whole it is impossible to review the methodological literature in the social sciences without reaching the conclusion that in
sociological research the ban on having feelings is of the nature of the
incest taboo. One scholar who has seriously considered the fusion of
thinking and feeling is Kurt Wolff. He addressed this issue while reviewing the anthropological and sociological research literature and as a
major focus of his reflections on his research experiences at Loma, a
small Mexican village, spanning two decades of work. Reviewing the
methodological writings, Wolff analyzed the common field research
phenomenon by which the observer transforms all interactional and
affective elements of an action into *cognitive* problems:

The relevance of what is observed is transformed into theoretical relevance, and the
relevance of the observer into theoretical interest. Even the field worker's confusion
has a purely theoretical meaning; when he writes, "I did not clearly see any reason
why I should enquire into one matter rather than another," there is no affective or
interactive component in his meaning: interaction and affect are limited for him

to interaction with and affect for cognitive problems, although they are more purely limited and more passionate, more unconditional within these limits than anywhere else in a community study that I know of. It is as if Bateson's humanity was absent from relations with the people he lived with and studied and had been wholly absorbed in his burning theoretical concern. [Wolff, 1964:256]

The Bateson study about which Wolff wrote is, according to his analysis, characterized by the transformation of all affective elements of living into cognitive problems. But he concluded that just the opposite occurred during his five field studies at Loma between 1940 and 1960:

It was years before I understood what had happened to me; I had fallen through the web of "culture patterns" and assorted conceptual meshes into the chaos of love; I was looking everywhere, famished, with a "ruthless glance." Despite admonitions to be selective and form hypotheses that would tell me what to select, I was not and did not. Another thing I sensed was that I was not content with the probable but wanted to *know*; and I thought I might *know* if, instead of looking for culture patterns, for instance, I looked directly — not through the lens of *any* received notion but the adequate lens that would come out of my being in Loma. "Culture pattern," indeed any conceptual scheme, had come to strike me as something learned *outside* Loma that I would import, impose, and that had been imposed on me. Instead, I was busy, even panicky at times, observing, ruminating, recording as best I could. Everything, I felt, was important, although the ways in which it was important would yet have to become clear. But then there was also the fear that I should be overwhelmed by the mass of my notes; I could not possibly keep in mind all the veins, lodes, and outcroppings of that growing mountain of typescript. [Wolff, 1964:235; emphasis in original]

The "chaos of love" Wolff subsequently conceptualized as "surrender." There were several distinct dimensions of meaning of surrender for Wolff, but he argued that the essential or core meaning is *cognitive love*. He made clear, however, that this concept represents a *retrospective* interpretation:

I can give no excerpts from my field notes that would exemplify or analyze these meanings. The reason is, as I have said, that I had not surrendered to Loma beyond the low degree of being most tensely alert to what was going on around me; what was going on in myself had not yet begun to announce itself as relevant to my enterprise. Hence there is no record — or at least none that I could present in a brief excerpt — of self-observation which would show involvement, identification, or hurt. [Wolff, 1964:237]

Wolff's reflections on his field research experiences are presented here in some detail because this is *the one stance* in the methodological writings where the fusion of thinking and feeling has been considered seriously, where this issue has been treated as something more than an anecdote. Wolff expressed a deep sense that his feelings were a crucial part of the project, even one of the fundamental determinants of what the observer saw and reported as findings of the investigation. And yet, no observations or records were made on these phenomena at the time.

There is no record to assess their influence, if any, on the validity of the observational data. All we have is a retrospective interpretation of a cognitive love for the members of Loma; no lust, feelings of sensuality, hatred, disgust, anger, ecstasy, bewilderment, or even stomach pains, but a cognitive love. Thus, in the one instance where the fusion of thinking and feeling was seriously addressed as one of the problematic relevancies of actual research conduct, our instruction is to believe that on those rare occasions when a scientific research observer feels, he only does so thinkingly.

The remainder of this chapter intends a partial discussion and analysis of some of the fusions of feelings and thoughts present in my field research investigations of social welfare (Johnson, 1975). The research project was undertaken to fulfill the requirements for a doctoral dissertation in sociology. The field observations were conducted with the Child Welfare Services (CWS) social workers in five satellite (district) offices located in two metropolitan county departments of public welfare. The project originated during the fall of 1969. The observations began at the Lakeside Office in May 1970, and the major portion of the actual field research was done at the Metro Office between July 1970 and May 1971. Irregular return visits to the offices and occasional contacts with the social workers have continued since the termination of the fieldwork.

When the field research investigation of CWS began, one of the original plans was to make the social research process itself a topic for recording and analyzing. As initially conceived, this plan was viewed as of secondary importance. My personal thoughts about the priority of a plan such as this are succinctly expressed in Peter Berger's observation that "in science as in love a concentration on technique is quite likely to lead to impotence" (1963:13). At the time, the plan only directed the observer's attention to what occurred and the social worker's definition of the researcher or research situation. The limited hope was to produce a methodological appendix to the research, a conventional practice in many field research projects. The anticipated relevancies of the plan were the conventional categorizations culled from the existing field research literature, topics such as gaining entrée, establishing trust, recording field notes.

Analyzing feelings or the relevancies of these phenomena to the issues of objectivity in the social sciences was not considered at the beginning of the research. The idea of doing this never entered my mind at the time. In candor, I have to say a substantial portion of my field observations involved features of the naive rationalistic perspective earlier attributed to Rob. Though some readers may consider the idealization unfair, it was constructed to reflect certain features of my early observational naiveté. Indeed, even the references to the remarks of Blau and Balzac were not thrown in gratuitously. Furthermore, I must partially associate my observational and recording practices with Wolff's reflections on his recording omissions. Even though I initially intended an investigation of the research process itself, my voluminous records contain relatively few explicit notes on my personal feelings. Had I not originally intended such an endeavor, it is likely I would have no records of these phenomena at all. For me Rob is a recognizable idealization of certain features of the early portions of the research. This chapter reflects some of the changes of perspective since then.

It is impossible for me to say precisely when it occurred to me to consider the relations between thoughts and feelings as possibly relevant for understanding everyday, practical action. I can say, however, that my first thoughts about this possibility concerned the social casework done by the CWS social workers, and not social research. Only after many months of field research and a long period of investigating this issue with respect to the practice of social welfare casework did the relevance of these relations to social research occur to me. To put this in a different perspective, the CWS social workers instructed me in some matters about which my teachers, mentors, colleagues, and professional associates were ignorant or considered pedagogically irrelevant.

After three years of reviewing the observational records, writing, and reflecting, my analyses led to the conclusion that the personal feelings of the observer become fused with the rational cognitions of the research project in five ways: as (1) initial anxieties, (2) gut-level reactions to situations, (3) personal relations with people in the research setting, (4) personal relations with colleagues, and (5) the desire for understanding that motivates and sustains the research. These are not appropriately thought of as levels of feelings, but there is a certain ascendancy, ranging from the most immediate to the more remote. The major theoretical and methodological questions raised by these issues ask for an assessment of their influences on what are subsequently reported as the findings of the empirical investigation. For some, it is relatively easy to judge their influence as negligible or trivial. For others, the assessment is more difficult. The remainder of this chapter highlights these issues.

Behind the rational self-presentations

In the traditional field research literature, reports of the affect or feeling of an observer, when noted at all, tend to be presented in anecdotal fashion. Despite this, it is still relatively easy to read between the lines and infer a widely shared recognition that the beginning moments of a field research project are frequently accompanied by feelings of many different kinds of anxieties. Though there is only one report on the first days in the field as such, many others have noted their initial experiences (Geer, 1964). Without actually reporting their own experiences, many others advise hopeful field researchers to delay recording any observations or other notes until several weeks of the project have passed and the anxieties subsided. The beginning of the field observations and the initial contacts with those in the research setting are widely recognized as intertwined with private anxieties, fears, apprehensions, feelings of ignorance, confusion, incompetence, and incomprehension. In the case of my field research in the social welfare offices, I experienced all these at the beginning and some periodically thereafter. In fact, upon returning to my apartment at the end of the first day of fieldwork at the Lakeside Office, several of the blood vessels in my nose broke. There was an explosion of blood over the floor. I was taken to the emergency room of a local hospital. The doctor said the event was inexplicable. Upon returning home, however, I recorded field notes for seven hours. In retrospect, that also appears to be a reflection of my feelings of anxiety, apprehension, and worry about doing a good job. For the remainder of my initial visit to the offices in the northern county, the physical manifestations of my anxieties were not as explosively dramatic as on the first day. But the indirect manifestations reflected by the demented recording ritual continued.

Starting the field observations at the Metro Office in the southern county was less dramatic in some respects, but in others it was more difficult. Because of my preentry preparations and personal contacts, I felt more or less at ease when I addressed a joint meeting of the social workers from the two CWS units to explain the purposes of the research. What occurred then, however, really caught me off guard. Largely because of the misadventitious timing of the beginning of the research in the context of other events perceived as threatening by the CWS social workers, several of those at the meeting accused me of being a spy from the governor's office or an efficiency specialist from the staff of the welfare director sent to check up on them. The event was subsequently called "the crucifixion" by several of the workers. My response to the accusations fostered the appearance of a lack of composure, and this was taken as tentative evidence by several at the meeting that the charges might not have been warranted. Behind the rational self-presentation of the observer, however, there were genuine anxieties, fears, and apprehensions.

The anxieties eventually diminished, but they remained for some time. The following excerpt from the field notes was recorded about six weeks after beginning at Metro:

Not sure whether these comments will ultimately have any relevance whatsoever, but I guess I'll add a couple of remarks to the notes to record some of my personal thoughts which I haven't noted before. I've been going down to [Metro] for nearly six weeks now. Even though I probably appear cucumber-cool to everybody down there, I am, for the most part, scared to death of some of those people. And in many cases, I don't know any good reasons for this. Every morning, around seven forty-five, as I'm driving to the office, I begin to get this pain in the left side of my back, and the damn thing stays there usually until around eleven, when I've made my daily plans for accompanying one of the workers in the field. Since nearly all of the workers remain in the office until around eleven or twelve, and since there's only one extra chair in the two units, and no extra desks as yet, those first two or three hours are sheer agony for me every damn day. Trying to be busy without has-sling any one worker too much is like playing Chinese checkers, hopping to and fro, from here to there, with not place to hide. But I guess the biggest thing that keeps gnawing at me is Bonnie's reaction to my presence in the office. [She flatly rejected all cooperation with the research.] If I had had any idea at all before I began this damn project that a field researcher could possibly cause anyone so much grief, you can bet I wouldn't be here.

Various anxieties experienced at the beginning of a research project mark the first way an observer's feelings become intertwined with the observations. I experienced many of these anxieties, as many others have. Mine were further complicated by distinct physical manifestations of various kinds. Still, a voluminous amount of notes were recorded during this time. I think I recorded even more notes during the early months than later, notwithstanding the advice of the traditional research literature to the contrary. As I subsequently reviewed the notes with these reflective understandings in mind, I found the notes not especially valuable, either descriptively or insightfully. But it is not at all clear that this necessarily results from the feelings of fear, anxiety, and apprehension. In retrospect, it is just as plausible to think their trivial, naive, and often mistaken character results from the observer's ignorance of the setting, its tasks, official rules, names, and terminology.

Field workers generally agree that the initial anxious feelings eventually subside, and all concerned tend to accommodate to the new expectations. But this does not necessarily mean all goes smoothly thereafter. The following excerpt from the notes was recorded during the tenth week at Metro. It describes my reaction to a talk with a worker called Buzz. It is fair to say the notes were recorded because of the unusual nature of my reaction:

Also had a talk with Buzz this afternoon. I began by asking him what had happened recently with the kids at the Young foster home, where we were last week. Buzz began his account by saying "Oh wow, J.J., you wouldn't believe how bad I blew it," and then he proceeded to describe the details of what he called his own ignorance, unprofessional conduct, erroneous judgments, sentimental and sloppy thinking, bad social casework, and so on. Now I'll admit that I don't know all there is to know about social workers or social casework, but I sure as hell know enough about it to know that all the examples he cited from this case wouldn't be similarly defined by *any* other social worker, that there isn't a social worker in the world who would see that as unprofessional conduct, or anything else. The account would've been implausible from nearly any worker, but it's (especially) implausible coming from Buzz. He's one of the brightest guys I've met so far . . . It's fairly obvious he was giving me some kind of short con this afternoon, although I'll be damned if I have any idea why. The thing today really got to me. After taking leave of the situation, I walked out of the office and over to the parking lot, whereupon I proceeded to break into a cold sweat, felt weak-kneed and nauseous.

This excerpt gives another illustration of the private feelings and the physical manifestations. Interestingly, it also notes the researcher takes leave of the situation to hide these feelings from others. Not wanting to give any of the social workers an opportunity for developing a fatal insight about the apparently rational self-presentation, an exit is made to the nearby parking lot, where the researcher tries to reconstruct the rational appearance. Also implicit in the field notes is an indication that, even relatively early in the research, the observer is oriented to a normal state of affairs at the office. The event was recorded only because it depicts breaches of these prior anticipations, even though the comments themselves show no awareness of this, because there was no such awareness. The excerpt is an excellent illustration of the self-organizing and essentially *conservative* nature of the observer's rationalistic perspective. When confronted with an account conflicting with the prior anticipations or other knowledge, the observer reflexively tries to remedy, or conserve, the foundations of the rationalistic vision by treating the appearance of conflict as epiphenomenal to some reason, albeit one that is not yet known.

Along with the intial moments of anxiety at the beginning of any new research, the early portions of the investigation additionally engage the researcher's feelings at a deeper, primordial level. As suggested above, these may involve commonsensical and taken-for-granted presuppositions about the essentials of social reality, such as the nature of rationality, as noted above. Also involved, in this sense, are those basic ideas others have termed world hypotheses and domain assumptions (Gouldner, 1970). The first anxious moments are likely to be relatively unimportant for the research observations, at least as compared with these primordial feelings about one's sense of reality. The latter are likely to be fundamental determinants of what one sees when observing.

When the rational appearances crack

The previous section documents the gap between one's rational self-presentation and one's private feelings. Furthermore, the point is made that the maintenance of the rational appearances is a self-organizing and managed enterprise of daily life. The two following excerpts illustrate the problematic nature of the enterprise.

The following event occurred relatively late in the observations at Metro. The account resembles, one might suggest, the folktale of the kid caught with his hand in the cookie jar:

I'm not sure I've recorded any notes about this, but ever since they added those partitions dividing all of the supervisor's offices in half, I've been ducking into the interviewing rooms on the other side of Frank's and Mary's offices to eavesdrop . . . [on conversations]. Well, today, because I got a lot of good dope from a discussion in the coffee room with Barrie and her gang, I ducked into one of the rooms in order to write a couple of pages of notes. About three or four minutes after I had been in the interviewing room, I heard Sherri begin a conversation with Mary on the other side of the partition. But, after hearing some of the opening remarks which indicated they were talking about Sherri's recent crisis with her boy friend, I just ignored the conversation and went on recording my field notes. Wow, I should've paid attention to the talking, at least enough to know when they'd stopped. When I finished my notes I stepped out of the interviewing room, and who should I meet walking around the corner. Yep, you guessed it. [Sherri.] My heart must have hit the floor. I felt like Portnoy must have felt when his mother was knocking on the bathroom door. I think I tried to force the appearance of a smile, but I'll bet it was obvious as hell that I was really shaking. I somehow managed to make it to the back door, and lost my breakfast out by the railroad tracks.

A noteworthy feature of this event is its out-of-the-ordinary character and the relations of the private feelings to physical signs, which one might plausibly interpret, without doing great violence to the phenomena, as one index of the socially sanctionable nature of the normal forms of social interaction.[1] Even though my reactions to the above event were serious enough to produce physical signs, my notes fail to record what the actual feelings were. Whatever feelings existed, they were not expressed, and this could be because they are inarticulatable, inexpressible ones, like many of our feelings. This underscores the great difficulty of understanding one's day-to-day, ordinary feelings and their relevance for one's perceptions or actions.

The next event is depicted in some detail by the field notes. They record my reactions and feelings about an incident that occurred one afternoon at the local juvenile court. The case involved a determination of the legal custody of a four-year-old boy, David. David's biological mother had officially relinquished her first four children for adoption several years earlier. But since his birth, David had been "unofficially placed in an unlicensed foster home," the official euphemism for saying she gave him to someone else. Such a practice is relatively common in the poorer areas of the city, much to the consternation of the foster home licensing officials.[2] David had been living with the Smiths for the last four years. On this day, the case came to court because David's biological mother wanted to take David away from the Smiths to send him to Oklahoma so that her relatives could receive more money from the local welfare agency. Incidentally, this is not common, but it does occur now and then. As the notes show, the Smiths had obviously come to regard David as their own son:

However, neither I nor all of the persons who had come to testify in the Smith's behalf were allowed to witness the proceedings. Even though I wasn't allowed inside the courtroom, I decided to wait around in the lobby until the case had been concluded. I waited both minutes.

The reference to waiting both minutes is literal, not ironic. And it is noteworthy that this time element is typical for juvenile courts, not out of the ordinary (Lemert, 1970). Having added those caveats, I should additionally note the reference to waiting both minutes masks my private feelings of smoldering indignation and outraged incomprehension about the unintelligible bases on which such consequential decisions are frequently made.[3] I say this, after having engaged in conscientious and concerted efforts to understand the juvenile court situation from the various perspectives of the participants.

Returning to the David Smith case:

As the parties allowed into the juvenile court proceedings reemerged into the lobby, the following events transpired. The first one through the door was Mrs. Smith's brother, a gargantuan man of about forty-five years, about six-four, with a neck like a circus strong man's. Was wearing one of those checkered shirts like lumberjacks wear, under his overalls. At the scales he'd probably weigh in at about 250 pounds. He was really broken up, crying heavily, and pounding his fist against the wall. David's foster mother, Mrs. Smith presented the appearance of one who had gone absolutely hysterical. Her bulky frame was being carried through the door on the shoulders of her long-time friend on one side and her next-door neighbor on the other. At the top of her lungs she demanded that divine intervention make its appearance on the scene in the name of justice. She called for God and asked for intervention to correct what she very obviously thought was a miscarriage of justice. She then turned on David's natural mother and threatened physical violence, but was restrained by her two friends and a burly sheriff. She screamed that justice had not been done, that David's mother did not deserve to have him returned as she had not bothered to even visit him once in four years, even though she lived only one block from the Smiths. She claimed that her life was now meaningless and not worth living anymore. She was ushered outside by her two friends, and they stood out on the sidewalk for a couple of minutes. During this time David began crying and screaming, claiming that he did not want to be returned to his natural mother, that he didn't want to go to Oklahoma. He said he hated his natural mother and didn't want to leave his foster home. Within a couple of minutes, after Mrs. Smith's brother had stopped crying, he threatened to kill David's mother on the spot, and reentered the building to make good his threat, whereupon he was almost literally smothered by what seemed like 500 onlookers and the entire Sheriff's Department, persons obviously sensing that his utterance was not what is called "an idle threat." He was finally "ushered" out of the lobby, and he and his sister and friends and neighbors adjourned to the parking lot, where they cried and hugged each other with what appeared to be a great deal of anguish and suffering.

David, of course, exerted all efforts to join his loved ones and had to be restrained by the sheriff's officer in the lobby. The scene proved too much for those onlookers in the lobby, and the guards, probation officers, and receptionist began crying profusely. Betty [the social worker] also appeared visibly shaken and ran to her car crying.

The notes refer to Mrs. Smith's brother as "almost . . . smothered," and I might add, "by a number of onlookers greatly exaggerated by the notes." This did not include myself. I was one of the few who did not join the restraining action. As best I can remember, I just stood there, stunned by the unfolding scenario. The conclusion depicts my reactions:

And how did the cool, objective, calculatingly rational social scientist react to all of this? Having quickly analyzed all of the formally rational courses of action open to me, and feeling confident that I had controlled for all spurious relations, I also began to cry. As we say in the trade, I presented the appearance of one who had lost all self-control. And then, when alone on the grounds of the juvenile facility several minutes later, I presented the appearance of a formally rational [expletive deleted] social scientist beating his [deleted] fist against a tree. Shortly after that, I doubled over and puked my guts out. What am I doing here anyway? To hell with the appearance of sociology and the horse it rode in on!

One noteworthy feature unrecorded here is that, after these events, I returned home and spent most of that evening crying. The field notes were not recorded in the heat of the moment, but the following day. This was one of the few occasions I did not record notes on the day of the observation. Given this added understanding of the elapsed time, note that the field notes do not explicitly say what the feelings were in the situation. Even though this was a very emotional event, the actual feelings are glossed and masked by cynicism. By adopting the observer's stance here, it is possible to read between the lines, and conclude it was more human in the situation to cry and lose self-control. But rather than recording a relatively straightforward expression of one's sense of injustice, feelings of sympathy, outrage, or whatever the feelings actually were in the situation, the tensions between one's primordial, gut-level feelings and one's rational thoughts are glossed by cynical phrases, such as "presenting the appearance" and "controlling for spurious relations." One might propose that the observer was just an incompetent recorder, or worse, lacked aesthetic sensibilities. There may be an element of truth in the proposal. As we recall Kurt Wolff's analysis of the common research tendancy for observers to transform all interactive and affective elements into cognitive problems, however, it is wiser to conceive of these tensions between thinking and feeling as necessary and inevitable ones. They are necessary and inevitable, that is, as long as one retains a moral commitment to the observations. To observe sociologically means that one deliberately cedes experiencing the things-in-themselves to the members of the setting; observation entails seeing phenomena as exhibits of the things-in-themselves. If one elects to observe sociologically, it is, and can be, no other way. In practice, of course, the distinction breaks down slightly. It is actually a mixture, and we bob in and out, to and fro. We participate, observe, experience, record, pause for reflection, and then return for more of the same. But the field researcher's valued commitment to observing and recording notes on the events of daily life means that there will always be, to some irreducible degree, a transformation of the actual experiences into something other than they were in reality. There is a sizable body of writings on the phenomenon of going native in the literature of anthropological and sociological field research (Paul, 1953). These writings attest to the problematic nature of the commitment and the existence of other plausible alternatives. That we make and are made up of the phenomena we seek to understand is the irremediable paradox of our enterprise.

When viewed in the broader perspective of the entire field investigation, the David Smith case was methodologically trivial and substantively unimportant. Personally, however, the experience had, and continues to have, a lasting biographical relevance. I had spent a decade of absolutist commitment to the causes of the American Civil Liberties Union, and as I reflected on the David Smith case the ironic contrasts were too obvious and painfully evident. Had the ACLU filed an amicus curiae brief in this case, it would have promoted the very outcome which resulted in my profound sense of injustice. The event was one of several leading to changes in my thinking about legalistic (or other rule-governed) remedies. My ACLU membership lapsed some time later and was not renewed. And that was no small decision for me.

Feelings and personal involvements

The overformalized rationalistic instrumentality that appears as the public account of one's methods is never the whole story of the research. The discussion to this point documents two ways an observer's personal feelings become fused with the rational accounts: the in-

itial anxieties at the start of the research and the gut-level reactions to
the situation at hand. The third way is decidedly more important and
involves the observer's on-going personal relations with the persons in
the setting where the research is conducted. All field investigations that
penetrate the rational appearances of the public fronts, that involve relations of trust with individuals to obtain a truthful, empathic, valid,
and reliable understanding of the actions occurring there, inevitably
involve complicated personal feelings between the observer and the
members. Instead of being dependent on one's gut-level reactions to an
immediate situation, many of these feelings are of a transsituational
character. Some accrue glacially over time, perhaps without explicit
awareness. Others involve an entirely different congeries of feelings. But
this does not mean these dimensions of feeling are less primordial than
the others or that they necessarily transcend the gut level because of
the time involved. In substantive terms, this realm of feeling may
include sympathy, love, hate, friendship, resentment, admiration,
respect, infatuation, identification, dislike, and all the rest. This is the
meaningful stuff of which the problems of overrapport and going native
(to use the euphemisms of the field research writings) are made.

The complicated feelings between an observer and the persons with
whom the investigation is conducted may involve, as Kurt Wolff has
taught us, cognitive elements, even a cognitive love. Based on my reflections, the concept of cognitive love precisely characterizes my feelings
toward one of the CWS social workers at Metro and one other worker
at another office. It cannot be said that the CWS worker at Metro and I
immediately hit it off together as a result of some mutual personal
compatibility. He was the one who lodged the first accusation that I
might be a spy from the governor's office at the initial meeting of the
two CWS units. For the first couple months, our interactions with one
another were cordial, but cool. Eventually we became friends, largely as
a consequence of our generally compatible personalities, manner, de-
meanor, past experiences, and interests. Personally, I liked him, felt certain about communicating such sentiments, and he responded accordingly. In retrospect, this particular friendship might have been anticipated because, in the terms used in the traditional field research literature to categorize types of informants one is likely to find in a given setting, this CWS worker was a natural — one of those rare reflective individuals capable of insightful analyses of daily events (Dean, 1954). As we
were around each other more and more, he gradually became even more
inclined to see his practical CWS actions as exhibits for analysis. By the
end of my stay at Metro he referred to these analyses as *his* participant-
observational research, and it is my judgment that I successfully turned
him out as an analyst of everyday affairs. On several occasions I told him

it was unfortunate that he was not the observer for the field investigation of CWS. And I meant it. A number of the insightful ideas I subsequently reported were, quite frankly, stolen from him.

In addition to being a natural, this CWS social worker happened to occupy *the* key position in the two CWS units with respect to informational control and caseload referral. Also, he single-handedly altered or subverted several existing official policies or practices directly affecting the character of the CWS work at Metro. Several of these actions were clandestine and others patently illegal (Johnson, 1973a). This may have been one of the reasons for his initial apprehension about admitting an outsider access to the official public secrets. In short, it would be impossible to obtain a valid understanding of what occurred at Metro CWS without befriending this worker. In this respect, I consider my friendship with him fortuitious for the research.

Wolff's abstract definition of the core meaning of surrender as involving a cognitive love does make some sense, then. On other counts, however, the idealization fails miserably in telling us how affective and interactional elements of action are involved in the research process and hence distorts our understandings. Conspicuously absent is any mention of the nonrational grounds of some of our pettier feelings. During the field observations at Metro, for example, I encountered two freeze-outs (i.e., individuals who refused any cooperation with the research purposes from the start). One was a girl who told her friends she was terrified by my presence. I agonized over this situation for months, resolutely rejecting others' explanations of this by invoking some typification of her personality, continually thinking of ways to put her at ease, and worrying about what I must be doing wrong. Emerging out of all this was my private irrational fear of her. I still do not know why, but the feelings of fear were real ones.

My relations with the second freeze-out mellowed over time, but they were none too friendly at best. Unlike the first instance, where my private feelings could be appropriately depicted as epitomizing an Adlai Stevenson consciousness almost until the end, my private feelings about this fellow were less charitable. I thought he was a betty, although I think I successfully masked that sentiment during the research.

Petty feelings emerged in other situations. On one or two occasions, I just got bored and fabricated some excuse to escape for a desired respite. On one occasion relatively late in the investigation, an older woman directed the wrath of her moral indignation at me because I had "lowered myself" by going with one of the male social workers to throw a glorious drunk at several infamous brothels in a neighboring community. I deferred to her judgment, but my private feelings consisted of deleted expletives. Wolff's emphasis on the cognitive character of one's affect ignores all these petty feelings, but they are all only too recognizable in everyday actions.

The research experiences of social welfare included several friendships. Some originated before the research, and some have continued for years afterward. Others came to bloom during the observations, but have atrophied over time. Only on one occasion did I have a sense that a friendship presented a problem for the research. This situation involved a personal struggle between a CWS supervisor and a CWS social worker, who was legally blind. The supervisor did not think a blind person should be in CWS. She set out to build a case against him, a preliminary to giving him the axe, one of the practical strategies for personnel transfers in the office. Because of his reliance on a paid driver for transportation, the blind worker was caught in a bind. He feared his own presence in the office during the working day would be used to constitute part of the case against him. He solicited my assistance as his cover for a period of about three weeks. Without hesitation, I agreed. For me, the problematic character of this consisted of the conflict between this course of action and the specific welfare activities I wanted to concentrate on at that time. It is doubtful whether my actions introduced any additional elements of selectivity to the research observations, but with different options, I would have chosen otherwise.

A claim that field research involves feelings of friendship deserves considered reflection. It raises the issue of a possible conflict between one's personal feelings and a rational course of action intended to effect the best observational results. This issue is raised by the comments in the preceding paragraph. If or when this occurs, it is incumbent on the observer to use his sociological competence to evaluate the effects. But there are other potential conflicts inherent in friendships, and these are little appreciated. The most obvious is a potential conflict between the substantively rational friendship sentiments and a formally rational body of codified rules, such as legal statutes.

Having spent much of my time for the past decade lingering in the bowels of official state bureaucracies, notably universities, welfare agencies, and military commands, I find it difficult to believe there are many adults who are not technically guilty of periodic violations of official rules, if one elects to view such actions in a legalistic perspective. Illegal drug use, for example, is common in these settings.[4] And yet, one almost never hears of one colleague's calling in the police on another or using the hot line to Washington. Unauthorized sexual liaisons are frequent. Some members do not even know what the official rules are about these, and the rules are rarely invoked.[5] Many are irrelevant. Playing around with the entries on official records and reports is common. These public secrets rarely inspire moral indignation. The potential for conflict between the absolutism of the formally rational legal codes and the moral pluralism of the substantively rational family, friendship, and colleague sentiments is obvious in these settings. When a conflict actually occurs, the members invariably elect a moral or ethical view over a legalistic one, at least with respect to their own or their friends' actions. This is no news to many parents; the game is typically a no holds barred affair when one is called to the police station in the middle of the night to extricate a son or daughter from the clutches of the officials. My personal thinking, then, has been undeniably colored by these experiences. But I am also aware that the situation is much different in other settings. Among the BaMbuti, for example, the possibility of such conflicts would not arise because of the homogeneity and un-codified nature of their moral sentiments (Turnbull, 1962). Even in our own teeming, conglomerated societies there are pockets of moral isolation, such as the Amish communities of northern Indiana and university laboratories, where it is possible to live without dealing with these complexities on a day-to-day basis. I am aware, then, of many others who do not share my views.[6]

Whether or not my suppositions are correct, if my field research conduct in the welfare agencies is viewed in a legalistic perspective, it can be seen that my actions involved my complicity in or guilty knowledge about literally hundreds of illegal activities. Some of the relevant legal categorizations include being an accessory before and after the fact of an illegal act, misprisioning of felonies and misdemeanors, and obstructing justice. On the basis of my understandings of the field research literature and especially of my many conversations and debriefings with my colleagues in sociology, I believe it wrong to report such role infractions to the legal authorities (cf. Polsky, 1967). I regard my ethical position on this issue as absolute: I am prepared to go to jail before violating the confidentiality of the research information.[7] It comes as a surprise to me, then, to learn that this is not the position taken by other sociological researchers.[8]

Observers of all kinds have remarked about the strength and pervasiveness of sexual desire. Modern psychology elevates this commonsense knowledge to scientific status and calls it a drive. Yet the methodological writings in the social sciences imply that we must believe one of two things about this: Either one must be a eunuch to conduct scientific research or, following in the vein of Wolff's argument, the desires of scientists involve only (or primarily) cognitive elements. My research experiences (and those of others) do not support this naive view. During my visit to one welfare office in northern metropolitan county, for example, I was virtually seduced by an attractive lady. We made home visits to see welfare clients during the day, played around like rabbits for the better portions of four nights, and, obviously, there is a peculiar four-day gap in my field notes. After the events had passed, I suffered from profound feelings of guilt about this, and a truly horrendous fear that my wife would find out about it. Several years later, the prospect still fills me with feelings of horror. Another series of events occurred near the end of my field research at Metro. They concerned what has long been called in literature the eternal triangle. The resolution involved feelings of bitterness, betrayal, hate, resentment, and shattered friend-ships. It produced a severe crisis for me personally and delayed the writing of the research reports. The situation involved a considerable amount of hurt, which is one of the elements of Wolff's definition of surrender. But it would be pure casuistry for me to consider the prime movers of these events as the *cognitive* elements of social action.

In one sense, the present discussion only brings out in the open what many have understood for a long time. These are some of the public secrets of scientific conduct. John Lofland aptly captured this common understanding and some of the reasons for masking one's research account:

One of my mentors has commented that what typically goes into "how the study was done" are "the second worst things that happened." I am inclined to believe that his generalization is correct. What person with an eye to his future, and who wishes others to think positively of him, is going to relate anything about himself that is morally or professionally discrediting in any important way? This is especially the case since field work tends to be performed by youngish persons who have longer futures to think about and less security about the shape of those futures. We delude ourselves if we expect very many field workers actually to "tell all" in print. [Lofland, 1971:132—3]

During the Watergate investigations, our brother sociologist Richard M. Nixon coined a phrase that expresses Lofland's observations in a more parsimonious fashion. When his aides were called on to reveal the method-ological protocol of the events, he advised a "limited hang out." My experiences and reflections tend to support the great wisdom of sociolo-gists Lofland and Nixon. I think the best we can expect from the method-ological literature is a limited hangout.

As one considers the complicated fusions of feelings and rational thoughts that become intertwined in any scientific investigation, two major theoretical questions are raised by these issues. The first question is whether some form of direct participation by an observer with the societal members introduces any greater degree of bias or error into an investigation than would otherwise obtain from an observer's reliance on his own commonsense thinking based on no direct personal involve-ment. The evidence on this is mixed, but it is clear that a detached in-vestigation based on no direct participation contains a great potential for not being a true one. Others have previously addressed this question, so it will not be dealt with in detail here (Douglas, 1972a).

The second major question is partially related to the issue of establishing relations of trust in anthropological and sociological field research. Many analysts agree that trusting relations are the essential ingredients if the research report is to be a true one. The question is whether the feelings and sentiments resulting from the observer's personal relations with the individuals in the setting necessarily mean that the research report will be biased. This does seem to be a distinct possibility, but there is clearly no a priori reason for thinking it will necessarily occur. These personal sentiments appear to become a potentially biasing feature of the research when the observer's intention to *empathize* with the individuals in the setting (i.e., to try truthfully to understand the situation from the actor's perspective) becomes transformed into a *sympathetic* stance (i.e., siding with or promoting the perspective of the group one studies). Such a distinction is often less than clear cut. The understanding leads some analysts to advise the wisdom of reading all field research reports with an eye to the tenuous nature of the distinction (Scott, 1959). The same understanding exists in commonsense thought. It is commonly expressed by the remark that one always views one's loved ones through rose-colored glasses.

Feelings about home

If a field researcher is able to honor the distinction between empathy and sympathy in his observations and analyses, it is perhaps most importantly because of his simultaneous relations with his professional colleagues. A field worker has a foot in two different camps at the same time: the on-going relations with those in the research setting and the on-going relations with his sociological friends, teachers, advisers, and peers. A researcher is able to move back and forth between these simultaneous roles. In one sense, then, the sociological colleagues, through informal conversations, seminars, talks, and debriefings, serve to keep the researcher honest (i.e., act as a check against the possibility of his taking a sympathetic stance toward the research observations). And, of course, many ideas for the research emerge from such contacts. Although there are several practical (even utilitarian) elements about these collegial relations that are necessary for the completion of any project, and although the colleagues provide a check on the objectivity of the research in many cases, the most fundamentally important aspect of collegial relations is that this is where the researcher lives. He lives here in the sense that his colleagues and friends are the ones who bestow or withhold those statements of praise, probity, or damnation out of which all of us try to put together some concept of a social self. This is home. Whether the researcher stays with the project to the end or says to hell with it is often dependent on these personal ties. This is another way his personal feelings become fused with the rational cognitions of the enterprise.

The same congeries of feelings that come into play between the observer and the individuals in the research setting may emerge in collegial relations as well. These personal ties are typically alluded to in the introduction, preface, or opening footnotes of a work. They cut across all known categories of theoretical perspectives, methodological programs, political beliefs, substantive interests, and value commitments. There is even a traditional format used to acknowledge these ties. It consists of mentioning one's colleagues and then absolving them of any moral responsibility for what is to be reported as the findings of the research. An example can be found in virtually any book, such as: "It goes without saying that [my colleague] is in no way to be held responsible for what follows. While there may be honor among thieves as well as among sociologists of knowledge, some crimes are committed together and some separately" (Berger, 1967:vii).

The traditional format is a quaint holdover from the past. It promotes a moral perspective honored only on such ritualistic occasions as writing prefaces; it distorts the actual truth. It is also poor sociology of knowledge, and many of the personal reflections of scientists show that few really take such statements seriously anyway, at least in theoretical terms (Horowitz, 1970; Watson, 1969). The tradition does point out, however, that all rationalistic sociological accounts are quintessentially social enterprises. As is true of some other forms of crime, we would probably be well advised to consider the moral responsibility as collective rather than individual.

Trying to understand the nature of one's personal relations with one's colleagues, the underlying feelings, and the effects of these on what gets reported is very difficult. It requires a second-order analysis — one that is probably impossible to do during the field investigation itself. There exist very few accounts of these phenomena, and these few fail for the most part to consider them in the context of scientific objectivity. But one should not mistake their crucial importance. To anyone who has spent some time sloshing about the methodological mesogasters of a research facility at the university, it is crystal clear that many of the empirical observations of the real world are hatched here; the rationalized research accounts of the methodological procedures used in the data collection represent a form of laundering the data to hide this truth from us. Just as Nixon's aides laundered checks through Mexican banks to construct the appearance of a rational compliance with the election campaign contribution laws, so do social researchers launder the data to maintain and promote their rational appearances.

During my investigations of social welfare I thought of the influences of one's collegial relations as the problems of the Faustus-Mephistopheles dialectic in sociological research. Some of the influences are relatively easy to determine; others, more difficult. There is little doubt in my own mind, for example, that the sociological relevance of the topic I eventually analyzed for the purposes of completing the dissertation (official records and reports), was implicitly suggested to me through the similar interests of two of my mentors: one who had done a previous research investigation of coroner's determinations of suicides, and another who was then investigating the official records of drinking drivers. Had it not been for my personal associations with these two men, and others, the relevance of official records and reports to other theoretical issues in sociology probably would not have occurred to me. Had my dissertation been submitted to a sociology department at a different school, the chances are great that it would not have been accepted. Other influences can be ascertained too. One consequence of my many collegial relations is that I brazenly stole some of my colleagues' ideas, as I did in the writing of this chapter. Simultaneously, I lent them some of my ideas. One mentor referred to this phenomenon as a symbiotic relationship, jokingly, as he scurried off to publish some of my ideas in one of his papers. I am still thinking about other subtle influences. This will undoubtedly continue for some time.

One's collegial relations can influence virtually all aspects of scientific investigation. The interest in the sociology of knowledge, so popular in recent years, is indebted to this insight for its good fortune of late. John Lofland's observations, cited earlier, also attest to this truth. Lofland's analyses of the possible factors involved in the decision not to tell all about a research project did not mention that the potential dangers of telling all stem from the members of our local communities, the police, other official control agencies, our families or churches. Lofland emphatically stated that the withheld information is of a *professionally* discrediting nature. Although a literal interpretation of the traditional ethics of scientifically conducted research leads one to anticipate a stance of ethical neutrality by scientists *on methodological issues*, we all know and recognize this inherited version as myth. These understandings are the ones urging us to think of the primordial, gut-level feelings involved in the observer's personal relations with his professional colleagues as feelings about home. We intuitively understand that this is where the heart is, and that the heart has reasons of which reason knows not, as Pascal put it. Using these intuitions often serves us well as a convenient escape from the arduous labor of critical reflection: To do otherwise is madness.

In several different ways the materials presented in this chapter point out the basic conflicts between substantive and formal rationality. These tensions reflect one of the fundamental ambiguities of our Western self-understandings. The profound irony of the sociology of knowledge is that it proposes we view ourselves as we have traditionally viewed others, the erstwhile subjects of our scientific inquiries, those constituting the objects of our interests. Always claiming a privileged exemption for its own questions, the sociology of knowledge fails to elucidate an understanding of the paradox it is. It hides from us our natural bonds of community and the ways we know one another as human. Additionally, it fails to enlighten us about the motivational sources of our common interests. This leads to the final consideration.

Rational accounts and passionate feelings: iron cages and enchanted gardens

Similar to other social actions, the daily conduct of scientific research involves a complicated mixture of thoughts and feelings, and this is further complicated on occasion by minor and for the most part relatively insignificant considerations of values or ethics. The problematic features of the research process are rarely settled, and any stability achieved during its course may be short-lived. In view of all these complicated fusions of thought and feeling, their physical manifestations and emotional anxieties, and all the other problematic exigencies of the research, one might wonder why more research projects do not atrophy before their completion. Many do; commonly, many more are delayed, sometimes for years, before some practical resolution is achieved by the researcher and the relevant peers or colleagues. As these elements of a research project are infrequently reported in the rational accounting of the observational realities, these facts are not as well appreciated as they should be. What is it that motivates a person to engage in scientific research or analysis? And, regardless of the reason he initially undertakes such an adventure, what motivates a person to transform those research experiences into a formally rational, written account, thereby modifying their actual nature? On these questions, the sociology of knowledge stands mute, necessarily and forever. Complete answers to such complex questions would entail nothing less than an unraveling of virtually all the mysteries of our existence. Our partial and tentative attempts at understanding must necessarily emanate from some combination of our own conscious awareness, our self-observations of daily conduct, and our reflections on these. Additionally, such attempts should be offered with the humility of and in the spirit of hypothesis.

The motivational wellsprings of an organized research project and any rational accounts issuing from it, like the actions occurring in most other settings, are always complicated and mixed. As the desire for critical self-understanding is no more prevalent among scientists than among other societal members, many are, for all practical purposes, unconcerned about their elucidation. But even when one tries, during moments of reflection, to unravel and sort out such motivations, a well-intentioned analysis produces only ambiguous results. The primordial feelings that motivate our daily conduct are inevitably and inextricably mixed. Each of us is to some degree limited in his individual desires and capacities to understand this flux. And the motivations do not remain fixed and unchanging over time, but instead require further analysis, which may in turn transform one's experiences or previous understandings.

The feelings that motivate the rational accounts of science are for the most part those that motivate men of practical affairs in their daily actions. In substantive terms, these include desire for acceptance, comfort, security, respectability, membership, and a place in the sun. It is not uncommon to find among scientists sex-like lust for status, wealth, power, fame, and all the other desires, resentments, and passions, from the big ones to the small. In Chapter 1 Jack Douglas enumerates many substantive illustrations of these from his personal experiences and observations in university settings. These indicate that the feelings motivating the rational accounts of science do not differ in kind from those involved in all conduct. This is not a trivial or unimportant point: understanding existing status or power relations within a given scientific subculture, for example, is often crucial knowledge for full understanding of who is saying exactly what about whom, for what audience, and for which purpose. Though important, these private meanings of scientific communications are commonly masked to a naive reader of the general public. Insiders, or those who have learned how to read between the lines of such accounts, are rarely mislead, however; actions are commonly predicated as much on the basis of what was communicated between the lines as what was literally stated.

Although the feelings that motivate rational wordsmiths are more akin to than distinct from those of used car salesmen, prostitutes, politicians, mothers, and other societal members, such accounts are also (but never exclusively) motivated by a passion for a more lucid self-understanding of ourselves and others. The passion that leads one to subject all or portions of one's own or another's existence to rational thought, reflection, analysis, and articulation is one which, according to

Max Weber, entails a "special motivation." For Weber this distinguished the theoretical stance adopted by scientists from the unreflective or commonsense attitude of ordinary men. But Weber was clearly wrong about this. For all of us, with no greater differences among us than those that obtain among scientists themselves, there is an unorganized but nevertheless natural community of our self-interested curiosities and passions for more complete understanding of our own lives and the world in which we live. These unite and divide us in everyday life. They brought many of us in hope to that very first sociology class and endure beyond that painful experience. We presuppose them when we experience the feelings of optimism or pessimism, joy or despair. Our feelings of membership in this natural community evidence themselves by our continued commitments to talking and listening, reading and writing, questioning and answering, acting and reflecting. And they are most evident when we care so much as to fight so bitterly and acrimoniously with one another, when we judge so unequivocally, and speak in anger. Such passions are barely concealed behind the facades of our rational accounts.

On those occasions when we momentarily pause to reflect and compare the truths we recognize about the complicated fusions of our passionate or situational feelings and the rational thoughts in our daily lives with the stilted, overformalized instrumentality implied in the writings on scientific methodology, we can see the existence of a certain historical irony confronting the development of an existential sociology. Max Weber and many others have for decades analyzed the trends in rationalization in modern societies, the gradual but increasingly evident shift in the thinking of societal members toward decision making based on rational and empirical grounds. Weber viewed this as a mixed blessing. On the one hand, he saw this shift as important for a more efficient industrial production and recognized the practical pay-offs of this. On the other hand, Weber feared that organizing everyday life on the basis of a formal or technical rationality carried with it the seeds for destroying the traditional, sentimental bonds of human community. He argued that such a form of rationality became an "iron cage" when separated from the sentimental infrastructures of daily life and was potentially destructive of our sensibilities about what he termed the "enchanted garden" of human existence. Weber and the others were correct in their assessments of the increasing importance of formally rational cognitive criteria. But he and all those who unthinkingly followed his lead failed to see that the socially sanctionable character of the rationality of our daily lives consists of making our ideas, plans, desires, purposes, and actions *appear acceptable to others.* For decades sociological research has taken the public appearances for the realities of existence. All have overlooked the ways and extent to which our words mask our private thoughts and feelings and our partial and tentative attempts at articulation and understanding. The historical irony is that the very social conditions that have been so important for the institutionalization of academic sociology have become a prison for our sociological understandings and imaginations. Academic sociology has a storehouse of answers to questions that have been forgotten.

The promise of existential sociology is to break away from those portions of our inherited rationalistic traditions that constrain our imaginations, to provide an intelligible understanding of the ways in which we know one another and the world we live in. Materials presented in this chapter about the fusions of thought and feeling in sociological research indicate that the immediate, deferred, and even the not-yet-fully understood feelings are the prime movers of the action. The rational accounts of science try to hide this fact, to enhance the accomplishment of some other worldly desire, or to make sense of it, for whatever reason or desire. The importance of understanding the primacy of the affective elements of everyday actions in order to understand their actual meanings has been repeatedly emphasized by the empirical data presented in the other chapters in this volume. In addition to Douglas's observations of university settings (Chapter 1), these include Altheide's discussion of the feelings and actions in TV newsrooms (Chapter 4), Anderson's discussion of his observations in a community mental health center (Chapter 6), Kotarba's discussion of the chronic pain experience (Chapter 9), Warren and Ponse's analysis of the sometimes deceiving rationality of the members of gay communities (Chapter 10), and my own researches on the necessarily deceiving construction of official statistics (Chapter 8). These researches represent the early beginnings of our efforts to achieve a more truthful understanding of the meanings of our actions in actual situations of daily life.

8

Occasioned transcendence

JOHN M. JOHNSON

Few would dispute a claim that sociology has been a pluralistic (or multiparadigmatic) discipline of social thought, given to a high degree of theoretical and/or methodological consensus only on rare occasions, and then only for brief periods. But whether or not this has always been the case, it seems especially true today as many challengers of the conventional sociological wisdom call into question the taken-for-granted (or commonsensical) nature of knowledge in the social sciences. The present situation is characterized by a proliferation of various methodological and theoretical perspectives within and throughout the discipline. But the absence of the well-developed mechanistic, physicalistic, or biologistic social theories so common in the last century is evidence for the fact that on one point (at least) all sociologists agree: Interactional activity interpreted as socially meaningful or meaningless by the members of society is the fundamental datum for sociology. Furthermore, these social meanings or their lack must be taken into account for any valid sociological understanding. This central idea of sociology has often been implicit or taken for granted in most sociological writings. None of the contemporary debates in sociology has seriously questioned this central idea concerning the fundamental datum of sociology. The analysis presented here proposes an alternative theoretical concept of socially meaningful action. This emerged from the observer's reflections on empirical materials gathered during an extensive field investigation of certain social welfare activities. As an introduction to this, the prevailing theoretical arguments concerning socially meaningful actions are presented.

Having provided sociology with many creative scholarly contributions since the 1930s, what is variously termed structuralism, functionalism, or (perhaps more commonly) structural functionalism has been the dominant theoretical perspective in sociology for several decades. The intellectual creativity of Talcott Parsons, Robert Merton, and many others has made this a plausible theoretical perspective for many sociologists. Structural functionalism was the major theoretical perspective self-consciously concerned with socially meaningful human activities. These sociological writings conceived of society (also called the social system) as constituted of various overlapping sets of social meanings. Substantively, these meanings have been variously referred to as values, beliefs, goals, norms, attitudes, expectations, opinions, and anticipations. Following the work of Parsons, it has been argued that there is a set of core values which is widely shared by the individuals in a society by virtue of their societal membership. Robin Williams's code-book listing of "core American values" is a popularly known substantive example of this idea. In addition to the assumption concerning the sharedness of meanings, structural functionalists conceived of these core meanings as external to the individual (i.e., as social facts, in the manner of Durkheim), unproblematically known by societal members, relatively stable over time, relatively homogeneous, unconflictual, and unchanging. This general theoretical concept is appropriately termed the *transcendence theory of social meanings*, in that the societal core meanings are thought to go beyond, extend above, or lie outside the immediate sense perceptions of the commonsense actors of society. In different terms,the core meanings are thought to constitute the underlying structural reality leading the commonsense members of society to produce the orderly appearances of everyday life. Following the lead set by Durkheim, Merton has repeatedly argued that commonsense actors of society may be quite unaware of these underlying structural realities. The commonsense actors see only "the appearances of things" (in Durkheim's words) or "the manifest functions" of actions (in Merton's words). But (allegedly) only a full-fledged sociologist can see "the real affinities of things" (Durkheim) or "the latent functions" of meaningful actions (Merton). According to Merton's argument, seeing latent functions of meaningful actions "represents a greater increment in knowledge than findings concerning manifest functions" (1957:68).

The theoretical arguments of structural functionalism have been criticized from various stances, perspectives, and orientations in sociology during the last decade. Specifically with respect to the theory of socially meaningful activities, a major critique has come from the work of Harold Garfinkel and other ethnomethodologists in sociology. Following the early critical appraisal of the work of Max Weber by the late philosopher-sociologist Alfred Schutz (1967), the research of various ethnomethodologists also has expressed a concern with studying meaningful human activity. They have concerned themselves with the elucidation of the commonsense properties of language and interpretation used by societal members to communicate intersubjectively and to understand the meanings of their actions. These emphases have led to various critiques of the traditional approaches in sociology. We are not concerned here with detailed exposition of these arguments. It is sufficient to note that, according to Garfinkel, traditional sociology accords the commonsense societal member the status of a "judgmental dope." He is a "puppet" who presumably acts out his obligatory social roles in such a fashion as to fit the omniscient sociologist's preconceptions. As an alternative to the structural functionalist argument, ethnomethodological investigators have repeatedly argued that the social meanings of any given activity are of an *indexical* or *occasional* nature for the members of society. The meaning of these terms is to some extent variable, but they generally refer to: (1) universal properties of the human knowing mind, (2) the practical necessity for commonsense speakers and hearers to index and take for granted their ongoing verbal (and paralinguistic) communications to understand their meaning, or (3) the practical necessity for commonsense actors to understand many taken-for-granted ideas to make sense of the other's remarks in a given setting. Whether the terms are taken to refer to properties of the human knowing mind, properties of linguistic accounts, or properties of commonsense action in practical situations, the general argument is that the social meaning of a given activity is necessarily determined by certain aspects of the practical situation in which it is understood and known. For this reason we refer to this as the *occasional theory of social meanings.* This phrase refers to the fact that meanings are conceived of as occasioned by the socially organized settings in which they are known. Several ethnomethodologists have argued that socially meaningful action is irremediably indexical in nature. This explicitly denies the transsituationality of meanings as conceived by structural functionalists. The two theories of social meanings are mutually incompatible.

Most of the remainder of this chapter presents detailed ethnographic materials gained from a year-long field research investigation in five district offices of two metropolitan departments of public welfare. Reflections on these materials have led me to formulate an alternative concept of meaningful action to those presented above. I call this *occasioned transcendence.* The term *occasioned* intends the idea that none of the events described were anticipated or preplanned by the members in advance of their occurrence. The materials clearly show that these activities are not easily conceived of as constituted by (or derivatives of) the members' values. On the other hand, the ethnographic materials also indicate the presence of various transsituational elements in the events to be described. These transsituational elements include not only some of the evaluative features of social action emphasized by structural functionalists (e.g., values, goals), but various cognitive and affective elements as well. The term *transcendence*, then refers to those trans-situational elements (whether evaluative, cognitive, or affective) used by the societal members in their continually on-going and self-organizing attempts to create, change, alter, or stabilize the nature of their everyday situations as they perceive them. Following a presentation of the empirical materials drawn from the research observations, we return to these theoretical interests.

The research setting and observations

The descriptive materials presented here were drawn from a year-long participant observational project that included five district offices of two large metropolitan departments of public welfare. The particular events described in this chapter stem from the observer's ten-month participation with Child Welfare Services social workers at the Metro Office in Southern Metropolitan County of Western State.[1] The research was organized to allow the integration of the observer into the everyday working routines of agency personnel. Tape recordings of actual interactions occurring in the setting, tape-recorded interviews, field notes, official records and documents, and the observer's experiences and reflections provide the data for the study.[2]

Being a social worker in a public welfare agency involves many different tasks, but the agency members studied commonly classified their diverse experiences in two broad categories: (1) working with people, a broad reference to face-to-face (and other) daily interactions taking place between social workers and public welfare clients; and (2) paperwork, a phrase that refers to the many and diverse forms of documentation routinely completed and used by agency members. The social workers studied during these research investigations were involved in the provision of child welfare services. Their assigned tasks included intervention in a wide (and ambiguously defined) range of family troubles. Public welfare activities such as these have been traditionally conceived of as a legal institution guided by various sets of formally codified rules (e.g., laws, statutes, regulations). But the formally codified rules related to these troubling features of family life (e.g., child battering, child neglect, sex molestation) were either unknown or considered too ambiguous (or even irrelevant) by the CWS social workers at the Metro Office. Therefore, the research investigation conceived of social work as a gloss for the complex understanding work whereby social workers used their commonsense knowledge of typical social events to define the problems of welfare clients. And this usually included preparing the existent interactional sequences for subsequent actions intending solutions to the problems. One crucial resource used by social workers in this process was the dossier (case record) of the welfare client, a collection of narrative and other forms of documentary evidence concerning the client's societal existence. This case record provided one of the resources for looking again at the facts of the client's life as conceived by the appropriate cognitive criteria of social work. The client's case record was one of the important forms of paperwork routinely accomplished by CWS social workers.

In addition to the client's case record, CWS social workers used various other reports, forms, statistical summaries, and tabulations. Many of these other forms of documentation were designed by and for higher administrative personnel interested in having some measure of the efficiency of the public welfare programs. To complete statistical summaries and tabulations successfully, the social workers were always asked to reduce their knowledgeable understandings of their daily activities in the linguistic terms provided by a given reporting format. The social workers were held rationally accountable to many different administrative structures and in many different terms, so only by making use of their understanding of the situated official reporting context could they make sense of a given report and guess the intentions of the reporting format. Thus, the situational reporting context was partially independent of the organized features of the other official work contexts, and this was commonly known by social workers as one of their organizational facts of life. The social construction of official records and statistics by agency members consisted of a continuous improvisation of practical procedures for achieving a solution to some problem immediately at hand. The various terms actually used by social workers to refer to their procedures for managing these contingencies included accounting, ball parking, claiming, clustering, cross checking, crystal balling, cutting corners, digging, doctoring, dredging up, drylabbing, estimating, faking, feeding (the computer), fudging, highlighting, juggling, justifying, overclaiming, padding, pinpointing, projecting, reviewing, revising, rounding (or rounding off), scratching, stretching, taking up slack, tampering, and totaling. The meanings of some of these terms were biographically unique (e.g., accounting, drylabbing). Others were widely shared and commonly used (e.g., faking, fudging, feeding the computer, estimating, overclaiming). Most represented practical resolutions to commonly encountered problems of official reporting. Some of the terms could be (and often were) used interchangeably by the social workers; others were specific for a given reporting format. To understand the social meaning of any one of these terms, it is necessary to understand the situation (or context) within which the term is used. For the social workers at the Metro Office, the immediate situation at hand exercised a determinant influence in judging the reasonableness of one or the other of the above practical procedures.

The practicalities of the official reporting context were many and often of an emergent nature. These included such features as the time available for completing a report, its temporal coordination with other activities, the space provided on a given form for particular entries, the importance (or relevance) then being placed on the report by others in the setting. In addition to such practicalities, however, there were some occasions when the relevance of the social workers' reporting activities was established by their futuristically rational determinations of the use of such reports in advancing what they (variously) defined as the desirable goals of the organization generally or of child welfare services specifically. The remainder of this chapter describes a series of events of this nature.

The annual time study

In addition to the routine record making the social workers at Metro did, and their constructions of various weekly, biweekly, monthly, and quarterly statistical reports, they were occasionally called upon to produce reports of a less routine nature. An example is the Annual Time Study, a report distributed every thirteen months by the State Department of Social Welfare. Preceding the two pages of additional department instructions for completing this report (attached as a department memorandum) were the following statements, all in capital letters, which presumably sought to establish the relevance and importance of this report for the social workers:

EACH EMPLOYEE OF THIS DEPARTMENT IS REQUIRED, BY STATE AND FEDERAL REGULATIONS, TO *COMPLETE* FORM XXX—93 FOR THE MONTH OF NOVEMBER, 1970.

IT IS IMPORTANT TO ALLOCATE TIME WORKED TO PROGRAMS AS ACCURATELY AS POSSIBLE BECAUSE THE FORM XXX—93 IS THE BASIS FOR COST-SHARING (FEDERAL-STATE-COUNTY) OF THE TOTAL ADMINISTRATIVE COSTS OF THE DEPARTMENT.

The Annual Time Study was usually distributed during the last week of the month immediately preceding the one the report was intended to measure. This report sought to measure (as accurately as possible) the exact amounts of time each social worker devoted to each of his welfare cases *according to the classifications listed on the report.* The allocations of financial resources (i.e., which one of the various cost-sharing formulas) were thought to be highly related to these classifications by the members within the setting (and other administrative officials as well).

Figuring it out

This particular Time Study was intended for November 1970. At Metro the two CWS supervisors received the report and the accompanying instructions during the last week of October. They distributed these to their respective units. The supervisor of Unit One distributed these forms to her workers individually, commenting only that the workers should fill out the report conscientiously because the entries would determine how much money the county could claim from state and federal governments. As with other such reports, several social workers received this one with mutterings of "another damn report to fill out!" Even though the workers' personal experiences with this report varied (as the following sections show), they commonly saw the Annual Time Study as another encroachment on their time, another contingency to manage.

Upon receiving the Annual Time Study and the instructions, three (of the five) workers in Unit One sat down to "figure it out," as they put it. They read the instructions contained in the department memo, and then the two additional pages of instructions on the reverse of the Time Study report itself. After finishing the instructions, the three workers began joking with each other regarding their feelings that, even after reading the instructions, they knew no more than they had before. This was followed by their respective speculations about what the various categories listed on the report might be taken to mean. One social worker commented about how incredibly funny it was for someone in the state administration to think there actually was something termed "pure social services" (see Table 1).

Most of the social workers appeared to regard most of the entries on the form as self-explanatory, meaning that many of the boxes at the top of the form (i.e., those not included in Table 1) did not warrant or receive any joint discussion. The discussion among the three workers of Unit One centered on one feature of the report that was not clarified by the instructions, and that remained problematic for them: the meanings of line C of Part I (titled "children") and line G of Part I (titled "child welfare"). The instructions defined "child welfare" (line G) as those duties pertaining to child welfare that were not being handled by the CWS social workers, apparently an anomaly from their perspective. During this discussion several of the workers from Unit Two (who had

Table 1. *The Annual Time Study*[a]

Part I: Pure social services									
Programs	1	2	3	4	5		29	30	31
A Aged									
B Blind									
C Children									
D Disabled									
E Medical aid									
F Adoptions									
G Child welfare									
I General relief									
K Joint programs									

[a]Table 1 includes only Part I of the Annual Time Study, as this is the only section of the report relevant for the CWS social workers' reports of time spent. Part II of the report included entries for welfare activities other than service activities, and a third section included boxes for time spent on special projects, time off (such as vacation or illness), or nonallocable time.

not yet received the Time Study report from their supervisor) joined this group around one of the desks in the office. Their discussion centered on the possible distinction between an entry on line C and an entry on line G. One of those present suggested the line titled "children" probably referred to those cases that were "aided" or "linked" — that the families receiving the services of the CWS workers were also recipients of one of the categorical aids (such as Aid to Families with Dependent Children or the medical aid program) dispensed by the county Department of Public Welfare (hence, under the shared subsidy of the state and federal government). Furthermore, the line titled "child welfare" probably referred to those cases that were "nonaided and non-linked" — that the county completely subsidized the administrative costs of the services. Another worker suggested the opposite. A third said both appeared equally plausible. Then another worker suggested that both these formulations were absurd. The form contained no spaces for reflect how the intake workers actually spent much of their time. All those present agreed that this was the problem at hand.

The supervisor of Unit Two and two of the three intake workers discussed the *possible uses* of the report. The statements at the top of the instructions noted that the report was in some manner related to the cost-sharing formulas used by federal, state, and county officials to determine the funding for the various welfare programs. But the exact nature of the relationship was not spelled out. Also, one question arising in these discussions related the status of funding for the present fiscal year to any changes the entries on the form might entail. After some discussion, this general conclusion was reached: The greater the numerical magnitude on the "child welfare" line of the report (i.e., the more time the workers indicated they spent on cases where the administrative costs were completely subsidized by county funds and where the families involved were not receiving any financial assistance from the cost-shared categorical aids), the more the statistical compilations could be used subsequently for one of two purposes by the workers. First, if the compilations of the Time Study reports indicated they were spending more time on the nonaided-nonlinked welfare cases (line G), then the results could subsequently be used to justify a request (or demand) to the county administration for a reduction of their yardstick number. The yardstick number is the number of cases each social worker is supposed to carry in his or her caseload at any one time. It is determined solely on the basis of the cost-sharing formulas and excludes any of their efforts in behalf of the nonaided-nonlinked welfare cases. The desirability of such a practical goal was not disputed by any of those present, as workers often commented about not having enough time to do all they would like to for their clients. Second, if the resulting compilations indicated that they were spending more time for their nonaided-nonlinked cases, meaning that such efforts were being accomplished in addition to the work done on those cases within the yardstick number, then it might be possible to make a subsequent case about how overworked the CWS workers had been. Hence, a request for increased allocations for additional social workers for the two units could be made. Those present also deemed this a desirable purpose.

With these emergent understandings of the potential meanings of the two categories and the potential uses of the report, the supervisor and workers formulated a practical strategy for completing the report. As the classifications did not easily fit much of the work done by the intake workers, all their screening out and one-shot service work would be placed under the "child welfare" category (line G). This would increase the likelihood of a subsequent justification for reduced caseloads and/or

entries on how they *really* spent their time, much of which was tak
up by paperwork, filling out various forms and requests, driving to
from home visits, making phone calls, and attending training sessio
So it would be absurd to suggest that either of the above formulati
would render an accurate account of their time.

What appeared an an insoluble impasse was (for the moment) resol
by the advice offered by a veteran of Unit One. He established the 1
vance of the advice by explaining how the report had been accomplish
the previous year. He suggested that line C was for the aided or link
cases and line G was for nonaided or nonlinked cases. Another work
then asked about cases involving families receiving general relief (the
only welfare program of financial assistance subsidized solely by cou
funds and not subject to the shared-cost formulas involving state or
federal financial participation). The veteran commented that such ca
did not easily fit the aided-nonaided and linked-nonlinked categories
He said, "Oh what the hell, throw them on line G," a reflection of hi
exasperation that the oversimplified entries of the form could not refl
the complexities of their everyday work. When departing the meeting
several commented on the irrelevance and unimportance of this parti
lar report. Several said they would be wasting their time by filling it out

"Fudging heavy"

On the same afternoon as the informal meeting described above, the
social workers of Unit Two who were still in the office were called to
unit meeting by their supervisor to discuss the completion of the Annual
Time Study. Attending this meeting were most, but not all, of the social
workers in Unit Two. Similar to the aforementioned discussion, the
conversation of this meeting focused on the possible meanings of lines
C and G. For the members of Unit Two, however, the nature of such a
distinction was much different from what it had been for the workers
in Unit One. All three of the CWS intake workers of these two units
were in Unit Two. The majority of their everyday work involved a
variety of screening out and one-shot service activities. These included
answering out-of-town inquiries (OTIs), responding to requests for information or referrals to other agencies (I&Rs), and investigating complaints by neighbors, which, if the problem turns out to be with the
neighbor, never reach the stage of becoming transformed into official
cases. Because of these, regardless of the criteria used to report their
various work activities, the Annual Time Study would not accurately

increased allocations for more workers. Even this decision, however, did not eliminate much of the ambiguity of the report categories. But the supervisor suggested they might be able to use such ambiguity to their own advantage. He informed his workers that, should any doubt remain about the appropriate category for their work, then they should "fudge heavy" on their entries on the "child welfare" line of the report.

On hearing the fudging heavy advice, one worker hastened to caution his colleagues. He established the relevance of his caution by commenting about what had occurred thirteen months earlier when the members completed the previous report. He enjoined his fellows to "show some moderation" in their fudging. He explained that on the basis of similar reasoning the previous year, he had padded his report to favor entries for the nonaided-nonlinked cases. But the administrative officials had kicked back the report for a recomputation of the entries. He offered an explanation of this. Although nearly all social workers shared an interest in reduced caseloads and assignment of new workers, administrative officials were interested in providing the numbers to justify as much state and/or federal money as they could get. The administrators, according to him, were interested in seeing that the entries on line C ("children") were much greater than those on line G, because the latter would imply an increased expenditure by the county without matching funds from state and/or federal agencies. The unit meeting concluded with this worker commenting that the success of their joint efforts would require some finesse.

The first time around: getting it done

Some of the social workers in the two CWS units expressed some interest in completing the Time Study report. A few clearly formulated their interests by viewing the report as a possible way of furthering their political goals or what they saw as the futuristically rational purposes toward which the organization should advance. But this was not true for all the workers in these two units. Most expressed little interest in this report. They frequently commented that it was useless for any of their purposes, irrelevant to their everyday tasks, and an encroachment on their (always limited) time. One worker remarked that the report "was just another example of bureaucratic red tape." Another noted, "it's just one of the many statistical forms we complete to keep the administrators off our backs, to keep 'em happy over there." Similar feelings were voiced by those who intended manipulating the entries on the report for what they saw as the broader goals of the organization. The Annual Time

Study was commonly seen as a relatively insignificant event by the members. But this did not preclude the possibility that it might have future uses.

A literal reading of the instructions accompanying the Time Study might suggest the appropriateness of daily entries on the report. But none of the members of either unit thought that such day-by-day record-keeping would be one of the sanctionable features of completing the report. None commented that the supervisors would apply pressure on a day-to-day basis; the report just was not considered important enough for that type of investment by the supervisors. The sanctionable feature of completing the Time Study report was seen to be its completion as such. Several conceived of the possibility of pressure at the end of the month, when the supervisors would be subjected to pressure from those above them in the organizational hierarchy. One social worker told me that the conscientious completion of the report was of no importance in and of itself. Rather, the importance of completing the report lay in the possibility that someone might remember, at some unspecified future time, that a given worker had been dilatory in completing the report (or turning it in) by the deadline specified in the instructions. Such facts were periodically used for building a case against a given worker, the documentary preparation for giving someone the ax, a practical strategy for personnel transfers within the organization.

One worker who expressed an awareness of the sanctionable features of completing the report managed this contingency by filling in all the daily entries for the month of November on the day the report was distributed (October 27). He termed this ad hocing procedure "faking it." The relevance of this procedure on this occasion was established reflexively, on grounds that the rules intended such a response in the first place. He reasoned that what would undoubtedly happen was this: A few of the other workers might record entries on a weekly or biweekly basis, but most would put it off until the end of the month, when they would be reminded of the deadline and would retrospectively record their entries for the entire month. He commented that he was hedging against this last minute rush by completing the report before the month began. Then he would have it ready for submission at the end of the month. As he completed the entries, I asked how he would determine the numbers he recorded. He reasoned that he presently had twenty four cases. Two of these involved families that were nonaided and nonlinked with any other welfare program. So he estimated that he would spend from one-tenth to one-twelfth of his time on these cases during the coming month. With this reasonable accuracy in mind, he recorded appropriate entries on lines C and G of the Time Study to construct a plausible image of one who had spent one-tenth to one-twelfth of his time on these nonaided-nonlinked cases. He further instructed me that such a plausible image did not mean he would record entries to reflect an expenditure of exactly forty five minutes per day for each of the thirty days of November. Rather, he would record entries to reflect, for example, the fact he had spent two hours on one day and none on another. He said it was common knowledge among the office workers that they were never that regular in their casework scheduling. So the plausibility of his entries would be assured by recording irregular a-mounts of time in each of the boxes.

During November the social workers in the two CWS units employed a variety of practical procedures in completing the Annual Time Study. Several workers, just as the worker above speculated, did wait until the end of the month before recording their daily entries for the entire month. Even in these cases, however, different procedures were used for the completion of the report. Reasoning the same way as the above worker, another constructed an image reflecting that she had spent ap-proximately one-eighth of her time on the nonaided-nonlinked cases. She reasoned that, as three of her twenty four cases were of this type, she probably spent about one-eighth of her time with them. Another worker who waited until the end of the month to complete her report reasoned differently. Even though only two of her twenty nine cases involved nonaided-nonlinked families, each of these involved many children. She spent a disproportionate amount of her time with them. Because she spent more time with these families, she established the appropriateness of entries that generally reflected the fact that she had spent about one-sixth of her time on these cases (i.e., line G, or "child welfare"). Like the worker mentioned previously, this worker did not record entries showing an expenditure of the same amount of time each day. Instead, she constructed her numbers in an irregular fashion to preserve the overall plausibility of the account. It is apparent that these workers used a generalized rule of plausibility rather than the rule of consistency routinely used in constructing other records at Metro.

Perhaps as many as half of the workers in the two CWS units record-ed all or some of their entries for the report on a weekly or biweekly basis. To do this they typically utilized the morning or afternoon when they were assigned phone duty for catching up on paperwork. This was a common strategy for managing the dual routines of paperwork and people work. One worker, whose phone duty fell on Monday, used this time to record entries for the previous week; another, whose phone assignment occurred on Thursday, used the time to record entries for that particular week; a third, whose day in the office occurred on Wednesday, used the time to record the entries for the three days of that week which had already passed, as well as for the two days which remained. (The worker had already scheduled her time for the next two days and, therefore, could reasonably determine how much time would be spent on the aided-linked cases.)

There existed some light bantering and joking related to how one might record coffee breaks, trips to the lavatory, the time spent on the Time Study itself. And, of course, there were several consuming preoccupations with "shooting beavers" mentioned by some office sportsmen.[3] But there were also discussions of a more serious nature about fundamental ambiguities regarding the appropriate classification of some activity. One such discussion involved the appropriate classification of time spent in training sessions, an activity to which nearly all members devoted a considerable amount of time, often to their consternation. A worker in Unit One said she had decided to record her time spent in training sessions on line C of the report, because this would justify the receipt of more state or federal monies. Another worker from Unit Two, not one of the three intake workers, informed me he had decided to record the time he spent in training on line G of the report. His reasoning was that this would take up some of the slack because the report did not adequately reflect the intake work of his unit.

During November there was little discussion among the workers regarding the Time Study. Most saw the report as relatively unimportant, and few attached much significance to it. This is not to say, however, that any of the members were inadequately motivated to do their best in completing the task, as time permitted. Several workers imputed enough importance to the report to take the time (and trouble) to cross-check their daily entries with other records (which reflected some index of where they had actually spent their time). One worker, for example, constructed the plausibility of his entries by cross-checking them with his mileage sheet. This was a record the workers were required to keep on a home-call-to-home-call basis if they desired reimbursement for traveling expenses. This worker reflexively established the intention of the Time Study report as reasonable accuracy. He noted that his mileage sheet allowed him to "come up with a ballpark figure" that would suffice for realizing this intention. While standing beside his desk as he recorded the entries, I asked why he entered a 6 in one of the boxes on line C for a given day rather than 6.278. I suggested, with a wry smile, the latter figure might reflect with greater accuracy the number of hours he had actually expended on the aided-linked cases for that day. As one of my trusted intimates, he presented his face in a manner truly difficult to describe. He called my attention to the size of the boxes on the form (which were approximately one-eighth inch square) and said the very size of the boxes necessitated the entry of only one digit per box. He termed this rounding off. Another worker, similarly motivated to take the time and effort to establish a more objective index than her memory afforded, consulted all the "317s" she had done during the month (i.e., the newly instituted computerized forms that replaced the dictated narratives in the client's case records).

To say the workers typically defined the relevance of their entries for the Time Study by referring to the various practical circumstances within the setting (e.g., time available, temporal coordination of this task with others, considerations of the reports of others, and spatial limits of the form), or that workers used various ad hocing procedures to complete the task in a manner deemed sufficient for the purposes at hand, is not to suggest they were less than adequately motivated to complete this task. Many of the situations described above involved various emergent features of social interaction that no set of formal instruction or supervisory rigor could have been designed (or planned) to anticipate. This is even more apparent in the following descriptions of the several occasions on which the Time Study was kicked back for recomputation of the entries. Given a generalized pragmatic motive for getting the job done or getting on with it, emergent situations such as these literally require the use of member's capacities for practical reasoning, for determining the relevance of the appropriate social rule for the situation at hand, for putting closure on such emergent features to get the job done.

The first kickback: putting the tin hat on it

The deadline for completing the reports was the first day of December. On that day, the supervisors collected the reports and forwarded them to the appropriate administrative station at the county administration building. Three days later the reports were kicked back (returned) to the Metro Office. The department memo accompanying the returned reports asked the supervisor of Unit Two (the unit with three intake workers who classified most of their work on the "child welfare" line to increase the likelihood of additional expenditures and resources for CWS) to have the social workers recheck their entries for this category. This meant, within the context, that the magnitude of the entries for this category should be (in some unspecified manner) reduced.

Upon receiving the reports and memo, the supervisor of Unit Two did not return the forms to the workers for a recheck. Instead, he formulated a strategy that he termed "juggling the numbers a little" for resolving this emergent problem. To accomplish this, the supervisor went through the six reports from his unit and altered the numerical

ratios (i.e., between the entries on lines C and G) in a minor fashion
that he considered sufficient for the purposes of responding to the (obviously ambiguous) department memo. In telling me about his actions,
he reflexively grounded the relevance of this by referring to his concern
not to inconvenience the workers further with this relatively unimportant matter. Seven weeks later, at the time of the third recomputation
of the report, he recalled these earlier efforts. He reflected that, at the
time, he thought his efforts had "put the tin hat on it."[4] Upon further
reflection on the unanticipated consequences that emerged during the
subsequent weeks, however, he noted that his earlier judgment was perhaps premature.

The second kickback: redefining the categories

Seven days after the Time Study reports were resubmitted to the Fiscal
Services Office, they were kicked back again, this time accompanied by
more elaborate instructions. The reports were not returned directly to
the supervisors. They were returned to the assistant chief at Metro. She
called the supervisors to a conference to discuss the problem at hand.
As the Time Study reports stood at that moment, she said, they would
entail a completely unrealistic budgetary request for the coming fiscal
year (owing to the large entries in the "child welfare" category). The
assistant chief then informed the supervisors it would be necessary to
return the reports to the individual social workers for a recomputation
of their entries in terms of the new instructions she had just received.[5]

The detailed instructions accompanying the returned reports were
elaborated in a departmental memorandum routed to the assistant chief
at Metro by the Fiscal Services Office. This memorandum was marked
"for limited distribution," which meant the assistant chief was to communicate the instructions verbally, not allowing the supervisors (or
workers) to read or possess copies of the memorandum. Such a device
reflects the insider understandings of the (actual or potential) evaluative
uses to which such documentary evidence might be put, especially its
possible use to build a case for some sort of adjudicatory process at
some (unspecified) future time when the social meanings of the events
might be redefined by others for different purposes, as in the case of
what the popular press termed "the My Lai Massacre." This is an especially delicate matter when the situation at hand involves actions that
could be plausibly interpreted by outsiders — those removed from the
immediate situation in time and space and, hence, lacking understanding of the emergent features — as clandestine, surreptitious, or immoral.
I have no direct experience with this, but trusted intimates at Metro

tell me that one can demonstrate organizational acumen by destroying such potentially dangerous documents before "they return to haunt you" in some unanticipated manner.[6] Such situation-specific tactics are typically subsumed under the more general rubric of "protecting yourself" or "covering yourself." These are commonly used terms from the organizational lexicon reflecting the omnipresence of politics in everyday life.

The two CWS supervisors returned from their meeting with the assistant chief with detailed notes on the new instructions pertaining to the recomputation of the Time Study. They immediately called a meeting of the social workers in their respective units. As before, the new instructions focused on the problematic meanings of the "children" versus "child welfare" categories. During one of these unit meetings the supervisor explained that the purpose of the new instructions (as well as the recomputation) was to delimit further the rules used for constructing the entries on the "child welfare" line. This intended a more realistic budgetary request related to child welfare services. For the purposes of the recomputation, the new instructions called for the inclusion of the following situations on the "children" line: (1) all cases where the only needs are medical (termed "medically needy only"); (2) all cases involving families who have been the recipients of some financial assistance from the welfare department within the last three years, and all families linked to such aid (these were termed "former cases" in the instructions); and (3) all cases involving family disorganization or any other indications of an unsuitable or unstable environment which, in the judgment of the social worker, would or could lead to the subsequent linkage of the family with one of the categorical aid programs (these were termed "potential cases"). In addition, there was a further specification of the meaning of "potential cases." Regardless of any social worker's judgment regarding the suitability or stability of the family environment, all families were to be classified as "potential cases" if their income did not exceed by 50 percent the figure for a family of comparable size receiving aid to families with dependent children.

On hearing this last instruction, all those present at the meeting burst into laughter. One worker commented that the new instructions had successfully managed to include everyone he had ever encountered as a social worker in the last ten years. Several of those present commented:

I. R.: Wait a minute, this is getting as ridiculous as that piece of shit we fill out every three months [referring to one particular portion of the State Statistical Report]. If it's a former case, then you don't have any records lying around to find out how much time you spent on it, and if it's a potential case, well then you don't have it yet. When you . . .

O. T.: No, this isn't the same. The former and potentials refer to those you've got now. The way you deter- . . .

I. R.: Jesus, does it really make any difference? I mean how many of your, tell me now, how many families have you seen in the field which couldn't be called a potential case. You've just got to be kiddin' me if you really . . .

O. T.: Yeah, you've got a point [begins laughing].

S. W.: What about the OTIs and the I&Rs? You mean after all of this rigmarole we still don't know what to do with the OTIs, the I&Rs, and the general file cases?

A. E.: Oh, for Christ's sake! Are you still worrying about that? Can't you see that [the assistant county director of the Department of Public Welfare] wants us to put everything on the first line?[7]

Even from these brief remarks it is apparent the members present understood the newly formulated instructions differently. One worker understood the new instructions in terms of the intention he imputed to them. Another noted certain ambiguities that the new instructions did not clarify. Shortly following these remarks, one intake worker again raised the question pertaining to the appropriate classification for Out-of-Town Inquiries (OTIs), Information and Referral requests (I&Rs), and cases that were "general filed" (i.e., those typifications of the daily work of intake workers that did not result in an official "case" for record-keeping purposes). The supervisor said, as the new instructions did not even mention such cases, he presumed the workers should classify these as before, that is, under "child welfare." The meeting then broke up. The workers returned to their other duties, expressing in various idioms their consternation, exasperation, anger, futility, and displeasure regarding this recent development.

Following the meeting, the supervisor for this unit commented to me:

G.U.: I just hate things like this. I originally told my workers to count all of the [nonaided-nonlinked] cases under child welfare, and if they were going to fudge, they should fudge heavy. That's how we get more workers. But now I have to tell them to do just the opposite, to fudge in the other direction.

J. J.: Well you couldn't have known that . . .

G. U.: These are the kinds of things I call completely useless actions. This is really what people are pointing to when they talk about all of the waste and inefficiency of bureaucracies. It's like, you know, it's like digging a hole in the morning and filling it up in the afternoon. When you ask your workers to do something like this it can only hurt their morale and diminish their respect for their jobs and the authority of their supervisors. Even their respect for the agency as a whole . . . and we keep on using these terms which don't mean anything, which are really covering up the inefficiency and waste of the system, like "delivery of services" and all those . . .

J. J.: It's really hard to see how so much hassle can be caused by such a seemingly simple report. Why do ya' think the administrators are getting so . . .

G. U.: That's what it's all over. One set of numbers versus another set of numbers. That's what's keeping the bureaucratic cogs rolling.

Shortly thereafter one of the intake social workers commented to me:

T. A.: It's like they're saying this: We want to find out something from you, and here's what we want to find out . . .

J. J: Yeah, it does sound like that all right.

I wasn't able to attend the unit meeting for Unit One, but later that same afternoon, as I was seated at one of the desks in the office reading a case record, the supervisor for this unit approached me and said:

P. Z.: I suppose you heard about classifying everyone as aided or linked if they've been aided any time in the last five years?

J. J: What?

P. Z.: We had this meeting around eleven. We got this new memo from . . .

J. J.: Oh? The Time Study?

P. Z.: [nods head] We're now supposed to reclassify all our [nonaided-nonlinked] cases as aided or linked if there is any deprivation or unmet need. Doesn't make any difference whether or not they're on welfare. If they've been aided or linked to an aided case within the last five years, if you think they might be within the next five years, or if, in your judgment, there's any chance of danger in the home. Oh I don't know. It looks like they want nearly all our hours recorded as aided in order to justify their budgets for their federal funding . . . The forms didn't justify what they had already decided they wanted for funding purposes, so they're asking us now to cheat on the numbers for them . . .

J. J.: Well how much difference is this from what you told them in the beginning, I mean . . .

P. Z.: I didn't tell them anything! The instructions seemed pretty clear to me, though I realize some complications from [the other supervisor's] unit. I just passed them out.

On the basis of my understanding of these events at this point, I think it is true to say that all the members of the two CWS units had developed a sense that the social rules were problematic, at least in this particular situation. This is not necessarily to imply, however, that such a sense led them to generalize from their understandings of this particular situation to other situations. The comments of the two supervisors above, especially with respect to their differential use of several plural pronouns to impute meanings of organizational membership, make clear that the workers are continually aware that the formal rules and regulations may be differently used by various members for different purposes. But the above transcription also reveals that such an understanding does not necessarily threaten the integrity of the common-sense assumption that social action is normative (rule-governed) in nature. In different terms, when confronted with such a problematic experience, the members may establish the truth of the assumption that social actions are rule-governed by either (1) referring to the uniqueness of the particular situation at hand or (2) calling into question the intentions or motivations of other users of the rules, which have apparently led to different interpretations of the same rule.

To accomplish the recomputation, none of the social workers (at least insofar as I was able to observe or learn about through informal conversation) made any attempt to recapture any data on their time spent during November by consulting some other form of documentation, to reinterpret the meanings vis-à-vis the new instructions. Several reasoned that however one might interpret the intentions of the new instructions, it appeared obvious that one intention had been eliminated; namely, that the Time Study intended some simple index of how they had really spent their time. As I observed one worker do the recomputation, he commented:[8]

> *J. J.:* You're back at the Time Study again I see.
> *O. L.:* Another day, another form. You should've learned that by now.
> *J. J.:* How're you determining the numbers there, I mean, what . . .
> *O. L.:* Well, I looked into my crystal ball this morning and . . . [looks up at me with a grin]
> *J. J.:* No, really.
> *O. L.:* Hell, how should I know. Fiscal apparently wants the ratios lower, so I'm lowering the ratios. Mine was about half and half before, so I'm just changing them to about seven to one, more or less.

Another intake worker managed this uncertainty by waiting until several of the others had already done their recomputations. He retrieved their completed forms from his supervisor's desk. He said to me that he "just juggled the numbers to come out somewhere between [the numerical ratios from the reports of two other workers]." The differences in the various ways of doing the recomputation versus the workers' initial efforts must be understood in terms of the different social meanings imputed to the intention of the Time Study at a subsequent time. This intention was established reflexively by referring to what had occurred before.

The third kickback: "kissing the gunner's daughter"

Following the successful completion of the recomputations, the reports were once again forwarded to Fiscal Services, arriving there around the middle of December. Within the next several weeks few comments were made about what had occurred and, I commonsensically presume, the details of these events receded from the memories of many of those at Metro.

Six weeks later, another official report that appeared to be very similar to the original Time Study report was distributed to the social workers in the two CWS units. Each of these forms was accompanied by two pages of instructions. The instructions carried the signature of one very highly positioned administrator. The supervisors distributed the new forms and instructions to the workers.

The new instructions began with a reference to the recent completion of the Annual Time Study. The first paragraph noted the figures representing the budgetary allocation for CWS for the present fiscal year and commented that the overall compilations of the recent Time Study would lead to a budgetary request for the coming fiscal year exceeding that figure by more than 300 percent. The first paragraph concluded with a statement to the effect that, given the present status of public welfare within Western State, such a request would be unrealistic.

The remainder of these two pages included detailed instructions for completing the attached form. The instructions noted that the form was not to be interpreted as another time study. Rather, it was a request for further information regarding those cases classified on the "child welfare" line of the previous Time Study. Instead of including entries for the "time spent" on such cases, however, this new form only asked the workers to record such cases by case name, case number, whether judged to be a "former case" or a "potential case" or within the nonaided-nonlinked category. The instructions defining how such categories were to be determined for the purpose of this report were substantially the same as those transmitted by word of mouth at the unit meetings six weeks earlier. Moreover, these new instructions clarified one previously ambiguous matter (and instructed the workers to classify this particular type of case as a "potential case" on the new form). On this new report there were no provisions for entries on how much time each worker spent on casework within the respective classifications.[9]

Within the unit meeting, these new instructions were initially greeted with expressions of anger, exasperation, chagrin, and routine bitching. When these subsided, the first issue raised concerned the *intention* of this new report. Was it the same as the Time Study? Or was it, as stated, not the same as the Time Study? The accompanying instructions began with several statements about the Time Study, and then, in the next paragraph, other statements disavowed any connection with it. Why would anyone want to know about their nonaided-nonlinked cases in the distinctive terms of the Time Study? This issue was discussed by the workers for some time, without apparent resolution.

Then several workers raised essentially the same questions about the form which had been raised at the meeting six weeks earlier (e.g., regarding the appropriate classification for Out-of-Town Inquiries). None of these was clarified in the new instructions. The supervisor departed the meeting momentarily to recruit the Metro assistant chief as a possible resource for clarification. The assistant chief joined the meeting, listened to the questions, commented on her uncertainty, and departed the meeting momentarily to solicit the aid of the chief of the Metro

Office. The chief could not be found at that moment. So the assistant chief telephoned the highly positioned person whose name appeared at the bottom of the instructions. She returned to the meeting with the knowledge sufficient for resolving these practical problems.

On returning, the assistant chief addressed each of the four or five ambiguous and vague features that had not been resolved by the new instructions. To make a long story short, the closure she suggested for each of these issues, with one exception, involved classifying each under "children" (or what would have been equivalent to line C of the initial Time Study). In other words, the new classifications would mean that virtually none of the CWS cases would be classified under "child welfare." On hearing this, the supervisor of Unit Two noted that if the workers used these new classifications, the report would not reflect the real nature of the work the CWS social workers did. The assistant chief told the supervisor that this new form should not be seen in the same manner as the initial Time Study. The supervisor then remarked: "We'll be digging our own graves if we fill out the form like that!" (a metaphorical reference to the possibility of budget cuts in the CWS allocations). The assistant chief made several comments that appeared to cool the supervisor off, comments suggesting the consequences of such actions would probably not be as grave as the supervisor suspected. The meeting adjourned on this note.

Immediately following this meeting, and for several days afterward as the social workers completed this new report, all were much more emphatic in expressing their interpretations of the events relating to the Time Study then they had been at any time previously. During the meeting itself one worker scribbled a note, which he passed on to me. It said: "This is bureaucratic absurdity at its peak — I don't recall Max Weber writing about this!" Several workers of each unit who had previously interpreted the Time Study as having little importance except as a relatively trivial matter of routine practicality, on learning of this recent twist, constructed new meanings for these events. Some of these involved what are commonsensically thought to be moral interpretations (e.g., lying, cheating). One worker who had expressed great concern three months earlier about using the Time Study as a potential resource for advancing what he defined as his own political purposes within social welfare continued to take action on this basis in spite of the new instructions promulgated in the meeting. He also expressed his feelings about the assistant chief (and "where her head is"). Another worker who had similar feelings three months earlier remarked that the recent events symbolized a defeat, a phenomenon to be expected periodically within the realm of political action. And another worker, although not having previously defined the Time Study in such political terms, appeared reflexively to reinterpret it as such at the conclusion of this final meeting. One of those in the setting who had witnessed these events as they unraveled over the three months was an ex-U.S. Navy chief. His observation at the conclusion of this final meeting was that recent events appeared to indicate that the CWS workers had "kissed the gunner's daughter" once again.[10] These interpretations were additionally reinterpreted over the course of the following weeks as well, and, in principle at least, are subject to further modifications.

Concluding remarks

These ethnographic materials describe how one official statistical report was successfully accomplished by social workers of two CWS units at the Metro office. And on several different occasions. The materials show that the intended purposes of the workers (at one or more times during the three-month period when the events occurred) were related to their futuristically rational estimations of the actual or potential uses of the statistical data they were asked to provide. Furthermore, this chapter shows that this particular reporting situation brought forth motivations to construct numerical representations as a presentational (or rhetorical) device. It was a way of presenting to others an image of looking good, for furthering their (variously defined) practical purposes concerning budgetary allocations and staffing policies.

Throughout most of this century sociologists and other social scientists have utilized the data provided by offical agencies to formulate or test their theories. For the theories first conceived and articulated by Emile Durkheim as well as many of the more contemporary variations (such as Robert Merton's theory of deviance discussed in the first pages of this chapter), the validity of official data is absolutely crucial. But rarely have sociologists invested the time and effort to study the conditions under which such statistical information is put together. This is because sociologists have failed to examine their assumptions about the mandates and practices of official organizations of social control. Sociologists have traditionally assumed (1) that official mandates reflect a homogeneous set of moral meanings (values, norms, interests, attitudes, beliefs, perspectives, orientations, or other social meanings) in the society; (2) that the moral meanings remain relatively stable over time; (3) that only the moral meanings and no others are important for understanding social actions; (4) that the societal members, and especially those working in formally rational, bureaucratized settings, unproblematically know what should be the correct meanings for their actions; and (5) that if any apparent conflicts or apparent differences are found to exist in a given setting, such differences may be properly understood as merely differential interpretations of the homogeneous set of moral meanings (presumably) definitive of competent societal or organizational membership. At the beginning of this chapter these assumptions are termed the transcendence theory of social meanings.

Comparing the traditional assumptions with our ethnographic materials about the Annual Time Study shows clearly that *none* of the assumptions is supported empirically by this evidence. The chapter points out the existence of various conflicts and different meaningful interpretations occasioned by this reporting situation. Moreover, instead of being mere differences of opinion, these conflicts and differences were the grounds for different moral assessments and valuations made by the social workers. The detailed account presented here also emphasizes that an organizationally correct reading and/or completion of the Annual Time Study was clearly not one of the givens of the Metro situation. It had to be figured out in light of other understandings of the setting's organized features, as they emerged or changed over time. All this is readily evident if one tries to place oneself in the shoes of the CWS social workers. Is the correct reading or completion of the report the one where the Out-of-Town Inquiries, for example, are recorded on line G? Or line C? There existed no absolute set of rational cognitive criteria exercising a determinant influence on the social workers in this case. To determine the reasonableness of a given construction at a particular time, the workers reflexively established the relevance of their (various) other understandings of the immediate tasks. These included various practical considerations and their various individual ideas, purposes, plans, goals, feelings, and values. Some of these were bounded by the immediate situations in which they occurred, such as Time Study entries influenced by one's immediate bodily feelings. Others were of a relatively transsituational nature such as the feelings of resentment between one of the CWS intake workers and the assistant chief or the political feelings expressed on several occasions by several (but not all) of the CWS workers.

This chapter began with an expressed interest in an appropriate theoretical concept of meaningful action that would reflect the actual experiences of the Metro CWS social workers with the Annual Time Study. The ethnographic materials provide clear evidence that, in actual situations of daily life, there are both situational and transsituational elements of social actions, both feelings and cognitions, practicalities and values. All these (and more) may be brought together in specific occasions. The Metro workers' successful completion of the Annual Time Study may be appropriately conceived of as an *occasioned transcendence* in that the Time Study report occasioned one or more opportunities for the participants to try to use this situation in their on-going and self-organizing efforts to stabilize or change the nature of their daily situations in accord with their individual desires, motives, intentions, plans, dreams, fears, hopes, interests, politics, and feelings. To understand the meanings of a specific social worker's actions on a particular occasion correctly, it was often crucial to understand the underlying feelings that motivated that specific course of action. These were often the prime movers of what occurred. The materials presented show clearly that the reasons and rationality of the verbal and written accounts typically came very much after the fact of these existent feelings. This is not intended to deny the realities of retrospective interpretations; these are necessary and inevitable insofar as we feel a curiosity further to understand our daily existence. Rather, it is an attempt to put first things first, the theoretical calling for the reflections and researches of existential sociology.

PART V

The existential self

9

The chronic pain experience

JOSEPH A. KOTARBA

Feeling physical pain is a universal element of human experience. Every-day life is filled with feelings of pain — headaches, a child's teething, muscular spasm, or unexpected minor accidents. Because everyday pain is such a common experience, we usually blurt an impulsive "ouch," rub the wound, maybe pop a few aspirins, and accept it all as part of life. Occasionally, we experience episodes of severe or unremitting pain as the result of a traumatic accident, a disease, or giving birth. In such situations we ordinarily consult professional health care personnel. Our common sense expects the expertise of modern medicine to locate the cause of the pain and eliminate it.

For a large segment of our population — the people who endure chronic pain — physical suffering is more problematic than the typical pain experience. For them, pain is a devastating element in their every-day lives with which they must contend. Shealy (1974) has estimated that there are at least 20 million Americans who constantly seek medi-cal help for chronic pain. Approximately 7 percent of serious injuries of all types result in chronic pain. The most frequently diagnosed dis-orders resulting in chronic pain are spinal (disc) diseases, postoperative complications, migraine headaches, digestive tract disorders, arthritis and rheumatism, cancer, and various traumatic injuries. The pain result-ing from these becomes chronic because it does not respond to conven-tional modes of treatment. Modern medicine's usual relief consists of overprescribed and habit-forming analgesic drugs (Lennard et al., 1971). Common sense suggests that constant pain affects one's activities, social interactions, self-image, and world view. Nevertheless, sociologists writing of health and illness have ignored chronic pain as an element of human behavior. Suchman (1965), Mechanic (1968), King (1972), and others have perceived pain as a sensory indicator or symptom that re-sults in a person's feeling that something is wrong physically. This symptomatic stage of illness is seen as the beginning of behavior patterns whereby the person interacts with the medical community to have the cause of pain diagnosed and eliminated. The literature has assumed that all these pain experiences are acute and will be alleviated in direct proportion to the success of the medical treatment in solving the physiological problems. This assumption, however, cannot be made for the person with chronic pain, for often there is no definable source of the suffering. In these cases pain becomes a disease itself and not just a symptom (Bonica, 1953). The existential relevance of pain as disease — and therefore an illness in its social implications — has been ignored by sociologists.[1]

The research described in this chapter was undertaken to obtain a sociological understanding of the everyday experiences of people who suffer chronic pain. Most such people appear normal to others and lead normal lives (i.e., they are not ordinarily hospitalized during the periods they feel pain, as those with severe medical disorders are). Therefore, a crucial research goal was an exploration of the ways an intense, existential feeling such as chronic pain affects otherwise normal lives. Another goal was an examination of the means used to alleviate this suffering, including various approaches outside standard American medical practice.

The methodological form of this research was participant observation, both by chance and choice. The chance resulted from the fact that the researcher is a natural member of the group studied. For several years I have had a chronic back disorder for which I have occasionally sought medical attention. During 1974 I decided to undergo a series of acupuncture treatments. The acupuncturist, a medical doctor who practices in Arizona, was knowledgeable about and interested in sociological perspectives on health and illness. We frequently engaged in lengthy conversations on these topics. Through these conversations and my reflections, it soon became obvious that people who suffer chronic pain are misfits, or deviants, sociologically and medically. Sociologically, they do not fit existing models of health and illness behavior, as is discussed in the concluding remarks of this chapter. Medically, in the words of that understanding acupuncturist, they are little more than " a pain in the ass" to family doctors and specialists. These frustrated professionals can do little more for their chronic pain patients than continue prescribing pain killers and muscle relaxers. This results from the fact that relief of chronic pain has been one of modern medicine's biggest failures. One afternoon, while my back and neck were riddled with six-inch needles, I asked the physician if he would be interested in being a resource for a study of acupuncture and people with chronic pain. He agreed.[2]

The first part of the research was complete at the point of my request. I had a store of vivid recollections of my own experiences with chronic pain and its effects. I had only to decide the means I would use to gather data on others with chronic pain. Participant observation was the most logical course of action, especially in light of the research objectives. I was interested in obtaining an understanding of the experience of living and dealing with chronic pain. Positivistically oriented procedures that would fit these people into an abstract model of behavior were unacceptable; my personal knowledge was that these people did not fit the sociological fantasies created to show that sick behavior is rule-governed like other social behavior.[3] The search for socioeconomic, cultural, and attitudinal indicators would have prohibited me from understanding the chronic pain experience from the actor's subjective, often emotional, and situational viewpoint.[4] As is stated in Chapter 1, only an understanding of social life based on commonsense, everyday experience allows a social researcher to maintain the integrity and inherent properties of it.

The reasonable starting point for collecting data was the physician's office where I received acupuncture treatments. In the United States the tremendous growth in popularity of acupuncture in recent years has brought the previously obscured reality of chronic pain to our attention. My own experience indicated that many people who shared the acupuncturist's waiting room with me were there in hopes that acupuncture would alleviate their chronic pain. During August and September of 1974 I continued the acupuncture treatments and maintained the sole identity of a graduate student with a bad back. Only the physician knew that research was taking place. At every opportunity I engaged other patients in casual conversation about their private lives, their encounters with the healing arts, and their pain. These conversations occurred in the waiting room, double occupance treatment rooms (where other patients and I waited for the nurse to remove the needles), and occasionally over coffee. When my series of treatments was completed, I exposed my hidden role to my contacts. I said I had decided to write a paper on acupuncture for a college class. Although this blew my cover, empathy with my contacts was already established. I soon became aware of a camaraderie among people who experience chronic pain, a closeness that exists because they feel that outsiders such as family, friends, and physicians do not really understand what it is like to experience pain all the time. This feeling is a result of the existential nature of the pain experience. Thus, openness and honesty were maintained in our following conversations.

The beauty of true participant observation is that the researcher's experience of self becomes data for the research. The researcher immerses his total self in the phenomenon in question, so that he experiences that phenomenon as a real actor — bodily, consciously, morally, and emotionally. His own experience thus serves four purposes in developing an understanding of the phenomenon.

1. Experience is a firsthand source of data. This is especially crucial for discerning the hidden aspects of human reality, such as physical sensations and emotions, that are not available from observation of others.

2. One's experience provides a basis for comparison with the experiences of others. For example, the awareness of my own fear of surgery gave meaning to the decisions of others with chronic pain to opt for conservative treatment.

3. One's experience generates points of inquiry. The fact that an educated and urbanized social scientist like myself decided to undergo an "unscientific" treatment like acupuncture led me to question the assumptions about marginal healing practitioners and their patients held by traditional sociologists.

4. One's experience helps the researcher attain a theoretical understanding of real events. The participant observer who operates with good faith and realizes the complexities he himself faces in making sense of the world is reluctant to espouse unrealistic and simplistic explanations for other people's behavior.

There were two other facets of the research. My physician was a valuable source for gaining access to other physicians and acupuncturists in Arizona, who, in turn, were sources for other chronically suffering people. Conversations with these people were usually more superficial than those with the first group, as expected. Nevertheless, my ability to empathize with their problems greatly enhanced rapport. Finally, I had the opportunity to attend a concentrated, weekend-long session in autogenic training offered by a pain clinic in Arizona. Fortunately, this session was held in December, near the end of my data gathering. This experience allowed interaction with twenty-four people who suffered chronic pain and who had never met me. I again assumed the sole identity of patient and was able to add to and verify much of the data gathered earlier. Throughout the research I interacted with approximately seventy-five people who suffer chronic pain. The following summarizes some of the most important research observations.

The secrecy of chronic pain

Chronic pain is a bodily sensation that is unique to the self, much like feeling and emotions. It is an experiencing of oneself that is not generally visible to others. Unlike blindness, paralysis, and other physical impairments that form part of the outward identity of a person, chronic pain is essentially known only by the person who suffers it. It is his own decision whether or not to make public his personal feelings of distress and attempt to communicate a sense of his pain to others.

There are several considerations that may lead a person to admit he is experiencing constant pain. He may seek the emotional support of family and friends. This occurs if the person feels that his pain is affecting his relationships with these significant others, or if he simply feels that he needs help in normalizing a problem that he cannot solve by himself. If the pain is severe enough to pose a threat to physical well-being or the normal management of his everyday life, the person may decide to divulge his pain experience to a doctor. The person may decide that it is beneficial to admit his pain to any of a number of other people who are relevant to his life, such as his priest, who can offer metaphysical consolation, or his boss, who may take the pain factor into consideration when judging the person's work.

These others form only one type of audience to the person who has chronic pain. The experiencing of oneself is also an audience to the self, and many people choose to keep the admission of pain to themselves. Because of the secrecy of these experiences, it is impossible to estimate their prevalence in our society, but it is obvious that millions of Americans suffer from hemorrhoids, continually sore arches, various vaginal discomforts, bunions, and other sources of chronic pain that are rarely seen in the doctor's office and are almost never mentioned publicly except to an understanding spouse. We can only speculate on possible reasons for this secrecy from our own experiences. Many people undoubtedly feel that their pain is too minor to admit or be concerned about. Others feel embarrassed to talk about hemorrhoids or vaginal problems, even to a doctor. People who try to maintain a healthy and youthful outward identity may decide that the public admission of aches and pain exposes their true physical condition and age. Finally, pain may be kept hidden because of fear of doctors or fear that the pain is a symptom of a more serious problem that will go away if ignored — or is so feared it cannot be faced.

Even those people who feel their pain is sufficient to admit to a doctor maintain a certain level of secrecy about their suffering. Mrs. Carlson, a sixty-year-old widow who injured her arm in a fall two years ago, explained the aspect of secrecy she maintained:

I don't complain to anyone about my arm. In the first place, it's nobody's business. People call you a hypochondriac if you complain all the time . . . It's better just to keep it to yourself and your doctor. I'm telling you about it because you're doing this for school. My sister complains all the time and everybody makes fun of her.

A person thus keeps his pain a secret in those situations where the acknowledgment of the pain is feared to be discrediting to the self. There is another level of secrecy that necessarily applies to all experiences of self, for feelings and emotions can be objectified through conversation and body language, but the uniqueness of one's body and self cannot be shared, even if so desired.

The people discussed in this research are those chronic sufferers who at some time felt that their problems were agonizing enough to warrant the exposing of self to a doctor. Among all people who must deal with chronic pain, they are only the tip of the iceberg. It must be kept in mind that the physical sensation of pain is the fundamental reality and that a person brings his private suffering to the forefront of social reality only when such action appears to him beneficial to the management of that pain or some other part of his life.

The management of chronic pain

Chronic pain becomes an element of a person's existence when he first feels it. The initial episodes of pain may be immediate and intense, as with traumatic injury. If a person feels the pain to be an indication of serious bodily damage, he seeks immediate medical care. Mr. Jackson, a thirty-seven-year-old heating repairman, related how his experience with chronic pain began with an occupational accident:

We were working this factory job out in Glendale about three years ago when it happened. I was working on the roof unit, so I was using the ladder a lot. I had to come down for something and when I got on the ladder it must have slipped. I fell about thirteen feet and landed right on my feet, you know, in a standing position. All I remember feeling was a crack in my back and I knew I busted it or something. The boys picked me up and took me to the hospital. The doctor there said that nothing was broken but my back sure hurt like hell, so they kept me there for a couple of days. All they did for me was make me take some pills and stay in bed.

Even though the pain involved with an accident may be severe, the person may not associate it with serious physiological damage. Assuming that it will go away in time, like other everyday pain, he ignores it or treats the injury himself with aspirins and heating pads. Judy, a twenty-four year old patient with spinal injury, took aspirins and stayed in bed for several days because she perceived her pain to be a result of overexertion and fatigue:

I remember first feeling pain in my legs right after a football game my senior year. I was a cheerleader then and I was really exhausted. My daddy said that I was hurting because I jumped around too much. I suppose I believed him . . . I thought the whole thing was stupid. I mean, I had to miss the high school winter formal because of what we thought was a pulled muscle or something.

My own experience with chronic pain began much like Judy's. In 1971 I was playing basketball after school with several students at a Chicago high school where I was a teacher. I remember coming down with a rebound and feeling a sharp pain in my right leg. My first reaction was that I had a pulled muscle. Assuming that I would shake it off, I tried to continue playing. Even though the pain never totally disappeared, I did not take any days off from school because I did not think it was sufficient reason to use up a sick day.

For many others, the discomfort begins subtly and gradually increases. This is especially true for people who have arthritis, migraine headaches, or postoperative pain. At the milder stages of discomfort, the pain is commonsensically attributed to such natural causes as getting old, tension, hard work, being on one's feet all day, or an expected result of letting a doctor cut you open. Mr. Ricci, a fifty-one-year-old retired labor leader, referred to his back problem as "railroad spine." When I asked him why he called it that, he replied that railroad workers almost always have painful backs because they work so hard. He assumed that his back pain was also the natural result of many years of physical labor. Mr. Ricci's medical charts indicated, however, that his condition was diagnosed as lumbar arthritis, a disorder that can also strike teachers and accountants.

When the chronic pain sufferer consults the healing arts is determined by several factors. As mentioned earlier, a person seeks professional attention immediately if he perceives pain as an indication of serious bodily damage that will not heal naturally. A person seeks professional care also if the pain is unbearable. Those who do not perceive the initial pain episodes as serious, however, do not consult a doctor or go to a hospital until they begin to fear something is wrong. This fear may result from the eventual realization that the pain has not gone away as expected, from an increase in the severity of the pain, from advice given by significant others, or from a combination of the above meanings given to the unending pain. The emotion of fear leads to action because the person's experience with bodily sensations, knowledge of health and illness, and attempts at self-treatment (i.e., either ignoring the pain or resorting to commonsense remedies such as aspirin and rest) have failed to alleviate the pain or give adequate reason to continue living with it. The fear is of the unknown meaning of the pain to the person's physical well-being and the threat it presents to the person's commonsense desire to lead a pain-free, pleasant life. In any event, a person usually takes action within three or four weeks of the initial episode of pain.

Whom one consults for relief is a consequence of one's practical knowledge of the healing arts. The family doctor is typically visited because most people have always gone to him first when they felt sick. The family doctor, incidentally, is usually a doctor of medicine, but he may be a chiropractor, osteopath, or other type of practitioner. Occasionally, the sufferer is sophisticated enough to go directly to a specialist, such as a neurologist or an orthopedic surgeon, but this happens rarely.

The usual response to one's complaint of pain is a prescription for conservative treatment. For the medical doctor, this means bedrest and Darvon tablets. An osteopath or a chiropractor schedules a series of manipulations.[5] A naturopath gives the patient a massage and a jar of vitamin E capsules. The treatment is conservative because the doctor usually says that the pain is a result of strained muscles, the osteopath and chiropractor blame it on the subluxation of a vertebra, and the naturopath says that the patient's total body harmony has been temporarily disrupted.

The above patient-practitioner interactions are, of course oversimplified. The important point is that all this has very little meaning or importance for the person with chronic pain. His primary concern is getting rid of the pain, and he trusts his family doctor to do this as expected. He is not accustomed to medical failure, so his anxiety increases when the conservative treatment fails to alleviate the pain. It then becomes apparent that his problem is serious. After several weeks of conservative treatment, the frustrated family doctor refers the patient to a specialist, or the patient pressures the doctor to refer him to a specialist, or the patient looks for his own specialist. Mrs. Carlson is one of the patients who used pressure: "My family doctor wouldn't believe me. He said that the X-rays were negative and that there was no reason why I should be hurting. I finally got him to send me to an orthopedic ... I don't blame my doctor for not knowing what was wrong with my arm; he's not a specialist, is he?"

At this point, the chronic pain sufferer still believes his problem will be solved: It is all a matter of finding the right doctor. His anxiety is mostly a result of feeling that the problem is serious. The person usually does not feel anxious over the still unknown but unbelievable notion that the problem is chronic and insoluble. The anxiety is lessened when the specialist defines the problem as serious but remediable. One elderly patient told me that she was in fact happy when her neurosurgeon said she needed a disc operation; at least, she said, it wasn't cancer or "something really serious." The radical treatment proposed by the specialist usually requires hospitalization and often surgery. Again, the patient's anxious response to this radical proposal relates to practical considerations such as taking extended time off from work, getting the medical insurance forms in shape, arranging for a babysitter. Every chronic pain patient who had surgery performed for his problem asserted that he agreed to surgery on the unquestioned assumption that it would be successful. The varying meanings of "successful" are enunciated later.

There are several reasons why some people decide not to undergo the prescribed surgery. An obvious reason is the high cost of surgery, hospitalization, tests, and x-rays. This is an important consideration for working-class people with inadequate medical insurance. They would never consider having surgery performed at the low-cost county hospital where all the welfare people "go for free," and they could never pay the cost of major surgery out of their own pockets. Nevertheless, the most prevalent and important argument given by those who refuse surgery is an emotional one. They fear surgery because of the danger they feel inheres in it. Judy decided against recommended surgery for this reason: "The orthopedic surgeon said that I needed surgery. Some friends of my parents said that back operations leave a lot of people crippled. This scared me, so my daddy took me to a chiropractor instead. Besides, daddy said that I was too young for an operation anyhow." Mrs. Reynolds is an eighty-six-year-old woman who has a painful nerve tic in her head. Her husband related how age was a factor in deciding against surgery: "The neurosurgeon said that the only thing that might help my wife would be to cut a big nerve in her neck. Now, let me ask you, how could I let him operate on a woman my wife's age?"

When the surgery is completed, it is invariably labeled "successful" on the surgery report form. To the patient, hearing that his operation was successful means that the cause of his pain has been eliminated and his troubles are finally over. His physician assures him that the pain he feels right after the operation is temporary. It will diminish in time with the help of some Darvon. In the course of this research, many nurses indicated that any surgery is labeled successful if the surgery crew is reasonably confident that the patient did not leave the operating room with a sponge or two sewed up inside him. Thus, the official declaration of success has no necessary relevance to the patient's original pain problem. After several weeks, he may realize that the postoperative pain has not diminished and he may be emotionally crushed when he finds that the surgery has resulted only in a huge medical bill, a jar of Darvon tablets, a scar, and more pain.

Whether or not the bout with the specialist results in surgery, the failure of this encounter inevitably changes the person's understanding of his problem. He now realizes that his pain is chronic, a depressing realization after putting total trust in the medical profession to solve his problem. His options are quite limited now. He can learn to live with it, as many frustrated doctors recommend or become a habitual drug user or a doctor hopper. I have never encountered a person with chronic pain who has learned to live with it. They just continue to contend with it. The last two options are those taken by most chronic pain sufferers.

The more severe a person's pain and the less he is able to integrate it into his everyday life (i.e., to minimize the pain's disruption of daily activities), the more he tends to maintain the search for the practitioner and treatment that will help him. As this search continues, the chronic pain sufferer is motivated less by trust in doctors than by sheer despair and hope. Mr. Herrin, a forty-seven-year-old insurance adjuster, related how his trust in doctors diminished:

> Don't ever go to an orthopedic if you have a back problem! Orthos are all traditionalists who have to actually see the cause of your pain on X-rays before they'll do anything for you. This one guy I saw said there was nothing wrong with me. He put me in traction for two weeks anyhow and that did no good. Later, I went to see a neurosurgeon I heard had a good reputation. He said I had a ruptured disc and did a laminectomy. It got rid of the pain in my right leg, but my back still hurt like hell. He said there was nothing he could do about it and told me to exercise and take some pain pills. I tell ya, you can't trust these doctors.

The despair and hope that motivates doctor hoppers result in some very unusual behavior. People who would never have considered consulting any other practitioner besides a medical doctor before the onset of their chronic pain find themselves going to hypnotists, chiropractors, osteopaths, naturopaths, yoga instructors, acupuncturists, and anyone else who offers hope. Several physicians have indicated that long-term sufferers come to their offices and literally dare physicians to cure them. In the search for a cure, many people undergo multiple surgeries; one man had eighteen operations performed on his back. And, as if their physical miseries were not enough, many chronic pain victims go heavily into debt in order to pay for the search. Mr. Moore, a seventy-five-year-old man with cervical disc disease, depicted his personal search for help in one simple sentence: "Forty thousand dollars' worth of work and I'm no better off!"

The role of habitual use of analgesic drugs in the chronic pain experience is noteworthy. Since I first injured my back, I have personally never taken pain killers. It is not because I am stoical; I just find an occasional shot of bourbon to be an effective analgesic. In any event, my nonparticipation in drug use probably left me insensitive to its crucial importance to the people involved in the research observations. It was not until the data-gathering portion was completed that I realized that for many veteran chronic pain sufferers the primary objective in undergoing bizarre therapies like acupuncture was not the elimination of pain but the elimination of their distasteful drug habits. They had already, more or less, accepted the fact that their pain was chronic, but they

were not prepared to spend the rest of their lives being stoned on down-
ers. They were looking to acupuncture primarily as a substitute for the
Darvon, Seconal, and codeine their physicians routinely prescribed. Mr.
Moore's wife related this aspect of her interest in acupuncture:

After my husband was operated on for his neck, he still hurt, so the doctor put him
on sleeping pills for nighttime and some other pills for the day. It worried me so because he would sit all day in front of the television like a zombie. You should know
that all these drugs are no good for anybody . . . Some friends of ours who went for
acupuncture themselves said that it can get some people off their drugs.

Mrs. Martin, a forty-year-old housewife who has suffered years of postoperative pain and related migraine headaches, relayed this evaluation
of doctors and drugs: "A good doctor . . . prescribes medication knowing its reactions and side effects. Before I came for acupuncture, my
doctor was prescribing about fifty dollars a month in drugs. Right now,
I'm only using a little Darvon once in a while." Penny, a twenty-nine-
year-old rheumatoid arthritis patient who miraculously was still teaching piano, told about the following experience with cortisone treatment:

From what I've heard, a physician is supposed to begin cortisone injections in small
amounts and gradually increase the dose if it's needed. My physician began with
massive doses. After ten years of cortisone, you can see what it's done to me. [All
her joints were greatly swollen and she had the typical cortisone-caused moon
face.] I was kind of hoping that acupuncture could help me without ruining my
body like cortisone.

Mrs. Jarvis, a fifty-five-year-old woman whose pain was a leftover from
postoperative peritonitis, bluntly stated her expectations of acupuncture: "Some of my friends told me about acupuncture and how they
use it to relieve pain instead of those goddam pills and dope all the doctors give out." Mr. Herrin described his encounters with drugs: "Since I
first hurt my back, I've collected more pills and capsules than any self-
respecting hippy."

Chronic pain and the communication of love

The search for a cure, although time consuming and financially burden-
some, is only one facet of the chronic pain sufferer's life. The need to
maintain ordinary daily activities forces him to negotiate between his
most personal feelings of distress and the expectations of the world
around him. The existential nature of the self to become rather than be
determined results in a continuous process of accommodating the
private reality of pain to the public reality of identity management and

social interaction. This process is difficult for most chronic pain sufferers because there are rarely any overt indications of impaired health that can be perceived by the commonsense eyes of family and friends or the professional eyes of doctors. Thus, the individual cannot play a Parsonian "sick role" (Parsons, 1951). Briefly, sick-role theory states that a sick person is allowed to be deviant (i.e., nonproductive and dependent) because his significant others are aware of his health impairment, define the problem as medically real, and therefore accommodate him until he is well. The chronic pain sufferer, however, is stigmatized as being sick only when his overt activities justify that reaction (e.g., when he is initially injured, when he is hospitalized). Most of the time he appears normal and is treated as such by others. His becoming of self is fundamentally influenced by his personal experience with pain and only secondarily by the interactive evaluations of the pain by others.

If the person's problem has a visibly recognizable cause, such as an injury or diagnosed disease, he and those he interacts with often attach a common meaning to the related pain. Common sense tells you that a bodily injury hurts and that an injury serious enough to warrant medical care, hospitalization, or surgery probably hurts a lot. Therefore everyone involved expects the person to behave like any other sick person and understands that the resultant inactivity, need for attention, and crabbedness disappear as the injury heals. The meaning of the pain usually becomes problematic after the injury heals, surgery is completed, or the expected recuperation period is completed. The victim still feels miserable even though he is up and walking and probably back to work. The people with whom he interacts, nevertheless, often begin to change their interpretation of the pain; more and more they blame him for not returning to normal behavior, using such explanations as, "He doesn't want to stop being babied," "He doesn't want to give up his disability compensation," "It's all in his head." The person's doctor may attach the last meaning to the pain by using the official definition "psychosomatic disease." If the pain does not originate in a commonly understood cause such as an injury or a diagnosed disease, as migraine headaches do not, the pain may be immediately defined by others as psychosomatic. The problem of psychosomatic pain is a medical issue I will not discuss as such. It is clear, however, that one cannot objectively decide whether another person is imagining sensations of pain. One sympathetic physician told me: "If a patient tells me he's in pain, there is nothing else I can reasonably do except believe him." This attitude, however, is rare among doctors.

The individual most often rejects the incorrect social definitions of his expressions of pain. To accept them would be destructive of the self, for the individual would then have to deny to himself his most personal and real bodily feelings. It is difficult continually to disregard the evaluations of others to whom the chronic pain sufferer looks for help, but the fundamental relationship of the self to its own body is the first reality, and the socially constructed reality is secondary. Mr. Herrin related his experience with this dilemma: "After a while you start believing what all the doctors tell you, that it's all in your head. Even my old lady thinks I'm a little goofy for seeing all these doctors . . . You'd think that by now someone would be able to help you. It's hard to believe that a person can imagine so much pain. It's just too real."

Maintaining the reality of chronic pain and the subsequent search for a cure by oneself is a lonely ordeal. An individual is better equipped to live with his pain if he gets emotional and financial help from significant others. In order to get this help, he must communicate a sense of the reality of his pain. He must symbolize verbally his most existential feelings. This type of existential communication must be based on love, for it is intensely personal and difficult to develop intersubjectivity of feelings. There must be a singularity of meaning attached to the pain by all parties involved for the individual to present a credible self to the world. In commonsense language, a person is better able to cope with his chronic pain if his family, friends, physician, and co-workers love, trust, and understand him. Judy described how her relationship with her husband affected her pain experience positively:

At first I didn't tell Mark about my bad back. I hated to use my back as a crutch; I never was much of a complainer. I soon realized that I wouldn't get over it so I told him. He was very understanding . . . I started feeling sorry for myself because I felt I was too young to stop all the activities I liked to do. Mark is a very athletic person and I felt bad that I couldn't keep up with him. He keeps telling me that it's not so important. He's always the one who decides to try a new doctor to help me out; it was his idea to come to Dr. Fitz for acupuncture . . . Yes, I get depressed and bitchy when my back hurts real bad, but Mark just ignores me until I feel better . . . I don't know what I'd do if he wasn't around to cheer me up.

It is the constant discomfort of the pain and not the definitions of others that most often leads to changes in the chronic pain victim's everyday activities. People with neuromuscular disorders tend to lessen the frequency and intensity of their sexual encounters. It just hurts too much to do a lot of sex. If true existential communication does not exist between the person with pain and his sexual partner, the partner may blame this paucity of sex on impotence, indifference, another lover, or other reasons because, again, there is no visible disability involved. The chronic pain sufferer may limit his body movement in other ways to lessen discomfort. He may begin by eating lunch in the office instead of walking all the way to the company cafeteria. He may spend all leisure time on sedentary activities such as watching television, instead of more social activities like visiting friends. The net result of lessened activity is threefold: (1) the person's social interactions tend to dwindle and he becomes a loner; (2) the inactivity frees the person's mind to concentrate solely on his pain and thus increases his depression; (3) the inactivity often increases the level of pain for the person with a neuromuscular disorder because he loses vital exercise.

Age is a crucial factor in a chronic pain sufferer's adjustment to his problem. A middle-aged or elderly person can combine his chronic pain with the normal discomforts of aging and get away with it, both to himself and others. A young person, however, may face a crisis of self because of his pain. The self is aware of being young and it presents a body-identity of youth and fitness. Yet the presence of constant pain results in the self's feeling alienated from its body. The body hurts, but for no apparent reason. Thus, many young people speak of their pain as if it were an entity in itself and not a sensation emitted by the body. A young person often tries to disguise the pain because he feels it is discrediting to his identity if it is discrediting to his self. This disguise is accomplished through avoidance of activities that divulge the pain and by lying to cover one's nonparticipation. The best example I can give of this behavior is my own experience. When I was a graduate student, the sociology department members played softball on Friday afternoons. The games were highly valued by the graduate students, especially when we thought about beating the professors. Forgetting about my back problem and thinking only about having a good time with friends, I played in the first few games. I limped home after every game, aching with back pain. I also became very self-conscious about hitting the ball and limping to first base. Nevertheless, I also felt self-conscious about telling those out-of-shape professors I wasn't going to play softball any more because of my back (as I was only twenty-seven and appeared physically fit). I avoided the embarrassing issue by scheduling observation time at a physician's office for Friday afternoons. I told everybody at school that I had to pass up the softball games to complete my research. I did not think they would understand because I myself could not understand why I was in pain.

Age is also a factor in self-evaluation when chronic pain forces a person in his prime earning years either to quit working or to take a less strenuous job. For a person who is used to being economically and physically productive, this may lead to a self-evaluation of inadequacy even with the support of significant others. Mr. Jackson, who was used to doing physical labor, found this adjustment highly disruptive of his image of self: "The thing that bothers me the most about my accident is that I gotta sit home all the time. Christ, I'm about going crazy!

Don't forget, I've been working most of my life, so I ain't used to sitting around like an old man."

Surprisingly, veteran sufferers of chronic pain are almost universally (and even unrealistically) optimistic about the future possibility of solution to their problem. This optimism is the result of the fact that they never learn to live with it and discard the incorrect definitions of the pain by others. After years of suffering and repeated failure to find a solution, they still struggle with their pain and believe they will eventually beat it. The reasons given for this optimism vary. Some believe that, because there is nothing pathologically wrong with them, the pain cannot go on forever. Others believe that modern medicine will eventually produce a solution because it has eliminated what they perceive to be more serious problems, such as polio. Finally, there are some diehards who believe that someone who can help them exists and he just has to be found.

Concluding remarks

The traditional sociology of health and illness has utilized two distinct conceptual models to explain the behavior of sick people: the sick role and illness as deviant behavior. The data presented in this paper indicate that neither model adequately explains the behavior of sick people. Both models have inaccurately asserted that human behavior is determined and shaped by one single element of social life.

The sick role (Parsons, 1951; Bloom, 1965; Sussman, 1965; Gordon, 1966) is based on the assertion that members of the American society share and esteem two values: independence and productivity. Physical disability is detrimental to the fulfillment of these values, so society makes provisions for emotional and medical care for the sick person, allowing him to be dependent and nonproductive during illness. In return, the sick person is expected to try to get well, accept his position of dependency, and seek proper medical care as provided by the scientific medical community. The society determines who is allowed to occupy the sick role according to its ability to support nonproductive members. In general, sick-role theory assumes that meanings of health impairment, proper medical care, and manners of behavior when sick are known or knowable by all societal members. For example, people who consult marginal modes of healing, such as acupuncture or chiropractic, are said to be emotionally unstable (Mechanic, 1968) or unsophisticated and undersocialized country bumpkins (Cobb, 1958).

The data presented here indicate that a person with chronic pain rarely conforms to this evaluative model. One's pain is first and foremost a private problem. When the pain is perceived as unbearable or a symptom of a more serious health problem, professional care is sought according to a person's practical knowledge of the healing arts. As pain persists, one feels little moral obligation to remain dependent on the definitions and treatments of scientific medicine. The desire for physical relief transcends any notion of how one ought to behave when sick. Thus, educated and sophisticated people — including many doctors of medicine — consult acupuncturists, chiropractors, and other healers who offer hope of relief when scientific medicine fails.

The concept of illness as deviant behavior (Mechanic, 1968; Freidson, 1970) is built upon the labeling theory of the symbolic interactionist perspective. When a person who feels sick either tells significant others about his bodily feelings or is observed by others as appearing sick, he is launched on a deviant career. The significant others — including the doctor — label the person as sick, define his health problem, and provide statements to the self of the sick person that are adopted as part of his self-image. In other words, the effects of bodily distress on a person's self-image are determined by the reactions of family, friends, and the definitive assessment of the doctor. Freidson (1970) went so far as to state: "Medicine creates the social possibilities for acting sick."

The person with chronic pain adopts the definitions of others when they are meaningful to the management of the pain. But this is frontwork, not reality. The primary definition of being sick comes from the person's body. Even the social definition, "it's all in your head" (or more professionally, "psychosomatic disease") that refers *directly* to the self is disregarded. One cannot reasonably deny bodily feelings because the body is the fundamental experience of life. Brute being is the foundation and overriding reality of life. As a result, the person with chronic pain seeks various modes of cure and adjusts his everyday life in response to the dictates of his body, whether or not the dictates of others correspond.

In developing an understanding of the chronic pain experience, we must remember that bodily distress is an existential feeling of the self. If the pain is not reflected in his outward identity, the person decides whether or not to make his pain an element of social interaction. If he decides to make his pain known to others, in order to enlist their help in managing the pain, he evaluates the reactions of others according to their usefulness to him. Throughout his experience with pain, the person is primarily motivated to interact with healers by his feelings of pain, trust, hope, and fear. It is up to the individual to make sense of his pain. Thus, the embodied self negotiates the appropiateness of social reactions according to its own feelings and sensations.

10

The existential self in the gay world

CAROL A. B. WARREN AND BARBARA PONSE

Since the emergence of modern individualism in the Renaissance, Western women and men have shared some general ideas about themselves, about what they are, about their very beings. Though there are undoubtedly great complexities to the commonsense ideas, people have shared a general belief that each person has a self, that each is a self. They have made use of complex ideas about *situated selves*. For example, they have believed that individuals have certain properties because they are involved in nation-states or in certain social class positions. They have believed that being an American, an Italian, or an English person leads one to be certain different things in different situations: "As an American, I feel I must support my nation's policies in Romania"; "As a member of the gay community, I must support the new 'sex among consenting adults' law." But they have also assumed, and more consistently, that behind such complex sets of situated selves there is a *substantial self*, the real me, the thing I still always am when I am all those different and varying situated selves: "He's been my doctor for years, but I never suspected what he was really like until I met him at the club and got to know him as a whole individual"; "She's really completely different when you get to know her off the job."

These basic ideas of situated selves and substantial selves lie behind all the early theories of the self in sociology.[1] The earliest sociologists, such as the mechanists, had no significant theory of the self, for they were not concerned with individuals. The structural funtionalists also had almost no theory of the self, for they too had only a minimal interest in individuals. They were concerned with studying structures and functions, not individuals' concepts of themselves or others. Even when they were concerned with explaining actions, they tried to do so with no direct observations or mentions of the men- and women-of-flesh-and-bone. They exhorted each other to "explain the social socially" and strove valiantly to avoid any hint of the sin of reductionism, which

273

would have committed them to looking directly at concrete individuals. They were interested in code-book law and official rates of crime, not in how criminals look at themselves. Even the action theorists, such as Talcott Parsons, had little to say about self-definitions, even when they talked about personality systems. Instead, they have been concerned with social roles, role sets, and so on. These roles were commonly assumed to make up individuals' definitions of themselves, at least for all sociological purposes, because they were assumed to determine the individuals' actions in the world.

Ethnomethodologists have been primarily concerned with invariant properties of mind. Though these properties can be assumed to constitute the individuals' beings, they do not say anything about the individualness of concrete persons or minds. They look only for the properties all individuals have in common, so individual selves of flesh-and-bone beings are just as totally irrelevant as all the vast differences in the things those concrete beings do. Why should one worry about the self-concept of the murderer when one is interested only in the things that make him the same as the victim? The other phenomenological theorists, such as Berger and Luckmann (1967), have been more concerned with the construction of selves, but with the important addition of the idea of alternation or *transformation* of self-concepts (see below), they have followed the symbolic interactionist theories rather closely.

The symbolic interactionists have made the major contributions in sociology to the theory of the self. There are many presentations of the symbolic interactionist theory of the self (e.g., Blumer, 1969), and we need give only the general outline here. Following Mead (1934), almost all interactionist theories made the commonsense distinction between the "me," which is the set of situated, socially defined selves (an American, a doctor), and the "I," which is the substantial self lying behind the me. The pre-Goffmanian interactionist theories were concerned primarily with ways in which both the I and the me are *determined* for the concrete individual through community socialization. In general they argued that significant others (i.e., the people with whom one is emotionally involved in primary, face-to-face interactions) symbolically define the self for the individual. These symbolic definitions, communicated and reinforced through the shared universe of symbols (e.g., hair length, color of clothes and walls), make up the looking-glass self, which becomes the individual's definition of her- or himself and then the determinant of actions. Goffman added an important dimension to the interactionist theory, though he assumed all of this as well. As we

saw in Chapter 3, Goffman was concerned with the individual's dramaturgical presentation of situated selves (learned social roles) to achieve
his purposes in a given situation.

All these earlier sociological treatments of the self were grounded in
the traditional commonsense ideas about situated selves and substantial
selves. The structural functionalists were concerned with situated selves
(role play). The symbolic interactionists and phenomenologists were
concerned with both the situated selves and the substantial selves. Goffman extended the interactionist theory by considering the ways in
which individuals construct or present situated selves to achieve goals in
the situation, but had little to say about the relations between the two.

Accordingly, all these theories shared the fundamental properties of
the commonsense ideas about the situated and substantial selves. Most
importantly, they looked at the self as determined or caused by society.
Society socializes the individual and he introjects roles and a looking-
glass self, the social definitions of himself. They saw one's actions as
caused by one's self-concept. They saw the self, the core of one's being,
that which gives integration and foundation to all the rest, as being a
concept, as being highly conscious and symbolic ("definitions"). They
saw these definitions as being clear and definite. They saw the self
as being unchanging when they were concerned with the I (substantial
self) and as being made up of unchanging social role material when they
were concerned with the me and situational presentations of self
(Goffman). And, finally, they saw the self as being independent of the
situation in which it is observed, as being object-like (a substance or
substantial role material) passed on from generation to generation. The
presentations may change from situation to situation, but the definitional material remains a given.

We have no doubt, either from our experience or from our studies of
gay communities, that all these ideas about substantial and situational
selves are partially true. They contain truths that have been important
in the lives of all Western men and women for centuries. But our research has led us increasingly to believe that they contain only part of
the truth, that the truths about the core of our beings, which we call
our *existential selves*, are hardly dealt with at all, and that our concepts of our selves are rapidly changing as the nature of our lives
changes and as we choose new selves. We have found that each of the
major properties of self assumed by even the interactionist theories
contains some oversimplification. We return to our considerations of
these general properties of our evolving selves after considering the details of our research on selves in the gay communities we studied.

A note on our data and their interpretation

Our data are derived from two participant observation and interview studies of two gay communities (see Warren, 1974; Ponse, forthcoming). Both gay communities were located in large urban areas of Southern California; one was the secret male community described by Warren (1974, 1976), and the other was an overt, politically activist and feminist group of lesbians (Ponse, forthcoming). (The comparison between the overt and secret reponses to stigma is a subsidiary theme, as this contrast elucidates the general features of various audience definitions of the self and of the self's response to such definitions.)

It is important to realize that our studies of the gay selves were part of a general study of the natural world of the gays. We did not start out with the assumption that self was a crucial variable in their lives and that we should focus on it. As in any existential study (see Chapter 1), we started out only with the conviction that we should study the gay world and try to understand it on its own terms before analyzing it. We did not assume the importance of the gay selves, we discovered it; we found that the gays themselves see their experiences and ideas of self as important.

One of the advantages of studying the nature of self in gay communities is that gays are highly conscious in their management of their selves. They feel forced by the stigmatizing treatment they often receive from society to look at their selves as problematic, as needing management. Their selves are thus more open for study, more observable in taped interviews. This makes it easier for the researcher to communicate her findings to readers. But, of course, there are two obvious possible disadvantages, even dangers, in this. First, it may well be that the symbolic interview material is very different from the natural realities. As we have already seen (Chapter 1), such symbolic accounts are often used as fronts in all society. This is certainly true of the gay world, where gays consciously construct dishonest, highly symbolic accounts of themselves as nongay for some audiences who might stigmatize them. We have dealt with this problem by using only those symbolic interview materials that are confirmed by the understanding we have of the gay communities and individuals derived from our observation of them. Most obviously, we let the members "speak for themselves in their own words" only when they are telling the truth.

Second, many readers may object that gay selves are by these very facts of stigmatization and the resulting conscious management of selves not representative of other selves. This may once have been true, but we think it is no longer so. Our society is now so conflictful and rapidly changing that most people are stigmatized from the standpoints of significant generalized others in their lives and, realizing this, they become quite conscious in managing their selves. Then, too, most individuals undergo basic changes in their selves and make basic, conscious choices of what they will try to become, which put them in potential conflict with their earlier selves. And, finally, most people have become aware that these are indeed important facts in their lives with important consequences for what they are becoming. Certainly there is a difference in degree between the problems and self-management of gays and most other people, but that difference seems to be decreasing, and there appear to be no basic differences. We suspect that looking at the general properties of gay selves reveals the direction in which other people are heading or have already arrived.

Reflections of stigma

Perhaps the most important facet of the self's experiencing of gayness is that "gay" is a stigmatized category in our society. It is stigmatized (as is income-tax evasion) in the courts of law and by the officials of the state, and (unlike tax evasion) it is stigmatized morally in the courts of public opinion and the give and take of everyday interaction. The generalized other, or society as a whole, teaches gayness — if at all — with stigma attached; the result is that people grow up either not knowing much about homosexuality or "knowing" a set of negative descriptive things about it that can be either confirmed or changed by later experiences. And people in the gay community have had later experiences: By one route or another they have undergone the process Berger and Luckman call *alternation*, in which the self is reinterpreted as a member of a new category. Thus a new identity emerges and the old is sloughed off. In this process of conflict and change, the self theorizes about itself. Biography is often recast to make of one's life a consistent and coherent whole, with a neat dovetailing of past, present, and future.

   The gay people we studied had in the past, and sometimes still, experienced themselves as structured and determined by environmental factors, both in the sense that the stuctures of society prevented the realization of their essential being or true nature, and in the sense that there was a lack of suitable alternative ways of conceiving of the self. Many reinterpreted their prealternation biographies as an example of preprogramming by society to adopt certain traditional behaviors and social roles:

Veronica:[2] I realize now I never liked men. I always related to women. I was simply doing what society told me to do when I got married. I was programmed for marriage.

Oliver: I did go to bed with one girl in high school because that was the thing to do and so I went ahead and did it. But I never did it again. It was against my nature.

Later with alternation, some of these roles or aspects of them were rejected. For example, Veronica saw her ten-year heterosexual marriage in terms of false consciousness, a denial of her real self. Still other roles, most particularly general social stereotypes of masculine and feminine were retained, at least for a time (see also Gagnon and Simon, 1967):

Brenda: Where I grew up there was a very strict line between males and females, and males did so and so and females did so and so and there was no question of crossing over. Men were strong and capable and women were passive and they were achievers only behind a man, and they were more docile and subservient. I never fit into that, so when I considered myself a masculine woman I *really* considered myself a capable, determined, strong woman . . . so when you clear away all the crap and all the bullshit you realize this really is not masculine necessarily at all, it's what society says is masculine. What it really is, is that I wasn't really masculine, I was what I really was, the things that I wanted to develop.

Drake: When I first came out I was outrageous — always getting into drag, and it wasn't even Halloween. Although I'm not always that masculine now [he laughs and flips his wrist], at least I don't wear a dress. And before I came out, you know, I was your typical jock.

The responses of the different people to traditional role expectations varied over time. Veronica did get married as expected, but later, unexpectedly from the standpoint of the predetermined (generalized other) self, entered into a lesbian relationship with another woman.[3] Brenda on the other hand, became a lesbian, but became a "masculine" one, an identity that at a later stage of her life became inauthentic to her — an illusion behind which her real self hid. Furthermore, in her "masculine" years she also played the role of one-way butch, a butch who makes love but is not made love to; this, too, she later perceived as inauthentic:

I didn't really like it because again I feel that I was cheated out of something. There was something that I should be getting, more than what I was getting. Somehow I felt frightened, because I felt that if I tore down that particular barrier and had a freer sexual exchange with people they might be frightened away.

Other gay people alternated from straight to gay identity, but experienced self-hate, an emotional residue of the society's stigmatization of the homosexual:

Int.: How did you feel about gayness when you first came out?[4]

Diane: When it first entered my consciousness I wanted to kill myself — I blocked. What I told myself was that I was no use, that I was no use to anybody. That I wouldn't be getting married and having children. That my life would be wasted. I felt there was no way I would ever be happy . . . I was desperate. Very. I had all these feelings and no place to take them . . .

Int: What did you think about it?

Diane: I don't think I thought it was a sickness, but you have to understand it was the way I was raised. I was given little dolls when I was a kid and tea sets. You know, girls are nurses and boys are doctors and girls marry boys and so it was a shock. It was a great shock to me.

Reynolds: I was raised in a very religious and a very fundamentalist backround. Then I went away to college — a religious college mind you. One night after we had been to the football game something happened with my roommate. The next day I felt just sick and guilty. I prayed to God, and I went to the minister and to the library to find out what was going on. I found the label I was looking for — "homosexual" — but I thought it was a terrible thing, and I did not accept it for many years.

The coming out process had many of the same emotional and definitional shocks for those who alternated from the secretive gay world to the overt gay world as for those who moved from the straight world to the secret gay world. In fact, most of those now in the overt gay community started out in some more secretive one. The later experiencing of the overt versus the secret community had salience for the subsequent ways of dealing with stigma.

In his analysis of overt gayness, Laud Humphreys distinguished between *stigma evasion* as the tactic of the secret homosexual, and the *stigma confrontation* of the overt homosexual: "*Passing* is the type of stigma evasion most common to homosexuals. By careful, even tortuous control of information, stigmatized individuals attempt to ward off social condemnation" (1972:138). "Stigma conversion . . . involves . . . conversion *from* stigma, in the sense of rebirth into a new identity" (1972:142). Although passing was the type of evasion used by the secret community, many members of the overt community in this study had gone beyond stigma conversion to *radical destigmatization*, which involves radically changing the meanings of the category to which stigma formerly obtained. Destigmatization of the category, a form of rejection of the rejecters, has increasingly superseded the development of an individualized liberated identity as a mode of praxis in the world:

Sherri: I define gayness and lesbianism as much more than sexuality . . . I think it's an attitude, and a perspective, and a way of dealing with problems . . . I don't think in today's society that straight is a very positive label . . . and I would prefer to think of that person as having a gay essence. I think straight means closed to being gay.

The elements of a radical destigmatization are contained here: A gay essence is seen as the basic universal human condition; being straight is a limitation of human nature. By radical destigmatization, the formerly stigmatized category becomes the standard by which the former stigmatizers are judged. Thus, the self accepts a variety of social labels, but changes their content and emotional valence:

> *Int.*: What do you think about the word *dyke*?
>
> *Diane*: Dyke means something different today than it used to. Women who call themselves dykes are very radical lesbians. I mean there's no shit about gay power or lesbians. It's like getting rid of the bullshit after getting rid of the bullshit. Sort of a high enema!

Stigma evasion through passing as straight[5] places the self in the category "gay," but only in selected settings (see below). In addition, in some covert gay circles the terms *gay*, *homosexual*, and *queer* are not radically destigmatized; secret members sometimes regard themselves as having a sickness, or condition, which deviates from the accepted and natural norm of heterosexuality. Whereas gay liberationists angrily question the propriety of causative explanations of homosexuality, many secret homosexuals use such explanations in the construction of their own biographies (see Warren, 1974).

Reflections of community

To analyze the self as it becomes reflected in a concrete community, the theorist moves from structural functionalism to symbolic interactionism. In the symbolic interactionist paradigm, the individual develops his or her identity in interaction with, and symbolic conversation with, significant others who mediate the generalized other. In the case of the prealternation gay person, the community of significant others is most often a world of heterosexual family and peers who purvey the societal definitions of the stigmatized category homosexual, often in a way that makes it impossible or difficult to consider homosexual as a way of viewing the self (Dank, 1971; Warren, 1974). Upon alternation, however, the secret or overt gay person has a new audience of significant others: the gay community. That community can provide definitions of gayness, homosexuality, lesbianism, and bisexuality, and sub-concepts such as masculine and feminine, butch and femme, which receive various degrees of acceptance by the individual. Some saw their entry into the social rounds of the gay community as coming home:

> *Boris:* I walked into that gay bar, and I thought "I'm home." The people in there were professional people like me, handsome, and they weren't creeps like I'd been told.

> *Beatrice:* It was an absolute relief. I always knew I was different, but I never knew what it was and it was suddenly like I was home . . . I finally found . . . I don't know if it was a structure or just an awareness of myself that I suddenly knew at last where I belonged in the world. As compared to constantly searching and knowing no matter where I was that I didn't quite fit. Not knowing, not being sure where I was in relation to people I was around.

Others, both in the secret and overt communities, did not locate their essential, unique selves in the gay community, although their continued interaction with the community involved them in playing the roles that were expected of them. (Still others rejected both roles and community after alternation, and theoretical consideration, but these are beyond the scope of this analysis.)

In the interview below, Doris discussed her experience of role playing in the lesbian bar community of some years back, in which women were expected to symbolize adherence to one or the other roles of butch or femme:

Doris: Role playing? Oh, sure I was into that. You know I'm really a green country kid. I was. I didn't know anything about homosexuals. I didn't know anything about anything. All I knew was how I felt and from adolescence on I felt inclined toward women. By the time I was twenty-four and ready to get involved with a woman, I went there [to the bar] not realizing that I had to be anyone other than me, when I got there, to that bar, I saw that there was a very definite division. Some women looked very masculine and some looked very feminine, and I really felt that I looked kind of in-between, but people took me to be feminine and I was *assigned* a role, really because of my appearance. It doesn't mean that I was overly feminine. It just means that I wasn't overly masculine. So I was classified. That was on the Missouri side in Kansas City. I got into realizing that so long as I was classified in that role I was restricted. I was limited in the kinds of people I could relate to and I found the kinds of people I was willing to relate to me as a femme were people I was not really interested in. They were not . . . It restricted it to a class of people that considered themselves butches and butches in the sense of how they look and how they dress. They were not really appealing to me. I had been on the receiving end of aggression from men for years and I wasn't interested . . . you know, it wasn't really that comfortable for me and so it was a time when I really didn't know what to do . . . so when I went to the Kansas side, I decided to experiment a little and I got to the point where I cut off my hair and so I would go to the Kansas side and I would dress very masculine in terms of men's pants, men's clothes, and men's sweatshirts and things like that, just jeans not really anything else you know . . . I would go to the Kansas side and I would slick my hair back and I'd be a butch and I could pursue more feminine women, as we see them, you know, and that was a little more satisfying, and I . . . so since that time . . . and people were calling me the "it" because, you know, they'd see me on one side and I'd be a butch and in Missouri I'd look like a femme, but I didn't want to be restricted. I didn't want to put restrictions on who I could relate to.

Although many of the gay people expressed their relief, delight, and feeling of coming home upon finding the gay community, this example illustrates that it, too, like society as a whole, can provide coercive definitions and roles that become constricting to the development of the real self. This constriction has two dimensions: by the subconcepts of the gay world, like butch and femme, and by the identification of oneself as gay, homosexual, or lesbian. Here, once more, there are differences between the overt and secret gay community.

Stigma gives the self a stake in the maintenance of an established identity within a community of like others, as sociologists of social conflicts have long noted (Simmel, 1950; Coser, 1956). Stigma and secrecy together, however, give a double stake: "When you keep one part of yourself secret, that becomes the most important part of you" (Miller, 1971:46). In both communities, then, there was a stock of interpretive knowledge which enabled the self to interpret experience and identity as a coherent past, present, and future of essential gayness. However, the double pressure of stigma and secrecy made this almost universal in the secret community, more members of the overt community expressed flexibility and openness about future conduct and identity and about past experience:

Nora: I think of myself as a woman, and after that I think of my sexuality. I think of myself as having a bisexual *consciousness* but *expressing* it through homosexuality.

Jim: By my personal definitions I was not and am not homosexual or heterosexual, not gay or straight, nor sick or healthy; I remain just plain old me. But society looked at what I did and labeled me quickly and permanently. [Murphy, 1971:40]

To this end, some of the activist women expressed hopes for a future beyond radical destigmatization that embodied bisexuality and freedom to experiment with sexuality rather than one in which gay remained the only available alternative sexual identity.

Among the significant others of the gay community (and outside it) are the intimate significant others who are lovers and friends and who provide an audience for the self. Even intimates may have quite different labels for the other than the other has for him or her self. For example, in the following statements, made separately by two lesbian lovers, there is a dichotomy of labels:

Frederika: I don't consider myself gay. I simply can't relate to that for me . . . I need a romantic involvement in my life and it happens to be with Veronica, but it was with a man before this. I love my husband in a way. I need the kind of anchoring or stability he gives me, which I think only a man can give.

Veronica: I wish I could identify as a lesbian, isn't that strange? But somehow I can't. But Frederika, if there's one thing I know for sure is that she is a *real* lesbian. That's where she really gets her emotional gratification. The real reason she stays with her husband is that she's afraid he will take the kids away from her if she leaves, and the kids mean a lot to her.

This is not to say, of course, that the self never accepts the audience's proffered labels. People can and do tailor actions, lives, and identities to the labels of others. But people can also make the choice to accept or reject such definitions quite freely and with full moral responsibility: "Man . . . will be what he makes of himself" (Sartre, 1964b:290).

Identity, the audience, and self-deception

Existentialism sees human beings as necessarily partially free, morally responsible creatures who construct meanings in the world for themselves (Kaufman, 1964; Lyman and Scott, 1970:1—2). Existentially, existence precedes essence; human consciousness is not determined by, and is not the sum of, the descriptive characteristics that set humans apart as an animal species (Sartre, 1964b:289—90). Existentialism defines human beings as selves capable of false consciousness, bad faith, or self-deception[6] (Kaufman, 1964b:13—19; Sartre, 1964b:261—264).

Sociologically, a moral category such as self-deceiving can be observed in audiences' reaction to selves. For example, it is commonplace for a person to say of someone else: "Oh, she is just deluding herself," as in the above example of Veronica's insistence that Frederika "really is" a lesbian, despite Frederika's own self-concept. And it is commonplace, if less so, for the inner self to accuse other self-formulations of self-deception. When the self responds to audience labels and presents an identity that is then or later perceived as inauthentic, as in Brenda's example of masculine and feminine responses, there is an engagement with the existential concept of self-deception:

Very often nowadays we are called upon to fill in forms establishing what is called our identity . . . I have not a consciousness of *being* the person who is entered under the various headings, thus: *son of, born at, occupation,* and so on. Yet everything I enter under these headings is strictly true . . . It is, in fact, against the existence of such garments that I have to protest: *I* am not this garment. [Marcel, 1973:119—200]

The realm of social labels reflects that aspect of the self which in existential terms can lead to the self-deception. In self-deception the human being is thinglike to itself. Some of the gay people in both communities expressed the longing to be, or feeling of being, labeled selves, while at the same time having a converse desire to be unique selves of their own choice.

Marcie: You know I met Cora socially with Teri and Sandra and some gay men. We were drinking and dancing and after the men left, I said to her "Are you a lesbian?" and she got very embarrassed . . . and I said, if you ask me about myself, the first thing I will tell you is that *I am a lesbian.*

Jim: Let's start with the gay thing. How far back does it go with me? From the time I was three or four, I imagine maybe earlier, maybe from the time I tripped out of the womb, maybe before that. [Bell, 1971:7][7]

Arthur: I am not going to take a job there — I have nothing in common with them. I'm gay and they are straight and we are just different types of people.

Int.: What does gay mean to you?
Nora: I think labels are used to define or make us more secure . . . Gay . . . it's

interesting because the word really doesn't mean anything to me. I understand the meaning that is used. To me it's just another label, the opposite of straight — except it's being used by homosexuals to feel more secure. Again it's gay meaning happy, gay meaning free . . . Lesbianism is one expression of [my life].

Int.: Does it permeate your life?

Nora: Well, I hope certainly more than that is expressed. I hope the essence that is expressed is that of a loving human being. If I choose to relate sexually with other women, that's fine . . . I don't deny that . . . but I hope my sexuality is not my essence.

On the other hand, the self may be aware of self-deception in the process of *not* affiliating with a particular category and *not* accepting the labels of a certain audience, as expressed in the derisive term *closet queen* for those who will not publicly admit their homosexuality.[8] Sartre discussed this form of self-deception among homosexuals:

Let us take . . . a homosexual . . . [who] while recognizing his homosexual inclination . . . refuses with all his strength to consider himself a pederast . . . Here is assuredly a man in self-deception . . . acknowledging all the facts which are imputed to him, he refuses to draw from them the conclusion which they impose.[Sartre, 1964b:261—4]

Sartre continued his meditations on the paradoxical relationship of sincerity or authenticity and self-deception in "the pederast" in a way that echoes the theories of several of the activist women. These women had a sense of themselves as unique selves which had, in addition, several layers of other identities, of varying degrees of usefulness and authenticity:

Int.: Have you come out? Does that term apply to you?

Diane: I would say that I made a transition from thinking I was straight to knowing I was gay.

Int.: Do you consider yourself a lesbian now?

Diane: Politically, yes.

Int.: Emotionally, do you consider yourself a lesbian?

Diane: I consider myself a bisexual who is living in a time of history when it is better to identify myself as a lesbian.

Int.: When you talk about this time in history what are you talking about?

Diane: I'm talking about the gay — revolution; I'm talking about the women's revolution.

Depending on the meanings of the process to the social actor, the arranging of one's self to fit the identity labels of the society or the stigmatized community can be just as much an act of authenticity as it can be of self-deception, and of self-deception just as much as of sincerity; the roles of homosexual and gay, of butch and femme can be played with wholeheartedness or distance, with authenticity or self-deception, and with feelings of joy or of regret.

The self as mask: dramaturgical sociology

Those roles that are played in contexts from which the self feels some distance come within the province of dramaturgical sociology. Dramaturgical sociology is linked to symbolic interaction in its concern with the immediate audience of significant others, but departs in its emphasis on the self as consciously or quasi-consciously presenting masks of the self to others, instead of as a socialized reflection (or effect) of significant others or the society. Goffman's dramaturgical sociology conceptualized the self, implicitly and explicitly, as a mystery lurking behind a variety of masks that are worn to placate, engage, strategically destroy and unmask a variety of audiences. The Goffmanic self is half-intentionally distanced from his or her audience in a manner expressed in playing the role of "Doris the butch" or "Doris the femme," who has an instrumental as opposed to a purely emotional investment in the roles played within the community. The Goffmanic masked self, then, most often comes into play when the audience is to some degree to be manipulated rather than for such motives as self-development, authenticity, or the development of a new style of life.

In the world of stigmatized gayness one obvious place for masks is the homosexual's relationships with nongay audiences, and there is a clear distinction here between the overt community and the secret one.[9] Members of the overt community, who had come out before many more audiences than just their own, dispensed with many of the masks worn previously in the presence of the family, heterosexual friends, and workmates (Ponse, 1976; Warren, 1976). They commonly went through a process of stigma confrontation, sometimes developed into radical destigmatization, which involved a long-term series of steps rather than a cataclysmic single declaration (Ponse, 1976). Stigma confrontation has some parallels with the politicized meaning of the term "coming out of the closet" in the gay community (i.e., presenting the gay self to successively wider audiences).

Sarah: Out of the closet, well that means different things to different people. It could mean you tell your mother you are gay, or it could mean you march on city hall . . . There are degrees, you know, of being out of the closet. I think essentially it just means to be more open and up front about your gayness.

Int: Would you describe yourself as more overt or covert vis à vis your gayness?

Sarah: Most of the areas of my life I'm out of the closet and the more out of the closet, the more I want to be. There are places, though, like at work that I'm not open about my gayness because . . . they're not open about homosexuality, and I don't like to use that word 'cause *that's* an old one too. They're, they're, you know, in the psychiatric field, they're very prejudiced, narrow-minded. So I don't feel like I'm . . . you know, that's just my own fears . . . I guess . . . I'm not open at work. But every place else I'm open and it feels good to be open and be honest about who I am.

Int.: How do you feel about people who are still in the closet?

Sarah: I have different feelings about them . . . Sometimes I feel sorry for them . . . because it's very hard to live that way . . . it's isolating, it's alienating to have to be frightened like that. I understand what that feels like. I think it's fear . . . people are afraid of losing their jobs or somebody finding out or whatever it is . . . I empathize with . . . I wouldn't . . . sometimes I get angry with them, thinking that they're sabotaging the gay community by not being open, but I'm not, you know . . . I can understand their fears and I wouldn't put a judgment on them for being in the closet . . . I think that once you've come out of the closet . . . you know . . . you open the door and feel the fresh air, and it feels so good you know you never will go back to being that closed . . . But it takes time to come out of the closet, you know . . . I think that older people who for years and years lived in the closet, there was no community, there was no openness about gayness, so they lived in the closet and still do and it's very hard to come out . . . I think the older you get and the longer you stay in the closet, the safer it feels in there. I think the younger people, I'm not trying to make it an age thing, but being involved in the center I would go on speaking engagements and talk about gayness and I was on educational television, on a panel about gayness and it was only afterward that I thought, God . . . appearing on television, you can't get much more out of the closet than that!

Members of the secret community, on the other hand, presented an assorted variety of masks, well thought out or hastily conceived, half-conscious or fully planned, and convincing or not to the audiences they sought to disarm (Ponse, 1976; Warren, 1976). Merle Miller described his lifetime of masks and his regret at laying them aside:

I never wanted to take off the mask; I wanted to wear it everywhere, night and day, always. And I suppose I still do . . . It took me almost fifty years to come out of the closet, to stop pretending to be something I was not, most of the time fooling nobody. [Miller, 1971:6]

The completeness of the mask and the purposes it serves vary. The mask may be an entire life style arranged around a storybook wife and children, or a simple omission of the mention of one's roommate. Reasons for the mask vary from not wanting to "kill" mother to a not unfounded fear of ridicule. The audience to whom the mask is presented ranges from everyone straight to just a few people with whom the gay person does not dare to come out of the closet — workmates, perhaps, or family:

Ronald: I have told lots of straight people — friends, that is. In fact, I don't think you can be a real friend to someone without letting them know the most important thing about you. But not my family. It would kill my mother, and she's going on seventy, so what's the point. And at work I keep up a big thing about this girl I'm dating.

A lesbian who was very much in the closet and had not confirmed her gay identity to any straight friend explained her feelings:

Int.: How do you react when you hear people saying things about other gay people or about lesbians and stuff? Does it make you mad?

Carrie: Yeah, well it does. It depends again on who's saying it and what they say. It does irritate me, yeah, it irritates me. But usually I'm so hung up on trying not to act like it means anything to me that I don't feel anything too much. I'm too concerned with the way I'm reacting. It's a real hangup of mine, I wish I didn't feel that way.

Int.: Why do you think you feel that way? Why are you so averse to anyone's knowing anything about you?

Carrie: I care less now than I used to. However, it's just a thing where for some people it could be a stigma . . . There are people that I think would, if they really knew for a fact . . . might just change the relationship just enough, you know, that I wouldn't like it . . . let them think what they want but I don't get into confessing it or discussing it or being blatant about it.

The felt necessity of wearing masks in settings other than the gay community leads many secret gays to conceive of the gay community as the only milieu in which they can express their real, existential selves. This, in turn, colors all other interactions with a sense of inauthenticity and falseness, however intimate in terms of conventional social roles such as mother-son or husband-wife, in which the self is not available to the other for real interaction (Warren, 1974; Ponse, 1976). A second implication of this is that the individual in the secret community, who already has a double stake in his or her identity as a gay person with a gay essence, derives a triple stake from the maskless experiencing of gay community interaction. "Letting down one's hair" is a commonplace expression for the dropping of the mask, and the resulting feeling of freedom and exhilaration experienced in the secret community. Members of an overt community, on the other hand, do not have this third stake.

Conclusions about existential selves

The most cursory overview of our findings about gay selves suggests that they are immensely complex and problematic. It seems obvious that theories of dramaturgy, structural functionalism, or symbolic interactionism could never capture their most important properties, though it seems equally obvious that each of the traditional theories captures some small part of the complex realities. Certainly many gays insist on looking at their gay selves as their substances, the thing they really are at all times and situations. But equally certainly others, especially those with the new freedom of being overt, have consciously given up the idea that gay is somehow totally different or even the ultimate thing in life. Certainly many gays appear to an outsider to be merely bundles of socially defined roles, but often this outsider is being taken in by frontwork and masks the gay does not believe in. And certainly some gays insist that their prealternation selves were determined by generalized others (i.e., that they were then looking-glass selves), but far more certainly they are insisting that what they really are won out over the socially determined selves, largely because they chose to assert themselves against the social definition, regardless of the conflict and anguish involved.

But it is much easier to see the failings of earlier concepts than to propose new ones that capture the complex, problematic, conflictful, and rapidly changing realities. Any existential theory of the self must be an emerging theory. We would like at this point to restrict ourselves to the major implications of our findings.

The three most important implications seem clear enough. First, almost without exception, the people we have studied have found themselves in fundamental, unrelenting, anguishing conflict with a social world that tried to deal with them in absolutist fashion, tried to force them into a mold they felt did not allow them to become what they really were or what they wanted to be. Although there are possibly many people our study did not get at (the negative cases), who did submit totally to such absolutist demands, it is clear that the people we studied did not. These people insisted on *choosing* to be what they wanted to be. They asserted their individual sexual desires and self-desires against the world.

Second, it seems clear that this assertion and choice of self begins with, is continually grounded in, and is pervaded by the individual's deepest feelings. Feelings are the foundation of self, the source of all else. The gays reported again and again that they were unhappy, restless, alienated — without knowing why. They often felt they were searching for gratification and fulfillment, yearning, but not knowing clearly for what or why, often not conscious of the whole process, often refusing to believe what they began to suspect from their new forms of behavior. At the base of it all, pushing all else, was the complex of bodily feelings — the *body self*, the individual's brute being. As the process of becoming increased and the individual became more aware, more conscious of it and thus able to symbolize it for himself, the *becoming self* emerged. The becoming self is a complex, often conflictful, partly conscious grasping of what one is becoming and may be. The individual often experienced a sudden awareness of *self-transformation* or alternation. As some said, they felt as though they had come home, that they belonged in what they knew to be a gay world. They had new *substantial self-images*, highly conscious, symbolized selves of the type symbolic interactionists speak of. But neither our inner lives nor our social lives seem static enough or homogeneous enough

to allow this to continue for long or, perhaps, ever to be the only reality of the individual. Almost all the individuals we studied felt that
they were still more complex than that; that the total experience of self
in the world, which is what we call the *existential self*, both because of
what the world is becoming and because of the individual's choices to
try to become some ideal self in the future, is always to varying degrees
in the process of becoming; and that there are always some forms of
complex self presentation going on to protect the complex realities of
the existential self.

Third, though it is clear that none of them acted as totally free persons, which might involve rejecting all demands of the gay world as well
as the others, it is also clear that most of them insisted on being partially free. It seems to us that, in general, they worked creatively to
construct complex, shifting, situated compromises with their changing
social world. These compromises were sometimes closer to being sur-
renders, as when they hid what they believe to be their real selves and,
above all, when they suffered the terrible internal conflicts between
what they wanted to be and what they could not stop being. But sometimes the compromises included tremendous room for freedom in
choosing one's self. Some people, though recognizing perils involved in
that partially free search for a self that best suited their brute beings
and the social world in which they must live, came to see that freedom
of searching for a new self, of creating a new self, as basic to their lives.
We believe people throughout our society are discovering the same
perils and the same rewards of this new freedom to create themselves,
to create new forms of expressing and gratifying their inner beings within their social world. The acceptance of this necessary freedom and the
search for new and better ways of becoming-in-the-world are basic to
our existential selves.

Appendix: the origins of existential sociology

JACK D. DOUGLAS

All educated men know something about existential philosophy. Few have yet heard of existential sociology. Given this fact, many readers may assume that existential sociology is simply a specialized branch of philosophical thought, or worse, a new brand of philosophical chic. Such an assumption is both wrong and conducive to many miconceptions about this work. It is important, therefore, to discuss the relations between the two.

As sociologists, we began with our experience in the social world and our research; came slowly to use phenomenological and, later, existential philosophy to help us achieve a new perspective on our social world; then moved beyond the philosophy, even to the extent of changing some of its basic ideas. The philosophy was vital in achieving a new perspective and remains a basic source of insights; it serves as an important part of the foundation of existential sociology, but must not be mistaken for the whole building or even for the whole foundation. Some of the fundamental ideas of existential sociology, especially those concerning objectivity, research methods, and the construction of social order, have hardly been touched upon by the philosophers.[1]

One of the oldest and most basic arguments in the history and philosophy of science concerns which came first, the theoretical perspective or the new facts. Do scientists (or philosophers) first change their ideas and thus come to discover new facts not encompassed by the earlier theoretical perspective, or do they first discover the new facts and then create new ideas to explain them because the old theory has proved inadequate? Recently, the sociology of knowledge has added a new question to deepen this quandary: Are there changes in the everyday life situations, the social situations, of the scientists that lie behind and in some way cause or shape both the changes in their theoretical perspectives and their discovery of new facts?

I suspect the historical developments of the many different sciences are so complex that some support will be found for each position in these disputes. Some scientific changes are more the result of new ideas than of new facts; others are stimulated more by new facts unexplained by old theories. Sometimes the new ideas and findings are stimulated by changes in the life situations of the scientists; sometimes they seem quite unrelated to anything but the scientists' own laboratory settings. These processes seem even more complicated because after one factor has stimulated the initial change, another may prove of crucial importance in determining whether the change is carried further and whether the new ideas are accepted or eventually rejected by the communities of scientists, scholars, intellectuals, and educated laymen.

Fortunately, the questions are a little less complicated in the relations between philosophy and the new forms of phenomenological and existential sociology, in good part because the creators of these events are still available as sources of information. It is obvious that all the sociologists developing these new ideas in sociology knew about phenomenology and existentialism in some general way long before they used them in sociology. These philosophical ideas have been common intellectual coin for decades, and these sociologists certainly learned about them at an early age. However, it is equally obvious that few if any of them made important connections between the philosophy and sociology in their early works.[2] Generally only much later, after experiencing definite problems in their more traditional research did they come to the new ideas in search of some way to solve their problems. It is clear that most sociologists who have faced these problems, such as the problems of official statistics on crime and deviance, which are known to all good students in these fields, have shrunk from converting to a new perspective. (In criminology and many other areas where the basic problems of official statistics and questionnaire data are apparent, there is even a basic pattern to this shrinking back from the abyss: The sociologist recounts all the problems of the data and analysis, making it apparent to anyone that there are more holes than vessel, and then asserts "but we really have no alternative, so we shall use them, while recognizing their weaknesses.") There are apparently personal and situational factors involved in the decision to accept the research problems as something that must be solved, even if it demands a change in theoretical perspective. The crucial point is that the sociologists who have done the most to create the new forms of sociology have commonly started with, and continually emphasized, the understanding of concrete social experience and, thus, of research problems. Instead of being the initial stimulus to observing the social world or to recognizing problems in understanding the social world, philosophical thought has been *used* to help gain a better understanding, though it also seems clear in retrospect that the use of such thought is not some highly rational, instrumental activity following upon a highly conscious decision. The primary movement has generally been from concrete experience and problems to philosophy, using philosophy to make better abstract sense out of our research and theoretical work after that work has been well launched. But beyond that beginning, there are complex interweavings and movements back and forth, with some individuals being far more oriented to philosophy and others far more oriented to concrete experience. The philosophers also appear to have a far greater influence on those who have come to phenomenological and existential sociology after it was created.

Three assertions are often made by opponents of the phenomenological and existential sociologies that demand brief treatment here because they often produce misunderstandings. First, it is often asserted that these basic theoretical ideas are really not new and not needed, as we can find those ideas in the works of symbolic interactionism, especially in the philosophical work of George Herbert Mead. I myself have argued (Douglas, 1970a) that we can indeed find some of the general forms of these ideas in Mead's work. But, just as it is untrue that phenomenological and existential philosophy were direct progenitors of their counterparts in sociology, so it is even less true that symbolic interactionism was their direct progenitor. There are two mainstreams of symbolic interactionism: the behavioristic form of the Iowa (Kuhn) tradition and the more symbolic constructionist (Blumer) tradition. The Blumer (1969) form of symbolic interactionism has rarely been found in pure form in any work except his own. Most of the work has been a mixture, with a heavy emphasis on the social determinism of the individual self, social roles, and, thence, social actions. Moreover, and more to the point, the general ideas of the phenomenological sociologists have generally been found in Mead's work after the phenomenologists showed their importance. Their importance in Mead's work and that of his followers was either previously unnoted or minimal. It is also obvious that the phenomenological sociologists did not make direct use of Mead's work because when they were first doing their work they thought of his as highly behavioristic and deterministic. Their generally shared understanding of Mead's work, however wrong, led toward the role theory and personality theory of the structural functionalists rather than toward a new perspective on society emphasizing the necessity of the individual's problematic creation of his self and his social world.

Second, it is often asserted that Alfred Schutz said it all (i.e., that the phenomenological sociologists, especially the ethnomethodologists, really got their ideas originally from Schutz and that their own writings are merely a working out of Schutz's basic ideas). Though it is obvious that some of Schutz's ideas became important in phenomenological sociology, the fact seems to be that this was an ex post facto mapping operation.[3] Furthermore, even ethnomethodology is very different from Schutz's phenomenology of the social world. A brief examination of the idea of indexicality or of the contextual determination of meaning helps make this clear. *Indexicality* is the term used by ethnomethodologists to refer to the ways in which the concrete occasion or situation in which a communication takes place is crucial for individuals' interpretations of the actual meanings of that communication. Indexicality is one of the cornerstone ideas of ethnomethodology (see Garfinkel, 1967). Undoubtedly one can find consideration of this idea in Schutz or, for that matter, in Mead. In fact, one can find all kinds of uses of the idea in everyday conversations: "It all depends on the circumstances" (or "on the situation") is an extremely common generalization in everyday life. Also undoubtedly, this idea did not form a cornerstone of Schutz's or Mead's thought; and certainly the man of common sense does not see the vast ramifications of the idea for the phenomenological sociologists' theories of social life. Schutz, Mead, and the man of common sense are no more the progenitors of the ethnomethodologists' theories of indexicality than Democritus was the progenitor of modern atomic theory.

Three, it is sometimes argued, more cogently, that the ethnomethodological ideas of indexicality are actually taken directly from linguistics, specifically from the work of Bar-Hillel (1954). This contention is more relevant, as Bar-Hillel did use the term "indexical expressions" and the ethnomethodologists have used and referred to his work in their own. Yet this too is a misunderstanding. It fails to note that the linguistic meaning of indexical expression does not deal with the whole situation of use that concerns most of the ethnomethodologists, but, rather, with the linguistic situation of use, the linguistic context. More importantly, this contention fails to note that the ethnomethodologists' recognition of the crucial importance of the idea grew directly out of their early work, such as Garfinkel and Bittner's work on psychiatric records (Garfinkel, 1967), rather than from a reading of Bar-Hillel or anyone else.

Further support for the idea of the crucial importance of the concrete research over philosophical work is found in the parallel development of the idea of "contextual (or situational) determination of meaning." This is the phrase used in my own early work (Douglas, 1967), and I believe in work of roughly the same period by Aaron Cicourel and, possibly, others, to refer to what ethnomethodologists were calling "indexicality." The idea was derived from the analysis of such things as case studies of suicide. It was not derived from knowledge of the ethnomethodologists' ideas of indexicality (which I did not understand at the time) and certainly not from linguistics or elsewhere. The term may well have been floating around when we used it, but the crucial thing, again, was that it *made sense out of* common aspects of the suicide cases and other concrete phenomena.

The dominant importance of concrete experience and research over philosophy was even more apparent, and important, in the development of existential sociology out of phenomenological sociology. The initial breaks with the traditional theoretical perspective retained the basic idea that society is highly patterned or ordered and that this order is in some way, however different from the way earlier theorists thought, the outcome of cognitive meanings.

For example, if we look at early ethnomethodological works, we find an implicit assumption that the social settings being analyzed are highly ordered. The ethnomethodological analysis consisted almost entirely of simply showing how that order is produced by (or constituted by) highly indexical communications (accounts). We also find that the emphasis of ethnomethodology was entirely on cognitive meanings, so much so that ethnomethodology was defined by Garfinkel (1970) in terms of accounts. Again, in Sudnow's early work on a city attorney's office (1965) and on death in a hospital (1967), we find a focusing of attention on the cognitive elements (patterns) used by these people in constructing their ordered accounts. The concern was with "normal crimes," rather than with the problematic aspects of constructions of meaning or order, or with attempts to produce disorder, or with attempts to reconstruct order. This emphasis on the cognitive and ordered is even more striking in the works of the linguistic ethnomethodologists, especially Harvey Sacks. There the emphasis was on the rules implicit in the use of language, such as the "chain rule," which states that a question is to be followed by an answer. In Cicourel's parallel work (1970a) the emphasis was on "deep rules" and even "social structure." In Wieder's (1970) analysis of meaning the emphasis was on "meaning by rule," and in Zimmerman's (1970) analysis of rule use the emphasis was on the ways in which (implicitly assumed) shared concepts of practicality were crucial in the use of rules to maintain the sense of a shared, ordered universe of meaningful activities. In my own early work on suicide (Douglas, 1967), even when the emphasis was on the problematic construction of meanings, the focus of the analysis was implicitly on the shared or shareable dimensions of meaning, and even when I was dealing with profound emotions, such as depression and anxiety, the emphasis was on how the individuals construct shareable cognitive meanings for each other, such as "showing that something is profoundly wrong." Implicitly, we were all dealing with the traditional problem of social order, and we were all focusing almost exclusively on the shared universe of cognitive meanings, even when we were showing that these meanings were not as simple as, or were not arrived at in the way, the traditional theorists had thought.

The philosophical perspective we adopted to provide an abstract rationale and foundation for this work was phenomenology, especially as found in the work of Schutz. This is clear in the use of some of his terminology, such as typifications (Sudnow, 1965); the explicit use of many of his basic ideas or principles of interpretive procedures, such as the principle of the reciprocity of perspectives (Cicourel, 1970b); and in some explicit statements to this effect (Douglas, 1971a). This was an extremely effective device for systematizing and communicating our ideas about the social world at the time. Though I was not consciously aware of the fact at the time, phenomenological philosophy itself retained a basic commitment, in very new forms, to the traditional ideas of absolute objectivity and a basically shared universe of cognitive meanings. Like us, the phenomenological philosophers had made only a partial break with basic assumptions of the traditional perspective and then reintroduced them in certain ways. Their abstract philosophical ideas thus provided a good model for systematizing and communicating those we had developed about specific realms of the social world.

But this fit between phenomenological philosophy and concrete understandings of American society did not last long for some of us. For me and others with whom I was working, the difficulties arose mainly over the nature of social rules and their uses, the relations of these rule uses to the construction of social order, the relations between social meanings and social actions, the relations between imputed definitions of the self and one's own self-concepts, and the nature of objectivity of the research procedures used to investigate such phenomena.

Many of these basic questions first became reasonably clear to me in doing the work for *American Social Order* (Douglas, 1971b) and, at about the same time, in some of my own commonsense experiences with the nature of rule uses in our society and with the problems any practical actor faces in figuring out what is going on, especially when he is trying to construct any kind of order.[4] As I tried to understand how rules are used and order constructed by political actors in our society, it became ever more clear that the phenomenological works of both philosophers and sociologists had not understood how pluralistic and even fragmented our society is; how conflictful meanings are even within individuals; how important emotions are in an individual's decisions about what rules to invoke and when not to invoke any; and, above all, how complex any attempt to construct social order through political action is. I came to see far more clearly how deceitful actors are, how highly adept at constructing fronts, even for their friends. I came thereby to see how difficult it is to know when one is getting from actors what they themselves believe to be true, or even when they themselves are clear about whether they know what the truth is. By similar routes, such as in the detailed analysis of a new case of attempted suicide (see Douglas, 1971b), I came to see that an individual's

self-concepts are themselves complex and often unclear to him and that the imputa-
tions of meanings to him by others are dealt with in complex and variable ways in
constructing his own self concepts. I came also to see that we had previously been
implicitly assuming the traditional rationalist view of actions — that they are the
result of (or caused by) social meanings — and at the same time, had implicitly
assumed that the primary goal of a sociological theory is to explain social actions,
by which we really meant externally perceivable behavior.

By the time I had finished writing *American Social Order*, I was aware that existential philosophy and literature were far more different from phenomenological
philosophy than I had earlier assumed. And it was clear that my own understanding
of American society as presented in the book was much closer to existentialism
than to phenomenology. For this reason, I used the name existential sociology in
the introduction (which, of course, was written after the rest of the book), whereas
in most of the book I had used the term phenomenological, often interchangeably
with existential. Subsequent to that, I took a more active interest in existential philosophy, and it proved stimulating to some new concrete work (e.g., Douglas,
1972b) and to the systematizing work that led to the more philosophical parts of
this book. (It is of some interest to note that this book was originally contracted
for publication as a reader of previously published material. But our work progressively diverged from previously published material so that eventually it had to be a
completely original work.)

Existential sociology originated with our attempts to make sense out of, to
understand adequately, to analyze or explain problems we encountered in working
with concrete phenomena we experienced in everyday life, either in our own commonsense activities or in our research. When we related our work to the ideas of the
philosophers, we generally, though not always, did so after the fact of the empirical
work as a way of clarifying and systematizing what we were doing for readers and,
perhaps sometimes, as a way of further legitimizing what we did or simply showing
how it fit into the bigger intellectual scene.

This is a vital point and one the reader must keep in mind throughout his reading
of this book. The most basic idea of all phenomenological and existential work is
maintaining the integrity of the phenomena. We begin with the world of experience
and always keep that immediately before us as the reality. Analysis, theory, and
philosophy come after and are largely determined by that experience, instead of experience of the world being molded by theory as it is by the experimental and
hypothetical methods of traditional science. It is true that this fundamental desire
to maintain the integrity of the phenomena is itself a presupposition of the philosopher and the sociologist, so I am not arguing that we begin or end with a presuppositionless knowledge, such as Husserl originally thought phenomenology would
give us. It is true that our basic commonsense ideas of reality, of what constitutes
experience of the real world, are commonly presupposed by sociological investigation, and I do not argue that we seek or find a reality completely undetermined by
presuppostions of common sense. And certainly each phenomenological or existential sociologist is greatly affected by his own personal experience and individual predilections, so I am not arguing that in some way this kind of sociologist is a tabula
rasa researcher, or a medium of social reality who is simply the vessel through

which social reality can be known. The crucial point is simply that, insofar as possible, we participate directly in social experience and develop our understanding of that experience, including the methods of knowing and analyzing it, in accord with the demands of that experience, in the way that seems best to allow us to maintain the properties of that experience. Just as an existential sociologist would argue that traditional sociology partially distorted social[5] reality from the very beginning by forcing social reality to fit the mold of experimental methods developed in the natural sciences to study a completely different kind of reality, so must he argue that philosophy, including an existential philosophy, must always be molded by the reality of his social experience, instead of by a set of abstract presuppositions. As existential philosophy was developed mainly by European philosophers out of their experience of their own societies, and as American society is so very different from those, this restriction of philosophy largely to the ex post facto function of helping us to systematize and communicate our findings is even more important for American sociologists.

Notes

Chapter 2. The emergence of existential thought

1 For an introduction to traditions of voluntarism in the West, see Bourke (1964); For discussions of the concept of agency, the journal *Philosophy and Phenomenological Research* (e.g., Boler, 1968) and Stanley (1973); for an agendum of the issues as philosophers now see them, Brand (1970) and McGowan and Gochnauer (1971).

2 In this chapter the term *positivism* refers essentially to those theories that are based on nonhumanistic assumptions concerning the nature of persons and of conduct; *humanistic* is meant in the sense defined in the text. Non-humanistic assumptions generally are couched in terms of two root metaphors: the organism and the machine (Pepper, 1942). Functionalism, for example deduces explanations of conduct from assumptions of evolution, homeostasis, and other biological functions that are taken as natural to social systems. Experimental empiricism has tended to use the machine as its model. Although functionalism bases itself in a realistic metaphysics of a priori principles and logical deductions, empiricism has stressed detailed factual research. For organicists the mode of explanation had tended to be telic, in terms of systemic purposes or ends (the relationship of the parts to the whole); for mechanists explanation has tended to be causal (the relationship of parts to parts *or* wholes to wholes).

Although some precision is lost by joining these approaches under the rubric positivism, we feel this is compensated for by the resultant stress on the common features that distinguish them from humanistic models. For example, to the extent that functionalism sticks to the data, it tends to assume that meanings are given and are objectively knowable to observers. This, in the humanist view, begs the central question of how actors themselves construct meaning interactionally. Conversely, by presupposing a social system, functionalism reifies such concepts as "function" and posits them as the end social conduct must serve. Likewise, both mechanists and organicists tend to view persons as the media or carriers of various functions or causes which lie "behind" the social reality that appears in the consciousness of actors. Organicists and mechanists themselves have tended to identify functionalism with theory and mechanism with data, thereby papering over some of the distinctions we have noted and keeping their two approaches within a presumptively common frame (Merton, 1957:3—120; Dore, 1961). For a discussion of the convergence of these approaches into a social theory based on the model of the computer, see Manfred Stanley (1973, 1975). For empiricists' efforts to distance themselves from functionalism see Peter Park (1969) and Ivan Vallier (1971).

3 We are not here assuming a cultural monolithism. Rather, for purposes of the argument we shall develop, we wish to highlight certain interrelated trends. Fideism, fundamentalism, and other pre- or antimodern beliefs or practices are easy to note. For arguments that rationalistic empiricism was the dominant movement, see Nef (1960) and Ellul (1964). Also see Nelson (1967), Grant (1962:612—16), and Beirstedt (1949:584—92). For general treatments of the rise of positivism, see Dijksterhuis (1961), Koyré (1957, 1968), Matson (1964), and Rossi (1970).

4 J. O. Wisdom (1968) has taken a contrary view, arguing that Descartes saw the mind-body problem "as in principle soluble and he did not regard the two domains as utterly disparate and unrelatable." Wisdom does allow, however, that "the impact of the problem upon almost all of Descartes's successors was so extreme that they planted upon Descartes a false interpretation of his actual view." Such qualifications, even if correct, do not affect the utility of taking the conventional interpretation of Descartes, for it is that interpretation which has come down to sociologists, who are our real interest.

5 Blauner (1960:399) has noted that not only was Marx a half century ahead of his time in using survey techniques, but that he understood even in 1880 the difficulties of getting at subjective feelings. For the entire questionnaire used by Marx, see Bottomore and Rubel (1956:204—12).

6 "Questions Concerning Certain Faculties Claimed for Man," "Some Consequences of Four Incapacities," and "Grounds for Validity of the Laws of Logic: Further Consequences of Four Incapacities, " reprinted in the *Collected Papers of Charles Sanders Peirce* (1960:V), edited by Charles Hartshorne and Paul Weiss. For echoes of Peirce in ordinary language philosophers see Quine (1964), Sellars (1963), and Feyerabend (1965). For something similar in an existentialist phenomenologist, see Heidegger (1962:24).

7 The pragmatists' insistence on experience as the context of inquiry may be compared to Kierkegaard's notion that concrete individual existence can never be *aufgehoben*. Likewise, Peirce's statement that "the idea of the other, of *not*, becomes a very pivot of thought" is similar to ideas expressed by Sartre in *Being and Nothingness* or *Critique of Dialectical Reason* (see Bernstein, 1971:182).

Chapter 4. The sociology of Alfred Schutz

1 Aaron Gurwitsch noted of Schutz's work: "No philsophical question is raised concerning the phenomenological constitution and the sense of the existence of either the world or the self conceived of as mundane. In the 'natural attitude' we are confronted with, and situated within, the world, the paramount reality whose existence we simply accept without even thematizing it. Such unformulated, implicit, and 'silent' acceptance of the existential thesis or belief is . . . the essential characteristic of the 'natural attitude'" (1964:399).

2 "Substantively, this construct in itself is like a utopia which has been arrived at by the analytical accentuation of certain elements of reality. It's relationship to the empirical data consists solely in the fact that where market-conditioned relationships of the type referred to by the abstract construct are discovered or suspected to exist in reality to some extent, we can make the characteristic features of this relationship pragmatically clear and understandable by reference to an ideal type . . . the ideal type is an attempt to analyze historically unique configurations on their individual components by means of genetic concepts" (Weber, 1949:90).

3 The ethnomethodologists, including many sociolinguists, have been seeking

the invariant process by which the natural attitude is constituted. One source for these investigations is language behavior of children. Cicourel (1970b; 1972) and his students have been focusing on the interpretive procedures by which social order is learned and replayed.

4 It is clear that Schutz overlooked the importance of power in his discussion of typification. Reciprocal typification is not necessary for interaction to occur between a public defender and a defendant (cf. Sudnow, 1964).

5 These data are selected from Altheide (1974). Tuchman (1973) has also employed a Schutzian framework in her studies of news.

6 Schutz (1970b) also discussed the process as a polythetic buildup to create a monothetic whole or completed act. Phenomenology attempts to reverse the process: to break the monothetic unity into the constitutive polythetic process.

7 Schutz also discussed intrinsic and extrinsic (imposed) relevance. The first is what we intend; this was clearly Schutz's focus. The second refers to the more obdurate character of one's surroundings (e.g., population, environment, technology, and energy). These "variables" are used by some sociologists to explain social behavior.

8 It should be clear that by "multiple realities" Schutz did not mean various orientations or interpretations of reality. To the contrary, he would argue that we all have the same basic multiple realities, which in turn are fundamentally dependent on an invariant natural attitude. I believe Schutz is mistaken on this point and suggest research will uncover alternative natural attitudes.

Chapter 7. Behind the rational appearances

1 One could also speculate the observer has a weak stomach, and there would be an element of truth to this. On several occasions while visiting friends in hospitals I have passed out, and I have a deep fear of hospitals.

2 The foster home licensing personnel were continually on the lookout for violations of the official rules on out-of-home care for children. They combed the classified ads in the newspapers daily for persons who might be so audacious as to advertise their services.

3 Many of the CWS social workers share these sentiments with me, some for entirely different reasons, however.

4 During the course of the research, for example, a questionnaire distributed to the social workers at Metro by the local Social Services Union revealed that about one-third of the workers used barbiturates during their work activities. There were even several pushers in the office, in the sense of persons who kept phenobarbital in their desks which others could draw upon as they wished. I never felt certain about what the questionnaire reported, but there was no apparent reason why anyone would exaggerate this.

5 To give just one example, at my present place of employment, many of my colleagues are unaware of a state statute that specifically proscribes the sexual liaisons of university professors.

6 This fact was dramatically emphasized to me through some of the journal reviews I received when I tried to publish several papers describing the field investigation. In his rejection of one paper, for example, an anonymous reviewer for *Social Problems* judged the author as having a "perverted sense of morality," and this was the only basis cited for the rejection. One of the few available public accounts of these phenomena is contained in Martindale's illuminating discussion of the aca-

demic reviews he received about one of his recent analyses (Martindale, 1973: 167—90).

7 While I was in the process of finishing the welfare studies, I became involved with about fifteen of my colleagues in another study where this possibility was a very real one. The study concerned the investigation of many different aspects of a national political convention, some of which were covert in nature. Given our understandings about the aftermath of the 1968 Democratic Party convention in Chicago, we·had to come to grips with the nature of our commitments and loyalties at the very beginning and decide what we would do if any of the research information was subsequently the subject of a court subpoena. With relatively few reservations, all of us committed ourselves to the possibility of "hunkering down" and "stone walling" to the end.

8 This reference is specifically to the discussion by Carl Klockars (1975) of his research bargains with the professional fences or receivers of stolen goods. Klockars reported that the research agreements he worked out with "Vincent" included the understanding that, if Klockars was hauled into court by a subpoena of his research information, he would reveal his information and sources before going to jail.

Chapter 8. Occasioned transcendence

1 Child Welfare services, Metro Office, Southern Metropolitan County, and Western State are pseudonyms to mask the identification of the actual research settings. For a more detailed description of these settings, see Johnson (1973a).

2 For a detailed description and analysis of the methods used to conduct the research investigation, see Johnson (1975).

3 In introducing me to the skilled craftsmanship of this activity, one of the more knowledgeable hunters within the office informed me that crucial regional differences exist regarding the linguistic usage of this phrase. As reported to me, only men do the shooting in the Midwest, while only women do the shooting in the West. In keeping with my scholarly purposes, I have tried to use the phrase here in an objective manner.

4 This phrase originates from the infantry. "Tin hat" is one of the soldiers' terms for a metal shrapnel helmet, and the phrase "to put the tin hat on it" means to bring some line of action to a conclusive termination. The supervisor using this phrase was a high-ranking officer in the U.S. Army reserves.

5 I first learned about what occurred at this meeting on the same day from one of those present; within the next few weeks, however, I received essentially similar accounts from the other two members present at the meeting.

6 I do not intend this comment to imply that the memo referred to in this instance was destroyed. I actually do not know whether it was. Dalton's (1959:111) researches of business management-labor union relations led him to conclude that such phenomena are commonplace for such activities. Other descriptions of these phenomena may be found elsewhere (Johnson, 1973a).

7 This conversation and the following comments by the two supervisors of the CWS units were tape-recorded within the setting. I have taken minor editorial privileges in presenting them, however, such as eliminating many interjections and disregarding separate conversations that occurred simultaneously.

8 This conversation was not tape-recorded, but represents my reconstruction of it which I was able to record within five to ten minutes after it terminated.

9 Several of the most knowledgeable members on such matters understood the new instructions in the following manner: As the previously complete Time Study

reports were seen as inappropriate by others in Fiscal Services, but as these others could not "properly" return them again with the instructions, these most recent forms would be used as a resource by those in Fiscal Services to rejuggle the original numbers themselves. It was never learned with any certainty if this actually occurred.

10 When asked to clarify this phrase, an unfamiliar one to the observer, this social worker said that it meant "getting screwed over." Further investigation by the observer revealed that the phrase originated in the folklore of the Royal Navy and (if literally defined) refers to the time when sailors were strapped face-down to the breech of a cannon in preparation for a flogging aboard ship.

Chapter 9. The chronic pain experience

1 Zborowski (1953), Suchman (1964), and others have attempted to link cultural differences to differential responses to pain. These studies do not give an understanding of the chronic pain experience because they concentrate solely on the verbal descriptions of the pain felt by patients in select hospital locations. The argument that culture determines a person's reaction to pain is suspect because differences within cultural groups are greater than differences among cultural groups.

2 The sociological implications of the practice of acupuncture in America are discussed in Kotarba (1975).

3 The problems inherent in attempting to explain social behavior in terms of the rule-following or normative paradigm are discussed in Chapter 8 of this volume and Wilson (1970a).

4 The lack of understanding of the emotional element of human suffering is not limited to sociologists. The mass media, in efforts to portray current social issues objectively, often miss the boat. A vivid example of this brand of professionalism occurred recently on a local television news show in Chicago. In one of a series of special reports on medical costs, the viewers were shown a woman with tubes coming out of her nose after heart surgery, not knowing that she was being filmed; an injured baby in an emergency hospital room, bitten by the family dog; and a woman weakened by a heart attack, hanging onto her husband's hand, and being asked by a reporter: "Do you know what your treatment costs?" It was obvious she couldn't have cared less.

5 Manipulation is one of the least understood words in medical terminology. For some reason, osteopaths and chiropractors never publicly state that a manipulation is like cracking your knuckles except that the practitioner does it to your vertebrae.

Chapter 10. The existential self in the gay world

1 In Western philosophy and sociology of the past few hundred years the self has been dichotomized into an essential unchanging core-of-self and a situated self that changes with the interactive context.

2 A female name denotes a female member of the overt community; a male name denotes a male member of the secret community, unless otherwise specified.

3 A structural functionalist sociology would view this as "faulty socialization" rather than as an expression of existential freedom of choice.

4 *Coming out* had several meanings in the different sectors of the gay community. In the secret community it referred either to the first homosexual experience or to the first public affiliation with the secret community. In the overt community it

had either of these meanings, plus another meaning that referred to public declaration of homosexuality in *straight* settings. In either public sense it may be expanded to "coming out of the closet."

5 See Lyman and Scott (1970) for a discussion of passing. Goffman and Humphreys noted, of course, other methods of stigma evasion, such as going to a psychiatrist for a cure, but these are not relevant to this discussion; neither is the second mode of stigma confrontation, the religious form of stigma redemption.

6 *Bad faith* is the usual translation of the existential concept here translated as self-deception. *False consciousness* has political currency and often refers specifically to class consciousness, whereas *repression* and *the unconscious* are the psychological conceptualizations of those facets of the self about which one is self-deceived. The societal and structural functional analog is latent functions.

7 This statement is taken from the published autobiography of a gay male activist who also made the earlier statement, "I remain just plain old me." This tension between the *en-soi* and the *pour-soi* is common in gay liberation writings and experience.

8 A *closet queen* for the overt community is one who will not admit gayness to straight audiences; for the secret community, it refers to one who will not affiliate with the gay community for fear of stigmatization.

9 Those closet queens who engage in homosexual behavior but who do not affiliate with the gay community have, of course, an even greater stake in wearing convincing masks before all audiences. Humphreys (1970) called the most elaborate of these masks "breastplates of righteousness" both because of their armorlike quality and because they are designed to blind the observer with the brilliance of the wearer's illusory heterosexuality and civic virtue.

Appendix. The origins of existential sociology

1 The failure to understand that we only *use* the philosophy, that we have gone far beyond it in some directions and disagree with it in others, has led to a number of important misunderstandings of our work. For example, our earlier work on phenomenological sociology (Douglas, 1970a) was roundly criticized by Thomas Luckmann for not "really" being the phenomenology of Husserl and Schutz. This is completely true and was, in fact, so obvious to us that we did not even take up the point. Because of these misunderstandings, I decided that we must discuss the relations of the philosophical ideas to our own sociological ideas.

2 This fact is strikingly illustrated in my first experience with the idea of existential sociology. As an undergraduate I had read a great deal of philosophy and became a sociologist only after carefully considering philosophy and physics. (They would not allow me to do much about social problems.) But I do not remember thinking about the possible relevance of phenomenology or existentialism to sociology, which I then thought of in quite structural and mathematical terms. I did, however, see the relevance of phenomenology to the study of personality and psychology generally, but even this remained largely at the level of an almost commonsensical insistence on the importance of subjective experience as the foundation of such studies. I did a very introspective paper on anxiety for David McClelland, who rejected it with the valid assertion that he was not William James.

I even did a sociology paper on stratification for Robert F. Bales, in which I attempted to analyze the vastly complex subjective experiences of class consciousness, status, class, and power. He rejected it with the kind suggestion that I might be suffering from megalomania and might need psychiatric help. My cognitive deviance was already apparent, but it was caused primarily by commonsensical proclivities, rather than by connections I then saw between existential philosophy and sociology.

I remember first thinking of such connections when I was a graduate fellow in mathematical models at Johns Hopkins. I do not remember which of us suggested it, but I and a friend in mathematical models, Lawrence Rose, spent some time *joking* about the creation of an existential sociology. The stark contrast between our mathematical models and the existential view of the world struck us as hilarious, especially when we regaled each other with ideas for mathematical models of an existential world. Despite the laughter, I was in some way intrigued by the idea, probably because I knew that in my own personal life, and in the life of my friend, who was experiencing deep anxieties, depressions, and suicidal impulses, the existential perspective was obviously more relevant and true. But given the assumptions of "the necessity of explaining the social socially" and "avoiding reductionism at all costs," I did not see the relevance of such everyday life situations to my social theories, and it was precisely at that time that I was writing a monograph (never published) on hostage commitments, which sought to explain social order in terms of a game theoretical analysis of interlocking webs of commitments. My next, and more serious, involvement with existential thought came a year later while teaching at Wellesley College and wrestling with my work on suicide. At some time I read Simone de Beauvoir's *An Ethic of Uncertainty* and was struck by its realistic value in dealing with concrete value problems in our society. I even gave a talk to an introductory class about adopting an open-ended approach to value problems, especially to sexual problems one of the girls had raised. (I was obviously still very much a rationalist.) But I did not relate that directly to my suicide work, which was still mathematical. (I had long ago read some of Kenneth Burke's analysis of Samsonic suicide as a rhetorical device, but did not at all see how that would later add to a new theoretical view of suicide as a socially meaningful act.) Meanwhile, my historical research on suicide and my work in deviance were leading me to see how unreliable official statistics were. I also came to see that my theoretical variables (such as felt control, which lay at the heart of my model of suicide) could not be directly related to the experience of the people killing themselves by anything except my own imagination and a few snatches of self-report data I might interpret to fit into my variables. In all honesty I could not do what I had planned and spent a year or more of anxious casting around for some new way to do it. Owing to simple job considerations, such as getting fired from Wellesley for proposing that the whole place be put into receivership and sold, I took a job at the University of California at Los Angeles, began reading Goffman, Burke, and early C. Wright Mills (who was then a pragmatist and interactionist) and talking with people like Garfinkel. Meanwhile, I had read Binswanger's existential study of Ellen West's suicide and almost all other case studies. All this slow development, combined with the social milieu at UCLA, the practical necessities of getting the suicide thesis done, and the alternative of a case study method, led me to start analyzing the meanings of suicide both in the available cases and in my own past. At no time then or since did I become deeply involved in reading phenomenological or existential philosophy. The perspective and a key idea here or there that fit the world I knew was what I found so valuable. I especially found the highly introspective, jargon-ridden, academic phenomenology unsatisfying. Instead of concentrating on the philosophy, I have almost always concentrated on looking into every corner of our society I could — both in research and, far more, in daily living — and in mulling over the meanings of these experiences. After its initial help in shifting to a new perspective on the social world — simply taking everyday life as the crucial experience for any sociology or other understanding of life — I have used the philosophy as an ex post facto mapping device, a more systematic way of showing where we are now in our understanding of the social world, and as a teaching device to help others see where we are and how it makes sense abstractly. I am now quite unsympathetic to any academic philosophy, including phenomenology, because it is too far removed from the hurly-burly of life in our tumultuous society. And questions of eschatology, of what philosopher really said what when, hold little interest for me.

3 Two things should be made clear in this discussion. First, not all works that are often thought of as phenomenological sociology are what I consider to be sociology. Some are best seen as philosophy. This distinction is not meant to be pejorative, as I see an important place for philosophy in the thinking and work of sociologists. The distinction is based on an obvious difference in methods used. A work such as that of Berger and Luckmann (1967) was meant to be an elucidation of the philosophy of Husserl and Schutz, not a work of sociological theory. (This is clear in the book, and in a personal discussion Luckmann himself has assured me that this book is only his philosophy, whereas his sociology is really quite Durkheimian. He clearly has made a distinction between such a philosophical work and his sociological work.) The book is obviously based not on systematic research, but on the philosophical ideas of Husserl and Schutz. Second, it is entirely possible that other phenomenological or existential sociologists have started primarily with the philosophy and then proceeded to the research. I can only say that those whose work I have seen in progress over the years did not do so. Obviously, the question is open to investigation by anyone who wishes to study it. Even if such a study is done, however, I expect there will remain considerable uncertainty about the complex relations between philosophical ideas and concrete experience and that the answer one gives, even in the light of all the "facts," will rest in significant part upon his personal construction of the past.

4 It seems useful to give a brief outline of what I am referring to, as these personal experiences had a great effect on all my work. Like so many other academics during the 1960s, I had the unhappy experience of becoming embroiled in the Great Campus Turmoils. (One outcome of this was my book, *Youth in Turmoil,* 1970d.) Owing in small part to my personal feelings (especially those of having my whole life's work and career threatened by what I saw as new hordes of barbarians, in the guise both of students and of politicians) and in far greater part to the peculiar circumstances of my university and departmental situation and to highly unpredictable situations, I became the supposed leader of a large, pluralistic grouping of faculty members who wanted to stop the effects of politics on the university. Although this group was partly dedicated to abstract ideas and the rhetoric of a politics-free university life, it was from the beginning more quietly committed to going for the jugular. Our old chancellor had resigned and a new one was to be appointed, but we knew that, if the normal procedures were followed, we would get a chancellor who would continue what we believed would be disastrous policies. We were faculty revolutionaries posing as royalists in an attempt to control another breed of revolutionaries and to keep state politicians from controlling the university more than they already did. I was faced with the problems of trying to determine what many different sides were up to and what they really meant; with trying to do some things without their knowing what we were up to, so they could not prevent our success; with constructing order within the group on one basis while constructing other orderings of events outside that group on other bases; with dealing with politicians of many different persuasions; with communicating with people through

the mass media, some of whose correspondents were indifferent, some friendly to us, and some out to get us; and with continually countering the attacks of our many enemies, including some regents and many students of different groups. Through this activity I learned about politics from the inside. I learned the difficulty of knowing what was going on, even of knowing what was happening with my closest associates. I learned how simple statements were distorted in the retelling. I learned how all sides, including our own, were involved in clandestine activities that they often did not understand. I learned how consciously the political labeling games were played. I learned about the difficulty of maintaining even a semblance of social order and that a semblance was often all there was and was often more effective than the real thing would have been. Importantly, I learned a great deal about the use of social rules, especially through an instance in which one group tried to invoke a rule against something I did. I had asked a secretary of the academic senate of the university if I could look at a college file. She gave it to me and said I should be sure to return it. The file contained some incriminating letters by an administrator, so the establishment was upset when they learned I had the file, apparently out of fear that it would be revealed to others.. (Actually, as I saw it, there was no way I could use the material effectively, but they must not have understood that. I chose to let them worry about such nonexistent dangers because I thought worry might exert a little pressure on them. In the same way, we chose at various times to leak to unreliable people information we had about some of their internal activities.) They insisted there was a rule against removing such files from the office and tried to have me censured by the faculty. Eventually, the rules committee decided that there was no such rule, but that in the future there should be. The censure failed. And, after a year and a half of struggling, we agreed, all very indirectly, upon a compromise administration.

Certainly it would be a mistake to see experiences such as these as the whole of our social lives. But throughout these practical activities I was intensely involved in trying to understand them and see their meaning for a better sociological theory. I believe they did reveal, in starker and more problematic forms, the kinds of struggles that go on all the time in the political arenas of our society in which social order must be constructed, with intense feelings often dominating and controlling events, with rules being formulated and waived as needed to achieve one's ends, and with great difficulty in understanding and uncovering the truth. It was undoubtedly the most important field research I have yet done and, even when I cannot reveal the exact details, it has formed the background information for some of my most important work in recent years.

5 I wish to emphasize that the distorting effect of traditional methods on the traditional sociological understanding of the social world was only partial. Most of the traditional sociologists always retained some commitment to understanding the social world of everyday experience. Their presupposed methods simply forced them to bootleg everyday meanings into their theories and to provide convoluted ex post facto translation devices to show how their abstract theories fit everyday life (Douglas, 1970a, 1972a). Their theories were always so complex and loose that they were able to bootleg a great deal of everyday reality into their works. This was especially true when their works were very concrete. (As almost everyone has noted, for example, the concrete, down-to-earth essays by Talcott Parsons contain many valuable truths about social reality in America, whereas his abstract theorizing distorts American society beyond recognition.) For example, the experimental designs of questionnaire sociology would have screened out almost every bit of truth about social reality had not the questionnaire sociologists always been able to

bootleg reality through the use of participant observation during the pretest stage and through the use of their commonsense interpretations, which they often presented at the beginnings of the works as hypotheses, but which were almost always formulated after the outcomes were already known. In research on suicide and any other topic involving official statistics this was blatantly obvious, as the sociologists always knew in general what the statistical relations were before they began. This bootlegging allowed the questionnaire sociologist to discover results that made sense commonsensically and had some relevance to understanding everyday life. Unfortunately, just as with bootlegging liquor, sociological bootlegging produced a skimpy product of inferior quality.

Bibliography

Adato, Al. 1971. "On the Sociology of Topics in Ordinary Conversation." Ph.D. dissertation, Department of Sociology, University of California, Santa Barbara.

Altheide, David L. 1974. "The News Scene." Ph.D. dissertation, Department of Sociology, University of California, San Diego.

    1975. "Newsworkers and Newsmakers: A Study in News Use." Unpublished paper, Department of Sociology, Arizona State University.

    1976. *Creating Reality: How TV News Distorts Events.* Beverly Hills: Sage.

Anderson, John P. 1972. "Objective Expressions." Unpublished paper, Duke University Medical Center.

Attewell, Paul. 1974. "Ethnomethodology Since Garfinkel." *Theory and Society* 1:179–210.

Ayer, Alfred Jules (ed.). 1966. *Logical Positivism.* New York: Free Press.

Bar-Hillel, Yehoshua. 1954. "Indexical Expressions." *Mind* 63:359–79.

Barrett, William. 1962. *Irrational Man.* Garden City, N.Y. :Doubleday.

Becker, Howard S. 1963. *Outsiders.* New York: Free Press.

    1970. *Sociological Work.* Chicago: Aldine.

Becker, Howard S., Blanche Geer, and Everett C. Hughes. 1968. *Making the Grade.* New York: Wiley.

Bell, Arthur. 1971. *Dancing the Gay Lib Blues: A Year in the Homosexual Liberation Movement.* New York: Simon & Schuster.

Berger, Peter L. 1963. *Invitation to Sociology.* Garden City, N.Y.: Doubleday.

Berger, Peter L., and Thomas Luckmann. 1967. *The Social Construction of Reality.* Garden City, N.Y.: Doubleday.

Bergson, Henri. 1950. *Time and Free Will*, 6th ed. London: George Allen & Unwin.

Bernstein, Richard. 1971. *Praxis and Action.* Philadelphia: University of Pennsylvania Press.

Bierstedt, Robert. 1949. "A Critique of Empiricism in Sociology." *American Sociological Review* 14 (October):584–92.

Bittner, Egon. 1965. "The Concept of Organization." *Social Research* 32:230–55.

    1967a. "The Police on Skid Row." *American Sociological Review* 32:699–715.

    1967b. "Police Discretion in Emergency Apprehension of Mentally Ill Persons." *Social Problems* 14:278–92.

Blau, Peter M. 1963. *The Dynamics of Bureaucracy*. Chicago: University of Chicago Press.

Blauner, Robert. 1960. "Work Satisfaction and Industrial Trends." In R. G. Galenson and S. M. Lipset (eds.). *Labor and Trade Unionism: An Interdisciplinary Reader*, pp. 120—45. New York: Wiley.

Bloom, S.W. 1965 *The Doctor and His Patient: A Sociological Interpretation*. New York: Russell Sage Foundation.

Blum, Alan. 1970a. "The Sociology of Mental Illness." In Jack D. Douglas (ed.). *Deviance and Respectability*, pp. 31—60. New York: Basic Books.

　　　1970b. "On Theorizing." In Jack D. Douglas (ed.). *Understanding Everyday Life*, pp. 301—19. Chicago: Aldine.

　　　1972. "Sociology, Wrongdoing, and Akrasia: An Attempt to Think Greek about the Problem of Theory and Practice." In Robert A. Scott and Jack D. Douglas (eds.). *Theoretical Perspectives on Deviance*, pp. 342—63. New York: Basic Books.

Blum, Alan, and Peter McHugh. 1971. "The Social Ascription of Motives." *American Sociological Review* 36 (1):98—109.

Blumer, Herbert. 1969. *Symbolic Interactionism*. Englewood Cliffs, N.J.: Prentice-Hall.

Boler, J.F. 1968. "Agency." *Philosophy and Phenomenological Research* 29(2): 144—63.

Bonica, J. J. 1953. *The Management of Pain*. Philadelphia: Lea & Febiger.

Bottomore, Thomas B., and M. Rubel (eds.). 1956. *Karl Marx: Selected Writings in Sociology and Social Philosophy*. London: Watts.

Bourke, V. J. 1964. *The Will in Western Thought*. New York: Sheed & Ward.

Brand, Myles (ed.). 1970. *The Nature of Human Action*. Glenview, Ill.: Scott, Foresman.

Burke, Kenneth. 1950. *A Rhetoric of Motives*. Englewood Cliffs, N.J.: Prentice-Hall.

　　　1965. *Permanence and Change*, 2nd rev. ed. Indianapolis: Bobbs-Merrill.

Burtt, E. A. 1954. *The Metaphysical Foundations of Modern Science*. Garden City, N.Y.: Doubleday.

Carnap, Rudolph. 1953. "Inductive Logic and Science." *Proceedings of the American Academy of Arts and Sciences* 80:154—80.

Chapin, F. Stuart. 1939. "Definition of Definitions of Concepts." *Social Forces* 18:110—28.

Churchill, Lindsey. 1971. "Some Limitations of Current Quantitative Methods in Sociology." Paper presented to the annual meetings of the American Sociological Association, Denver, Colorado

Cicourel, Aaron V. 1964. *Method and Measurement in Sociology*. New York: Free Press.

　　　1968. *The Social Organization of Juvenile Justice*. New York: Wiley.

　　　1969. "Generative Semantics and the Structure of Social Interaction." Paper presented at the International Days of Sociolinguistics, Rome.

　　　1970a. "Basic and Normative Rules in the Negotiation of Status and Role." In Hans Peter Dreitzel (ed.). *Recent Sociology No. 2*, pp. 44—9. New York: Collier.

1970b. "The Acquisition of Social Structure." In Jack D. Douglas (ed.). *Understanding Everyday Life*, pp. 136—68. Chicago: Aldine.

1972. "Delinquency and the Attribution of Responsibility." In Robert A. Scott and Jack D. Douglas (eds.). *Theoretical Perspectives on Deviance*, pp. 142—57. New York: Basic Books.

1974. *Cognitive Sociology.* New York: Free Press.

Cicourel, Aaron V., et al. 1975. *Language Use and School Performance.* New York: Academic Press.

Cicourel, Aaron V., and John I. Kitsuse. 1963. *Educational Decision Makers.* Indianapolis: Bobbs-Merrill.

Cobb, B. 1958. "Why Do People Detour to Quacks?" In E. Gartley Jaco (ed.). *Patients, Physicians and Illness*, pp. 283—7. New York: Free Press.

Cohen, Morris R. 1930. *A History of Modern Culture.* New York: Holt, Rinehart and Winston.

1949. *Studies in Philosophy and Science.* New York: Holt Rinehart and Winston.

Coleman, James. 1968. "Review Symposium." *American Sociological Review* 33 (February):126—30.

Collins, Randall, and Michael Makowsky. 1972. *The Discovery of Society.* New York: Random House.

Coser, Lewis. 1956. *The Functions of Social Conflict.* New York: Free Press.

Dalton, Melville. 1959. *Men Who Manage.* New York: Wiley.

Dank, Barry. 1971. "Coming Out in the Gay Community." *Psychiatry* 34:180—97.

Dean, John P. 1954. "Participant Observation and Interviewing." In John T. Doby (ed.). *Introduction to Social Research*, pp. 225—52. Harrisburg, Pa.: Stackpole.

Denzin, Norman K. 1969. "Symbolic Interactionism and Ethnomethodology: A Proposed Synthesis." *American Sociological Review* 34 (December):922—34.

1970. "Symbolic Interactionism and Ethnomethodology." In Jack D. Douglas (ed.). *Understanding Everyday Life*, pp. 261—87. Chicago: Aldine.

Descartes, René. 1912. *Philosophical Works.* (M. Haldane and R. Ross, trans.) London: Oxford University Press.

Dijksterhuis, E. J. 1961. *The Mechanization of the World-Picture in the 17th Century.* Oxford: Clarendon Press.

Dilthey, Wilhelm. 1957—60. *Gesamnelte Schriften.* Stuttgart: Teubner.

Dore, Ronald Philip. 1961. "Function and Cause." *American Sociological Review* 26 (December): 843—53.

Douglas, Jack D. 1967. *The Social Meanings of Suicide.* Princeton, N.J.: Princeton University Press.

1970a. *Understanding Everyday Life.* Chicago: Aldine.

1970b. "The Relevance of Sociology." In Jack D. Douglas (ed.). *The Relevance of Sociology*, pp. 185—233. New York: Appleton.

1970c. *Youth in Turmoil.* Washington, D.C.: G.P.O.

1970d. "Freedom and Tyranny." In Jack D. Douglas (ed.). *Freedom and Tyranny in the Technological Society*, pp. 3—41. New York: Random House.

1971a. "The Theory of Objectivity in Sociology." Paper presented at the annual meetings of the American Sociological Association, Denver, Colorado.

1971b. *American Social Order.* New York: Free Press.

1972a. "Observing Deviance." In Jack D. Douglas (ed.). *Research on Deviance*, pp. 3—33. New York: Random House.

1972b. "The Experience of the Absurd and the Problem of Social Order." In Robert A. Scott and Jack D. Douglas (eds.). *Theoretical Perspectives on Deviance*, pp. 189—213. New York: Basic Books.

1973. *Defining America's Social Problems.* Englewood Cliffs, N.J.: Prentice-Hall.

1974. *Drug Crisis Intervention.* Washington, D.C.: G.P.O.

1976. *Investigative Social Research: Individual and Team Field Research.* Beverly Hills: Sage.

1977. "Creative Deviance and Social Change." Unpublished manuscript, Department of Sociology. University of California, San Diego.

Douglas, Jack D., and Paul K. Rasmussen, with Carol Ann Flanigan. 1977. *Nude Beaches.* Beverly Hills: Sage.

Dreitzel, Hans Peter (ed.). 1970. *Recent Sociology No. 2.* New York: Macmillan.

Duncan, Otis D., and Leo P. Schnore. 1959. "Cultural, Behavioral, and Ecological Perspectives in the Study of Social Organization." *American Journal of Sociology* 65: (September):132—46.

Durkheim, Emile. 1951. *Suicide.* New York: Free Press.

Edie, James M. 1967. "Transcendental Phenomenology and Existentialism." In Joseph J. Kockelmans (ed.). *Phenomenology: The Philosophy of Edmund Husserl and Its Interpretation*, pp. 237—51. Garden City, N.Y.: Doubleday.

Ellul, Jacques. 1964. *The Technological Society.* New York: Random House (Vintage Books).

Emerson, Joan. 1970. "Behavior in Private Places: Sustaining Definitions of Reality in Gynecological Examinations." In Hans Peter Dreitzel (ed.). *Recent Sociology No. 2*, pp. 73—97. New York: Macmillan.

Emerson, Robert M. 1969. *Judging Delinquents.* Chicago: Aldine.

Farber, Martin. 1940. "The Idea of Presuppositionless Philosophy." In Martin Farbeı (ed.). *Philosophical Essays in Memory of Edmund Husserl*, pp. 46—64. Cambridge: Harvard University Press.

Feigl, Herbert. 1943. "Logical Empiricism." In Dagobert H. Runes (ed.). *Twentieth Century Philosophy*, pp. 119—44. New York: Philosophical Library.

Feyerabend, Paul K. 1962. "Explanation, Reduction and Empiricism." In Herbert Feigl and Grover Maxwell (eds.). *Minnesota Studies in the Philosophy of Science*, vol. III, pp. 199—228. Minneapolis: University of Minnesota Press.

1965. "Problems in Empiricism." In Robert Colodny (ed.). *Beyond the Edge of Certainty*, pp. 22—51. Englewood Cliffs, N.J.: Prentice-Hall.

Fite, Warner. 1930. *The Living Mind.* New York: Dial Press.

Freidson, Eliot. 1970. *Profession of Medicine.* New York: Dodd, Mead.

Friedrichs, Robert W. 1970. *A Sociology of Sociology.* New York: Free Press.

Gabaglio, Antonio. 1888. *Teoria Generale de la Statistica: Parte Storica*, vol. I. Milan: Hoepli.

Gagnon, John, and William Simon. 1968. "Homosexuality: The Formulation of a Sociological Perspective." In Mark Lefton, James K. Skipper, Jr., and Charles E. McGaghy (eds.). *Approaches to Deviance: Concepts, Theories and Research Findings.* pp. 75—91. New York: Appleton.

Garfinkel, Harold. 1967. *Studies in Ethnomethodology*. Englewood Cliffs, N.J.: Prentice-Hall.

Garfinkel, Harold, and Harvey Sacks. 1970. "On the Formal Structures of Practical Actions." In John C. McKinney and Edward A. Tiryakian (eds.). *Theoretical Sociology*, pp. 337–64. New York: Appleton.

Geer, Blanche. 1964. "First Days in the Field." In Phillip E. Hammond (ed.). *Sociologists at Work*, pp. 372–98. Garden City, N.Y.: Doubleday.

Goffman, Erving. 1959. *The Presentation of Self in Everyday Life*. Garden City, N.Y.: Doubleday (Anchor Books).

    1963. *Stigma*. Englewood Cliffs, N.J.: Prentice-Hall.

    1967. *Interaction Ritual*. Garden City, N.Y.: Doubleday.

Gordon, Chad. 1968. "Systemic Senses of Self." *Sociological Inquiry* 38:161–78.

Gordon, G. 1966. *Role Theory and Illness*. New Haven: College & University Press.

Gouldner, Alvin W. 1970. *The Coming Crisis of Western Sociology*. New York: Basic Books.

Grant, Edward C. 1962. "Hypotheses in Later and Early Modern Science." *Daedalus* 17:612–6.

Gurwitsch, Aaron. 1964. *The Field of Consciousness*. Pittsburgh: Duquesne University Press.

Habermas, Jurgen. 1970. *Knowledge and Human Interests*. Boston: Beacon Press.

Hamilton, Wallace. 1973. "Male Homosexuals and Their 'Worlds.'" In Judd Marmor (ed.). *Sexual Inversion*, pp. 79–95. New York: Basic Books.

Hayek, F. A. 1955. *The Counter-Revolution of Science: Studies on the Abuse of Reason*. New York: Free Press.

Heidegger, Martin. 1962. *Being and Time*. New York: Harper & Row.

Hildahl, Spencer.1970. "A Note on . . . 'A Note on the Sociology of Knowledge.'" *Sociological Quarterly* 11:405–15.

Holzner, Burkard. 1968. *Reality Construction in Society*. Cambridge: Schenkman.

Horowitz, Irving Louis. 1970. *Sociological Self-Images*. Beverly Hills: Sage.

Hughes, H. Stuart. 1958. *Consciousness and Society*. New York: Random House (Vintage Books).

Hull, Clark L. 1943. *Principles of Behavior*. New York: Appleton.

Hume, David. 1961. "An Enquiry Concerning Human Understanding (1748)." In *The Empiricists*, pp. 307–430. Garden City, N.Y.: Doubleday (Dolphin Books).

Humphreys, Laud. 1970. *Tearoom Trade: Impersonal Sex in Public Places*. Chicago: Aldine.

    1971. "New Styles in Homosexual Manliness." *Transaction* 8 (March–April): 38–46.

    1972. *Out of the Closets: The Sociology of Homosexual Liberation*. Englewood Cliffs, N.J.: Prentice-Hall.

Husserl, Edmund. 1931. *Ideas: General Introduction to Phenomenology*. (W. R. Royce Gibson, trans.) London: George Allen & Unwin.

    1962. *Ideas: General Introduction to Pure Phenomenology*. (W. R. Royce Gibson, trans.) New York: Collier Books.

    1965. *Phenomenology and the Crisis of Philosophy*. (Quentin Lauer, trans.) New

York: Harper Torchbooks.

1970a. *The Paris Lectures.* The Hague: Martinus Nijhoff.

1970b. *Cartesian Meditations.* The Hague: Martinus Nijhoff.

Hyman, Herbert. 1960. *Survey Design and Analysis.* New York: Free Press.

Jacobs, Glenn. 1970. "Life in the Colonies: Welfare Workers and Clients." In Glenn Jacobs (ed.). *The Participant Observer,* pp. 246—59. New York: Braziller.

Jacobs, Jerry. 1967. "Symbolic Bureaucracy." *Social Forces* 21:107—30.

James, William. 1890. *The Principles of Psychology* (2 vols.). New York: Holt, Rinehart and Winston.

Johnson, John M. 1972. "The Practical Use of Rules." In Robert A. Scott and Jack D. Douglas (eds.). *Theoretical Perspectives on Deviance,* pp. 215—49. New York: Basic Books.

1973. "The Social Construction of Official Information." Ph.D. dissertation, University of California, San Diego.

1975. *Doing Field Research.* New York: Free Press.

Kafka, Franz. 1971. *The Complete Stories.* New York: Schocken Books.

Kant, Immanuel. 1949. *The Philosophy of Kant.* (Carl J. Friedrich, ed.) New York: Random House (Modern Library).

1965. *Critique of Pure Reason.* (Norman Kemp Smith, trans.) New York: St. Martin's Press.

Kaufman, Waldo (ed.). 1964. *Existentialism from Dostoevsky to Sartre.* New York: New American Library (Meridian Books).

Kierkegaard, Sören. 1944. *Either/Or: A Fragment of Life.* (David F. Sorenson and Lillian M. Sorenson, trans.) Princeton, N.J.: Princeton University Press.

1946. *The Concept of Dread.* (Walter Lowrie, trans.) Princeton, N.J.: Princeton University Press.

King, S. H. 1972. "Social-Psychological Factors in Illness." In H. E. Freeman et al. (eds.). *Handbook of Medical Sociology,* pp. 129—47. Englewood Cliffs, N.J.: Prentice-Hall.

Klockars, Carl. 1975. *The Professional Fence.* New York: Free Press.

Kockelmans, Joseph. 1967. *Phenomenology.* Garden City, N.Y.: Doubleday (Anchor Books).

Kolakowski, Leszek. 1969. *Toward a Marxist Humanism: Essays on the Left Today.* New York: Grove Press.

Konvitz, Milton R., and Gail Kennedy. 1960. *The American Pragmatists.* New York: New American Library (Meridian Books).

Kotarba, J. 1975. "Acupuncture and the New Entrepreneurs of Hope." *Urban Life* 4 (July):149—78.

Koyré, Alexandre. 1957. *From the Closed World to the Infinite Universe.* New York: Harper & Row.

1968. *Metaphysics and Measurement: Essays in the Scientific Revolution.* Cambridge: Harvard University Press.

Kroeber, Alfred L., and Clyde Kluckholn. 1952. "General Features of Culture." In A. L. Kroeber (ed.). *Culture, a Critical Review of Concepts and Definitions.* Cambridge: Papers of the Peabody Museum.

Kuhn, Thomas S. 1962. *The Structure of Scientific Revolutions.* Chicago: University of Chicago Press. Second edition, revised, 1970.

1970. "Logic of Discovery or Psychology of Research?" In Imre Lakatos and Alan Musgrave (eds.), *Criticism and the Growth of Knowledge*, pp. 61—80. New York: Cambridge University Press.

Kwant, Remy C. 1963. *The Phenomenological Philosophy of Merleau-Ponty*. Pittsburgh: Dusquesne University Press.

Lakatos, Imre, and Alan Musgrave (eds.). 1970. *Criticism and the Growth of Knowledge*. New York: Cambridge University Press.

Lauer, Quentin. 1958. *Phenomenology: Its Genesis and Prospect*. New York: Harper Torchbooks.

1965. "Introduction." In Edmund Husserl. *Phenomenology and the Crisis of Philosophy*, pp. 1—71. (Quentin Laver, trans.) New York: Harper & Row.

Lazarsfeld, Paul, and Allen Barton. 1951. "Qualitative Measurement in the Social Sciences." In Daniel Lerner and Harold Lasswell (eds.). *The Policy Sciences: Recent Developments in Scope and Methods*. Stanford: Stanford University Press.

Lazarsfeld, Paul F., and Morris Rosenberg. 1955. *The Language of Social Research*. New York: Free Press.

Lemert, Edwin M. 1970. "Records in the Juvenile Court." In Stanton Wheeler (ed.). *On File: Records and Dossiers in American Life*, pp. 355—88. New York: Russell Sage Foundation.

Lennard, Henry L., et al. 1971. *Mystification and Drug Misuse*. San Francisco: Jossey-Bass.

Lofland, John. 1969. *Deviance and Identity*. Englewood Cliffs, N.J.: Prentice-Hall.

1971. *Analyzing Social Settings*. Belmont, Calif.: Wadsworth.

Louch, A. R. 1966. *Explanation and Human Action*. Berkeley: University of California Press.

Luckmann, Thomas. 1972. *The Structures of the Life-World*. (Richard Zaner and Tristram Engelhardt, Jr., trans.) Evanston: Northwestern University Press.

Lukacs, George. 1968. *History and Class Consciousness: Studies in Marxist Dialectics*. (Rodney Livingstone, trans.) Cambridge: MIT Press.

Lundberg, George. 1955. "The Natural Science Trend in Sociology." *American Journal of Sociology* 61 (November):191—202.

1964. *Foundations of Sociology*. New York: McKay.

Lundberg, George, Clarence C. Schrag, and Otto Larsen. 1954. *Sociology*. New York: Harper & Row.

Lyman, Stanford M. 1961. "The Structure of Chinese Society in Nineteenth Century America." Ph.D. dissertation, University of California, Berkeley.

1974. *Chinese Americans*. New York: Random House.

Lyman, Stanford M., and Marvin B. Scott. 1970. *A Sociology of the Absurd*. New York: Appleton.

MacIver, Robert. 1937. *Society: An Introductory Analysis*. New York: Holt, Rinehart and Winston.

Manis, Jerome J., and Bernard N. Meltzer (eds.). 1967. *Symbolic Interaction: A Reader in Social Psychology*. Boston: Allyn & Bacon.

Manheim, Karl. 1936. *Ideology and Utopia*. New York: Harcourt, Brace Jovanovich.

1952. *Essays on the Sociology of Knowledge.* (Paul Kecskemeti, ed.) London: Routledge & Kegan Paul.

Marcel, Gabriel. 1973. "The Embodied Self." In Richard M. Zaner and Don Ihde (eds.). *Phenomenology and Existentialism.* New York: Putnam.

Martindale, Don. 1973. "The Mentality of the Crusader." In Don Martindale and Edith Martindale. *Psychiatry and the Law*, pp. 167–90. St. Paul: Windflower.

Marx, Karl. 1946. *Capital.* New York: Everyman's Library.

1959. "Theses on Feuerbach." In Lewis S. Feuer (ed.). *Marx and Engels: Basic Writings on Politics and Philosophy.* Garden City, N.Y.: Doubleday.

Matson, Floyd W. 1964. *The Broken Image: Man, Science and Society.* New York: Braziller.

May, Rollo, Ernest Angel, and Henri F. Ellenberger (eds.). 1958. *Existence: A New Dimension in Psychiatry and Psychology.* New York: Basic Books.

McGowan, R., and M. Gochnauer. 1971. "A Bibliography of the Philosophy of Action." In R. Binkley et al. (eds.). *Agent, Action and Reason*, pp. 310–26. Toronto: University Press.

McHugh, Peter. 1970. "On the Failure of Positivism." In Jack D. Douglas (ed.). *Understanding Everyday Life*, pp. 320–35. Chicago: Aldine.

McHugh, Peter, Stanley Raffel, Daniel C. Foss, and Alan F. Blum. 1974. *On the Beginning of Social Inquiry.* London: Routledge & Kegan Paul.

McKinney, John C. 1970. "Sociological Theory and Process of Typification." In John C. McKinney and Edward A. Tiryakian (eds.). *Theoretical Sociology*, pp. 235–69. New York: Appleton.

Mead, George Herbert. 1934. *Mind, Self and Society.* Chicago: University of Chicago Press.

Mechanic, David. 1968. *Medical Sociology.* New York: Free Press.

Mehan, Hugh. 1974. "Accomplishing Classroom Lessons." In Aaron Cicourel et al. *Language Use and School Performance*, pp. 76–142. New York: Academic Press.

Mehan, Hugh, and Houston Wood. 1975. *The Reality of Ethnomethodology.* New York: Wiley.

Merleau-Ponty, Maurice. 1962. *Phenomenology of Perception.* London: Routledge & Kegan Paul.

1964a. *Signs.* Evanston: Northwestern University Press.

1964b. *Sense and Non-Sense.* Evanston: Northwestern University Press.

1964c. *The Primacy of Perception.* Evanston: Northwestern University Press.

1968. *The Visible and the Invisible.* Evanston: Northwestern University Press.

Merton, Robert K. 1957. *Social Theory and Social Structure.* New York: Free Press.

Meszáros, Istvan. 1970. *Marx's Theory of Alienation.* London: Merlin Press.

Miller, Merle. 1971. *On Being Different: What It Means To Be a Homosexual.* New York: Random House.

Miller, S.M. 1953. "The Participant Observer and Over-Rapport." *American Sociological Review* 28:97–9.

Moore, Omar K., and Alan R. Anderson. "Puzzles, Games and Social Interaction." In David Braybrooke (ed.), *Philosophical Problems of the Social Sciences*, New York: Macmillan.

Morris, Charles. 1932. *Six Theories of Mind.* Chicago: University of Chicago Press.

Morselli, H. 1903. *Suicide: An Essay in Comparative Moral Statistics.* New York: Appleton.

Murphy, John. 1971. *Homosexual Liberation: A Personal View.* New York: Praeger.

Natanson, Maurice. 1963. *Philosophy of the Social Sciences.* New York: Random House.

1970a. *Phenomenology and Social Reality: Essay in Memory of Alfred Schutz.* The Hague: Martinus Nijhoff.

1970b. "Phenomenology and Typification: A Study in the Philosophy of Alfred Schutz." *Social Research* 37:1—22.

Nef, John U. 1960. *Cultural Foundations of Industrial Civilization.* New York: Harper & Row.

Nelson, Benjamin. 1967. *The Early Modern Revolution in Science and Philosophy: Fictionalism, Probabilism, Fideism and Catholic "Prophetism."* (R.S. Cohen and M. Wartofssky, eds.) Boston: Boston Studies in the Philosophy of Science.

O'Neill, John. 1974. *Making Sense Together.* New York: Harper & Row.

Ortega y Gasset, José. 1964. "Being in One's Self and Being Beside One's Self." In Richard M. Zaner and Don Ihde (eds.). *Phenomenology and Existentialism,* pp. 215—31. New York: Putnam.

Park, Peter. 1969. *Sociology Tomorrow.* New York: Pegasus.

Parsons, Talcott. 1937. *The Structure of Social Action.* New York: Free Press.

1951. *The Social System.* New York: Free Press

Paul, Benjamin D. 1953. "Interview Technique and Field Relations." In A.L. Kroeber et al. (eds.). *Anthropology Today.* Chicago: University of Chicago Press.

Peirce, Charles S. 1960. *Collected Papers.* (Charles Hartshorne and Paul Weiss, eds.) Cambridge: Harvard University Press (Belknap Press).

Pepper, Stephan. 1942. *World Hypotheses.* Berkeley: University of California Press.

Peters, R.S. 1960. *The Concept of Motivation.* London: Routledge & Kegan Paul.

Petrovic, Gajo. 1967. *Marx in the Mid-Twentieth Century.* Garden City, N.Y.: Doubleday.

Polanyi, M. 1967. *The Tacit Dimension.* Garden City, N.Y.: Doubleday.

Pollner, Melvin. 1970. "On the Foundations of Mundane Reasoning." Ph.D. dissertation, Department of Sociology, University of California, Los Angeles.

Polsky, Ned. 1967. *Hustlers, Beats and Others.* Chicago: Aldine.

Ponse, Barbara. 1974. "The Meaning World of Lesbians." Unpublished paper, Department of Sociology, University of Southern California.

1967. "Secrecy in the Lesbian World." *Urban Life* 6 (October): 313—38.

forthcoming. *Identities in the Lesbian World.* Westport Conn.: Greenwood Press.

Popper, Karl F. 1959. *The Logic of Scientific Discovery.* New York: Basic Books.

1970. "Normal Science and Its Dangers." In Imre Lakatos and Alan Musgrave (eds.). *Criticism and the Growth of Knowledge,* pp. 51—8. New York: Cambridge University Press.

Psathas, George (ed.). 1973, *Phenomenological Sociology.* New York: Wiley.

Quine, Willard Van Orman. 1964. *From a Logical Point of View.* Cambridge: Harvard University Press.

Quinney, Richard. 1970. *The Social Reality of Crime.* Boston: Little, Brown.

1972. "From Repression to Liberation: Social Theory in a Radical Age." In
   Robert A. Scott and Jack D. Douglas (eds.). *Theoretical Perspectives on Devi-
   ance*, pp. 317—40. New York: Basic Books.
Rasmussen, Paul K., and Lauren L. Kuhn. 1976. "The New Masseuse." *Urban Life*
   5 (October):271—92.
Ricoeur, Paul. 1964. "Existential Phenomenology." In Richard M. Zaner and Don
   Ihde (eds.). *Phenomenology and Existentialism*, pp. 87—98. New York: Put-
   nam.
Riley, Matilda, John Riley, and Jackson Toby. 1954. *Sociological Studies in Scale
   Analysis.* New Brunswick, N.J.: Rutgers University Press.
Rossi, Paolo. 1970. *Philosophy, Technology and the Arts in the Early Modern Era.*
   (Benjamin Nelson, ed.) New York: Harper & Row.
Roy, Donald. 1970. "The Study of Southern Labor Union Organizing Campaigns."
   In Robert W. Haberstein (ed.). *Pathways to Data*, pp. 216—44. Chicago:
   Aldine.
Sacks, Harvey. 1963. "Sociological Description." *Berkeley Journal of Sociology*
   8:1—16.
Sallach, David L. 1971. "Critical Theory and Critical Sociology." Paper presented
   to annual meetings of the American Sociological Association, Denver, Colo-
   rado.
Samuelson, Kurt. 1961. *Religion and Economic Action.* (E. Geoffry French, trans.)
   Stockholm: Scandinavian University Books.
Sartre, Jean-Paul. 1939. "Erostate." In *Le mur.* Paris: Gallimard.
   1945a. *Le sursis.* Paris: Gallimard.
   1945b. *Les chemins de la liberté*, vol. I. Paris: Gallimard.
   1945c. *L'age de la raison*, vol. II. Paris: Gallimard.
   1947. "Huis-Clos." In *Théâtre.* Paris: Gallimard.
   1948. "Qu'est-ce que la literature?" In *Situation.* vol. II. Paris: Gallimard.
   1949. *Le Mort dans l'âme*, vol. III. Paris: Gallimard.
   1951. *Le diable et le bon Dieu.* Paris: Gallimard.
   1956a. *Being and Nothingness.* (Hazel E. Barnes, trans.) New York: Philosophical
   Library.
   1956b. *Nekrassov.* Paris: Gallimard.
   1960. *Critique de la raison dialectique.* Paris: Gallimard.
   1964a. *Les mots.* Paris: Gallimard.
   1964b. *Nausea.* New York: New Directions.
   1965. *Situations.* New York: Braziller.
   1968. "Existentialism as a Humanism." In Waldo Kaufman (ed.). *Existentialism
   from Dostoevsky to Sartre.* pp. 287—311. New York: New American Library
   (Meridian Books).
Scheff, Thomas J. 1966. *Being Mentally Ill.* Chicago: Aldine.
Scheffler, Israel. 1967. *Science and Subjectivity.* Indianapolis: Bobbs-Merrill.
Scheler, Max. 1958. *The Nature of Sympathy.* (Peter Heath, trans.) London: Routledge & Kegan Paul.
   1961. *Ressentiment.* (William W. Holdheim, trans.) New York: Free Press.
Schumpeter, Joseph A. 1954. *History of Economic Analysis.* New York: Oxford

University Press.

Schutz, Alfred. 1962. *Collected Papers.* vol. I, *The Problem of Social Reality.* (Maurice Natanson, ed.) The Hague: Martinus Nijhoff.

——— 1964. *Collected Papers*, vol. II, *Studies in Social Theory.* (Arvid Brodersen, ed.) The Hague: Martinus Nijhoff.

——— 1966. *Collected Papers*, vol. III, *Studies in Phenomenological Philosophy.* (I. Schutz, ed.) The Hague: Martinus Nijhoff.

——— 1967. *The Phenomenology of the Social World.* (George Walsh and Frederick Lehnert, trans.) Evanston: Northwestern University Press.

——— 1970a. *Reflections on the Problem of Relevance.* (Richard M. Zaner, ed.) New Haven: Yale University Press.

——— 1970b. *On Phenomenology and Social Relations.* Chicago: University of Chicago Press.

Schutz, Alfred, and Thomas Luckmann. 1973. *The Structures of the Life World.* (Richard M. Zaner and Tristram Engelhardt, Jr., trans.) Evanston: Northwestern University Press.

Scott, Marvin B., and Stanford M. Lyman. 1970. *The Revolt of the Students.* Columbus, Ohio: Merrill.

Scott, W. Richard. 1959. "Field Methods in the Study of Organizations." In James G. Marsh (ed.). *Handbook of Organizations*, pp. 272—82. Skokie, Ill.: Rand McNally.

Sellars, Wilfred. 1963. *Science, Perception and Reality.* New York: Humanities Press.

Shapere, Dudley. 1964. "The Structure of Scientific Revolution." *Philosophical Review* 73:383—94.

Shealy, C.N. 1974. "The Pain Patient." *American Family Physician* 9 (March): 130—7.

Shroyer, Trent. 1970. "Toward a Critical Theory for Advanced Industrial Society." In Hans Peter Dreitzel (ed.). *Recent Sociology No. 2*, pp. 210—34. New York: Macmillan.

Simmel, Georg. 1950. *The Sociology of George Simmel.* (Kurt H. Wolff, ed. and trans.) New York: Free Press.

Simon, William, and John H. Gagnon. 1967. "Feminity in the Lesbian Community." *Social Problems* 15:212—21.

Sjoberg, Gideon. 1959. "Operationalism and Social Research." In Llewellyn Gross (ed.). *Symposium on Sociological Theory*, pp. 175—210. New York: Harper & Row.

Skinner, B.F. 1953. *Science and Human Behavior.* New York: Macmillan.

Sorensen, Theodore C. 1975. *Watchmen in the Night.* Cambridge: MIT Press.

Sorokin, Pitirim. 1941. *Social and Cultural Dynamics.* Totowa, N.J.: Bedminster Press.

Speier, Matthew. 1967. "Phenomenology and Social Theory: Discussing Actor and Social Acts." *Berkeley Journal of Sociology* 2:193—211.

Spiegelberg, Herbert. 1967. "Husserl's Phenomenology and Sartre's Existentialism." In Joseph J. Kockelmans (ed.). *Phenomenology*, pp. 252—67. Garden City, N.Y.: Doubleday.

Stanley, Manfred. 1977. "The End of Citizenship: The Intellectual Pursuit of a Post-Industrial Future." In Richard H. Brown and Stanford M. Lyman (eds.). *Structure, Consciousness, and History.* New York: Cambridge University Press.

Staude, John R. 1967. *Max Scheler, 1874—1928, An Intellectual Portrait.* New York: Free Press.

1972. "The Theoretical Foundations of Humanistic Sociology." In John F. Glass and John R. Staude (eds.). *Humanistic Society: Today's Challenge to Sociology,* pp. 5—31. Pacific Palisades, Calif.: Goodyear.

Strasser, Stephen. 1962. *The Soul in Metaphysical and Empirical Psychology.* Pittsburgh: Dusquesne University Press.

1964. *Phenomenology and the Human Sciences.* Pittsburgh: Duquesne University Press.

Suchman, E.A. 1964. "Sociomedical Variation Among Ethnic Groups." *American Journal of Sociology* 70:319—31.

1965. "Stages of Illness and Medical Care." *Journal of Health and Human Behavior* 6 (fall):114—28.

Sudnow, David. 1965. "Normal Crimes: Sociological Features of the Penal Code in a Public Defender's Office." *Social Problems* 12:255—75.

1967. *Passing On: The Social Organization of Dying.* Englewood Cliffs,N.J.: Prentice-Hall.

Sumner, William Graham. 1906. *Folkways.* Boston: Ginn.

Sussman, M.B. (ed.). 1965. *Sociology and Rehabilitation.* Washington, D.C.: American Sociological Association.

Swanson, Guy. 1968. "Review Symposium." *American Sociological Review* 33 (February):122—4.

Szasz, Thomas S. 1961. *The Myth of Mental Illness.* New York: Harper & Row.

1970. *The Manufacture of Madness.* New York: Harper & Row.

Szymanski, Albert. 1970. "Toward a Radical Sociology." *Sociological Review* 40: 3—25.

Taylor, Charles. 1964. *The Explanation of Behavior.* New York: Humanities Press.

Taylor, Richard. 1966. *Action and Purpose.* Englewood Cliffs, N.J.: Prentice-Hall.

Thomas, William I. 1902. *Source Book for Social Origins.* Boston: Badger.

1966. *On Social Organization and Social Personality.* (Morris Janowitz, ed.) Chicago: University of Chicago Press.

Thurstone, Louis Leon, and E.J. Chave. 1929. *The Measurement of Attitude.* Chicago: University of Chicago Press.

Tiryakian, Edward A. 1962. *Sociologism and Existentialism.* Englewood Cliffs, N.J.: Prentice-Hall.

Tolman, Edward C. 1961. *Behavior and Psychological Man.* Berkeley: University of California Press.

Tuchman, Gaye. 1973. "Making News by Doing Work: Routinizing the Unexpected." *American Journal of Sociology* 79:110—21.

Turnbull, Colin M. 1962. *The Forest People.* New York: Simon & Schuster.

Turner, Ralph H. 1962. "Role-taking: Process Versus Conformity." In A. Rose (ed.). *Human Behavior and Social Process,* pp. 20—40. Boston: Houghton-

Mifflin.

Unamuno, Miguel de. 1954. *Tragic Sense of Life.* (J.E. Crawford, trans.) New York: Dover.

Urmson, J.O. 1956. *Philosophical Analysis.* London: Oxford University Press.

Vallier, Ivan (ed.). 1971. *Comparative Methods in Sociology: Essays on Trends and Applications.* Berkeley: University of California Press.

Vehinger, H. 1924. *The Philosophy of "As If."* London: Routledge & Kegan Paul.

Vico, Giambattista. 1948. *The New Science of Giambattista Vico.* (Thomas G. Bergin and May H. Fisch, trans.) Ithaca, N.Y.: Cornell University Press.

Wallace, Anthony F.C. 1968. "Review Symposium." *American Sociological Review* 33(February):124—6.

Warren, Carol A.B. 1974. *Identity and Community in the Gay World.* New York: Wiley.

1976. "Women Among Men: Females in the Male Homosexual Community." *Archives of Sexual Behavior* 5 (April):157—69.

Warren, Carol A.B., and John M. Johnson. 1972. "A Critique of Labeling Theory from the Phenomenological Perspective." In Robert A. Scott and Jack D. Douglas (eds.). *Theoretical Perspectives on Deviance*, pp. 69—92. New York: Basic Books.

Watson, James. 1969. *The Double Helix.* New York: New American Library (Signet).

Wax, Rosalie H. 1952. "Reciprocity as a Field Technique." *Human Organization* 11:34—7

Weber, Max. 1913. "Uber einige Kategorien der verstehenden Soziologie." *Logos*, vol. IV. Gesammelte Aufsätze zur Wissenschaftslehre.

1947. *The Theory of Social and Economic Organization.* (Talcott Parsons, ed.) New York: Free Press.

1958. *The Protestant Ethic and the Spirit of Capitalism.* New York: Scribner.

Weinberg, Martin S. 1965. "Sexual Modesty, Social Meanings and the Nudist Camp." *Social Problems* 12:311—18.

Weyl, H. 1949. *Philosophy of Mathematics and Natural Science.* Princeton, N.J.: Princeton University Press.

Whyte, William F. 1955. *Street Corner Society.* Chicago: University of Chicago Press.

Wieder, D. Lawrence. 1970. "On Meaning By Rule." In Jack D. Douglas (ed.). *Understanding Everyday Life*, pp. 107—35. Chicago: Aldine.

1973. *Language and Social Reality.* The Hague: Mouton.

Wilson, Edward C. 1975. *Sociobiology: The New Synthesis.* Cambridge: Harvard University Press (Belknap Press).

Wilson, Thomas P. 1970a. "Conceptions of Interaction and Forms of Sociological Explanation." *American Sociological Review* 35:697—709.

1970b. "Normative and Interpretive Paradigms in Sociology." In Jack D. Douglas (ed.). *Understanding Everyday Life*, pp. 249—75. Chicago: Aldine.

1971. "The Infinite Regress and the Problem of Evidence in Ethnomethodology." Paper presented to the annual meetings of the American Sociological Association, Denver, Colorado.

Winch, Peter. 1958. *The Idea of a Social Science and Its Relation to Philosophy.* New York: Humanities Press.

Wisdom J.O. 1968. "Anti-Dualist Outlook and Social Inquiry." In Imre Lakatos and Alan Musgrave (eds.). *Problems in the Philosophy of Science*, pp. 79—102. Amsterdam: North Holland.

Wiseman, Jacqueline P. 1970. *Stations of the Lost.* Englewood Cliffs, N.J.: Prentice-Hall.

Wittgenstein, Ludwid. 1953. *Philosophic Investigation.* (G.E,M. Anscombe, trans.) Oxford: Blackwell.

Wolff, Kurt H. 1964. "Surrender and Community Study." In Arthur J. Vidich, Joseph Bensmen, and Maurice Stein (eds.). *Reflections on Community Studies*, pp. 233—64. New York: Wiley.

Wood, Houston. 1968. "The Labeling Process on a Mental Hospital Ward." Unpublished M.A. thesis, Department of Sociology, University of California, Santa Barbara.

Young, T.R. 1971. "The Politics of Sociology: Gouldner, Goffman, and Garfinkel." *American Sociologist* 6 (November):276—80.

Zborowski, M. 1953. "Cultural Components in Response to Pain." *Journal of Social Issues* 8:16—31.

Zetterberg, Hans L. 1964. *On Theory and Verification in Sociology.* New York: Tressler Press.

Zimmerman, Don H. 1966. "Paper Work and People Work." Ph.D. dissertation, University of California, Los Angeles.

　　1969. "Record Keeping and the Intake Process in a Public Welfare Agency." In Stanton Wheeler (ed.). *On File: Records and Dossiers in American Life*, pp. 319—54. New York: Russell Sage Foundation.

　　1970. "The Practicalities of Rule-Use." In Jack D. Douglas (ed.). *Understanding Everyday Life*, pp. 221—38. Chicago: Aldine.

Zimmerman, Don H., and Melvin Pollner. 1970. "The Everyday World as Phenomenon." In Jack D. Douglas (ed.). *Understanding Everyday Life*, pp. 80—104. Chicago: Aldine.

Zimmerman, Don H., and D. Lawrence Wieder. 1970. "Ethnomethodology and the Problem of Order." In Jack D. Douglas (ed.). *Understanding Everyday Life*, pp. 287—302. Chicago: Aldine.

Znaniecki, Florian. 1968. *The Method of Sociology.* New York: Octagon.

Index

323